300 BEERS TO TRY BEFORE YOU DIE!

ROGER PROTZ

CAMPAIGN
FOR
REAL ALE

'There's always time for one more beer'

Bert Grant, founder Yakima Brewing and Malting Co, Yakima, Washington State, USA

First published in 2005 by Campaign for Real Ale
230 Hatfield Road, St Albans, Hertfordshire AL1 4LW

www.camra.org.uk

ISBN 1 85249 213 9

A CIP catalogue record for this book is available from the British Library

Printed and bound in the United Kingdom by Butler and Tanner Ltd, Frome, Somerset

Head of Publications: Joanna Copestick
Editor: Helen Ridge
Editorial Assistance: Emma Lloyd
Design: Alison Fenton
DTP Assistance: Dale Tomlinson and Cressida Feiler
Picture Research: Sarah Airey and Nadine Bazar
Marketing Manager: Georgina Rudman

ACKNOWLEDGEMENTS

The Publisher would like to thank the breweries for their kind permission in reproducing these photographs.

All photographs have been provided by the breweries except:

Beerlabels.com 19, 55, 143, 174, 200 left, 215, 259, 272

CAMRA Archive, 5, 7, 8, 16, 23, 28, 37, 46, 54, 58, 67 above left, 68-69, 72-73, 77, 80, 82, 108, 122, 132-133, 136, 146,148, 156, 161, 163-164, 167, 180, 185, 199, 200 right, 220, 224, 238-239, 243, 252, 256 below, 258, 274-275, 278

Cephas/Martin Walls 113
Cephas/Nigel Blythe 271

National Hop Association 6

Vanessa Courtier 11, 15, 81, 128, 142, 152-153, 165, 181, 196, 198, 202, 208, 228, 231, 232, 235, 237, 242, 244, 249, 250-251, 253-254, 256 above, 260, 269, 285

Contents

Introduction

Beer has never been more fascinating. In Britain and the United States, small craft breweries appear like mushrooms at dawn. There are close to 500 'micro-breweries' and family-owned regional companies in Britain and more than 1,000 in the US. In France, a country indissolubly linked to wine, an almost-lost brewing tradition has been revived in the ancient regions of Artois, Flanders and Picardy. Across the border into Belgium, the amazed store-house of beery riches there – beers brewed by monks, made with spices, deliberately soured or fermented with wild yeasts – has been brought to the attention of an astonished world.

With the old political barriers in central Europe swept away, we can marvel at the brilliance of the lager beers in the Czech Republic, where the first golden Pilsner was made in the middle of the 19th century. In Germany, thought of as the home of lager brewing, older styles such as wheat beer and golden ales, are being rediscovered and relished. Craft brewers in Australia and Canada are challenging the hegemony of bland, sweet lager with pale ales, stouts, India Pale Ales, Pilsners and Belgian-style beers.

With revival has come interest in styles. Craft brewers are not content to go down what used to be the English route of making 'a drop of mild, a decent bitter and some strong stuff for the winter'. Eager brewers have dug deep into history and old brewing books. Now our taste buds are regaled by porters and stouts based on 18th- and 19th-century recipes. There are many fine examples of true India Pale Ale, a style that revolutionised brewing in the 19th century and which should be strong and genuinely pale, not just a beefed-up version of bitter. Old ales and barley wines, with enormous depth and complexity, enliven the winter months. New golden beers, bursting with fruity hops, refresh us in summer.

In the United States, craft brewers have an historian's zeal for digging out the truth from brewing's past. Brewers who have toured Britain and been inspired by the warm-fermenting ales of those islands produce pale ales, IPAs, porters, stouts and barley wines of great quality. From cities and regions where the people are of German rather than British descent, dark and golden lagers, March beers, Bocks and Oktoberfest beers challenge the best that even the homeland can muster.

All of this pleasure and discovery has to be set against the backdrop of a brewing world in which a handful of global giants dominate production and force-feed consumers via slick and expensive advertising. Only a handful of beers made by big brewers feature in this book, as their main interest is churning out vast amounts of uninspired pale apologies for lager beer. The future of good beer and the history that has shaped it lies in the hands of people who love the product and ignore any corners that bigger brewers love to cut.

Fritz Maytag, who saved the Anchor Brewery in San Francisco in the 1960s and helped spark the American beer revival, says 'You don't make good beer, you get everything together as best you can. Then you let the beer make itself.' This book is dedicated to Fritz and the legion of craft brewers throughout the world who search for the soul of good beer. They take the finest malts and hops, avoiding cheap ingredients, place them in their brewing vessels and then let nature, rather than computers, take its course.

I hope, above all, that this book will prove that beer is more, far more, than just a quick refresher. Good beer is complex. It offers a range of aromas and flavours that no other alcohol can deliver. It is as welcome at the dining table as it is at the bar. In this book, you will find beers ranging from pale gold to jet-black and, in between, every colour and flavour imaginable. Enjoy the journey and keep travelling.

Making beer

We take beer for granted. We assume, as it is an everyday drink rather than one for special occasions, that it is easily and quickly made. It is true that most beers are not matured for long periods, as is the case with single malt whiskies or vintage wines. But there are vintage beers, too, and there are also beers that are matured for long periods. Not all whiskies are stored for 12 or 18 years, while most wines are also meant for everyday consumption.

At its simplest, wine can be made by crushing grapes and allowing the wild yeasts on the skins to turn the juice into alcohol. If you crush an ear of barley, all you will get is dust on your fingers. Long before the brewer can start work, a maltster has to take the grain from the fields and turn it into malt, the vital ingredient that will launch the fascinating journey that ends with a delicious glass of beer in your hand.

Malt

Barley is the preferred grain of brewers. It has a husk, which acts as a natural filter during the mashing stage, and it delivers a clean, sweet, biscuity character to the finished product. Even wheat beers are made with a blend of barley and wheat. Oats and rye are also occasionally used but in small amounts for fear that their oily, creamy or bready notes will overwhelm the essential character of barley malt.

The finest type of barley is known as 'two-row', so called because there are two rows of grain within each ear. The best two-row is called maritime barley, as it grows close to the sea in rich, dark soil. In regions away from the coast, six-row barley is the norm. It produces coarser malt and is often blended with other cereals such as rice or corn. Craft brewers in the United States who want to create specific, refined flavours from their beers will import malt from Britain or mainland Europe and will avoid 'adjuncts', or cheaper grains. Ale brewers prefer winter barleys sown in the autumn with robust, biscuity tastes, while lager brewers prefer the softer notes that are derived from spring varieties.

When barley reaches the maltings, it is thoroughly washed in deep vats to clean it and remove any harmful bacteria. The grain absorbs moisture, vital to encourage germination. When the correct level of moisture has been achieved, the grain is spread on heated floors or placed in large rotating drums. Germination will last from between four to 10 days, depending on the method used.

During germination, the embryo of the plant starts to grow, while tiny roots break through the husk. The process is known as modification. As the embryo grows it triggers complex chemical changes that turn proteins into enzymes, while the starch in the grain becomes soluble. When the embryo has fully grown and the rootlets stand proud of the husk, modification is complete. Ale brewers want a fully modified malt so that enzymes will work quickly to convert starch into sugar during the infusion mashing process. In traditional lager brewing, malt is poorly modified, with substantial amounts of protein remaining. This is caused by the poorer quality of lager malts with a high nitrogen level that require a more thorough decoction mash.

The grain is loaded into a kiln, where the malt is laid out on a mesh floor and heated from below, or in a drum where the heat is applied externally. The heat is gentle at first. It dries the malt, stops germination and preserves the vital enzymes. The heat is then increased. All brewers need pale malt, as it is rich in enzymes, and this type of malt is gently roasted. The heat is increased to produce darker malts such as amber, brown, black, chocolate or roast. Unmalted roasted barley, often used in stout brewing, is also kilned at a high temperature. Some malts are stewed and arrive at the brewery with the starch already converted to malt sugar. Crystal malt, widely used in English ale brewing, is a type of stewed malt. It gives both colour and a pleasing nutty flavour to beer but must be used in small quantities. Similar malts are known as caramel malt or caramalt.

TOP
Brewers call barley 'the soul of beer', as it is the finest grain for brewing, creating a juicy and biscuity flavour as well as essential sugars for fermentation.

ABOVE
Grain has to be malted to start the brewing process.

Hops – described as 'the grapes of brewing' – give bitterness, aroma and flavour to beer. There are many varieties of hops grown throughout the world. Shown here are the classic English Fuggles (top) and Phoenix from the United States (below).

Hops

The hop is a remarkable plant that provides bitterness to beer to balance the sweet, juicy and biscuity nature of malt. It also delivers superb aromas and flavours reminiscent of pine, resins, citrus fruit, fresh-mown grass and floral notes. The Latin name for the hop is *Humulus lupulus*, the wolf plant, because, left to itself, it would run wild across the ground. Hop growers train plants to climb up tall trellises to absorb sun, warmth, wind and rain. The male and female plants grow separately. Most brewers, especially lager makers, prefer unfertilised female hops, while ale brewers want the earthier and more pungent character of fertilised plants. The cone of the plant contains acids, oils and resins that give aroma and flavour to beer, help stabilise the wort during the brewing process and attack bacteria.

Hops are picked in the autumn and dried in oast houses. The cones are laid out on perforated drying room floors and heated from below. Once dry, the hops are packed into large sacks called pockets or taken to a specialist factory and turned into pellets by milling and reducing under great pressure. There is a tendency in giant breweries to use hop extract, which is a thick liquid like damson jam created by crushing the hops. Craft brewers prefer not to use extract, which can give a harsh note at the back of the throat.

There are scores of different hop varieties. Germans call the types that grow in the vast Hallertau region near Munich 'noble hops' as a result of their fine aroma and gentle bitterness. Many lager brewers will buy Saaz hops from the Czech Republic for their superb aroma. American hops, many descended from European stock, are famous for their distinctive and robust citrus fruit character. English hops have resiny aromas and flavours, with a medium bitterness. Hops are grown in many countries, including Russia, Poland, Slovenia – well known for the Styrian Golding – Northern France, Belgium, Australia, New Zealand, Canada, Japan, South Africa, Zimbabwe, South and Central America, Greece, Turkey and parts of Scandinavia.

Just as with grapes, each hop variety will have its own character and distinctive aroma and flavour. Many brewers will blend two or more varieties to achieve the balance of flavour they are looking for. In England, for example, two long-established varieties, the Fuggle and the Golding, are often used in tandem: the Fuggle primarily for bitterness and the Golding for aroma. Several European countries, with England leading the field, have developed new types of hops known as dwarf or hedgerow varieties that grow to only half the height of conventional hops, are easier to pick and are less prone to attack by pests and disease.

Water

Even the strongest beer is made up of 93% water. The quality of water is therefore crucial to brewing. For centuries, long before brewers were able to adjust water to suit their recipes, breweries developed around natural supplies in the form of wells or springs. River water was used before such sources were ruined by pollution.

In a brewery, water is always known as liquor. Its formulation will depend on the minerals present in the rocks and soil of a particular area. Soft water is the result of rain falling on insoluble rock such as slate or granite. Where soluble rock is present, water will pick up such sulphates as calcium and magnesium, also known as gypsum and Epsom salts. It is these salts present in the waters of the Trent Valley that made Burton-on-Trent a key town in the development of brewing. The hard waters help acidify the mash, encourage enzymes to work, ensure the best extraction of aromas and flavours from malt and hops, and discourage astringency. Yeast thrives on magnesium. On the other hand, the soft waters of such famous lager brewing towns as Pilsen emphasise the soft malty character of the beer. The total salts in the waters of Burton amount to 1,226 parts per million. In Pilsen, on the other hand, the figure is just 30.8. Brewers can now adjust their liquor to suit their purposes: many ale brewers 'Burtonise' their waters by adding gypsum and magnesium salts. All brewers thoroughly cleanse their liquor to remove impurities and such agricultural chemicals as nitrates, which can create a haze in beer.

Yeast

It was not until the 18th and 19th centuries that scientists, including Louis Pasteur, were able to explain yeast's role in brewing. Until then, fermentation was looked on as some kind of witchcraft. The foam produced by this strange alchemy was known as 'God-is-good'. Pasteur demonstrated with the aid of a microscope that the production of alcohol was the result of a natural chemical reaction in which yeast cells multiplied as they turned sugars into alcohol and carbon dioxide.

Yeast is a fungus, a single cell plant that can turn a sugary liquid into alcohol and CO_2. There are two basic types of brewer's yeasts: ale and lager. Ale yeast is classified as *Saccharomyces* [sugar fungus] *cerevisiae*, while lager yeast is labelled *Saccharomyces carlsbergensis*, as the first pure strain of lager yeast was isolated at the Carlsberg breweries in Denmark. It is also known today as *Saccharomyces uvarum*. The two types are often referred to as 'top fermenting' and 'bottom fermenting' strains. This is because ale yeast creates a thick collar of foam on top of the fermenting beer, while lager yeast produces a smaller head and sinks to the bottom of the vessel. The terms are misleading, as both yeasts must work at all levels of the liquid to convert malt sugars into alcohol. I prefer the terms warm fermenting and cold fermenting yeasts, for ale yeast will only work at 12˚C (55˚F) and above, while lager yeast is tolerant of cold and will happily work at temperatures as low as 5˚C (40˚F).

Yeast is not a neutral substance. It does more than produce alcohol. As the same strain reproduces itself many times over during fermentation, it does not die out. There is always a fresh supply of refrigerated yeast on hand. A brewery's yeast culture picks up, retains and passes on vital flavour characteristics from one brew to the next. Breweries not only safeguard their cultures but lodge samples in yeast banks. If a brewery has the misfortune to get a yeast infection, fresh supplies can be obtained from the bank.

The role of wild yeast strains in the production of Belgian lambic and gueuze beers is explained in the relevant section of the book (see pages 240–1).

Brewing

In the brewery, the malt is ground, or 'cracked', in a mill. The mill has several settings, and the malt is reduced to flour, coarser grain and the husks. The mixture is known as grist. In an infusion mash system, malt and pure hot liquor are mixed in a large circular vessel known as a mash tun. The thick, porridge-like mixture is left to stand for an hour or two as saccharification takes place. This means that the enzymes in the malt convert starch to sugar. Two principal types of sugar are produced. Maltose is highly fermentable, while dextrin can be only partially fermented by brewer's yeast, and the dextrins left give body and flavour to the beer. The sugars dissolve in the hot liquor and produce an extract called wort. When the brewer is satisfied that full conversion has taken place, he opens the slotted base of the vessel and the wort filters through the spent grain. To make sure no vital sugars are left behind, the spent grains are then sprinkled, or 'sparged', with more hot liquor to wash them out.

The wort is pumped to the copper, a domed vessel made from either copper or stainless steel. Boiling wort gushes up a central tube inside the copper, while hops are added through a hatch in the top of the vessel at specially selected times to extract the maximum aroma and bitterness. They are usually put in at the start of the boil, half way through and just a few minutes before the boil ends. Special brewing sugars may be added during the copper boil for colour, flavour and to encourage a powerful fermentation. At the end of the boil, the 'hopped wort' is filtered through the bed of spent hops into a vessel called a hop back. The liquid is cooled and run into fermenting vessels, which may be round or square, open or covered, where liquid yeast is mixed, or 'pitched'.

Ale fermentation lasts for around seven days. During that time, enzymes in the yeast turn sugar into alcohol and carbon dioxide. Fermentation also creates natural chemical compounds called esters that are similar to fruity aromas. They are present in the atmosphere in the fermentation rooms and may be reminiscent of apples, oranges, pineapples, pear drops, liquorice or molasses. Eventually the

BELOW
A classic lager brewery showing the burnished copper vessels used in the mashing process.

yeast will be overcome by the alcohol it has produced. The cells will clump together and rise to the surface. The unfinished, or 'green', beer will spend several days resting in conditioning tanks and purging itself of rougher and unwanted alcohols. Finally, the beer will be run or racked into kegs or casks. It may be filtered and pasteurised or, if it is cask-conditioned real ale, it will be left to mature and enjoy a secondary fermentation in cask. Extra hops may be placed in each cask for additional aroma and flavour, while finings will start to clarify the beer.

In lager brewing, where the malt is less modified than ale malt, a decoction mashing system is used. A third of the mash will be pumped from one vessel to another, heated to a higher temperature and returned to the first vessel. A further third of the mash will receive similar treatment. The aim of the system is to degrade protein in the mash and gelatinise the starch so it can be attacked by enzymes and converted to sugar. When saccharification is complete, the mash will be pumped to a lauter tun with a false bottom, where the liquid is run off and the spent grains are then sparged.

Following the copper boil with hops, the hopped wort is cooled and pumped to fermentation vessels – which are usually enclosed – where yeast is pitched. As a result of a lower temperature, the yeast will work more slowly, and conversion to alcohol may take as long as two weeks. Finally, the liquid goes to the lager cellar and is run into tanks for a long, slow second fermentation and ripening at a temperature just above freezing point. Lager tanks may be upright conical vessels but purists prefer horizontal vessels, where the yeast works more slowly and produces a fuller-flavoured beer. There is a growing tendency to speed up the lagering time but classic beers such as the Czech Budweiser Budvar enjoy 90 days in the cellar. When lagering is complete, the beer will be filtered, as a heavy sediment of yeast and protein will have settled in the tank, and is then racked into kegs. The lagering process removes many of the fruity characteristics associated with ale.

By two very different routes, classic ale and classic lager brewing and fermentation, we now have beer to drink and savour.

Tasting beer

A little care, skill, and appreciation of the art of the brewer is required to appreciate beer at home. First, the glass. You can use a conventional pint or half-pint beer glass, or similar measures in metric countries. You may be lucky enough to have one of the glasses designed to accompany a particular beer. Or you may use any suitable glass container in your home. Whatever you use, it must be scrupulously clean and, above all, it should contain no residue from cleaning agents. If you take a glass from a dishwasher, rinse it thoroughly under running cold water. Washing-up liquids and detergents will not only leave a vile taste in the glass, but will also kill the head on the beer. Avoid pouring and drinking beer in a kitchen area. Oil or fats used in cooking infiltrate a beer glass, leave unpleasant flavours and also kill the head.

There is more to pouring beer into a glass than merely emptying the liquid from one container into the next. Hold the glass and bottle at eye level. Slowly pour the beer into the glass, raising the glass from the horizontal to the vertical as it fills. Let the beer trickle down the side of the glass. When the glass is two-thirds full, raise it to the vertical and pour more quickly: this should give the required healthy head of foam. Don't pour too slowly or the head will fail to materialise. Pouring at eye level is important when a beer contains yeast sediment. You can monitor the passage of the yeast, which will rise from the bottom of the bottle towards the neck, and stop pouring just before it leaves the bottle. If some of the yeast does get into the glass, don't worry: it will do you no harm and is full of healthy nutrients.

If you are pouring a German wheat beer, you cannot avoid the yeast sediment getting into the glass. It's meant to be served that way. A German beer waiter will deliberately rotate the bottle as he or she pours, and will give a final dramatic roll of the bottle to ensure all the yeast enters the glass.

If you are giving a beer tasting at home, you may find that large stemmed glasses intended for red wine are the most suitable containers, as they allow the aroma of the beer to develop, while the stem on the glass enables drinkers to swirl the beer to release the aroma to the full.

Whether you are drinking for pleasure or taking part in a tasting, begin by appreciating the aroma. Depending on the style, you will detect malty and hoppy aromas plus a fruitiness from either the hops or as the result of natural chemical esters created during fermentation.

As the beer passes over the tongue, you will detect more malt, hop and fruit notes. The tongue spots sweetness, bitterness and saltiness. Finally, let the beer slip down the back of the tongue and throat to appreciate the aftertaste or finish. This is an important part of the tasting process, as a beer that starts malty on the aroma may finish with a pronounced degree of hop bitterness, or vice versa.

If you are organising a beer tasting, you will need a good supply of glasses. If you reuse glasses, rinse them thoroughly between beers. You should also have a good supply of uncarbonated mineral water to drink between beers, plus plates with crackers or other kinds of dry biscuits to cleanse the palate further. Many tasters like to have small squares of cheese as well, but these should be of the mild variety, as the likes of blue Stilton or mature Cheddar are too overpowering, especially if you are tasting delicately flavoured beers.

You should involve only one style of beer in a tasting: there is little point in attempting to match, say, pale Pilsners with English barley wines. Using the beers mentioned in this book, you could arrange tastings of Bocks, wheat beers, Belgian ales or English pale ales.

Draught beer can be difficult to handle for a tasting at home. If you know a pub or bar with a friendly landlord and an upstairs room, you could arrange a tasting there. In Britain, many brewers of cask-conditioned beer supply their products for home drinking in polypins containing 18 or 36 pints. Follow the simple instructions on the box to set up the beer, which must be allowed to settle for 24 hours. It is crucial that cask beer is kept in a cool place with a temperature of 11–12°C (52–55°F). The Charles Wells Brewery in Bedford, England, has pioneered cask beer in a take-home can containing eight pints of Bombardier Best Bitter. The cans are easy to set up and serve from, and other brewers may follow the example.

Bottled beers should be kept in a cool place prior to serving. Many brewers will suggest a serving temperature on the bottle label. A simple rule of thumb is that lager beers should be served cold, ales served cool: 8–9°C (46–48°F) for lager, 11–12°C (52–55°F) for ales. You will have to experiment with your refrigerator and a thermometer to see how long beers should be stored. Beers containing sediment should be stored upright unless the bottles have corks, in which case they should be laid down to keep the corks moist. Sedimented bottles should be opened and left to stand for five or 10 minutes to vent off some of the carbonation created by bottle conditioning and to stop the beer 'fobbing' or gushing out of the container. Strong ales such as barley wines can be served at a slightly higher temperature of around 13–14°C (55–57°F) to allow the full aroma and palate to develop.

You will need tasting sheets with the names of each beer and with columns that allow the tasters to give marks out of 10 for appearance (clarity), aroma, palate, finish, and adherence to style. With some styles, you may wish to add marks for colour. Many beers called India Pale Ale, for example, are too dark, while a true Irish Dry Stout should be jet-black but with just a tiny hint of ruby around the edge when held against the light.

Above all… enjoy!

India Pale Ales

India Pale Ale is a conundrum. As the title is often abbreviated to IPA, many people are unaware of the full name. Others call it *Indian* Pale Ale, assuming its origins lie in the subcontinent. To muddy the waters further, many modern IPAs are both too dark and too weak to deserve the title. The first IPAs were truly pale, using no coloured malts, and had robust strengths of 6% or more. I have assembled some beers I believe to be true to the style: to mix the grain, if not the metaphor, I have sorted the wheat from the chaff.

These beers underscore the way in which India Pale Ale transformed brewing on a world scale. Until the Industrial Revolution of the 18th and 19th centuries, all beers were brown in colour, as barley malt was roasted, or 'kilned', by wood fires that tended to scorch the grain. The result was brown malt, which, in turn, produced brown beer. Small amounts of paler malts were made using coal fires, but coal gave off gas that impregnated the malt with unpleasant flavours. As soon as coke – coal without the gas – was developed, pale malt started to be made in substantial quantities.

Brewers in Britain welcomed this development. They could produce attractive, sparkling pale beers, quite different in taste and appeal from darker porters and stouts, using malt that had a higher proportion of the natural enzymes that turn starch into sugar during the brewing process. As a result, it took smaller amounts of pale malt to make beer. This was a significant factor when brewing became a fiercely competitive industry rather than a homespun trade carried out by publicans in their cellars.

The term IPA was coined because the first pale, strong beers were made for export to India and eventually to other parts of the British Empire. An East London brewer called Hodgson, who had easy access to the East India Docks, made the first 'India Ale' at the end of the 18th century. But he was soon supplanted by bigger brewers such as Allsopp, Bass and Worthington, all based in Burton-on-Trent in the English Midlands.

As a result of the Napoleonic Wars (1799–1815), the Burton brewers had lost their lucrative trade in nut-brown ales exported to Russia and the Baltic, and were desperate for new foreign markets. They were able to replicate Hodgson's beer and to improve on it with the help of the spring waters of the Trent Valley, which are rich in the sulphates that tease out the best character from malt and hops.

During the early decades of the 19th century, the Burton brewers built a substantial trade with India and then moved on to Australia, the Caribbean and even the United States with their new pale beers. In order to withstand the rigours of long sea journeys, the brewers realised that the best defence against spoilage was alcohol and hops. The natural acids, resins and tannins in the cone of the hop plant are anti-bacterial and helped keep the beer, which was stored in wooden casks, free from infection. Prodigious amounts of hops – four times as many as in a conventional beer – were used.

The heyday of India Pale Ale was brief. By the end of the 19th century it had been replaced in most of the British colonies by German or German-inspired lager beers, which were less bitter and kept cool by refrigeration. The British brewers turned to an offspring – pale ale – for the domestic market, but IPA lingered on as a speciality for some brewers.

Today IPA is enjoying a resurgence of interest on both sides of the Atlantic, and some – in the finest traditions of the style – even make the sea journey.

Burton Bridge Empire Pale Ale

Source: Burton Bridge Brewery, Burton-on-Trent, Staffordshire, England
Strength: 7.5%
Website: none

Let us begin at the beginning with a beer from Burton, one that has a terrier-like devotion to the style. Burton Bridge is a micro-brewery behind an inn, or 'brewery tap'. The company owns three other pubs in the small town that was once the centre and great innovator of British brewing. The owners, Geoff Mumford and Bruce Wilkinson, worked for the national group Allied Breweries before launching Burton Bridge in 1982, and have many years' experience of the brewing art.

Empire Pale Ale is matured in cask for a minimum of three months in the brewery to replicate the length of a sea journey from England to India in the 19th century. The beer is then bottled with live yeast and will continue to improve and mature under glass.

In the exact style of Victorian times, it is brewed from Pipkin pale malt and brewing sugar, with no darker grains, and is hopped with English Challenger and Styrian Goldings hops from Slovenia (British brewers often used sailing ships to bring both malt and hops from abroad). A pronounced orange fruit note from the hops and house yeast dominate the aroma and palate. The fruitiness is balanced by biscuit malt and deep, tangy, spicy and resiny hops, with a long and lingering finish with juicy malt, tart fruit and bitter hops.

The beer won the Guardian/CAMRA Bottle-Conditioned Beer of the Year award in 1997. It's worth buying for the 'British Raj' label alone, which shows an army officer and a cricketer enjoying tankards of beer. Both IPA and cricket were introduced to the Indian subcontinent by the Raj; cricket today is the greater passion.

TASTING NOTES
Appearance
Aroma
Taste
Overall score

Caledonian Deuchars IPA

Source: Caledonian Brewing Company, Edinburgh, Scotland
Strength: 3.8%
Website: www.caledonian-brewery.co.uk

TASTING NOTES
Appearance
Aroma
Taste
Overall score

The Caledonian Brewery dates from 1869. It draws on the hard waters that bubble up from red sandstone underground strata known as the Charmed Circle, which made Edinburgh a great brewing centre and enabled it to compete with Burton as a leading producer of IPA.

Robert Deuchar owned a brewery that closed in the 1960s, and Caledonian acquired the name for this pale bronze beer that is both succulent and controversial: Scottish IPAs were darker and maltier than the English style, as can be seen in McEwan's Export, whereas Deuchars is pale with a fine hop character. It's brewed from Scottish Golden Promise malt with a touch of darker crystal: at 12.5 units of colour on the brewers' scale, this is a pale beer by any standards. The hops are English Fuggles and Styrian Goldings. The beer has a luscious citrus fruit note on the aroma balanced by tart, spicy hops. Juicy malt, tart hops and tangy fruit dominate the mouth, followed by a long finish, in which peppery hops linger with pronounced lemon fruit and biscuity malt.

At just 3.8%, the beer has a modest strength for the style; a filtered bottled version is widely available in supermarkets and specialist beer shops at 4.4%. The draught beer was named Champion Beer of Britain by CAMRA in 2002, since when sales have soared.

Some of the character of Caledonian's beers comes from the unique boiling coppers fired by direct gas flame (originally coal). The brewers claim this creates a good 'rolling boil' when hops are added to the sweet extract, draws intense bitterness and aroma from the hops, and stops the sugary extract, or wort, becoming stewed.

Concertina Bengal Tiger

Source: Concertina Brewery, Mexborough, South Yorkshire, England
Strength: 4.6%
Website: None

TASTING NOTES
Appearance
Aroma
Taste
Overall score

As befits the style, you will have to travel to sample Bengal Tiger, as it's available only in a workingmen's club in Mexborough and a few pubs in the immediate area. The club's full title is the Concertina Band Club – known locally as 'The Tina' – and it's the only private club left in Britain that brews on the premises.

As the name suggests, the club was founded (in the 1880s) to enable members to sustain a band based solely on the concertina. The Mexborough band was of high repute: it gave a private performance to King Edward VII and won a thousand guineas prize in a competition at London's Alexandra Palace in 1906. Concertina bands have long since disappeared and the Mexborough club went into decline until Kenneth Pickering bought it in 1986. He encouraged his son Andy, a keen home brewer, to install a brewery in the club cellar.

The brewery was launched in 1992 with equipment from Mansfield Brewery in Nottingham and from Whitbread. It can brew just eight barrels of beer at a time, with a mash tun, copper, four fermenters and settling tanks. Andy uses pale and crystal malts, and Fuggles, Styrian Goldings and Target hops in his beers. He started with Club Bitter and Old Dark Attic but he always wanted to brew an IPA. A member of the club found an image of a Bengal tiger on his computer and he designed a clip for the handpump on the bar. The beer has a complex aroma of biscuity malt, spicy hops and tangy fruit, with a malty/hoppy palate underscored by citrus fruit. Tart fruit, juicy malt and bitter hops dominate the finish.

To sample the beer, you can enter the club at 9a Dolcliffe Road, Mexborough, by signing the visitors' book or pay £2 for a year's membership. The club is open 12–4 and 7–11 Monday to Saturday, and 7–10.30 on Sunday. The club is just off the high street and a few minutes' walk from Mexborough railway station.

Darwin Rolling Hitch

Source: Darwin Brewery, Sunderland, England
Strength: 5.2%
Website: www.darwinbrewery.com

TASTING NOTES
Appearance
Aroma
Taste
Overall score

Darwin is both a commercial brewery and a research facility for students attending courses at Sunderland University's Brewers Laboratory (Brewlab). As well as a range of bitters and dark beers for the pub trade in the North-east, Darwin in conjunction with Brewlab re-creates old beer styles, most famously Flag Porter, using yeast found in a bottle rescued from a shipwreck.

Rolling Hitch was launched commercially in 2004 but was first brewed by a trainee American brewer, Jeff Holcomb, on a Brewlab course. The name comes from a traditional sailor's knot, and the bottle label features a clipper ship, the City of Adelaide, which was built on the River Wear and plied its trade between Sunderland and the colonies.

Rolling Hitch is brewed with just pale malt and American Amarillo hops, a new variety that is grown on only one farm in Washington State. The aroma and palate of the beer burst with tangy hop resins, lemon fruit and biscuity malt. The finish ends bitter and dry, but is balanced by juicy malt and fruit, with hints of fennel. It was chosen by customers in the Asda chain of supermarkets as their favourite beer and, as a result, enjoys a national presence in the stores. A draught version is planned: check the website for availability.

Goose Island IPA

Source: Goose Island Beer Company, Chicago, Illinois, USA
Strength: 5.9%
Website: www.gooseisland.com

TASTING NOTES
Appearance
Aroma
Taste
Overall score

John and Gregg Hall, father and son, built a Chicago brew-pub and turned it into a major commercial company, revered by beer lovers throughout the US via the Beer Across America Club, which offers micro-brewed beers to members.

The original brew-pub, with a large bar room with burnished mahogany fittings, is at 1800 North Clybourn, while a second bar and brewery opened in Wrigleyville at 3535 North Clark Street. Goose Island, named after an island in the Chicago River, is best known for its copper-coloured Honkers Ale (see page 90), but the IPA is the standout beer, arguably the finest modern interpretation of the 19th-century style.

The Halls don't stint on ingredients for their beers, using both North American and European malts, and Cascade and Mount Hood hops from the US, Czech Saaz and Styrian Goldings. Water is drawn from Lake Michigan and carbon filtered. Yeast strains for ales, lagers and wheat beers are imported from Europe to ensure the correct aromas and flavours.

The bottle-fermented IPA is true to style in two important particulars: it is truly pale, with just 10 colour units (only fractionally darker than a Pilsner), and heavily hopped, with 58 units of bitterness, making it one of the bitterest beers in the world. It has an entrancing aroma of bitter oranges, spicy hops and a cracker biscuit maltiness. In the mouth a full, rich fruitiness balances the bitter edge of the hops, and there is a superb underlying juicy malt note. The persistent finish has an iron-like intensity from the hops, more bitter, tangy fruit and a lingering, delightful malt character. (For British stockists, contact James Clay & Sons: beersolutions.co.uk.)

Grant's India Pale Ale

Source: Grant's Yakima Brewing and Malting Company, Yakima, Washington, USA
Strength: 4.2%
Website: www.grant.com

TASTING NOTES
Appearance
Aroma
Taste
Overall score

Bert Grant, who died in 2001 at the age of 74, was a brewing pioneer. He was born in Scotland but his family moved to Canada when he was only two. When he left college, he worked as a chemist in the brewing industry, then crossed the border to run a hop-processing plant in Yakima in Washington State's hop-growing region. His friends relished his home-brewed beer, and when production reached 500 barrels a year, he decided to go into business.

His first brewery was in Yakima's former opera house. Success enabled him to build a new plant on a greenfield site on the edge of town, alongside the hop fields. He also opened a brew-pub in the old railroad station: it was the first legal brew-pub in the US since the repeal of Prohibition in the 1930s, and it concentrates on cask-conditioned beers.

Bert's IPA has been tweaked slightly since his untimely death, down from 4.5% alcohol to 4.2%, while the original bitterness of 60 units is now 50. But the beer, made from pale malt only and hopped with local Cascade and Galena varieties, is still a marvellously potent brew with a pungent floral hop aroma, an apple-like fruitiness, luscious malt and tart hops on the mouth, and a lingering finish that becomes dry and bitter but with balancing fruit and malt. Grant's beers are available in just about every State of the Union.

When I visited Bert in the 1990s, I toured the main brewery, then was taken into the Cascade mountains for a meal in a log-cabin restaurant. When we drove back to Yakima, Bert was heading for my hotel but decided to go to his brew-pub instead. 'There's always time for one more beer,' he said. I hope they put that on his tombstone.

Hogs Back BSA

Source: Hogs Back Brewery, Tongham, Surrey, England
Strength: 4.5%
Website: www.hogsback.co.uk

BSA stands for Burma Star Ale. It was first brewed in 1995 as a tribute to the Burma Star Association, which marks the contribution made by soldiers and prisoners of war involved in the Burma campaign in World War Two. Stocks of beer are sold at the Imperial War Museum in London, and a donation from each sale goes to BSA's welfare funds.

Hogs Back is one of Britain's most successful micro-breweries. It was launched in 1992 in restored farm buildings that date from the 18th century. As well as a wide range of cask beers, Hogs Back produces several bottle-fermented beers that stand out from the crowd as a result of both their quality and the gold-embossed labels designed in-house by one of the brewery's partners. Their beers can be bought in local branches of Sainsbury's, at the on-site shop or by mail order: see website.

BSA is brewed from Maris Otter pale malt, with touches of crystal and chocolate malt, which combine to produce a deep bronze colour with a hint of red. The hops are the traditional English ale varieties: Fuggles and Goldings. The result is a beer with a deep and abiding aroma of crisp, nutty malt, orange fruit and spicy, resinous hops, with a palate of biscuit malt, tangy fruit and bitter hops. The finish lingers with pronounced orange fruit notes, rich malt and a firm underpinning of bitter, peppery hops.

The label depicts servicemen at the time of the Burma campaign and carries the moving wartime lines: 'When you go home tell them of us and say – for your tomorrow we gave our today.'

TASTING NOTES
Appearance
Aroma
Taste
Overall score

TASTING NOTES

Appearance	
Aroma	
Taste	
Overall score	

Marston's Old Empire
Source: Marston, Thompson & Evershed, Burton-on-Trent, Staffordshire, England
Strength: 5.7%
Website: www.fullpint.co.uk

Curiously, Marstons has been brewing in Burton since 1834 but never made an IPA until it launched Old Empire in 2003. Even more curious is the fact that the current site is Marston's second in Burton and it was bought from the London brewery Mann Crossman & Paulin, which had moved to Burton specifically to brew IPA for the London market. Marston's concentrated instead on a range of beers led by the world-famous Pedigree pale ale (see page 59) that is still fermented in the 'union rooms' packed with giant oak casks. Yeast from the unions is used to produce Old Empire.

Marston's invited me to give my views on several trial brews and my response was always the same: 'More hops!' The beer that emerged in both cask and bottle has 40 units of bitterness and I would still prefer a tad more.

It is made with Optic pale malt only and has 12 units of colour. The hop varieties are English Fuggles and Goldings and American Cascade. It's a rich and luscious beer. It starts with the usual sulphury note you expect from Burton-brewed beers as a result of the high levels of sulphates in the water. Floral hops, succulent malt, vanilla and light citrus fruit soon break through on the nose, followed by juicy malt, hop resins and tart fruit in the mouth. The long finish is packed with biscuity malt, spicy hops and lemon fruit, and is wonderfully quenching.

It took Marston's more than a century and a half to make an IPA but it was worth waiting for.

Pike IPA

Source: Pike Brewery, Seattle, Washington, USA
Strength: 6%
Website: www.merchantduvin.com

TASTING NOTES
Appearance
Aroma
Taste
Overall score

Originally called Pike Place Brewery after its first location in Seattle's restaurant and food market area, the pub and brewery have moved to 1415 First Avenue with a considerably up-rated production of 15,000 barrels a year. The brewery was founded by Charles Finkel's Merchant du Vin company that now specialises in the fruit of the barley rather than the vine: it is the major importer of Samuel Smith's beers into the US from Britain, for example.

Head brewer Kim Brusco has fashioned a stunningly hoppy India Pale Ale, using Chinook, Magnum and Willamette American hop varieties and pale, crystal, Munich and cara malts. Munich malt gives the signature red/bronze colour to the famous Oktoberfest beers of the Bavarian capital, while cara malt is similar to crystal, a stewed malt that gives a nutty flavour to beer.

The finished beer has an appealing burnished brass colour with a massive burst of floral hops and grapefruit, typical in particular of the characteristics of the Chinook. Underlying the hops is a rich, nutty and cracker biscuit maltiness. Juicy, quenching malt, citrus fruit and bitter hops combine in the mouth, followed by a punchy finish with creamy malt, earthy, resinous hops and tangy fruit. It's a memorable beer and the perfect companion for the fresh food in local restaurants.

Shipyard Fuggles IPA

Source: Shipyard Brewing Co, Portland, Maine, USA
Strength: 5.8%
Website: www.shipyard.com

TASTING NOTES
Appearance
Aroma
Taste
Overall score

Shipyard's beers are all about yeast. Alan Pugsley is a young British brewer who trained at the Ringwood Brewery in Hampshire under Peter Austin, renowned as the father of British micro-brewing: Ringwood was one of the earliest new-wave micros in the late 1970s. When Pugsley moved to the United States, he reached an agreement with Ringwood to reproduce its Old Thumper strong ale – one-time winner of CAMRA's Champion Beer of Britain award – along with the Hampshire brewery's yeast when he created Shipyard Brewing in 1992.

The Ringwood yeast strain gives a rich and rewarding fruitiness to Pugsley's beers. The current brewery, which is the second site used, is close to the home of the poet Henry Wadsworth Longfellow, as well as the city's historic shipyard. An IPA makes sense in a city with such powerful links to the sea.

Fuggles IPA is a 'single varietal' beer, which means it is brewed with just one hop, the English Fuggle. The hops give a characteristic earthy, resinous, spicy and piny aroma and flavour to the beer. The grains are pale, crystal and malted wheat that combine to produce a biscuity, nutty and creamy note. Malt and hops are underscored by the distinctive orange fruitiness of the Ringwood yeast culture. This is a much-travelled culture: before Peter Austin founded Ringwood and then travelled the world building small breweries, he was head brewer at the Hull Brewery in North-east England and brought samples of their yeast south with him. The giant American brewer Miller has taken a stake in Shipyard: let us hope the character of the beers is not dumbed down.

Worthington's White Shield

Source: Coors Brewers, Burton-on-Trent, Staffordshire, England
Strength: 5.6%
Website: www.coorsbrewers.com

We finish this section with the granddaddy of IPAs. William Worthington was one of the great Burton brewing entrepreneurs of the 19th century who joined the scramble to export new pale ales to India and further afield.

Worthington's main claim to fame was the high quality of its bottled beers, a sector of the market that boomed when commercial glass-blowing developed in Victorian times. At one time, bottled beer accounted for more than half of Worthington's production. Although Worthington merged with Bass in the 1920s, its bottled beers continued to appear under its own name. In the 'keg revolution' days of the 1970s, when it was often difficult to find real draught beer in British pubs, White Shield, with its natural sediment of yeast, kept legions of beer lovers happy.

White Shield was shunted around various regional breweries when Bass lost interest in brewing, but it has now come home to Burton. The American brewing giant Coors bought the old Bass complex in 2000. This includes a fascinating museum of brewing and a small brewing plant in a former engine shed. The brewery, run by master brewer Steve Wellington, re-creates old Bass beers from the past, but White Shield is by far the biggest product.

It's brewed from pale malt with a tiny amount of crystal and hopped with English Challenger, Fuggles and Goldings. It is interesting to note that, as the classic IPA, it has 26 units of colour, making it quite dark for the modern interpretation of the style. The hops create 40 units of bitterness. This wonderfully enticing and complex beer has spices, peppery hops, light apple fruit and sulphur on the nose, with juicy malt, tart and tangy hops, hop resins and spices in the mouth. The lingering finish has a bitter hop character but is balanced by rich malt and apple fruit: apple is a defining note in Burton pale ales and is also found in Marston's Pedigree (see page 59).

To prove that bottle-fermented beers improve with age, I kept a White Shield in my cellar for 10 years. When opened, it was darker and fruitier than a young version, with a muted hop bitterness. Buy some and lay some down.

TASTING NOTES
Appearance
Aroma
Taste
Overall score

Pilsners

Pilsner, in common with India Pale Ale, transformed brewing in the 19th century, but its impact was more profound and enduring. The name comes from the Bohemian city of Pilsen, now the great industrial heartbeat of the modern Czech Republic. It was not the first lager beer but it was the original golden beer made by the new system of cold fermentation and ageing. For centuries, brewers in central Europe had struggled to keep beer free from infection during hot summers. In Bavaria, beers were stored in deep, icy caves in the Alps. (The German word for 'store' is *lager*.) The cold kept wild yeasts and bacteria at bay, and fermentation was slower due to the low temperatures.

BELOW
Pilsner Urquell is the original golden lager from Pilsen. Weihenstephan's Bavarian interpretation is regarded as a classic of the style.

This empirical method was turned into a commercial system as a result of the Industrial Revolution and the invention of ice-making machines. Following primary fermentation, beer was stored in cellars deep beneath breweries and kept cold by ice packed in rooms above. The yeast worked slowly, turning remaining sugars into alcohol with a lively, natural carbonation.

The first commercial lager beers, which were brewed in Munich and surrounding areas of southern Germany, were dubbed 'Bavarian beer'. They were dark brown in colour, as the method for brewing pale malt that had been developed in England had not yet reached central Europe.

Change was sudden in the 1840s. The spark came in neighbouring Bohemia when the disgruntled citizens of Pilsen poured an entire batch of the local brewery's beer down the drains. It was sour and undrinkable, and a clamour went up to open a brewery that would use the new methods developed in Munich. Local businessmen and tavern owners clubbed together to raise the funds to build the Burghers' [Citizens'] Brewery. A modern malt kiln was imported from England to enable pale malt to be made, while a Bavarian brewer called Josef Grolle, who was skilled in the arts of lager brewing, was hired.

Grolle's first brew appeared in 1842 and it was a sensation. Its golden appearance and clarity in the glass were appealing, while its complexity of aromas and flavours, at once rich and malty yet enticingly hoppy and bitter, entranced all who drank it.

The beer was called in the German fashion Pilsner, meaning 'from Pilsen', just as a Hamburger steak came originally from Hamburg and a Frankfurter sausage from Frankfurt. Pilsner's reputation spread rapidly, aided by canals and a new railway system that carried supplies to all the great cities of the Austrian Empire, across into Bavaria and up the Elbe to Hamburg and beyond. A Pilsen Beer Train left every morning for Vienna. The beer became a cult drink in Paris, and by 1874 the style had reached the United States.

While the conservative Bavarians were slow to switch from dark to golden lagers, brewers in other parts of Germany met the consumer demand for the new pale style. A sudden rush of competing Pilsner beers forced the Bohemian brewery in 1898 to register its beer as Pilsner Urquell (*Urquell* means 'original source' in German); it is known in Czech as Plzensky Prazdroj.

But the brewery stable door had been left open too long and the dray horses had bolted. Just before World War One, the Czechs took several German brewers to court in an attempt to stop them using the term Pilsner. The result was a compromise. The Germans agreed either to shorten the term to Pils or to state the place of origin on their label to avoid any suggestion the beer came from Pilsen. The Rhineland brewery Bitburger, the first to brew a German Pilsner, has ever since called its beer Bitburger Pils. Others have adapted the spelling slightly to Pilsener. These tinkerings had little effect. Most of the world thought Pilsner was a German beer, a misconception deepened by the Cold War, when Czechoslovakia disappeared behind the Iron Curtain as a Soviet satellite.

As lager brewing spread throughout the world, more and more Pils beers appeared. Many are travesties of the original. They are often too pale – a true Czech Pilsner is burnished gold with a hint of colour in its cheeks. A true Pilsner is never bland but has the classic signature of a floral, hoppy aroma and a dry and bitter – often intensely bitter – finish.

My first visit to Pilsner Urquell in the 1980s was a revelation. Both primary fermentation and lagering were in wooden vessels. Secondary fermentation and ageing took place in giant oak casks deep below ground in sandstone cellars. The casks were lined with pitch, which helped create a natural carbonation and a rich aroma and flavour. I learnt at both Pilsner Urquell and other Czech breweries that ageing beer in horizontal tanks or casks leads to a slower second fermentation, with some unfermented sugars left in the beer for fullness of palate. Today many

ABOVE
A Belle Epoque promotion for the original golden lager from Pilsen.

LEFT
Christoffel bier from the Netherlands is a fine example of a full-bodied modern Pilsner.

brewers have switched to upright conical tanks with faster and shorter ageing. The result, even at Pilsner Urquell, is beer with diminished character.

For this section of the book, I have chosen a handful of beers that I consider to be true to style, but I had to think long and hard before including the 'Original Source Pilsner'.

Bitburger Pils

Source: Bitburger Brauerei Theo Simon, Bitburg/Eifel, Germany
Strength: 4.8%
Website: www.bitburger.de

Bitburger not only brews a fine example of a Pilsner beer but it also played a central role in the development of the style. It was the first brewery outside Bohemia to label a beer Pilsner, an act that infuriated the Czechs. The result was a court case just before World War One that led to an agreement that German brewers would include the place of origin on the label of their Pilsner beers to avoid any suggestion that the beers came from Pilsen.

Bitburger and most other German brewers went a step further and shortened Pilsner to Pils. For decades the label has made it clear the beer comes from Bitburg, a small town in the Eifel lake district, close to both the Luxembourg border and the historic city of Trier, birthplace of Karl Marx.

The company was founded in 1817 by Theo Simon, whose head, topped by a smoking cap, still adorns the label. It was a humble farmhouse brewery that at first made warm fermenting beers, but by 1884 was producing a golden lager, using ice from the lakes for cold conditioning. Its fortunes were boosted when a rail line was built to supply the Prussian army with cannons from

the steelworks at Saarbrücken. The Simon family, which still owns the company, used the rail links to export its beer to northern Germany. The original brewery, with fine copper vessels, is in the centre of Bitburg and continues to make some beer, but the main production unit, built in the 1980s, is on a greenfield site outside the town.

Enormous care is devoted to selecting the finest raw ingredients: Alexis, Arena and Steiner spring barleys, and Hersbrucker, Hüller, Perle and Tettnang hops, plus a small amount of the locally grown Holsthum variety. The beer has three hop additions in the kettle and 38 units of bitterness.

Bitburger is lagered for six to eight weeks and emerges with a rich toasted malt nose balanced by floral hops and light citrus fruit. Juicy malt and tangy hops dominate the palate, while the long finish has a delicious bitter-sweet note of biscuity malt, piny hops and light fruit before finally becoming dry.

Bitburger Pils is widely exported and uses the famous advertising line '*Bitte Ein Bit*' – a Bit Please.

Brand-UP

Source: Brand Bierbrouwerij, Wijlre, Netherlands
Strength: 5.5%
Website: www.brand.nl

Brand is the oldest brewery in the Netherlands, dating from 1340, when it was part of the estate of the local lord. According to legend, the peasants on the estate spent more time drinking beer than attending church services and the brewery was sold. It came under the control of the Brand family in 1743 – what happened in the intervening centuries is unclear – and the brewery was modernised in the 19th century to switch to cold fermentation. In the 1970s, the company became the official supplier of beer to the Dutch royal family, which enabled it to be called the Royal Brand Brewery, though it lost the title in 1990. In 1989, Brand became part of the Heineken group but it enjoys considerable autonomy.

Brand makes a Premium Pilsener, brewed from 90% pale malt and 10% maize and aged for 42 days. But, unusually, Brand makes a second Pilsner. Brand-UP is not a soft drink: UP stands for Urtyp Pilsner, or Original Pilsner. The name is not designed to cause confusion with Pilsner Urquell but to emphasise that it's true to the style. Several Dutch and German brewers use *Ur* in their beer names to stress their originality or dedication to style.

Brand-UP is an all-malt brew and is hopped with German Hersbrucker, Spalt and Tettnang hops, varieties known as 'noble hops' as a result of their fine and delicate aromas. The beer is aged for up to 56 days, and has 36 to 38 bitterness units. It has a superb floral hop aroma with gently toasted malt and lemon fruit, with hop resins, juicy malt and tart fruit in the mouth. The finish is long, finely balanced between hop bitterness, citrus fruit and mellow malt. On a visit to Maastricht, I introduced some sceptical CAMRA members to Brand-UP and they were entranced. Brand beers are fresh and unpasteurised. The head brewer says: 'Pasteurisation serves to lengthen the shelf life of a beer but only marginally and at enormous costs to the taste and aroma of the beer.' Amen to that.

Christoffel Blond

Source: Bierbrouwerij St Christoffel, Roermond, Netherlands
Strength: 6%
Website: www.christoffelbier.nl

By alphabetical good fortune, the Brand brewery is followed by a second brewery in Dutch Limburg that was founded by a member of the Brand family. Leo Brand studied at the world-famous brewing faculty of Weihenstephan near Munich and then worked in the German brewing industry. In 1986, he returned home to launch his own brewery behind his house in the old coal-mining town of Roermond, where St Christopher is the patron saint. Brand moved to a new site in 1995 but kept the handsome domed and brick-clad copper kettle that he had found in a barn. He brewed strictly to the German *Reinheitsgebot*, the 16th-century Purity Law that permits only malted barley or wheat, hops, yeast and water: no sugars, chemicals or cheap 'adjuncts' such as rice or corn are permitted.

Brand was so dissatisfied with many beers labelled Pilsner that he called his interpretation Christoffel Bier, which was later changed to the even more undistinguished Blond. Don't let the name put you off: this is one of the finest modern Pilsners, bursting and booming with hop character and a massive 45 units of bitterness. It's brewed from pale barley malt only and hopped with Hallertau and Hersbrucker hops that give a superb piny and resinous aroma, with toasted malt and spicy hops in the mouth, followed by a finish of great length that becomes dry and bitter, with hints of iodine, rich malt and a late burst of citrus fruit.

When some drinkers complained the beer was too bitter, Leo Brand declared: 'I am not brewing to please everyone!' With that dedication to quality ringing in drinkers' ears, he retired in 2001, but his successors have remained true to his beliefs.

TASTING NOTES
Appearance
Aroma
Taste
Overall score

TASTING NOTES
Appearance
Aroma
Taste
Overall score

Grolsch Pilsener

Source: Grolsche Bierbrouwerij, Nederland, Boeklo, Netherlands
Strength: 5%
Website: www.grolsch.nl

TASTING NOTES
Appearance
Aroma
Taste
Overall score

This book proves, I hope, that small is beautiful. Grolsch is one of the few large breweries to figure in these pages but in Dutch terms it is a minnow compared to the global giant Heineken/Amstel. It has won a deserved international reputation for the quality of its beers by concentrating on good brewing practice and the finest raw materials.

In 2004, Grolsch moved from it historic sites at Enschede and Groenlo to a new brewery at Boeklo. Brewing water is pumped 7km (4 miles) from Enschede to ensure consistency of product, and Perle hops are sourced from the German

hop-growing area of Hallertau. The only significant change to the beer is that the brewery has phased out the use of a small amount of corn [maize].

In spite of the company's close proximity to the German border, it has concentrated on Dutch and international sales. But it is now keen to build sales in Germany, where it wants to adhere to the *Reinheitsgebot*, or Pure Beer Law, that forbids the use of any grains apart from malted barley and wheat.

Grolsch can trace its history back to 1615, but the modern company was the result of a merger in 1922 of two separate breweries in Enschede and Groenlo. It's now the second biggest brewing group in the Netherlands after Heineken/Amstel, though that's a bit like saying Manchester United and Oldham Athletic are both professional football clubs in North-west England. Grolsch is no slouch, though. The new site can produce 3.4m hectolitres (74.8m gallons) of beer a year: 600 bottles and 550 kegs are filled every hour.

The Pilsener is made from a complex blend of spring barleys grown in Belgium, England, France, Germany and the Netherlands. It is lagered for 10 weeks and has 27 units of bitterness. It has a grassy hop resins aroma balanced by lightly toasted malt, with a good tingle of hop bitterness and juicy malt on the tongue followed by a quenching, dry and gently bitter finish with a good underpinning of malt.

The beer is best known for its traditional 'swing-top' stoppered bottle. Drinkers in Britain are advised to drink this version, as conventional bottles and draught versions are brewed under licence by Coors in Burton-on-Trent. The swing-top beer is not pasteurised, which adds to its appeal and freshness. The survival of this delightfully old-fashioned bottle is due to consumer preference in the area of the Netherlands where Grolsch is based. People there have a reputation for being careful with their cash and prefer to drink only half a bottle at a time and reseal it to keep it in good condition for the following day.

Jever Pilsener

Source: Friesische Brauhaus zu Jever, Friesland, Germany
Strength: 4.9%
Website: www.jever.de

The old moated town of Jever (pronounced 'Yay-ver') and its brewery are in German Friesland, the region with a group of islands divided among Germany, Denmark and the Netherlands. The islands, which once formed an independent buffer state, were the setting for the first modern spy story, Erskine Childer's *The Riddle of the Sands*.

The Frisians enjoy bitter drinks, and Jever Pilsener, with a redoubtable 44 units of bitterness, satisfies their tastes: the word '*Herb*' on the label means bitter. The brewery was founded in 1848 by Diedrich Konig and would be dubbed a micro today. It soon passed to Theo Fetkoter, who not only expanded the business but also drew water from a nearby well. The well is still used today, and its silky softness helps create the beer's taste and allows the aroma and bitterness of the hops to shine through.

The brewery has had a seesaw history. It has been taken over several times and is now part of the Brau & Brunnen brewing group. During World War Two, it was starved of raw materials. It recovered and was able to expand as a result of the growing popularity of Pilsner beers.

Jever Pilsener is made from pale malt and is hopped with Hallertau and Tettnang German varieties. First-time drinkers should be warned that this beer has an uncompromising and shattering bitterness. It has a herbal, grassy and resinous aroma balanced by toasted malt and a faint hint of honey sweetness. Bitter hops burst on the tongue, while the finish has an iron-like bitter intensity with only a small walk-on part for malt.

The beer is the perfect companion for the fish dishes that dominate the cuisine in Friesland.

TASTING NOTES
Appearance
Aroma
Taste
Overall score

Malt Shovel James Squire Original Pilsener

Source: Camperdown, New South Wales, Australia
Strength: 5%
Website: www.malt-shovel.com.au

Only the Australians would name a brewery and its beers after a convict, recalling their colonial past and the infamous British practice of transporting 'criminals', often on trumped-up charges, Down Under. James Squire from Kingston in Surrey was arrested in 1785 and transported for the heinous crime of stealing chickens. While he was still a convict, he started to brew ale for the governor of New South Wales. When he was freed he was encouraged to brew commercially to counteract the illicit importing of rum. By 1805 Squire had successfully grown the first hops in the country and a year later he had opened a new brewery on the shores of the Parramatta River at Kissing Point. He followed this by building the Malt Shovel Tavern between Parramatta and Sydney. He is commemorated as the father of Australian brewing.

Chuck Hahn, an American with a love of Pilsner beers, built the modern Malt Shovel Brewery, which is now part of the Lion Nathan group. Unlike most Australian lagers, which are brewed with substantial amounts of cane sugar and are syrupy sweet as a result, Hahn's Original Pilsener uses pale and Munich malts without any brewing sugars. The hop varieties are Belgian and Czech Saaz. The delectable beer has a floral, herbal and spicy hop aroma, with mellow malt and tart hops in the mouth, and a lingering quenching finish that finally becomes dry with hop bitterness dominating. Hahn pays tribute to 'the industrious people of Plzen [Pilsen]' on the bottle label.

TASTING NOTES
Appearance
Aroma
Taste
Overall score

Moravia Pils

Source: Holsten-Brauerei, Hamburg, Germany
Strength: 4.8%
Website: www.hosten.de

TASTING NOTES
Appearance
Aroma
Taste
Overall score

The north-west region of Germany based around Bremen, Hamburg and Kiel has had a long association with brewing. These great ports were important members of the medieval Hanseatic League, a trading group that exported and imported energetically before the rise of modern nation states. As a result of its trading links, the modern German state of Schleswig-Holstein, formed in 1864 when Prussia annexed part of southern Denmark, has been open to brewing influences from further afield.

The first golden lager beer from Pilsen reached Hamburg in the 1840s via the River Elbe and won an award in 1863 at a brewing exhibition in the city. As a result, breweries in the region were quick to fashion their own interpretations of the style. The biggest brewery in the region today is Holsten, an Anglicised version of Holstein. It produces more than 1m hectolitres (22m gallons) a year for the domestic market, while its unremarkable Holsten Pils is brewed under licence in other countries.

For the German market Holsten brews a 5% Edel Pils, which is malty, hoppy and dry: *edel* means noble. Its best beer is the least known. Moravia Pils, once brewed in the neighbouring town of Lüneberg, with its cobbled streets, an impressive central square and many fine beamed and gabled buildings. Holsten has closed the brewery and moved production of Moravia Pils to Hamburg.

While much stress is rightly placed on the importance of Czech Saaz hops to the character of a Pilsner, the original Kronen [Crown] Brewery in Lüneburg also recognised the major contribution made to the flavour of the style by the barley grown in Bohemia's neighbouring region of Moravia. Both malt and hops came to Schleswig-Holstein via the Elbe. Moravia Pils has 38 units of bitterness, is brewed with pale barley malt and hopped with Hallertauer varieties; it is late hopped in the copper for maximum aroma and bitterness. The beer offers a floral, resinous aroma with notes of lightly toasted malt and citrus fruit. Juicy malt and tangy hops compete on the tongue, while the long finish becomes dry and hoppy but with balancing malt and fruit.

Holsten's brewery in Lüneburg was modern and functional but the site of the former Kronen brewery now houses a museum with fascinating artefacts from the early days of lager brewing, including a horizontal oak ageing vessel. The brewmaster's house is also open to visitors. It proves that brewers in the 19th century lived in some style. The house, which can be booked for functions, has wood-panelled walls and wide, sweeping staircases. The gabled exterior is one of the most impressive in the town.

For further information about the museum, visit the website: www.lueneburger-heide-attraktionen.de/brauereimuseum-lueneburg.

Pilsner Urquell

Source: Pilsner Urquell Brewery/Plzensky Prazdroj Pivovar, Pilsen, Czech Republic
Strength: 4.4%
Website: www.pilsner.urquell.com

TASTING NOTES
Appearance
Aroma
Taste
Overall score

On my most recent visit to Prague, I dropped into the Café Slavia, a famous haunt of writers and artists. It stands across the road from the impressive bulk of the National Opera House that was built by public subscription in the 19th century in order that operas could be performed in Czech when German was the official colonial language of Bohemia. As my first beer arrived, the heavens opened and Prague was drenched in heavy rain for several hours. I had no choice but to spend the afternoon drinking Pilsner Urquell. There are worse ways to lose a few hours and there is no doubt it is still a fine beer. But it's not the beer it used to be. As it's the original Pilsner, once the benchmark for how a true golden lager should taste, it's worth asking the question: why?

At first, all is strictly and reassuringly traditional in Pilsen. The brewery entrance is a stupendous 19th-century Napoleonic arch (see picture, page 30) that proclaims the pride and pomp of the industrial age. In the brewhouse, malt is mashed in an intricate system of linked, burnished copper vessels. The system is known as triple decoction. Once mashing is underway, one third of the grain is transferred from the first vessel to a second, where the temperature is raised, and the grain is then returned to its first home. Another portion of grain is then moved to a third vessel where the temperature is raised still higher before the grain returns to the first vessel. The system ensures that enzymes in the grain fully convert starch to sugar, while protein that would cause a haze in the finished beer is degraded.

When mashing is complete, the sweet extract, or wort, is pumped to direct-flame boiling coppers where whole flower Zatec hops are added three times. The copper boil is protracted, around 2½ hours (90 minutes are the norm in most breweries). This long boil extracts as many acids, resins and tannins as possible to give the beer a fine aroma and palate, as well as ensuring the clarity of the beer. The hops create 40 units of bitterness.

Before major change arrived in the early 1990s, the hopped wort was transferred to 30-hectolitre (660-gallon) open oak tuns for primary fermentation. Then the 'green', or unfinished, beer was taken underground to deep, dank, cold sandstone cellars where ageing and secondary fermentation took place in 35-hectolitre (770-gallon) horizontal oak casks. The casks were lined with pitch; periodically each cask was taken to the brewery yard to be relined, the air rich with the autumnal, piny smell of the burning pitch.

In the early 1990s, following the fall of the communist regime and the privatisation of the brewery, the oak vessels were replaced in stages by conical steel fermenting vessels. Today a few of the old wooden vessels are confined to a small on-site museum as an example of the quaintness of the past.

We are now getting close to unravelling the mystery of the beer's change of character. The long ageing in pitch-lined wooden vessels, allied to the soft spring waters used by the brewery, gave the beer a complex aroma and palate that was malty, creamy and buttery but underscored by a deep, firm bitterness and a fine floral, herbal, resinous hop aroma. Fermentation in conicals is faster and turns more malt sugars to alcohol; the result is a more austere beer in the North German style, with pronounced bitterness but a lack of the old malty complexity.

There is also controversy surrounding the length of time the beer is now aged. Pilsner Urquell claims that ageing lasts for 40 days and that has always been the case. But I am not alone in disputing this. In his *Beer Companion* (1993), Michael Jackson wrote: 'The beer is said to be lagered for between two and three months.' In two of my books, *The European Beer Almanac* and *The Ultimate Encyclopedia of Beer*, published in the early and mid-1990s respectively, I said even more emphatically that the beer was aged for 70 days. Michael and I did not make up the figures: we were given the information when we visited the brewery – separately – in the 1980s. Did the communists dupe us? Unlikely. The regime was proud of Pilsner Urquell and welcomed visitors, who were shown films in different languages about the history of the brewery and the brewing processes.

It's not a case of 'You pays your money and you takes your choice'. Younger drinkers can never taste the old Pilsner Urquell. Enjoy what is on offer. I can only regret that you will never have the opportunity to drink the original, the classic, the peerless Pilsner.

PS: The global brewing giant SABMiller now owns Pilsner Urquell. SAB stands for South African Breweries, which has merged with the American brewer Miller (brewer of Miller Lite, 'a fine Pilsener beer!). Pilsner Urquell is now brewed under licence in Poland and may also be made in Russia. How can the 'Original Pilsner' be made anywhere else than at source? By the river of Pilsen, there I sat down, yea, I wept when I remembered Urquell.

Spendrup's Old Gold

Source: Spendrup's Bryggeri AB, Varby, Stockholm, Sweden
Strength: 5%
Website: www.spendrups.se

While Jens and Ulf Spendrup are the fourth generation of the family to run a brewing business that bears their name, the modern company is the result of a merger of several brewers that formed a major independent counter to the might of Sweden's brewing giant Pripps.

Brewing is a difficult business in a country where beer is heavily taxed. Until Sweden joined the European Union in 1995, beer could be bought for home consumption only in state-owned shops. Stronger beers were taxed almost to oblivion and could not be sold in bars and restaurants; this restriction has now been relaxed. Pripps enjoyed government patronage as a nationalised industry and responded by producing astonishingly bland and undistinguished pale lagers (its main brand is called Bla, which means blue in Swedish, but could be taken as a consumer comment on the quality of the beer). The group was privatised in the 1990s and is now part-owned by the Volvo car group.

Spendrups has carved out an important niche in the market by concentrating on top-quality, all-malt golden lagers sold in attractive packaging. The group has several plants in Sweden, including a large, modern but attractive facility with copper vessels in the Stockholm suburbs, with fine views over a tree-fringed lake.

Spendrup's Old Gold is firmly in the Pilsner camp, to the extent of enjoying the burnished colour of a true member of the family. It's hopped with German varieties and has a luscious toasted malt, floral hops and light citrus fruit aroma. Juicy malt and bitter, spicy hops dominate the palate, while the lingering finish is finely balanced between creamy malt, tangy hop resins and tart lemon fruit.

This is a beer that deserves wider recognition and approval. The packaged version comes in a distinctive ridged brown bottle.

TASTING NOTES
Appearance
Aroma
Taste
Overall score

TASTING NOTES
Appearance
Aroma
Taste
Overall score

TASTING NOTES
Appearance
Aroma
Taste
Overall score

Trumer Pils
Source: Trumer Brauerei, Obertrum, Salzburg, Austria
Strength: 4.9%
Website: www.sigl.co.at

Trumer Pils is widely regarded as the finest Pilsner brewed in Austria. The independent, family-owned Sigl brewery has been producing beer since 1601 in a scenic Alpine location with access to an inexhaustible supply of fine brewing water from the surrounding mountains.

Austria was part of the 'golden triangle' of brewing innovation in central Europe: lagering techniques were pioneered in Munich, the first golden beer made by cold fermentation came from Pilsen, while the great Austrian brewer Anton Dreher produced the 'Vienna Red' style of lager beer that still finds expression in the March beers brewed in Munich and stored until the Oktoberfest.

Sigl's Trumer Pils is made with pale German malting barley and hops from Austria and the German Hallertau region. The hops create 26 units of bitterness, comparatively low for the style, but the softness of the water and the light malt character enable a delicate bitterness to permeate the beer from aromas to finish.

To avoid any harsh flavours from the malt, the husk is removed from the grain before mashing begins. The beer is kräusened during the ageing period: this means that a portion of unfermented, sugary wort is added to the lagering tanks to encourage a strong secondary fermentation. The beer that emerges from the long brewing and fermenting process – it is aged for six weeks – has a rich aroma of toasted malt, cornflour, noble hops and lemon fruit, with juicy malt and gently bitter hops in the mouth, and a quenching finish dominated by tart citrus fruit, spicy and bitter hops and sweet malt. It's an exceptional beer but, as I have criticised the owners of Pilsner Urquell for brewing the beer under licence, I must report that since 2004 Trumer Pils has also been brewed in Berkeley, California. It's made under the strict supervision of Sigl brewmasters using exactly the same ingredients, with the exception of the water, which flows from the Sierra Nevada mountain range rather than the Alps.

Weihenstephaner Pilsner
Source: Weihenstephan Brauerei, Freising, Munich, Germany
Strength: 5.1%
Website: www.weihenstephaner.de

Signs throughout the brewery, repeated on bottle labels, proclaim that Weihenstephan is the '*Ältester Brauerei der Welt*' (the oldest brewery in the world). *Weihenstephan* means Holy Stephen, and a religious community was built on a hill near Munich in 724 by Irish Benedictines to commemorate St Stephen, the first Christian martyr. The monks built a brewery in 1040 to sell beer locally to aid their work in the community, but it's likely they were making beer much earlier, as they were growing hops by 768.

The location was ideal for brewing, as beer could be stored in cellars dug into the hill. The monastery that developed on the site has been sacked and attacked many times over the centuries. It was secularised in 1815 and owned first by the Bavarian royal family and now by the state. The site today includes a brewery and the world-famous brewing faculty of Munich University that runs training courses for students from around the world. Directed by Professor Ludwig Narziss, the faculty works closely with the German health service to evaluate the healthy properties of beer. It has carried out important research in to the contribution that hops can make to help prevent cancer.

The brewery is best known for its wheat beers but it produces superb lagers as well, and the Pilsner is one the finest of the breed. It is brewed from German pale barley malt and hops from the neighbouring Hallertau region. The beer is wonderfully refreshing, with a malty and biscuity aroma balanced by tart lemon citrus fruit and spicy hops. Juicy malt, tangy fruit and hop resins dance on the tongue, while the finish is lingering and beautifully balanced between rich malt, bitter hops and fruit. Magnificent.

Brown & Mild Ales

Brown beers provide a link to two quite disparate brewing periods: the bucolic pre-industrial age and the smoke-stacked period of the late 18th and early 19th centuries. As I explained in the section on India Pale Ale (see page 10), before the Industrial Revolution most beers were brown in colour. Malt was cured in kilns in which wood provided the fuel: wood was cheap and plentiful, whereas coal and coke were taxed and expensive. The beers of the time had a smoky aroma and palate, sometimes with a touch of lactic sourness that resulted from long periods of maturation in giant oak vessels known as tuns.

Beers that most closely recall this method of brewing are the well-matured oud bruin, or old brown, beers of the East Flanders region of Belgium and which feature powerfully in its cuisine. And as many beer styles cross-pollinate, there is a further link with the well-matured 'country' beers that survive in the shape of Greene King's Strong Suffolk Ale and the 'sour red' beers of West Flanders.

Brown beers of the pre-industrial age that were stored for only a short time were often known as mild ale, as they lacked the sour bite of beers aged for lengthy periods. This type of mild ale was one of the constituents of the early porters and stouts. The term was resurrected in the later 18th and 19th centuries when brewers were anxious to reduce the cost of maturing beer in wood. A demand from industrial workers for a sweeter, lighter and cheaper beer than porter and stout coincided with the commercial needs of the brewers. A new type of mild ale was born. It was brewed at first using brown, well-cured malt but this was replaced in the 19th century by pale malt, which by then had become more widely available, and blended with such darker grains as crystal, black and chocolate malts. Brewing sugar and caramel were also used to give the beer the sweetness demanded by drinkers who wanted to restore the energy lost after long shifts in the sapping heat of factories and mines.

Mild ale, in common with the dark, or dunkel, lager beers of Bavaria, became the dominant beer style of the industrial age. While most modern milds are low in strength, the term 'mild' has nothing to do with weakness. It was used to define a style that, compared to pale ale, was sweeter and low in hop bitterness. In 1871, in Herbert's *Art of Brewing*, the typical gravity of mild was given as 1070 degrees, which is around 7% alcohol in modern measurement. At the turn of the 20th century the average strength of beer was 5.5% at a time when mild was the dominant style. This potent type of mild is still occasionally available, as can be seen in the remarkable Sarah Hughes' Dark Ruby, brewed in the West Midlands.

In Britain, mild did not lose its hegemony until the 1950s, when heavy industry went into decline and paler beers became the fashion. Mild's decline was hastened by its perceived old-fashioned, cloth-cap image. Several brewers responded to this problem

SARAH HUGHES
DARK RUBY
Established 1921
ALC 6% VOL

LEFT
Sarah Hughes' Dark Ruby is a fascinating example of the type of strong mild ale brewed in Victorian England.

In England, brown ale means a bottled version of mild. It is also the name for a stronger type of brown beer confined to the North-east corner of the country. Brewers in such important industrial centres as Newcastle and Sunderland responded to the popularity of the pale ales and bitters of London and the Midlands with strong but darker russet-coloured beers called brown ales. They are sweeter than pale ale but with more hop bitterness than traditional milds. North-east brown ale is represented in this section by Double Maxim, which originated in Sunderland and, to my mind, is a finer example of the style than a better-known beer from Tyneside.

by dropping the term 'mild' but continuing to brew beers that belong firmly to the mild family: see for example Banks's Original and McMullen's AK. The latter also stands as a reminder that not all members of the mild clan are dark in colour. In the 19th and early 20th centuries, many brewers produced several mild ales, among them light milds that were similar to pale ales or bitters in colour but which lacked their hop bite.

In some areas of England, mild has never gone away. Banks's Original is the main brand made by the country's leading regional brewer. Other brewers in the Black Country district of the West Midlands also remain major mild producers. South Wales and Merseyside may have lost their industries but dark milds nevertheless remain popular drinks in those regions. In general, mild has seen a small resurgence due to the rapid expansion of the micro-brewing sector, where brewers rather than accountants decide the beer portfolio and there is a keen determination to maintain Britain's rich heritage of beer styles. That determination has crossed 'the Pond' and several American small craft brewers now fashion brown ales, although the term 'mild' is not used in the United States.

Banks's Original

Source: Wolverhampton & Dudley Breweries, Wolverhampton, West Midlands, England
Strength: 3.5%
Website: www.fullpint.co.uk

This beer was called 'Mild Ale' until the 1990s when Wolverhampton & Dudley, the biggest regional brewing group in Britain, decided the word 'mild' would not appeal to younger drinkers and brought in the meaningless Original. But let's not quibble. This is a brilliant example of the Black Country style and is by far the biggest selling mild ale in Britain. The name Black Country comes from the time when factories belched black smoke into the atmosphere and industrial workers favoured a dark beer to quench their legendary thirsts.

In the 1890s a number of Black Country breweries, including Banks's of Wolverhampton and Hanson's of Dudley, merged at a time when mild was far and away the leading beer style of the region. The group, which now includes Marston's of Burton-on-Trent, remains a major mild ale producer, with Hanson's Mild Ale also in its portfolio, although the Dudley brewery is long closed.

Banks's has a fine traditional brewery in the centre of Wolverhampton. It malts its own contract-grown Maris Otter barley and also has its own hop 'yards', or fields, in Worcestershire where it grows Fuggles. The brewery even makes its own finings to clear beer: a section of the brewery has a stock of swim bladders from the sturgeon and other fish that are boiled on the premises. Banks's Original is comparatively light in colour – tawny or amber – registering 40 units. It's brewed from pale malt and caramel and hopped with Fuggles and East Kent Goldings: the hops contribute 25 units of bitterness. The beer has a rich vine fruits aroma with a gentle underpinning of hops. Sweet malt, dark, burnt fruit and hops mingle on the tongue, while vinous fruit contributes a port wine character to the finish, which also has a hint of vanilla and a gentle, fading hop bitterness. It's the caramel – burnt sugar – that gives Banks's Original its distinctive fruity and

vinous appeal. They call it 'empty glass beer' in the locality: as soon as you finish one pint, you'll want another.

Banks's Original is the brewery's flagship beer, accounting for 60% of production. It's available in bottle, but this is a beer to savour in cask-conditioned draught form.

TASTING NOTES
Appearance
Aroma
Taste
Overall score

Bateman's Dark Mild

Source: George Bateman & Son, Salem Bridge Brewery, Wainfleet All Saints, Lincolnshire, England
Strength: 3%
Website: www.bateman.co.uk

Bateman's is one of the most idyllic breweries in Britain. It stands on the banks of a small river and is dominated by a windmill that recalls the time when grain was milled on the site. George Bateman opened his brewery in 1874 and it is still run by members of his family, including another George, the current chairman. When the brewery was threatened by closure in the 1980s, George, his wife Pat and children Stuart and Jaclyn threw themselves into a battle to save the company. They were victorious in 1986 and, as though some divine hand had written the script, won CAMRA's Champion Beer of Britain competition that year.

Bateman's has won several awards in the competition since then, including a gold for Dark Mild in 1997. The beer is now widely available in cask form: several other regional breweries that had phased out their own milds take Bateman's beer in their pubs. While it has a modest strength, it is packed with rich malt and dark fruit notes and is unusually bitter for the style due to the blending of Challenger and Goldings hop varieties. The colour rating is 124, the bitterness units 24. The grains are Maris Otter pale malt, crystal malt and wheat malt, with small amounts of wheat syrup and caramel. It has a rich biscuity malt, burnt fruit and hazelnut aroma, with dark chewy malt, raisin fruit and hop resins in the mouth. The finish is far from sweet: it is dry with dark malt and caramel notes balanced by tangy hops.

The brewery includes a visitor centre and the Brewing Experience that follows all the stages of making beer. Dummies of brewery workers include look-alikes of Luciano Pavarotti and Bill Clinton: the former American president is cast in the role of cask sniffer. Wainfleet is on the Peterborough to Skegness railway line.

Batham's Mild Ale

Source: Batham's Delph Brewery, Brierley Hill, West Midlands, England
Strength: 3.5%
Website: www.bathams.co.uk

Batham's small brewery, with its 'brewery tap', the Vine pub next door, is a shrine for lovers of Black Country mild. The fascia of the pub bears a quotation from Shakespeare's *Two Gentlemen of Verona*: 'Blessings of your heart, you brew good ale', and the brewery richly deserves the Bard's accolade. The pub is best known by its nickname of the Bull and Bladder: a butcher's shop and slaughterhouse were part of the site when Daniel Batham took over the brew-pub in 1881 after he had lost his job in the local coal-mining industry.

Batham's had been in business for 70 years before it first brewed a bitter. Its success was rooted in its dark mild. Today, the brothers Tim and Matthew Batham are the fifth generation to run the brewery and its 10 pubs. Tim is the brewer and is justly proud of the small plant run on strict utilitarian Victorian 'tower brewery' lines, with the brewing process flowing logically from floor to floor without the aid of pumps. The hot liquor tank feeds the mash tun with water from the public supply that has been 'Burtonised', or hardened with the addition of gypsum salts. The malt is Maris Otter pale: the mild's colour comes from the use of caramel. Herefordshire Northdown and East Kent Goldings hops are added in the copper. After the boil, the hopped wort is cooled and pumped to wooden fermenting vessels, some of which are more than 100 years old. Mild and bitter are 'parti-gyle beers': additional brewing water or liquor is added to

the 4.3% Best Bitter to reduce it to 3.5% for the mild. Caramel is added in the fermenter and Tim adds twice the rate of yeast for mild as he does for the bitter. The acidity of the wort is lower in the mild than the bitter as a result of breaking it down with liquor and it is vital to get a vigorous fermentation going as quickly as possible.

Batham's Mild Ale is remarkable in several ways. A mild ale brewer would normally prefer soft to hard water, so the addition of gypsum to the brewing liquor gives the beer a flinty dryness missing from most milds. The beer is also dry hopped, which means additional Goldings are added to each cask of beer. The result is a mild with a pronounced bitter hop character. Finally, the combination of caramel and the Whitbread B yeast strain brings a rich blackcurrant fruit note to the aroma and palate. The ruby red beer, fruity, biscuity, hoppy and quenching, is best enjoyed in the Vine, a great Black Country institution, where regular live jazz concerts are staged in a large back room.

TASTING NOTES
Appearance
Aroma
Taste
Overall score

Brains Dark

Source: S A Brain, the Cardiff Brewery, Cardiff, Wales
Strength: 3.5%
Website: www.sabrain.com

TASTING NOTES
Appearance
Aroma
Taste
Overall score

Brains Dark is a Welsh legend. Visitors to Cardiff are immediately regaled by the brewery's products, as almost every pub seems to carry the name, while brewery drays, posters and bus sides inform all and sundry that 'It's Brains You Need'. As Cardiff develops into a modern metropolis, based on commerce rather than heavy industry, Dark still charms and refreshes beer lovers. It is now sold far from its home base as a result of winning many awards, including the Best Mild category in CAMRA's 2004 Champion Beer of Britain competition.

Samuel Arthur Brain took over a small brewery in central Cardiff in 1882. It expanded rapidly to keep pace with the astonishing development of Cardiff from an insignificant small town into a major port and city. The success of the brewery was based on its Dark Mild. It was known for many years as Red Dragon Dark, using the Welsh national symbol, and it's disappointing that this commitment to nationhood has been dropped at a time when Wales has gained its own elected assembly. With 212 pubs, Brains is a major force

in beer retailing in Wales and English counties that border the principality. It marked its commitment to brewing in 1999 when it moved from the city centre to the substantially bigger site vacated by Welsh Brewers, a subsidiary of Bass.

Dark remains a vibrant member of the beer portfolio, its signature being a rich chocolate character due to the generous use of chocolate malt, a grain that resembles coffee beans in appearance and which imparts a delightful aroma and palate. Pale malt, from Regina and Pearl varieties, are blended with chocolate malt. Brewing sugar and caramel are also used, and the beer is primed in cask with brewing sugar to encourage a powerful second fermentation. The colour rating is 110. The hop varieties are Challenger, Fuggles and Goldings, and the units of bitterness are 22. Light hops and rich chocolate dominate the aroma, while the palate encounters more chocolate, hops, dark malt and nuttiness. The finish is bitter-sweet, quenching, with a good, gentle underpinning of hops and a vinous note from the caramel.

Brooklyn Brown Ale

Source: Brooklyn Brewery, Brooklyn, New York City, USA
Strength: 5.6%
Website: www.brooklynbrewery.com

Brooklyn Brown Ale is the beer that launched the modern style version in the United States. The brewery was the brainchild of Steve Hindy and Tom Potter, journalist and banker respectively. At first the F X Matt Brewery in upstate New York brewed for them, but Hindy and Potter opened a dedicated brewing plant in Brooklyn in 1996.

Before Prohibition and the Great Depression, Brooklyn had been a major brewing area, dominated by German styles, but one by one all the breweries had closed. Hindy and Potter called on a veteran brewer named Bill Moeller, a man with German ancestry, to fashion first a Brooklyn Lager (see page 276) and then Brooklyn Brown Ale. The Brown Ale was meant to be a seasonal beer but its popularity caused it to become a regular brew.

The brewmaster at Brooklyn is Garrett Oliver, a celebrated beer connoisseur in the US, a man dedicated to re-creating classic styles. He gives regular seminars and is the author of the magnificent book on matching beer and food, *The Brewmaster's Table*. Since he arrived at the brewery in 1996, he has tweaked Brown Ale considerably and it is now very much his own beer.

Garrett is a fan of English brown and mild ales, but while he finds them light and refreshing, he looks for greater depth and complexity in his own beer. In particular, he wants some roasted malt character missing from most English interpretations of the style. He is also aided by a robust strength, something English milds have not enjoyed for many years. He blends English pale ale malt with Belgian aromatic malts and American caramel, chocolate malt and roasted barley. The colour rating is 35. The hops are all home-grown varieties: Cascade, American Fuggles and Willamette, which create 28 bitterness units. The finished beer has a burnished mahogany colour and a rich and inviting aroma of chocolate, dark, burnt fruit, roasted barley and tangy hops. Caramel, roast and chocolate dominate the palate, followed by a finish that is dry from the malts and roast, with a continuing chocolate note and a solid underpinning of tart hops.

Garrett recommends the beer as a companion for steaks, venison, ham and roasted pork and also for such cheeses as Cheddar, Gouda, Gruyère and Stilton.

TASTING NOTES
Appearance
Aroma
Taste
Overall score

Buckerfield's Appleton Brown Ale

Source: Buckerfield's Brewery, Swan's Hotel, Victoria, British Columbia, Canada
Strength: 5%
Website: www.swanshotel.com

Swan's Hotel in the centre of Victoria is a hotel in the grand manner, with many Art Nouveau flourishes, spacious rooms, deep leather sofas, an English-style pub, an art collection and its own brewery. It was fashioned in the 1980s from old grain and grocery warehouses by Michael Williams, a shepherd from Shropshire, England, who emigrated to Victoria, the most English of Canadian towns with its black taxis and red buses.

Williams trained dogs and bought grain from the warehouses that had been created in the 1800s to help feed the hordes of prospectors who used the town as a base while they searched for gold in the Klondike. Eventually, Williams was able to buy the buildings and transform them into Swan's Hotel, so called, he said, because the site had been an ugly duckling. As well as the on-site pub, complete with imported English handpumps to serve cask-conditioned beer, Williams got Frank Appleton to design a small brewery for him and then named one of his beers in the designer's honour.

The malts and yeast are imported from England, though the hops are grown in Washington State. Williams knew he couldn't sell beer with the low strength of an English mild, so Appleton Brown Ale has a robust strength and flavour. It's brewed using pale, crystal and chocolate malts with a touch of roasted barley. The hops are Cascade and Willamette in pellet form. The beer has a pronounced aroma of apple fruit and cinnamon, with dark fruit in the mouth and a creamy, bitter-sweet finish. There is a generous tart and fruity hop character underpinning the malt flavours and a pleasing, chewy and burnt note from roasted barley.

Michael Williams was a generous and engaging host when I visited Swan's in the 1990s, and I was saddened to hear that he has since died. He has left Swan's and Buckerfield's to the local university, which benefits from the profits made.

Cains Dark Mild

Source: Robert Cain & Co, Liverpool, England
Strength: 3.2%
Website: www.cainsbeers.com

Robert Cain came from Cork in Ireland to Liverpool and opened a striking red-brick Victorian brewery in 1850 that became one of the top 50 industrial companies in Britain. After several changes of ownership and closure for a while, Cains was bought in 2002 by two young entrepreneurs, Ajmail and Sudarghara Dusanj, who have restored the fortunes of the brewery and produced a special beer to mark the fact that Liverpool will be the European City of Culture in 2008.

Throughout its roller-coaster life, Dark Mild has been the bedrock of Cain's success and is now promoted with renewed vigour by the Dusanj brothers. The beer has a fascinating history. As a result of Liverpool's large Irish community, Guinness Stout has always had a big following there. Even when Guinness had a London brewery, the stout sold on Merseyside was brewed in Dublin. But Guinness was comparatively expensive and beyond the reach of impoverished Liverpudlians in the late 19th and early 20th centuries. As a result, Cains and other local brewers fashioned dark milds that were similar in character to Guinness while being considerably weaker and cheaper. The key ingredient was roasted barley, which gives a burnt, slightly acrid and bitter fruit flavour to beer. Cains has continued this tradition.

Dark Mild is brewed from a blend of Maris Otter pale barley malt, roasted barley and chocolate malt. The colour is 140. The hops are Styrian Goldings for aroma and Target for bitterness, with 23 bitterness units. To encourage a good hop character, Styrians are added late in the copper boil and also to each cask of beer as it leaves the brewery. The result is a distinctive beer with greater hop bitterness than is the norm for the style. It has a pronounced dark fruit, chocolate, roasted grain and bitter hops aroma, with roast and fruit dominating the palate. The finish is smooth, chocolaty and grainy but with a solid underpinning of hops.

Double Maxim
Source: Frederic Robinson, Unicorn Brewery, Stockport, Cheshire, England
Strength: 4.2%
Website: www.dmbc.org.uk

Double Maxim is a stalwart of Sunderland and Wearside, a fine example of a strong North-east brown ale. It's now being brewed on the other side of the country following the closure of Vaux of Sunderland in 1999. Two Vaux directors, Doug Trotman and Mark Anderson, and former head brewer Jim Murray, bought the brand, brew it at Robinson's and sell the beer nationally as a bottled product. They are still based on Wearside. Cuthbert Vaux founded his brewery in Sunderland in 1837 to meet the demands of shipbuilders and miners in the area. A beer called Maxim Ale was brewed to mark the activities of Captain Ernest Vaux, who had led a raid during the Boer War in South Africa using a Maxim machine gun. A stronger version of the beer, called Double Maxim, was introduced in 1938, no doubt to offer some choice and competition to the high-profile Newcastle Brown Ale brewed since 1927 on neighbouring Tyneside.

The beer is brewed with pale and crystal malts with a touch of caramel and is primed with sugar to encourage a powerful fermentation. Fuggles are the only hops used, giving the beer a superb earthy, spicy and resinous aroma. It is fruity – plums and apricots – and nutty in the mouth, and comes dry in the finish with some tart fruit and spicy hop notes. It has 22 units of bitterness. It's good news that this important North-east beer is still brewed. The only sadness is that, after years of lobbying by CAMRA, Vaux relented in the 1990s and produced a cask-conditioned version of Double Maxim but today only the filtered bottled version remains.

TASTING NOTES
Appearance
Aroma
Taste
Overall score

TASTING NOTES
Appearance
Aroma
Taste
Overall score

Elgood's Black Dog Mild

Source: Elgood & Sons, Wisbech, Cambridgeshire, England
Strength: 3.6%
Website: www.elgoods-brewery.co.uk

Elgood's, in the North Brink area of Wisbech alongside the River Nene, is one of the finest brewery sites in Britain. It dates from 1795 and was one of the first classic Georgian breweries to be built outside London. It came under the control of the Elgoods in 1878, and the fifth generation of the family runs the company today. Managing director Belinda Sutton is an Elgood and one of the few women to direct a major brewery in Britain. As well as an attractive brewhouse and fermenting rooms, Elgood's also has magnificent grounds and gardens administered by one of Belinda's sisters. It is possible to tour both the brewery and gardens: see the website for information.

Black Dog Mild is a reminder that mild ales were not just brewed to refresh industrial workers – agricultural workers also needed refreshment, and dark milds, with both sweetness and bitterness, were in great demand in the fenlands of Cambridgeshire between the 18th and mid-20th centuries.

Black Dog, which takes its name from the brewery's logo of a dark hound with a key in its mouth, was a finalist in CAMRA's Champion Beer of Britain competition in 2004 and has won many other CAMRA awards. Its signature comes from the use of roasted barley, which gives the beer a chewy, grainy appeal. The malts are Maris Otter pale and crystal, with some flaked maize and torrefied wheat, which are used mainly to give the beer a good collar of foam: they are virtually identical to cornflakes and popcorn respectively, and in the wrong hands (i.e. some American and Australian lager brewers) are used in large quantities for cheapness and clarity. Clarity in Black Dog is not a major consideration with a colour rating of between 80 and 100. Fuggles hops contribute 25 units of bitterness. The beer has a pleasing aroma of roasty and toasty grain balanced by the familiar earthy hop resins imparted by Fuggles. Dark malt, vinous fruit, roasted grain and light hops dominate the mouth, while the lingering finish is finely balanced between fruit, hops and dark grain.

Highgate Dark Mild

Source: Highgate Brewery, Walsall, West Midlands, England

Strength: 3.4%

Website: www.astonmanor.co.uk

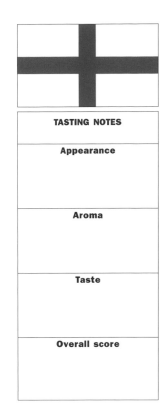

The Highgate Brewery stands as testament to the importance of mild ale to the Midlands region of England. The imposing red-brick brewery – standing somewhat incongruously on rising ground in a residential area of Walsall – was opened in 1898 with a capacity of 100,000 barrels a year to make just dark mild for workers engaged in the local leather industry. In 1938, Highgate was taken over by the giant Birmingham brewery of Mitchells & Butlers, another major mild producer. M&B planned to close Highgate but kept it open during World War Two, when every brewery received rations of malt and hops, and the Birmingham brewery didn't want to lose the raw materials earmarked for Walsall. When M&B became part of Bass, Highgate continued to brew as the smallest plant in the Bass group. It was bought by its management in 1995 and is now owned by the Aston Manor brewing company of Birmingham.

Much of the equipment in the spacious and spick-and-span brewery still dates from Victorian times. Mashing takes place in two ancient tuns, originally made of wood, relined with stainless steel but retaining hand-raised wooden lids. Boiling is carried out in two burnished and cherished coppers with internal heating columns topped by funnels known as Chinese Hats. The splendid fermenting room is packed with a variety of round and square wooden vessels. Head brewer Neil Bain describes the Highgate house yeast as 'a beast': unusually, it is a four-strain type, with each strain attacking elements of the brewing sugars at different times.

The recipe for Highgate Dark Mild calls for 2 tonnes/tons of Pearl pale malt, 65kg (143lbs) of black malt and 15–20kg (33–44lbs) of crystal malt for every 100 barrels brewed. Maltose syrup and caramel are also used to increase fermentability and colour. The colour rating is 70. Brewing liquor, rich in iron, is drawn from a bore hole on the site. Whole hops are Goldings and Progress, which create 22 units of bitterness. The finished beer has a complex aroma of dark fruit, chocolate and liquorice with chewy dark grain, chocolate and light, spicy hops in the mouth. The lingering finish is malty and fruity with a good underpinning of hops. Dark Mild is the base from which Highgate's strong winter beer, Old, is brewed.

TASTING NOTES
Appearance
Aroma
Taste
Overall score

TASTING NOTES
Appearance
Aroma
Taste
Overall score

Holt's Mild Ale

Source: Joseph Holt, Derby Brewery, Cheetham, Manchester, England
Strength: 3.2%
Website: www.joseph-holt.com

Joseph Holt is a phenomenon. Year in and year out, it is one of the most successful and profitable breweries in Britain, but it has achieved this success by remaining determinedly independent and family-owned. In the 1990s, it withdrew from the London Stock Exchange for fear it might put its independence at risk. The company owns 127 pubs, a considerable estate, but all within a 25-mile radius of the brewery. It still supplies its pubs with its bitter in giant 54-gallon hogsheads and refuses to supply beer festivals that are outside its trading area. It neither seeks nor requires publicity. In 1992, I was the first journalist ever allowed through the doors, and I asked about the Holt's advertising policy. I was met with a bemused look from company secretary Tom Dempsey. 'Do you mean our beer mats?' he asked.

Joseph Holt, the son of a weaver, founded the brewery in 1849. As the population of Manchester exploded in the middle of the 19th century from 70,000 to more than 300,000 due to the demand for cotton, brewers set up in business to meet the insatiable demand for refreshing mild ale. Joseph went to work as a carter for a Manchester brewery and then, supported by wife, Catherine, opened two small breweries of his own before moving to the present site. While considerable sums have been spent upgrading the business in recent years – it now has something as modern as a website and even makes its own lager – it nevertheless remains firmly traditional, still using many brewing vessels from the 19th century.

The mild is sensational. At a small beer festival in the North-west some years ago, surrounded by a fine choice of local beers, I drank nothing but this remarkable dark and bitter ale. It is yet another example of the more bitter style of mild made in the North-west, with Goldings and Northdown whole cone hops creating 30 units of bitterness. It is brewed with Halcyon and Alexis pale malt, crystal malt, flaked maize and dark invert sugar. Chocolate, liquorice, tart fruit and peppery hops coat the tongue, while the long finish is dry and bitter, but quenching with tart fruit and chocolate notes.

Hydes Dark Mild

Source: Hydes Anvil Brewery, Manchester, England
Strength: 3.5%
Website: www.hydesbrewery.com

The demand for mild is still so strong in the Manchester area that Hydes produces three versions of the style: Light Mild, Traditional Mild and Dark Mild, all 3.5%. The family-owned company, which has 72 pubs, dates from 1863, when Alfred and Ralph Hyde bought a small brewery from their grandfather, Thomas Shaw. In step with the development of Manchester into a vast, thriving and humming industrial city, the Hydes moved three times before settling on the present site in the Moss Side district. The name was changed to Hydes Anvil Brewery in 1944 to incorporate the anvil trademark, a sign of strength, craftsmanship and durability. The brewery has enjoyed considerable expansion in recent years, installing new brewing, fermenting and conditioning capacity to increase annual production from 60,000 barrels to 100,000.

The milds are essentially the same brew with the addition of darker grains for colour and flavour. The classic Dark Mild is distinct from Light and Traditional due to the use of chocolate malt. The recipe comprises Fanfare pale ale malt, crystal malt and chocolate malt, with a colour rating of 115. It is a single hop varietal beer, using just Fuggles, which create 23 units of bitterness. The aroma is roasty and chocolaty, with juicy malt and gentle, spicy hops. Rich smoky, roasted grain and chocolate fill the mouth, while the finish is bitter-sweet, with dark, roasted malt, tart fruit and light hop notes.

TASTING NOTES

Appearance

Aroma

Taste

Overall score

Liefman's Oud Bruin

Source: Liefman's Brouwerij, Oudenaarde, Belgium
Strength: 5%
Website: www.liefmans.be

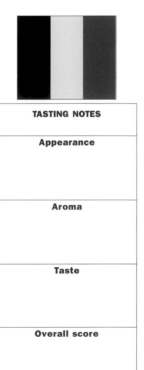

The Oud Bruin, or Old Brown, beers of East Flanders are a powerful link to the long-matured brown ales that were the dominant feature of brewing before the industrial revolution of the late 18th and 19th centuries. The region also has another claim to fame: it is home to one of the great beer-based culinary dishes, *carbonade flamande*, the classic beef stew, in which the meat is tenderised with Old Brown beer. The fact that Old Brown beers are also known as 'provision beers' stresses the point that their roots lie in pre-industrial societies where agricultural workers needed hearty food and drink to sustain them in their labours.

Oudenaarde is the historic capital of East Flanders, on the River Scheldt that flows to Ghent and Antwerp. The town has striking Gothic architecture and was once the capital of the

whole of ancient Flanders. It was central to the textile industry and was the birthplace of Jean Gobelin, the celebrated tapestry designer. Another famous citizen was the 11th-century Benedictine monk Arnold of Oudenaarde, who was a brewer and one of two Saint Arnolds from the area referred to as the patron saint of brewers.

Liefman's brewery has some history, too. It opened in 1679, which places it at the dawn of modern brewing and predates the early porter brewers of England who created a commercial industry there. While the current vessels at Liefman's do not date from the 17th century, the practice of long maturation and multistrain yeast cultures are a powerful reminder of ancient brewing methods that impart a characteristic bitter-sweet flavour with a hint of sourness. In the 1970s, when the owner of the brewery died

TASTING NOTES

Appearance

Aroma

Taste

Overall score

suddenly, it was taken over by the brewer's secretary, Rose Blancquaert-Merckx, who was known to everyone in the brewery and the town as 'Madame Rose'. A former ballet dancer, she occasionally surprised visitors by kicking off her shoes and dancing inside one of the brewery vessels. Her passion and verve helped build awareness of Liefman's beers, and the passion continued when she retired from the brewery to run De Mouterij (The Maltings) in Oudenaarde, a restaurant that specialises in beer dishes, including *carbonade flamande*.

Madame Rose's retirement coincided with the takeover of Liefman's by the Riva brewing group, best known for its Dentergems spiced wheat beer. For reasons I have never grasped, Riva decided to mash and boil Liefman's beers at its own brewery in Dentergem. The liquid is then trunked back to Oudenaarde where it is fermented, matured, blended and bottled with live yeast to encourage a second fermentation.

For Oud Bruin, Pilsner malts are blended with Munich and Vienna malts and a touch of roasted barley. Whitbread Goldings Variety – actually a type of Fuggle – is the main bittering hop with German and Czech varieties: they contribute 20 units of bitterness. The house yeast strain is carefully stored and cultured in the brewery but it came originally from the Rodenbach brewery in Roeselare, famous for its 'sour red' beer: it is the yeast that gives the lactic edge to Liefman's beers.

Another characteristic is the brewing liquor: instead of adding the traditional sulphites beloved by ale brewers, Liefman's uses sodium bicarbonate, which adds a softness to the beer and presumably guards against any ill effects from too generous portions of *carbonade flamande* in the town's restaurants.

After primary fermentation, Oud Bruin is matured for four months in metal tanks, an astonishing period for an ale and, again, a powerful link to brewing practices from earlier times. The beer that emerges from this long process has a rich aroma of dark fruits, roasted grain, a hint of chocolate and peppery hops. Sweetness is evident in the mouth but is balanced by the lactic note and the hops. The lingering finish is bitter-sweet, with rich, dark malts, spicy hops and the persistent hint of sourness.

A stronger version of Oud Bruin is known as Goudenband (Gold Riband). This 6% beer is the result of blending Oud Bruin with a stronger beer that has matured for between six and eight months. Both beers are centrifuged to remove the yeast and then reseeded with a dosage of fresh yeast and priming sugar to encourage fermentation in bottle. The bottles are matured for a further three months in the brewery's cellars before being released.

Goudenband has the characteristic Liefman's sourness but is balanced by an even greater fruitiness and spicy hop than Oud Bruin. It has 60 colour units and 20 units of bitterness. If bottles are laid down for several years, the beer will take on a pronounced 'sour wine' note that some drinkers compare to dry Spanish sherry.

There are more joys yet. Once a year, the brewery adds cherries or raspberries to Goundenband, which is then fermented for a further two months, creating beers with strengths of 7.1% for the cherry beer and 5.1% for the raspberry version. When young, these beers are fruity, even cloying, but laid down for a year or more, the sweetness diminishes and the sourness breaks through, making them wonderfully refreshing.

All the Liefman's beers, presented in attractive stoppered bottles and wrapped in coloured tissue paper, should be treasured as remarkable examples of the rich tapestry of beer and brewing history.

McMullen's AK

Source: McMullen & Sons, Hertfordforshire, England
Strength: 3.7%
Website: www.mcmullens.co.uk

McMullen's AK is, like Winston Churchill's description of Soviet Russia, 'a riddle wrapped in a mystery inside an enigma'. It is that rare beer in modern times: a light mild, and a splendidly full-bodied, full-tasting member of a much-depleted style. But where does the curious name come from? There is nothing in the brewery's records or archives, even though it's the company's biggest-selling brand that has existed since at least the late 19th century.

AK was once widely used as a brand name, most notably by the large Kentish brewery Fremlins. One suggestion for the name comes from brewing historian Martyn Cornell who argues that the 'K' may derive from a medieval Dutch beer called Koyt, which came in two strengths: Single and Double Koyt. Single in old Dutch was Ankel, therefore the weaker of the beers would have been branded AK. Flemish weavers who settled in Kent in the 15th century brought with them a considerable thirst for beer and may have handed on the AK designation to local brewers.

My own theory is more prosaic but is also based on the system of branding casks with letters long before beer mats, bar towels and pump clips were in use. For centuries, a widely used form of branding was the 'X' to denote strength, still in use (and even abuse) today with such beers as Castlemaine 4X. It was a simple system: the more Xs on the cask, the stronger the beer. In Victorian times, two main beer styles developed: mild and pale ale or bitter. Pale ale casks continued to be branded with Xs. If you split an X vertically, you get a K, which became the 19th-century method of branding mild. At a time when many breweries produced several versions of mild, AK meant either the weakest mild or it was used to distinguish light mild from dark.

McMullen, a family with Irish connections, dropped the term 'mild' in the 1990s in an attempt to rebrand AK for the modern market. The brewery dates from 1827 when Peter

McMullen, a cooper, decided it would be more sensible and profitable to put his own beer in the casks he built. Today, the striking red-brick Victorian site supplies beer to 134 pubs in Hertfordshire, Essex and London.

AK is brewed with water from an artesian well beneath the brewery, Halcyon pale malt, a tiny amount of chocolate malt, flaked maize and maltose syrup. The single hop variety is Whitbread Goldings. The colour is 24, the bitterness 22. There is another Whitbread connection: the yeast culture is known as Whitbread B and originated in the Mackeson Milk Stout brewery in Kent. It imparts a rich and fruity character to the beer. AK has a floral and spicy hop nose with juicy malt and tart orange fruit. Biscuity malt, tangy fruit and delicate hop resins dominate the mouth while the finish is dry with a good malty character balanced by orange fruit and hop resins. It's a great beer by any name.

Manns Original Brown Ale

Source: Burtonwood Brewery, Warrington, Cheshire, England
Strength: 2.8%
Website: www.refreshuk.com

TASTING NOTES
Appearance
Aroma
Taste
Overall score

For once, the overused word 'original' is apt. The large East London brewer Mann Crossman & Paulin launched the beer in 1902 as a mixer with draught mild. Drinkers at the time complained that draught mild was rough and badly kept, and the head brewer at Manns, Thomas Wells Thorpe, introduced the first example of bottled mild, which he dubbed brown ale, as an antidote. At just 2.8%, it was extremely low in alcohol for the time but its sweetness and smoothness took the edge off the harshness of the stronger draught versions available. Thorpe described it as 'the sweetest beer in London'.

Many brewers followed Manns but the Cockney beer dominated the market. Manns was taken over by the giant brewing group Watneys in 1958 and the Whitechapel brewery eventually closed. But Manns Brown had such a large following that Watneys continued to brew it. For a while it was produced at another Watneys subsidiary, Ushers of Trowbridge in Wiltshire, where it accounted for an astonishing 200,000 barrels a year. Ushers, too, closed and for several years Manns Brown has been brewed at the Burtonwood brewery in North-west England, a long way removed from its Cockney heartland. But the Cockney traditions of the beer had been diluted in the 1990s when it was promoted with the aid of the *Daily Mirror* cartoon character Andy Capp, who came from Sunderland and was more likely to sup copious amounts of Double Maxim than ale from London.

The drinks group Refresh UK, which also owns the Brakspear and Wychwood breweries in Oxfordshire, now owns Manns Brown and has promoted it with some zeal, though it doesn't stress the point that it was the favourite tipple of the vast and exploding Mr Creosote in *Monty Python's The Meaning of Life*.

Manns now commands a 90% share of the sweet brown ale market. Brewed with pale and crystal malts and a touch of roasted barley and wheat malt, and hopped with Target, it has a sweet toffee and light sultana fruit aroma, with more toffee, coffee, dark fruit and roasted grain in the mouth. The finish is sweet but not cloying, and is dominated by rich malt and vine fruits, with only the lightest hint of hops.

Mighty Oak Oscar Wilde

Source: Mighty Oak Brewing Co, Maldon, Essex, England
Strength: 3.7%
Website: www.mightyoakbrewery.co.uk

TASTING NOTES
Appearance
Aroma
Taste
Overall score

Oscar Wilde, an archetypal 'champagne socialist', is an unlikely drinker of dark mild. But this is Cockney rhyming slang and Oscar Wilde stands for mild, though I cannot recall from my East End youth ever hearing anyone order 'a pint of Oscar'. Perhaps I frequented the wrong pubs.

Mighty Oak is an award-winning micro-brewery founded in 1996 by John Boyce and his partner Ruth O'Neill. John worked for many years at the now-closed Ind Coope brewery in Romford, while Ruth is that most useful of people in a brewery: an accountant.

In the brewery's short history, it has moved to bigger premises and increased production to 70 barrels a week to supply pubs in London and the surrounding counties. John Boyce will remember from his previous employment that Ind Coope brewed a mild ale, as did the great brewers close by in East London, which was the base – as a result of good water supplies – for the likes of Charrington, the previously mentioned Manns, and Truman: Truman brewed Trubrown, the first mild ale to be advertised on British television in the 1950s.

Oscar Wilde is strong for the style and has a good hop character. It's brewed with Maris Otter pale malt, crystal malt and chocolate malt. The only hop is Challenger, which creates 21 units of bitterness. It has smoky malt and espresso coffee on the aroma with dark fruit notes and hop resins. Coffee and chocolate flavours dominate the mouth with dark and bitter fruit and the tang of hops. The long finish has tart and bitter hops, vinous fruit, chocolate and dark malt.

Would you Adam and Eve it, it's a great pint of pig's ear.

Moorhouse's Black Cat

Source: Moorhouse's Brewery, Burnley, Lancashire, England
Strength: 3.4%
Website: www.moorhouses.co.uk

Black Cat gave an enormous boost to the mild ale sector in England when it won CAMRA's Champion Beer of Britain award in 2000. Its success proved that mild ale was a beer style fit for a new millennium. The championship was also a boon for a company that had had a helter-skelter existence since a Burnley businessman, William Moorhouse, launched it in 1865. He concentrated at first on making mineral waters but his success prompted him to build a bigger site and add beer and 'hop bitters' to his portfolio.

Hop bitters were in vogue in the late 19th and early 20th century as a result of lobbying against the 'demon drink' by a powerful temperance movement. Moorhouse's hop bitters were less than 2% alcohol and were sold in special Temperance Halls set up to wean working people in Burnley's mills away from strong liquor.

When the descendants of William Moorhouse sold the business in 1978, it went through several hands and was on the point of closing in 1985 when Bill Parkinson had a pint of Moorhouse Bitter and – like the American who loved his Remington razor so much he bought the company – made a bid for the brewery and owned it within seven days.

Mr Parkinson had made his fortune from Lifting Gear Hire, a heavy engineering firm that, for example, supplied the equipment to lift the stricken Russian submarine *Kursk* from the bottom of the Barents Sea. He has since invested more than £1 million in the company and added new brewing equipment with the aim of boosting production to 20,000 barrels a year.

Moorhouse's is best known for its strong bitter, Pendle Witches Brew (see page 106), named after the terrifying old crones who inhabited the Pendle Moors outside Burnley in the 16th and 17th centuries. But Black Cat has also established itself as a major national brand, winning an award in the International Brewing competition in 1998, the overall CAMRA championship in 2000, and silver and bronze awards in the same competition in 2001 and 2002.

It's a brilliant example of a North-west dark mild, brewed with Halcyon pale malt, chocolate malt, invert sugar and flaked maize. The only hop is Fuggles. It has a succulent aroma of dark, roasted grain, bitter chocolate and light hop resins. Chocolate dominates the palate but there are also notes of dark fruit and light, spicy hops. The finish has some dark fruit notes, with a continuing chocolate presence and gentle hops. Above all, it is wonderfully refreshing.

Sarah Hughes Dark Ruby

Source: Sarah Hughes Brewery, Beacon Hotel, Sedgley, West Midlands, England
Strength: 6%
Website: None

This is the way dark milds used to be in the 19th and early 20th centuries: strong. I have seen the beer described as 'old ale' but I disagree and regret that brewery owner John Hughes has pandered to this view by dropping 'mild' from the title.

When the Beacon Hotel was built in 1850 the site included its own tiny 'tower' brewery in the yard at the rear. Sarah Hughes bought the hotel in 1921 and ran it for 30 years, handing it over to her son and daughters when she retired. She died in 1951. The brewery had always made just one beer: the strong dark mild. The Hughes family closed the brewery in 1958 but Sarah's grandson, John, decided to reopen it in 1987. All the old wooden vessels had rotted away and were replaced by stainless-steel ones faced with wood. John had the good fortune to discover Sarah's recipe for her mild in an old cigar box locked in a bank security vault.

To watch the brewing process, you have to clamber up narrow wooden stairs to the top of the building. Maris Otter pale malt is blended with 10% crystal malt. After mashing, the extract is dropped a few feet into a tiny underback and from there into the original open-topped copper where it is boiled with Fuggles and Goldings. It then falls to a hopback for clarification and then into five fermenters converted from cellar tanks from the old Ansells brewery in Birmingham. John Hughes won't reveal the source of his yeast but says it comes from another Black Country brewery, which narrows the field.

John has lovingly restored the hotel and turned it into a shrine to Victoriana, complete with tap room, smoke room and snug, all with open fires and tiled floors. Each room is supplied with beer from a central servery, with glasses pushed through a hatch. Every item is Victorian, including the gas lamps, wallpaper and out-of-tune piano.

Dark Ruby, brewed by Guy Perry, has a rich and fruity nose with blackcurrant dominating, laced with earthy Fuggles hop resins. The palate is amazingly complex, summoning up every dark fruit imaginable: it is like chewing all the dark sweets from a tube of Maynard's Wine Gums. The finish is dry, with spicy and peppery hops balancing the tart, tangy, bitter fruits and dark malt. As well as being available on draught, Dark Ruby also comes in bottle-fermented form and is suitable for vegans.

TASTING NOTES
Appearance
Aroma
Taste
Overall score

Pale Ales

The boundary between pale ale and bitter is – unlike the beers themselves – often a hazy one. Some books on beer do not trouble to make the distinction, merging the two styles. Even brewers are sometimes confused. Marston's Pedigree is a classic Burton pale ale, and I include it in this section, but it's marketed as a bitter.

Pale ale should live up to its name: the earliest versions were brewed only with pale malt and brewing sugar, whereas bitter made use of a new type of malt called crystal that gives a bronze or copper colour to the finished beer. Both styles are bitter in the sense that hop rates are generous, and brewers tend to choose varieties that impart tangy, spicy, peppery, citrus fruit and resiny aromas and flavours. But, to paraphrase the old philosophy joke, we must not put Descartes before the dray horse. Pale ale predates bitter by some years. While there are some references to 'bitter beer' in 19th-century books, the word was used as a descriptor rather than as a generic term. Bitter, as is made clear in the next section (see pages 66–7), developed as a style at the turn of the 20th century. Pale ale appeared much earlier.

The success of India Pale Ale abroad encouraged the Burton brewers to make IPA available to the home market, a task made easier by the new railway system that was faster and more direct than coaches and canals. But many drinkers found IPA too strong and too bitter. British brewers hurried to produce a type of pale ale that would better suit the domestic market, with less alcohol and fewer hops. They were aided by dynamic changes in brewing practice made possible by better-quality malt, hops and refrigeration. Louis Pasteur in France and Emil Christian Hansen in the Carlsberg laboratories in Copenhagen developed a scientific understanding of yeast that led to pure cultures being developed, with improved fermentations free from infection. The brewers were anxious to move away from the expense of storing or vatting beer for long periods, a system that became out of date with new yeasts that packed down quickly and allowed beer to 'drop bright' within weeks rather than months. When tax was lifted on glass in the late 19th century, brewers were able to produce bottled beer for the first time in substantial quantities.

Bottled pale ale acquired snob appeal as British society changed dramatically with the growth of a new and large middle class. Pale ale was not cheap and its price was pitched above those for mild and porter. Richard Wilson, writing in *The British Brewing Industry 1830–1980*, argues that 'Quality and cost… made it [Burton pale ale] a status drink for the expanding lower middle class of clerks and shopkeepers, the armies of rail travellers and those "aristocrats of labour" [skilled workers] whose standards of living rose appreciably after 1850.' Wilson described bottled pale ale as 'the high-fashion beer of the railway age'. It was consumed at home by 'respectable' middle-class drinkers who did not wish to rub shoulders with the hoi polloi in common ale houses. Here was the dividing point: pale ale, unlike the milds and porters of the time, and the bitters or 'running beers' that came later, became identified as a bottled, rather than a draught, product. The gap became wider as large brewers, such as Whitbread in London, made bottled pale ale a leading brand in their portfolios and eventually filtered and pasteurised them for ease of home delivery and consumption.

Confusion and the blurring of the distinction between pale ale and bitter took place in the 20th century as draught bitter increased rapidly in popularity. While the likes of Bass and Worthington continued to produce sedimented pale ales in bottle, many brewers preferred to cut costs by bottling filtered and pasteurised versions of their bitters and labelling them light ale or pale ale. The result has been that a style pioneered in Britain, and a descendant of the revolutionary IPAs of the early 19th century, is now confined to just a handful of beers. For this reason, the beers represented in this section are largely 'New World' pale ales brewed in the United States. In the US, in particular, there is a passion for faithfully and passionately re-creating great beer styles. As the term bitter is rarely used in the US, American pale ales bursting with rich malt and hop character have rescued and revived a style that has been largely bowdlerised out of all recognition in the land of its birth.

Anchor Liberty Ale

Source: Anchor Brewing Co, San Francisco, California, USA
Strength: 6%
Website: www.anchorbrewing.com

Liberty Ale is a revolutionary beer. It was first brewed in 1975 to commemorate the 200th anniversary of Paul Revere's ride from Boston to Lexington to warn the American rebels that the British Redcoats were marching to arrest them: his ride signalled the start of the War of Independence. And Liberty Ale sparked the resurgence of pale ale brewing in the US, a style that was almost totally extinguished by Prohibition in the 1920s.

The Anchor Brewery is best known for its Steam Beer (see page 238), but Liberty Ale stands free of its shadow. Ironically, Fritz Maytag, the man who saved Anchor from closure and turned it into one of the most highly regarded craft breweries in the US, was prompted to brew his pale ale following an extensive tour of Britain.

Marston's Pedigree from Burton-on-Trent, the home of pale ale, Timothy Taylor's Landlord from Yorkshire and Young's Special Bitter from London inspired him to produce a pale, sparkling and hoppy ale.

However, inspiration did not lead to subservience. Maytag's beer is strong, straw-coloured, an all-malt beer without additional sugars, and massively hopped. It's an all-American, love-me-or-leave-me beer, and it's the hops that give Liberty its profound character. Unlike the restrained spicy and peppery notes of traditional English varieties, Cascade hops from Washington State distend the nostrils with their assault of pine and grapefruit.

When I saw the hop store at Anchor I was astonished by the fresh vibrant green of the hops. When I flew from California to the Yakima Valley hop-growing region of Washington State, below the Cascade mountains, I discovered the secret of the hops and their intense aromas and flavours: plenty of rain but also blazingly hot summers that encourage the hops to swell on the bine and develop their rich fruity/citrus character. Cascade hops are used in abundance in Liberty Ale, both in the fermenters and in the maturation tanks. They dominate the nose and palate but are complemented by juicy malt from two-row barley. Many big American brewers use six-row barley (i.e. six rows of grain in each ear of grain), but craft brewers prefer the smoother, biscuity flavour of two-row varieties. The finish of Liberty is long and lingering, becoming dry and bitter but with a fine balancing act of malt and citrus fruit. An awesome ale.

TASTING NOTES
Appearance
Aroma
Taste
Overall score

Boston Ale

Source: Boston Beer Company, Boston, Massachusetts, USA
Strength: 5%
Website: www.samueladams.com

TASTING NOTES
Appearance
Aroma
Taste
Overall score

This is another beer with revolutionary credentials. The brewery has a split personality: officially it's the Boston Beer Company, but Boston Ale and its other brands all carry the name of Samuel Adams, as does the website.

Adams was a brewer (some records suggest maltster) in Boston. He was an active campaigner for American independence, he was involved in the Boston Tea Party and was a signatory to the Declaration of Independence, drafted by another keen beer drinker, Ben Franklin.

Adams, holding a foaming tankard, stares sternly from the label of Boston Ale, which is subtitled Stock Ale. Stock was an 18th-century English term meaning strong ale matured for a year or more that was used for blending with younger beers. In New England it took on a different meaning and indicated a beer similar to an IPA that was vatted for several months.

Jim Koch, who is descended from a family of German immigrants that ran several breweries, founded the Boston Beer Company. His forebears include Louis Koch, whose brewery in St Louis, Missouri, fell victim to another St Louis brewery, Anheuser-Busch, manufacturer of American Budweiser. Jim Koch's father went out of business in Ohio during a bout of merger mania in the 1950s. Jim, a graduate of Harvard, became a successful management consultant but brewing was in his genes. In 1985, he launched Samuel Adams Boston Lager, produced under contract. In 1988 he moved into the former Haffenreffer brewery in Boston, where he launched Boston Ale.

Boston Ale is brewed from two-row pale barley malt and caramel malt: the last named is similar to English crystal malt. The hops are German Spalt and English Fuggles and Goldings. Hops are added three times during the copper boil and there is a massive addition of Goldings in the maturation tank. The pale bronze beer has rich biscuity malt, tart fruit and perfumy, spicy hops on the aroma. Juicy malt, tangy fruit and hop resins fill the mouth while the finish is malty and fruity and dries to a long, hop-bitter finale. The beer is based on a family recipe and is kräusened. This means that some sugar-rich and unfermented wort is added to the maturation tank to encourage a strong second fermentation: it's a method borrowed from classic lager brewing. Boston now brews one million barrels a year in plants strategically placed around the US and is the biggest craft brewery in the country.

SAMUEL ADAMS
BOSTON ALE
BREWER · PATRIOT
STOCK ALE

BridgePort Blue Heron

Source: BridgePort Brewery, Portland, Oregon, USA
Strength: 4.9%
Website: www.bridgeportbrew.com

BridgePort has a striking façade. It's based in a warehouse built in 1888 for the Portland Cordage Co that made rope for ships using the Columbia and Willamette rivers that service the town and which are criss-crossed by bridges. The exterior is covered in climbing plants, including some hop bines from the surrounding Oregon hop fields.

When I first visited, the American-Italian Ponzi family owned the brewery. They had made their money from wine but spotted a niche in the market in the 1980s as craft brewing began to blossom in the US, in the Pacific North-west in particular. Their investment had made it possible to install a modern stainless-steel brewhouse open to view for drinkers in the spacious bars in the refurbished building. The beers included a cask-conditioned ale called Coho, a rarity in the US at the time. There was alarm in beer-loving circles when the Ponzis sold the business in 1995 to Gambrinus of Texas, best known for importing the Mexican lager Corona into the US. But to date the new owners have invested massively in BridgePort and expanded the range of naturally conditioned beers.

Blue Heron, named after the emblem of Oregon State, remains one of the flagship beers. It's brewed from barley grown in the North-west region and has a complex grist of pale, crystal, black and chocolate malts. The dark grains are used in tiny proportions to give subtle nuances of aroma and flavour, and to imbue the finish with a burnished bronze colour. The hops come from the Willamette area: the Willamette is an offspring of the English Fuggle but has developed

its own character in American soil. Surprisingly, Blue Heron has only 18 units of bitterness, extremely low for a pale ale, but nevertheless the hops give a fine sappy and citrus fruit aroma and palate to the beer, balanced by soft, creamy malt in the mouth, and a long finish with pronounced hop resins, tart fruit and juicy malt. It's a splendidly refreshing beer.

TASTING NOTES
Appearance
Aroma
Taste
Overall score

Coopers Sparkling Ale

Source: Coopers Brewery, Adelaide, Australia
Strength: 5.8%
Website: www.coopers.co.au

TASTING NOTES
Appearance
Aroma
Taste
Overall score

Coopers was for long an oddity in Australia. It produced ale when sensible brewers made lagers for a torrid climate. Its flagship brand Sparkling Ale often didn't sparkle: the beer was naturally conditioned with live yeast in keg and bottle, and threw such a heavy sediment that in the glass it was often cloudy. (When a rival Adelaide brewer launched its own sparkling ale, it used the slogan 'A new cloud on the horizon'.) And then, in the 1970s, in step with the 'real ale revolution' in Britain, beer connoisseurs bored with bland lagers discovered Coopers and turned Sparkling Ale into a cult drink. It is no longer confined to South Australia but is a national brand and is also widely exported.

Coopers is now revered rather than reviled, and is the only major brewery in Australia that is still in family hands. The founder was a most unlikely brewer. Thomas Cooper came from the Skipton area of Yorkshire. He emigrated with his wife to Australia in 1852. Cooper was a Methodist lay preacher who disapproved of drinking but his wife was the daughter of an innkeeper and she made beer at home. Cooper worked as a shoemaker and a dairyman but one day turned his hand to brewing when his wife was taken ill. His friends were so impressed with his home brew that they encouraged him to open a commercial brewery, which he did in 1862. When his first wife died, Cooper remarried and fathered 16 children. Today, members of the fourth and fifth generations of the family run the business. They have their own maltings near Adelaide where two-row barley varieties are turned into pale, crystal and roasted malts, while Pride of Ringwood hops come from Tasmania.

For many years, the beers were fermented in a system similar to the 'double drop' method widely used in England in the 19th century (see Brakspear Bitter, page 70). Primary fermentation was in wooden casks made from jarrah hardwood. The beer was then dropped into 108-gallon wooden puncheons where a cleaner fermentation continued. Sadly, this historic system has been replaced by stainless-steel conical vessels, and some devotees feel the beer has lost a little of its character as a result.

Sparkling Ale is nevertheless a wonderfully complex and rewarding beer. It is brewed from pale and crystal malts with around 18% cane sugar. Cane sugar is used widely in Australian brewing and has been since the early settlers arrived, when it was used to make a rough kind of ale before barley was cultivated. In the wrong hands, too much cane sugar can create a sweet, cloying beer, but Cooper's vigorous ale yeast attacks the sugar and turns it into alcohol. Pride of Ringwood hop pellets create 27 units of bitterness. The gold/amber beer (10 colour units) is intensely fruity, with apple and banana dominating. The hops give a tempting peppery note to the aroma and a good underpinning of bitterness through the palate to the finish. Citrus fruit also makes an appearance in the long finish with juicy malt and spicy hops. After primary fermentation, the beer is filtered and a dosage of sugary wort is added to encourage a secondary fermentation. Both kegs and bottles are then conditioned in the brewery for six weeks before being released to the trade.

De Koninck

Source: De Koninck Brouwerij, Antwerp, Belgium
Strength: 5%
Website: www.dekoninck.be

TASTING NOTES
Appearance
Aroma
Taste
Overall score

De Koninck means 'the king' and it is unquestionably the monarch of all it surveys in Antwerp. Large banners drape from buildings displaying a glass of the amber beer. Blow-ups of the glass hang from the ceilings of bars. The beer is so celebrated in the Flemish region of Belgium that nobody has to order it by name. Drinkers merely mention the word *bolleke**, which means little goblet, and a beer swiftly arrives on the bar top or table. 'The king' is not idle boasting but the name of the man, Joseph Henricus De Koninck, who opened a small brew-pub and beer garden in Antwerp in 1833. Following World War One, the Van Den Bogaert family joined the business, and Modeste Van Den Bogaert and his son are now in charge.

On my first visit, the brewery, despite being based on the outskirts of a mighty city, was charmingly rustic, with the beer made in traditional vessels, including a brick-clad boiling copper. When I returned a few years later, these vessels had become part of a small museum. Brewing now takes place in a modern brewhouse that appears to have been designed by draughtsmen from Cape Canaveral: the new stainless-steel copper, sited on a gantry, seems on the point of departure for a moon landing.

For once, change has not impaired the character of the beer. It's ale, made by warm fermentation and, in common with many Belgian pale ales, was inspired by the English versions. But it does more than merely pay homage to

them. De Koninck is made with Pilsner and darker Vienna malts with no brewing sugars. The hops are exclusively Saaz, most from the Czech Republic but some grown in Belgium; they are added three times during the boil. The finished beer (22 colour units, 23 bitterness) has an enticing amber colour, a dense rocky head of foam and an entrancing aroma of biscuity malt, hop resins and a spicy, cinnamon-like note. The spice comes from the house yeast. I asked Modeste Van Den Bogaert if the yeast was single strain or multi-strain. He answered enigmatically, 'Perhaps', which is the reply he gives to most questions. Juicy malt, tangy hops, spice and citrus fruit dance on the tongue while the persistent finish becomes dry but is preceded by further delights of toasted malt, spice and fruit. The beer is superb in bottle but is best drunk – filtered but unpasteurised – on draught. It is conditioned in the brewery for two weeks before being released. The Café Pelgrim opposite the brewery not only serves De Koninck but also has a bucket of fresh yeast delivered every day for those drinkers who enjoy a shot of the bitter, frothy liquid as a tonic.

*Antwerp waiters and bar staff feign not to know why the word *bolleke* causes such amusement to British visitors. But the servers take great delight, and with perfectly straight faces, in asking tourists 'not to drop one' as they hand round glasses of De Koninck.

TASTING NOTES
Appearance
Aroma
Taste
Overall score

TASTING NOTES
Appearance
Aroma
Taste
Overall score

Doc Hadfield's Pale Ale

Source: Spinnakers Brewpub, Victoria, British Columbia, Canada
Strength: 4.2%
Website: www.spinnakers.com

When I arrived at Spinnakers, I enjoyed a splendid lunch and sampled the beer range, then went outside to walk on the beach that fronts the pub, restaurant, brewery and guest house complex. I could have been in Cornwall, with the fine sand and dark rocks, but thoughts of home were quickly dispelled when I suggested to Paul Hadfield that I would take a stroll in the woods behind Spinnakers. 'Don't,' he advised. 'Bears!' Victoria may be frightfully British but Newquay it isn't.

Victoria also had a long fight to establish a brew-pub, the first in the whole country. Spinnakers was the dream of Paul Hadfield, an architect, and businessman John Mitchell. Both are from Vancouver, where John had run a bar. He returned from a trip to Britain with 14 ales. When John, Paul and their friends sampled them a whole new world of beer opened before them. In a vast country dominated by two brewing giants and little choice, they were determined to brew their own British-style ales. The local council refused to give permission but, after lobbying by locals, said it would grant a licence only if a majority approved in a referendum. Ninety-five per cent of those voting said 'Yes'. Even then, Paul and John had to wait for an amendment to federal law before they could fire their mash tun and copper. But from opening day in 1984, Spinnakers has been a huge success, with the brewhouse, built by a British company based in Manchester, expanded twice to meet demand.

Malts are imported from Simpsons in England, while the ale yeast strain was acquired from the National Yeast Collection in Norwich. The Pale Ale, brimming with snappy, fruity Cascade hop character, is made from pale malt, with the hops added twice in the brew kettle and then again in the hop back where the beer rests prior to fermentation. It has a piny and citrus fruit aroma balanced by biscuity malt. Hops, malt and fruit dance across the tongue while the long finish becomes dry, spicy and hoppy but with a good balance of tart fruit and juicy malt. It's enough to make a bear turn to drink.

Geary's Pale Ale

Source: D L Geary Brewing Company, Portland, Maine, USA
Strength: 4.5%
Website: www.gearybrewing.com

The two Portlands – Maine and Oregon – stand on east and west coasts of the US, separated by a vast continent, but they share a love of quality beer. Geary's was one of the earliest American micro-brewers and helped kick-start the brewing revolution.

MADE IN MAINE

There were only 13 micros in the entire country when David and Karen Geary opened their plant in 1986. David had learned the brewing skills on several short stints in Britain. He pays tribute to the late David Maxwell Stuart, the laird, or lord, of Traquair in the Scottish Borders, who had re-opened the ancient brewhouse in his stately home and passed on the brewing skills to the visiting American. David also visited the Ringwood brewery in Hampshire and returned with a supply of the house yeast. The trip led to Peter Austin, owner of Ringwood, and his brewer Alan Pugsley, building David's plant. Alan later set up the Shipyard brewery in Portland where he also uses the Ringwood yeast strain.

Geary's Pale Ale holds a special place in the affections of American drinkers, for it proved that there was more to beer than cold, bland and fizzy quasi-lagers, and encouraged a new generation of brewers to follow Geary's path. The copper-coloured beer bears the hallmark of the Ringwood yeast strain, a fruity and spicy note. The beer is brewed with pale, crystal and chocolate malts and is generously hopped with Cascade and Mount Hood from the US, Fuggles from England and Tettnang from Germany. It has a massive floral hop, spicy and citrus fruit aroma with biscuity malt, tangy fruit and hop resins on the tongue. The big finish is fruity and malty but is underscored by a lingering spicy hop note.

Marston's Pedigree
Source: Marston, Thompson & Evershed Brewery, Burton-on-Trent, Staffordshire, England
Strength: 4.5%
Website: www.fullpint.co.uk

In any country where a brewer makes pale ale, he or she will genuflect in the direction of Burton-on-Trent. This small and otherwise unremarkable town in the middle of England was the engine room of brewing in the 19th century. Beer from such revered breweries as Allsopp and Bass refreshed all parts of the British Empire and were even acceptable in post-revolutionary America. Burton Pale Ale became a hallmark and a benchmark, and even encouraged the first makers of pale lager beers in Bavaria and Bohemia.

TASTING NOTES
Appearance
Aroma
Taste
Overall score

The Burton Unions at Marston's Brewery in Burton-on-Trent. Fermenting beer rises from the giant oak vessels into the troughs above, where the yeast is trapped.

The secret of Burton's success lay not in the town but under it: the springs that bubble to the surface of the Trent Valley are rich in sulphates – calcium and magnesium in particular, better known as gypsum and Epsom Salts respectively. The salts enhanced the flavours of the new pale malts developed in the 19th century and also new and improved varieties of hops. The result was IPAs and pale ales with delicious and refreshing juicy malt and bitter hop character.

The Burton brewers also needed to present their new pale beers in the most attractive fashion, especially as glass was replacing pewter as the preferred container for draught beer in pubs. Beer needed to be clear, sparkling and clear of dregs. Peter Walker, a brewer from Warrington, one of many who set up new plants in Burton to capitalise on the water there, developed a system known as the 'Burton Union'. It was based on a medieval method used by monks. As beer fermented in wooden casks, yeast frothed out of the bung holes of the casks and was collected in buckets below for reuse.

It was a messy system and Walker turned it on its head. He placed troughs above the fermentation casks, and connected troughs and casks with swan-necked pipes. The fermenting wort and yeast rise from the casks up the pipes and drip into the trays above. The troughs are slightly inclined, enabling the beer to run back into the casks while the yeast is held behind. The method is brilliant in its simplicity: the beer is aerated, encouraging a powerful, continuing fermentation; it is cleared of unnecessary yeast; and the yeast propagated by the system can be stored and used again. Casks and troughs, linked together, were said in Victorian times to be 'held in union', hence the name of the system.

At one time, all the Burton brewers used the union system but it was phased out on the grounds of cost. But Marston's has remained true to the system and spent £1 million in the 1990s adding a third room of union casks. The oak casks, each one holding 144 gallons, have to be repaired at regular intervals, which means Marston's has to employ coopers, and the finest oak has to be imported from Europe and the US. But the company won't compromise, as the flavour of Pedigree is paramount.

Pedigree is a true Burton pale ale, not a bitter. It is brewed from Maris Otter pale malt, which comprises 83% of the recipe, and 17% glucose sugar. The hops are the whole flowers of Fuggles and Goldings. The colour rating is 20, the bitterness units 24. This is an authentic 19th-century Burton pale ale recipe. Maltose, which is the brewing sugar derived from malt, cannot be entirely fermented into alcohol: some maltose is left and gives fullness, or 'body', to the beer. Glucose, on the other hand, can be 'fermented out', giving more alcohol and dryness to the finished beer. The units of bitterness contributed by the hops show how the Victorian brewers responded to public demand for a less bitter and 'narcotic' beer. The gold/bronze Pedigree has a delightful aroma of juicy malt, hop resins and tart fruit, all overlain by a renowned waft of sulphur that comes from the salt-rich water. It's an aroma known locally as 'the Burton snatch'. Biscuity malt, spicy hops and apple fill the mouth: apple fruit is another defining characteristic of Burton pale ale. The finish has earthy, peppery hops, juicy malt, slight saltiness and further hint of apple.

I once described the Marston's union rooms as 'the cathedrals of brewing'. On a subsequent visit I was welcomed to the brewery by a member of staff dressed in the full regalia of a bishop. I hope he'll put in a good word for me with St Peter.

Mendocino Blue Heron Pale Ale

Source: Mendocino Brewing Company, Hopland, California, USA
Strength: 5.5%
Website: www.mendocinobrew.com

TASTING NOTES
Appearance
Aroma
Taste
Overall score

The address – Hopland – is a marketing man's dream. Hops were grown in this area of California until an outbreak of mildew in the 1950s destroyed the plants. As a result, cultivation moved north to Oregon. Mendocino's beers are packed with hop bitterness, aroma and flavour. Most of the hops come from the Pacific North-west but the owners of the brewery have restored pride and tradition by planting new hop bines amid California's vineyards.

Mendocino is a company with a short but stormy history. In the 1970s, Jack McAuliffe launched the New Albion brewery in Sonoma, the first new micro-brewery in the US since Prohibition. McAuliffe served in Britain with the US Navy and acquired a taste and a passion for English ales, as his choice of name for his brewery shows. His beers were good but the enterprise was ahead of its time and lasted for only six years.

Some of the equipment, along with the English yeast strain and two of the brewers, helped set up Mendocino in 1983. The company expanded rapidly to meet the demands for its ales and lagers. But nemesis stalked hubris: a new brewery in Ukiah in 1996 overstretched the company and it was rescued by Vijay Mallya, the billionaire owner of United Breweries of India, best known for Kingfisher lager. The acquisition has enabled Mallya to expand sales of Kingfisher in the US but Mendocino survives as a craft brewery.

Most of the beers are named after birds, including the Blue Heron, which nest in the Russian River area of California. Blue Heron Pale Ale is an all-malt beer that uses only pale malt from two-row barley. The hops are Cascade and Warrior. The beer – colour eight units, bitterness a massive 45 units – has a stunning aroma of pine and tart citrus fruit, with grapefruit dominating. Hops meld with juicy malt on the nose and in the mouth while the finish is long and finishes dry and bitter but with powerful contributions from biscuity malt and citrus fruit. Blue Heron, on draught or bottle fermented, is the perfect companion to the excellent cuisine in the brewery's restaurant.

TASTING NOTES

Appearance	
Aroma	
Taste	
Overall score	

TASTING NOTES

Appearance	
Aroma	
Taste	
Overall score	

Palm Spéciale

Source: Palm Brouwerij, Steenhuffel, Belgium
Strength: 5.2%
Website: www.palm.be

Palm beers are the biggest-selling pale ales in Belgium. Owned by the Van Roy family for 250 years, the brewery is substantial and the company expansive: it now also owns the Rodenbach brewery in Roeselare. But the Steenhuffel site has a country air, recalling its origins as the De Hoorn farm in the 16th century. A brewery has been in operation since 1747 and was called De Hoorn until 1975, when the name changed to Palm to strengthen the identity of its main brands. Pale ales were introduced after 1918, when a member of the family who was a priest suggested the ales should be called Palm as a symbol of peace following World War One.

The brewery is a blend of old and new vessels, with copper ones dating from the late 19th and early 20th centuries in one brewhouse, alongside a new 1990s brewhouse built with stainless-steel equipment. Unusually for an ale, the brewing cycle begins with a decoction mash. The brewery's wells provide soft water high in calcium carbonate. Pale malt is blended with darker malt and a little maize to produce a rich amber-coloured beer: colour is around 14 units. Kent and Styrian Goldings create between 25 and 30 units of bitterness. A complex, three-strain yeast culture ferments the beer to a biscuity dryness with rich orange fruit and peppery Goldings on the aroma, juicy malt, citrus fruit and hops in the mouth, and a finish finely balanced between toasty malt, tart fruit and herbal and spicy hops.

The brewery's beers are marketed with the symbol of the local sturdy, white-maned Brabant working horses. The horses are bred at a stud run by Palm, which also owns the adjoining chateau of Diepensteyn. After a tour of the brewery I was taken to admire the horses and then to enjoy a superb lunch in the chateau, where each dish was matched by a different beer: Palm also brews a spiced wheat beer, a Pils, a 7% ale called Aerts and a seasonal Dobbel, or double, Palm at 5.5%. Groups may tour the brewery and the chateau.

Pyramid Pale Ale

Source: Pyramid Ales, Seattle, Washington, USA
Strength: 5.1%
Website: www.pyramidbrew.com

Pyramid started life as a small craft brewery in the logging town of Kalama near the Oregon border. Beth Hartwall and Tom Baune founded the company as Hart Brewing but Beth had the idea of renaming it Pyramid after one of the peaks in the Cascade mountains.

Beth and Tom established a good reputation for their beers, which include a barley wine and a wheat beer, but they were bought out in 1989. The brewery was resettled in Seattle and later merged with the Thomas Kemper Brewery that concentrates on lager beers. Pyramid also now runs a brew-pub in Berkeley, California, but is best known as one of the many Seattle craft breweries that have made the city one of the best places to drink beer in the United States.

Seattle is known as Emerald City not as a result of the Irish who live there but because of the high level of rain that keeps the grass a lush green and, more importantly, seeps down through the Cascade mountains to produce magnificent brewing water. Seattle is also well placed to buy hops from the Yakima Valley across the Cascades, and barley from both the US and Canada.

Pyramid Pale Ale is a little on the dark side for the style, using caramel and carapils malts alongside two-row pale. The hops are exclusively Cascades and used in generous amounts. The finished beer is a rich, burnished copper colour with a superb aroma of nutty, toasted malt, topped by lilting hop resins and tart citrus fruit, the hallmark of Cascade hops. Bitter hops and tangy fruit dominate the mouth but with a good balance of juicy malt. The big finish becomes finally dry with powerful hop bitterness, but is preceded by nutty malt and the ever-present citrus fruit.

Samuel Smith Old Brewery Pale Ale

Source: Samuel Smith Old Brewery, Tadcaster, Yorkshire, England
Strength: 5.2%
Website: www.merchantduvin.com *

TASTING NOTES
Appearance
Aroma
Taste
Overall score

Sam Smith's is one of the oldest family-owned breweries in England. It is fiercely loyal to its Yorkshire base, but some of its 200 pubs are in London, among them the Olde Cheshire Cheese in Fleet Street, once a haunt of such literary giants as Dr Johnson and Charles Dickens.

Tadcaster has been an important brewing town since the 14th century, sitting on an underground lake of limestone water. The town became known as the 'Burton of the North' as a result of the importance of the water supply. Today there are still three breweries in the town, a former Bass plant now owned by Coors, Sam Smith's and John Smith's. Sam and John came from the same family but a row early in the 20th century led to John walking up the hill and opening his own plant. Now it is part of the Scottish & Newcastle group, a fate that Humphrey Smith, the current chairman of Sam Smith's, would never tolerate. His brewery dates from 1758 and still uses 'Yorkshire square' fermenters. This system, in common with the Burton union system, was designed to separate fermenting beer from yeast and also created the thick collar of foam beloved by Yorkshire drinkers.

The first brewery to use squares was Bentley & Shaw of Huddersfield, and it is thought that the system was the result of work in the 18th century by the Yorkshire scientist Dr Joseph Priestley, who lived next door to a brewery in Leeds. He unravelled the mysteries of 'fixed air', or carbon dioxide, and the absorption of gases in liquids. His research led to the development of carbonated water and later soft drinks.

A few Yorkshire brewers still use squares but Sam Smith is the only one that employs vessels made of Welsh slate: most modern squares are built of stainless steel. A square is a two-storey vessel. The two chambers are connected by a porthole with a raised rim and also by 'organ pipes'. The bottom chamber is filled with wort and yeast. As fermentation gets under way, yeast and wort rise through the porthole into the top chamber. The rim traps the yeast while the wort drains back into the bottom chamber via the organ pipes. The result is a beer with a high level of natural carbonation and a full-bodied, malty body.

Sam Smith's Pale Ale is a notable member of the Yorkshire family of beers. It is brewed from pale malt and 10% crystal malt, and hopped with the traditional English varieties, Fuggles and Goldings. It has 35 colour units and 26 bitterness units. The aroma has a malty, biscuity character with a hint of toffee or butterscotch, and a spicy and herbal note from the hops. The rich palate is dominated by biscuit malt, spicy, herbal hops, butterscotch and a hint of vinous fruit. The finish is long and broad, with delicious juicy malt and a lingering hop bitterness, with touches of fruit and toffee.

*Samuel Smith does not have a website. The one listed belongs to Merchant du Vin of Seattle, which distributes Smith's beers in the US.

Sierra Nevada Pale Ale

Source: Sierra Nevada Brewing Company, Chico, California, USA
Strength: 5.6%
Website: www.sierranevada.com

TASTING NOTES
Appearance
Aroma
Taste
Overall score

For beer lovers both within and without the US, Sierra Nevada is the benchmark pale ale of modern brewing. It was the inspiration for many of the revivalist pale ales and IPAs that now make beer drinking such a pleasure in North America.

The brewery dates from 1981 and was launched by two keen home-brewers, Ken Grossman and Paul Camusi, in the university town of Chico, where there is a fine supply of water from the Sierra Nevada and Cascade mountain ranges. They started with converted dairy tanks but the success of their venture enabled them to buy a state-of-the-art plant with copper vessels from Germany. That plant has also been replaced, and the current site produces 800,000 barrels a year. It is one of the ironies of modern craft brewing that Sierra Nevada is considered to be a micro in the US but is bigger than many British regional breweries that each make around 25,000 barrels a year.

Sierra Nevada now has a wide range of beers but Pale Ale made the company's reputation.

It has won many awards at the Great American Beer Festival and won a gold medal in the 2004 Brewing International Awards. The bottled version (which is bottle fermented with live yeast) is made from two-row pale malt and caramel [crystal] malt. It is hopped with Magnum and Perle for bitterness and late hopped with Cascade for aroma: it has 37 units of bitterness. The draught version is slightly darker and also a degree or two lower in strength. Pale Ale has a pale bronze colour with a hint of amber, topped by a big fluffy head of foam. The aroma is spicy and peppery from the hops, balanced by biscuity malt and tart citrus fruit from the Cascades. In the mouth there is a superb balance of hop resins, juicy malt and tangy fruit, while the long, deep finish offers a hint of vanilla pods and marzipan before it finally becomes dry, bitter and hoppy but underscored by sweet malt. It is a beautifully balanced beer with an uncompromising hop character.

Younger's Special Bitter

Source: Rogue Ales, Newport, Oregon, USA
Strength: 6.5%
Website: www.rogue.com

British readers may think this beer has a connection with Younger's, the brewery that became part of the giant Scottish & Newcastle group. But the name is more prosaic: it pays homage to Bill Younger of the Horse Brass pub in Portland, Oregon, an enthusiastic purveyor of Rogue beers.

'Enthusiasm' is the key word at the brewery. Jack Joyce, a former advertising executive with Nike, founded the small craft brewery in 1988 in Ashland, Oregon, and named it after the local Rogue river. Jack had a vision of small batch, well-brewed beer made without preservatives or cheap cereal adjuncts, and that vision married with the skills of brewmaster John Maier, who had previously brewed with the Alaskan Brewery.

When a flood destroyed their original site, they set up shop in Newport and have expanded to a 50-barrel production line. They don't want to get big or take part in mergers and takeovers but want to concentrate on making great beers that boom with hop character from local varieties. Younger's Special Bitter was originally called Rogue Ale and is brewed with two-row pale malt and crystal malt, with imported East Kent Goldings and local Willamette. It has a colour of 17 units and a powerful 35 units of bitterness. It has an overwhelming nose of apricot fruit and floral hops, underscored by rich biscuity malt with a hint of toffee. The palate is full-bodied, with chewy malt, peppery, mouth-puckering hops and tart fruit, while the long and lingering finish has an amazing punch of hops with an almost iodine-like bitterness but wonderfully balanced by biscuity malt and citrus fruit. At 6.5%, this beer might bc considered an IPA rather than a pale ale, but Rogue avoids any dispute by brewing an IPA as well.

TASTING NOTES
Appearance
Aroma
Taste
Overall score

Bitters

Bitter was a beer style born as much by the demands of brewers' cash flow as consumer preference. The 19th century was a turbulent time for the British brewing industry. In 1830, a Beer Act allowed anyone to open a pub or beer house on payment of two guineas (£2.40) for a licence. 46,000 new beer houses opened, almost doubling the number of licensed premises in Britain. Nicknamed Tom and Jerry Houses, they were often no more than the front rooms of private houses. Most of the new publicans had no business acumen, let alone the ability to store and serve beer, often in premises without cellars or any rudimentary form of cooling.

But the brewers, confronted by thousands of new licensed premises, rushed to dominate them by offering publicans 'loan tie' agreements: in return for loans and discounts, the publicans agreed to take beer only from the donor breweries. This beer retailing experiment in a free market was a disaster. One of the supporters of the Parliamentary Bill that led to the Act, Sydney Smith, wrote: 'Everybody is drunk. Those who are not singing are sprawling. The sovereign people are in a beastly state.'

When the law was tightened to prevent such easy access to beer retailing, many of the new pubs crashed and the brewers lost their investments. In 1896, the London brewer Barclay Perkins was owed £2 million by bankrupt publicans. Allsopp of Burton-on-Trent was so badly affected that it went into receivership and had to be restructured. Undeterred, other brewers rushed to buy the thousands of failed pubs on the market. The property scramble sent prices soaring. The brewers paid extravagant amounts to establish estates of 'tied pubs'.

As many of the breweries had become public companies and were responsible to their shareholders, urgent action was necessary to restore profitability. Brewers and shareholders were no longer prepared to lock up beer – liquid capital – in vats and casks, waiting months and even years for the cash to come in. They moved away from porters, stock ales and IPAs, and developed a new type of draught ale known as 'running beer'. The scientific understanding of yeast was a powerful impetus to producing running ales. Pure strains meant that fermentation could be better controlled. Yeast packed down and cleared in cask within a few days, enabling beer to 'drop bright' and be served within a few days of reaching the pub cellar.

Running beers – today's cask-conditioned beer, or real ale – quickly came to dominate the pub market by the turn of the 20th century. Mild made up a substantial proportion of the draught market, but a lighter beer, an offshoot of pale ale, quickly challenged mild's hegemony. The brewers were conscious that running beers, which enjoyed only a brief secondary fermentation in cask, lacked the smoothness and maturity of vatted beers. The problem was overcome by the development of a new type of malt called crystal. It is stewed malt made by a process similar to making toffee that turns the starch inside each kernel of malt into crystallised sugar. It cannot be fermented by brewer's yeast but adds a rich nutty and biscuity character to beer and a fullness of palate. While crystal has to be blended sparingly with pale and other standard malts (usually not more than 10% of the total), it gave running beers the characteristic bronze and copper colours that became the hallmark of a style dubbed 'bitter' by drinkers to distinguish it from less heavily hopped mild ale.

Bitter became the style of beer that distinguished Britain from every other brewing nation. Visitors from overseas, even though affronted by the assault of hop bitterness on their mouths and throats, find a visit to a British pub and a glass of bitter high on their itineraries. Even though the insipid versions of lager brewed in Britain now vie with ale in popularity, bitter – low in carbonation, malty, nutty and with fruity, spicy and peppery hop notes – remains a staple of pub life.

Bitter comes in different strengths but the differences are often confused by labelling. Standard bitters should come within the band of 3.6–4% alcohol, best bitters 4.1% and above. Nevertheless, as this section shows, some brewers call standard bitters 'best'. Perversely, a few bitters are known as 'ordinary', as in the case of Brakspear's and Young's bitters. Only the English, with their tight-lipped refusal to admit to doing something well, could downplay one of the glories of the beer world with such a dismissive shrug of the shoulders.

TASTING NOTES
Appearance
Aroma
Taste
Overall score

Adnams Bitter

Source: Adnams Sole Bay Brewery, Southwold, Suffolk, England
Strength: 3.7%
Website: www.adnams.co.uk

Adnams has both history and location on its side. Southwold is on the Suffolk coast, with a whitewashed, inshore lighthouse standing as a stubby sentinel over the small market town. Brewing has been carried on in Southwold for 650 years: in 1345, Johanna de Corby was fined by local magistrates for serving her ale in unmarked tankards. For centuries, brewing took place at the back of the Swan Hotel, a magnificent coaching inn. The brewery grew over time and was bought by George and Ernest Adnams in 1872. In 1902, the Anglo-Irish Loftus family joined them in a long-running partnership: members of both families still control the company today.

When I first visited Adnams in the late 1970s, it enjoyed a fine reputation for its beer but, apart from a small amount of free trade in London and the Home Counties, sales were confined to its own estate of pubs in Suffolk. Enormous demand for the beer saw sales increase dramatically. In 2001, £1.8 million was invested to double fermenting capacity. As a result, Adnams' beers are now available nationally but there has been

no decline in quality. The attitude of chairman Simon Loftus and head brewer Mike Powell-Evans is simple: if you don't like our beers, drink someone else's. Adnams refuses to compromise and produces spectacularly hoppy and tangy beers with a hint of salty sea breeze: they are to beer what Islay is to malt whisky.

Bitter is the flagship product, a pale copper beer brewed with Maris Otter pale and crystal malts, invert sugar and a touch of caramel for colour adjustment (26 colour units). The hops are First Gold, Fuggles and Goldings, used in whole flower form, with dry hopping in cask (33 units of bitterness). The Adnams' yeast culture gives the beer a pronounced orange fruit tang on the nose and palate, with peppery hops and juicy malt. The finish lingers and is finely balanced between biscuity malt, tart citrus fruit and bitter and peppery hops.

I hesitate to call it a beer to die for, as one of the brewery's founders, George Adnams, went to Africa where he was eaten by a crocodile, proof that a career in brewing is the safer option.

Black Sheep Best Bitter

Source: Black Sheep Brewery, Masham, North Yorkshire, England
Strength: 3.8%
Website: www.blacksheepbrewery.com

TASTING NOTES
Appearance
Aroma
Taste
Overall score

The wealth of Wensleydale, where the market town of Masham is based, comes from sheep and wool. The name of the brewery is a joke within a joke, reflecting both the rural economy and the fact that founder Paul Theakston is the black sheep of the famous brewing family. Paul was a director of Theakston's brewery in Masham (see Theakston Best Bitter, page 77) until it was taken over by the national group Scottish & Newcastle in 1988. He walked out and founded his own brewery in 1992 in the former maltings of another old Masham brewery, Lightfoot's. He toured Yorkshire and the surrounding counties to buy the finest traditional brewing equipment, including a vast domed copper and Yorkshire square fermenters.

Paul doesn't own a single pub but he has built a free trade of 800 outlets, while the bottled versions of his beers are available nationally. A new brewhouse was built in 2003 and further expansion will increase production to 80,000 barrels a year, an impressive success story for a company that is less than 15 years' old. The site includes a visitor centre, shop and an excellent bistro run by Paul's wife Sue.

Black Sheep Best enjoys a vigorous fermentation with a multi-strain yeast culture and emerges with a pale gold colour (19 units) and a heavy collar of foam in the Yorkshire manner. It is brewed with Maris Otter pale and crystal malts and a tiny amount of roast malt for colour and flavour. The hops are Challenger, Fuggles and Progress; Fuggles are used as a late copper hop (31 units of bitterness). The beer has a spicy and earthy Fuggles character on the nose, balanced by biscuity malt and citrus fruit. Full-bodied, slightly toasted malt fills the mouth with tangy hop resins and tart fruit, followed by a finish bursting with complex malt, fruit and hop notes, finally becoming dry and uncompromisingly bitter. Great Yorkshire beer, baa gum!

Brakspear Bitter

Source: Brakspear Brewing Co, Witney, Oxfordshire, England
Strength: 3.4%
Website: www.brakspear-beers.co.uk

Drinkers may call for 'a pint of Ordinary' but Extraordinary would be a better description. It is one of the joys and mysteries of the beer world that so much flavour and complexity can be packed into a beer of such modest strength.

W.H. Brakspear traces its history back to 1779 in the riverside town of Henley-on-Thames. The Brakspears were distantly related to Nicholas Breakspear who, as Adrian IV, became the first and so far only English-born Pope in 1154. The Brakspears pronounce their name in the same way as their illustrious forebear and use the symbol of the bee on his mitre as the company logo. The brewery was founded by Robert Brakspear and briskly expanded by his son William Henry, who built a chain of pubs in Oxfordshire and Buckinghamshire.

The character of the Henley beers owes much to the fascinating 'double drop' fermenting system that is used. The wooden vessels are ranged on two storeys. Fermentation starts in the top bank of vessels and after 16 hours the liquid is literally dropped down into the second storey of vessels below. Dead yeast cells, unwanted protein and other detritus are left behind, encouraging a cleaner and faster fermentation in the second bank of vessels. The result was beers that were full-bodied, quenching and clean tasting, and with a butterscotch note

known as diacetyl that is a bi-product of fermentation and which most brewers struggle to keep out of their beers.

In 2002, the brewery, by now a public, listed company, was threatened with closure, as its riverside site was worth a fortune as private housing. In spite of a vigorous campaign by drinkers, the brewery did close but the drinks group Refresh UK, which also owns the Wychwood Brewery in Witney, bought the rights to the beers. Refresh built a new, separate brewhouse alongside the Wychwood plant and installed the double-drop fermenters in a raftered building that was once a maltings. Brakspear Bitter and Special were unveiled in 2004 to great acclaim. The water supply in Witney is almost identical to Henley's and the same recipes are used for the beers.

The Bitter is brewed with Maris Otter pale and crystal malts with invert sugar added in the copper. The hops are whole flower Fuggles and Goldings. The deep bronze beer has 22 units of colour and 38 units of bitterness: this is 'boy's bitter' with hair on its chest. The aroma has pungent, earthy hops, biscuity malt, butterscotch and tart orange fruit. Sappy malt, bitter hop resins and fruit vie for attention on the tongue, while the finish has a wonderfully clean maltiness balanced by tangy fruit, butterscotch and bitter hops.

Brunswick Triple Hop

Source: Brunswick Inn, Derby, England
Strength: 4%
Website: None

The Brunswick is a remarkable inn that was once part of a row of cottages built for railway workers in 1842. The triangular, end-of-terrace pub is at 1 Railway Terrace, just a minute's walk from Derby railway station. The pub closed in 1974 and fell into disrepair but was rescued and restored to its Victorian glory by the Derbyshire Railway Trust. It reopened in the 1980s and has flagstone floors, a warren of small, intimate rooms off a central corridor, old station waiting-room furniture, coal fires, lamps and railway memorabilia by the yard. It's an atmospheric cross between a pub, a country station and a working men's club. Shortly after the reopening, a brewery was added in rooms at the back of the pub and the Brunswick rapidly won a reputation as a classic Victorian ale house serving superb beers.

The range of beers is vast and ever-changing, with monthly, seasonal and one-off brews backing such regulars as Railway Porter and Old Accidental. Triple Hop is the session beer brewed with pale malt only and a pinch of torrefied wheat for clarity and a good head of foam. The three hop varieties used are Challenger, Goldings and Northdown. The beer is pale gold with a rocky head of foam, a pungent, earthy and spicy hop nose with biscuity malt, tart lemon fruit and a hint of sulphur from the water (Derby is just down the road from Burton-on-Trent and also enjoys similar pungent and salty water). The palate has rich, juicy malt, tangy fruit and bitter hop resins, with a lingering finish that becomes exceptionally dry and bitter but balanced by rich malt and citrus fruit. It's a pale, quenching and uncompromisingly bitter beer.

The pub is now owned by Everards, the Leicester-based regional brewery, but the Brunswick enjoys almost complete autonomy under manager and brewer Graham Yates, who can usually be found pulling pints behind the bar in the main corridor when he's not 'mashing in'.

There's good lunchtime food, a family room where children are welcome, and live jazz on Thursday evenings.

Butcombe Bitter

Source: Butcombe Brewery, Cox's Green, Wrington, Somerset, England
Strength: 4%
Website: www.butcombe.com

Butcombe opened for business in 1978 and for the first 18 years of its life was a one-beer brewery, producing only Bitter. It has since added to the range but Bitter accounts for three-quarters of its output.

The founder was Simon Whitmore, who downsized from executive posts with Guinness International and Courage to set up one of the first of the 'new wave' micro-breweries in the 1970s. He sank his redundancy money from Courage into the brewery, built at the back of his house in the countryside. The acclaim for Bitter was so great that he had to expand the site twice to cope with demand. In 2003, after a lifetime in brewing big and small, Simon finally retired and sold the company to a small group of friends led by Guy Newell, who had set up the national wholesaling company The Beer Seller. A new brewery was built in 2005, just a few miles from Butcombe and using the same water supply. The recipes, which avoid any added sugars or colourings, remain unchanged but annual output will rise to 30,000 barrels a year, making Butcombe bigger than several family-owned regional breweries.

Bitter is made from Maris Otter pale malt with 5% crystal (20 units of colour). The hops are Northdown, German Northern Brewer and Yeoman (31–35 units of bitterness). The pale bronze beer has a superb aroma of pungent, spicy hop resins, tart fruit and biscuity malt, followed by full-bodied juicy malt, peppery hops and light fruit in the mouth. The finish is long and deep, beautifully balanced between smooth grain and bitter hops, with a continuing bridge of tart fruit.

Butcombe owns seven pubs, and one warm summer day I enjoyed with Simon Whitmore a pint or two of Butcombe Bitter and a proper ploughman's lunch of tangy, crumbly cheese and fresh crusty bread in the garden of one of them.

TASTING NOTES
Appearance
Aroma
Taste
Overall score

TASTING NOTES
Appearance
Aroma
Taste
Overall score

Coniston Bluebird Bitter

Source: Coniston Brewing Co, Coniston, Cumbria, England
Strength: 3.6%
Website: www.conistonbrewery.com

Coniston sprang to fame – and raised the profile of the entire micro-brewing sector – when Bluebird Bitter won CAMRA's Champion Beer of Britain competition in 1998. The beer became nationally available and, thanks to its success, the Ridgeway Brewery in Oxfordshire produces a stronger, bottle-conditioned version at 4.2%. Coniston enjoys one of the finest locations of any British brewery. It stands at the end of a road that leads up to a Lakeland peak called the Old Man of Coniston. The brewery is fronted by the Black Bull, an ancient coaching inn that dates from the time of the famous Elizabethan sea dog, Sir Francis Drake, conqueror of the Spanish Armada.

It's a more recent mariner, though, who is commemorated in the inn. Donald Campbell used it as his base for his ill-fated assault on the world water speed record on Coniston Water in 1967. There are photos of Campbell and his team on the walls of the inn, and the brewery's main beer is named after his boat, *Bluebird*.

Brewer Ian Bradley, whose parents own the inn, has access to the finest brewing water, with a beck – local dialect for a stream – running alongside and fed by water from the surrounding mountains and fells. Ian uses Maris Otter pale malt and 5% crystal in the beer. Bluebird is a 'single varietal' beer, using just one hop, Challenger. Colour is 21 units, bitterness 22. The pale bronze beer has a rich and enticing aroma of hop resins and elderflower backed by rich, biscuity malt. The palate is full, balanced between juicy malt, tart fruit and bitter hops, followed by a long, smooth and quenching finish that becomes dry, bitter and hoppy but with mellow notes of biscuity malt and fruit.

Ian Bradley lost a leg in a motorcycle accident a few years ago but, with great courage, has overcome his disability to manage the brewery with enormous verve and enthusiasm. As the mood takes him, he will either wear a false leg or hop around the place on his good 'un like yet another sea dog, Long John Silver.

Harveys Sussex Best Bitter

Source: Harvey & Son, Lewes, East Sussex, England
Strength: 4%
Website: www.harveys.org.uk

TASTING NOTES
Appearance
Aroma
Taste
Overall score

Lewes is an ancient town close to the sea and the Sussex Downs, and guarded by a castle. It has its own bibulous 'cathedral', the locals' affectionate name for Harvey's brewery. The site was built in 1784 alongside the River Ouse that meanders through the town. It came under the control of John Harvey in 1790 and, in 1880, his family rebuilt the site in red-brick Victorian Gothic style (see picture), though the Georgian fermenting rooms and cellars remain. The architect was the celebrated William Bradford, who also designed the Hook Norton, Shipstone and Tolly Cobbold breweries. His constructions are known as 'tower breweries', as the brewing process flows logically from floor to floor by gravity, without the aid of mechanical pumps.

The seventh generation of the Harvey family is still in evidence at the brewery. In the 20th century, the Jenners, who had run a south London brewery since the mid-18th century before moving to the coast, joined the Harveys. Miles Jenner represents his family today in the role of head brewer. His father arrived in Lewes in 1938 and worked for Harveys for the following 60 years as head brewer, managing director and, finally, chairman. Miles has been head brewer since 1986 and lives with his family in 'the brewer's house' in the grounds of the brewery. He makes sensational beers that deserve to be better known, but the company has avoided the high-risk strategy of going national and selling its products at deep discounts to the voracious pub groups. Harveys instead concentrates on supplying its 45 pubs as well as the free trade in London and South-east England.

Best Bitter is a classic of the style, a complex and rewarding blend of malt and hops. The malts are Maris Otter and Pipkin pale malts, with crystal malt, flaked maize and brewing sugars. No fewer than four hop varieties – Bramling Cross, Fuggles, Goldings and Progress – are used and added at different stages of the copper boil to extract the desired aromas and bitterness (colour 33 units, bitterness 38 units). The amber beer has a tempting nose of pungent, grassy and spicy hops, biscuity malt and tangy fruit. It fills the mouth with sappy malt, hop resins and citrus fruit, followed by a long and deep finish that becomes dry, bitter and hoppy but beautifully balanced by juicy malt and fruit.

Holden's Black Country Bitter

Source: Holden's Brewery, Woodsetton, Dudley, West Midlands, England
Strength: 3.9%
Website: www.holdensbrewery.co.uk

TASTING NOTES
Appearance
Aroma
Taste
Overall score

In the 19th and early 20th centuries, just about every town and village in the Black Country had a brewery or a pub that brewed on the premises. Their task was to satisfy the enormous demand for refreshment from the army of workers in factories and mines. Most of the small breweries have gone but Holden's, along with its near neighbour Batham's, continues. They have more than just beer in common. Both families are keen supporters of 'The Baggies' – West Bromwich Albion football club – and the breweries' taps or adjacent pubs sport literary quotations above the doors.

As we have seen in the case of Batham's (see page 37), Shakespeare is the inspiration, but Holden's goes one better with a Latin phrase from Horace's *Odes*: *Nunc Est Bibendum*, or Now Is the Time for Drinking. Wise words indeed, suggesting that Black Country folk were remarkably literate long before education was universal.

The Holden's involvement in brewing goes back four generations when Edwin and Lucy Holden first made beer in the Park Inn. They were so successful that they built a substantial brewery next door, which is one of the neatest and most attractive I have visited, with gleaming metalwork and tiles, and mashing, boiling and fermenting laid out on two floors. The brewery now owns 21 pubs and supplies an additional 60 outlets in the area. The Holdens have renovated, to much acclaim, a Grade II listed railway building in Codsall, where their beers are sold, and have also restored the Park Inn to its full Victorian splendour, with fascinating photographs of the family and its workers over several generations.

Black Country Bitter is a classic, brewed with Maris Otter pale malt and a high proportion of crystal malt (12%) with some torrefied wheat for clarity and head. Fuggles is the only hop variety used and the beer is dry hopped in cask (colour 24, bitterness 26). The beer has a copper colour with crisp, earthy hop resins, biscuity malt and a vinous fruitiness on the nose. Sappy malt, ripe fruit and bitter hops dominate the mouth, with a finish in which the nutty and fruity character of crystal malt plays a full part, balanced by a gentle but persistent earthy hop bitterness. Stonkin' good beer, as they say in the Black Country, echoing Horace.

Holt's Bitter

Source: Joseph Holt, Derby Brewery, Cheetham, Manchester, England
Strength: 4%
Website: www.joseph-holt.com

Holt's Bitter, in common with the brewery's Mild (see page 44) is a beer that takes no prisoners. If you don't like hop bitterness, then you'd be advised to drink a different brew, as this beer puckers the tongue and leaves a furrow down the back of the throat. With 40 units of bitterness, it is one of the bitterest beers regularly brewed in Britain.

Aficionados not only revel in the pungent aroma and flavour of the beer but are also aware they are helping to contribute to a good cause. The Holt family has long been a supporter of Christies Hospital in Manchester, one of the first to specialise in analysing and treating cancer. In the 1930s, the Holts helped sponsor the pioneering work of Dr Ralston Paterson at Christies. Today a donation from every pint of the brewery's beers goes to the hospital.

The Bitter is so popular in Holt's pubs that the brewery still supplies the beer in casks called hogsheads that each holds 54 gallons of beer. Most other breweries have long since phased out such giant casks but it's not unknown at Holt's to send a hogshead to a pub in the morning and for it to return empty to the brewery in the evening.

The Bitter is almost identical to the Mild except that it is stronger, and dark invert sugar in the recipe is replaced by a light version. The grains are Halcyon and Alexis pale malt, crystal malt and black malt, and the hops are Goldings and Northdown. It has a piquant, nostril-widening aroma of spicy and peppery hops, juicy malt and tart fruit. The palate is quenching, dominated by sappy malt, tangy citrus fruit and aggressive bitterness, followed by a persistent finish bursting with snappy and spicy hops, biscuity malt and bitter-sweet fruit.

On my first visit to the brewery, the head brewer refused to reveal any information about the ingredients he used on the grounds of commercial confidentiality. Not long afterwards, though, he spoke at a meeting of one of the CAMRA branches in Manchester and was asked the same question. 'I'll tell you my recipes as long you don't pass them on to that b*****d Roger Protz,' he said. The branch duly reported his speech in their newsletter, revealing the recipes to posterity as well as to me.

TASTING NOTES
Appearance
Aroma
Taste
Overall score

Shepherd Neame Master Brew Bitter
Source: Shepherd Neame Brewery, Faversham, Kent, England
Strength: 3.7%
Website: www.shepherd-neame.co.uk

TASTING NOTES
Appearance
Aroma
Taste
Overall score

Shepherd Neame is more than a brewery – it's a living museum of beer. The company dates from 1698 and is Britain's oldest brewery, but it's thought that brewing was carried out on the same site many years earlier. It's known that monks were brewing in an abbey in Faversham from the 12th century, though they would not have made use of Kentish hops, which were not grown until the 15th century, when Flemish weavers settled in the area and planted hop bines, as they couldn't acquire a taste for unhopped English ale.

Shepherd Neame is still run by the Neame branch of the two founding families and they fashion marvellous tangy bitter beers full of the piny and floral aromas of fresh hops plucked every autumn from the surrounding fields.

The brewery and its offices are a maze of wood-panelled rooms, unlined teak mash tuns dating from World War One and a steam engine that can still be used in the event of a power failure. Demand for the beers is so great that the brewhouse was substantially extended at the turn of the present century.

Master Brew Bitter is known among brewers as 'cooking bitter', a dismissive name for a beer of modest strength. But this is a beer of enormous character, due to the generous use of locally grown Goldings and Target hops, which create a punchy 37 units of bitterness. The grains are Halcyon pale and crystal malts and the colour rating is 25. The copper-coloured beer, topped by a lively head of foam, draws the drinker in with a stunning aroma of hop resins, biscuity malt and tangy fruit. Juicy malt, peppery hops and a fruitiness reminiscent of a confectionery from my youth called orange-and-lemon slices fill the mouth. The long and deep finish is beautifully balanced between juicy malt, bitter-sweet fruit and a lingering and persistent peppery and bitter hoppiness.

Theakston Best Bitter

Source: T&R Theakston, Masham, North Yorkshire, England
Strength: 3.8%
Website: www.theakstons.co.uk

TASTING NOTES
Appearance
Aroma
Taste
Overall score

Theakston's is one of the oldest surviving breweries in Yorkshire and dates from 1875, though Robert Theakston had been brewing earlier, from 1827, at the Black Bull inn. His son Thomas built the current brewery in 1875 on the aptly named Paradise Fields. In 1919, Theakston's bought the rival Lightfoot Brewery, not for strong commercial reasons but in retaliation for Lightfoot's always winning the annual cricket match between the two companies.

Theakston's today, with its high-sided wooden fermenters and traditional mash tuns and coppers, is a fascinating antique brewery. Tours are available, the centrepiece of which is the cooper's shop where wooden casks are still fashioned by a resident cooper using ancient and time-honoured tools. The company is best known for its world-famous strong ale Old Peculier (see page 132) but it brews a range of beers, including a fine example of bitter.

The brewery's greatest achievement has been its survival, for it has experienced great turbulence over the past 25 years. It merged in the mid-1980s with Matthew Brown of Blackburn, which in turn was bought by Scottish & Newcastle.

The Theakston's beers lost considerable credibility when they were brewed at both Masham and S&N's Tyneside beer factory. Then in 2003, S&N, with a dramatic turnabout, sold Theakston's back to the family. Simon Theakston and his three brothers are now firmly in control once more, though S&N will continue to brew part of Theakston's annual production, as the Masham site is too small to meet demand.

One of the first acts of the independent Theakston brewery was to increase the strength of Best Bitter from 3.6 to 3.8%: it had been reduced by S&N to save on duty. Best Bitter is brewed with pale and crystal malts, wheat and maize: it is a truly pale bitter with just 15 units of colour. The beer has a highly complex hop recipe, using Bramling Cross, Challenger, Fuggles, Progress, Styrian Goldings and Target varieties (24 bitterness units). The beer, not surprisingly, has a fine floral, grassy, resiny and lemon-and-lime aroma balanced by a good biscuity malt note. Sappy malt, tangy fruit, and piny and spicy hops coat the mouth, followed by a complex finish that becomes finally dry but has good notes of tangy fruit, bitter hops and rich malt.

Uley Bitter

Source: Uley Old Brewery, Uley, Gloucestershire, England
Strength: 4%
Website: www.uleybrewery.com

TASTING NOTES
Appearance
Aroma
Taste
Overall score

Perhaps it's the alcohol, but laughter and brewing are often intertwined. Chas Wright, who, with his beret, beard and striped jumper, looks like a cross between a pirate and a French onion seller, has a ribald sense of humour. With the exception of his Bitter, his beers have a porcine character, including Old Spot – a local Gloucestershire breed of pig – Pigor Mortis and Pig's Ear, which is Cockney for beer. Chas once chanced his arm and brewed a beer called Oil of Uley. To nobody's surprise, he received a threatening letter from the manufacturer of a well-known brand of beauty products. Chas told the company it could sue him if it wished but he was just a small, struggling brewer with no money in the bank. The threat of legal action was not carried out.

The small town of Uley is in the Cotswolds, and the hills have an abundance of fine brewing water. A natural spring bubbles away at the side of the brewery and provides pure brewing liquor.

Uley is based in part of a brewery called Price's that dates from 1833 when the sylvan area had a thriving pottery industry. When the industry declined, Price's went out of business and the buildings lay derelict for years. Chas Wright set up shop in 1985 and Uley is now one of the longest running of Britain's micro-breweries.

He uses only Maris Otter malt from the specialist maltsters Tuckers, in Devon, and whole Herefordshire hops: he has no truck with additives or brewing sugars. The amber-coloured Bitter has some crystal malt alongside the pale, with Fuggles and Goldings whole flower hops. It has an intense aroma of biscuity malt, with a hint of toffee, tart citrus fruit and peppery, spicy and earthy hops. Rich juicy malt, hop resins and tangy fruit fill the mouth, with a lingering finish that becomes dry and hoppy, but with a good underscore of orange fruit and sappy malt.

Welton's Pridenjoy

Welton's Brewery, Horsham, West Sussex, England
Strength: 2.8%
Website: www.weltons.co.uk

At last, a living example of a South of England 'boy's bitter', so low in alcohol it would have been legal under American Prohibition but bursting with rich malt, hops and fruit character.

Ray Welton is a character, a man with laughter on his lips and a sharp eye for business opportunities, which includes brewing a low-strength beer at a time when all the industry emphasis is on stronger 'premium' products. He has alcohol in his blood, so to speak. His grandfather was a cider maker in Surrey and his father ran a drinks wholesaling company. Ray was taught to brew by the retired head brewer at King & Barnes in Horsham.

Welton's was first based in Dorking but, when King & Barnes closed, Ray moved to Horsham to pick up some of the slack left by the collapse of a substantial regional brewery. He has useful engineering skills that have enabled him to pick up brewing kit on the cheap and refashion it to his own needs. It's not the prettiest micro-brewery in the world but it works and produces a large range of beers. The fermenting vessels are remodelled Carlsberg tanks, the mash tun came from a brew-pub in Croydon, while Ray found the copper on a waste dump with a tree growing inside it. Talk about 'beer from the wood'! 'It's the Steptoe in me,' Ray grins, recalling a British television comedy about a rag-and-bone man.

Pridenjoy is spelt without any spaces, as Ray knows that London regional Fuller's is highly protective of its flagship beer London Pride (see page 89): Ray hopes the lack of spaces will keep m'learned friends at bay. The beer has a remarkably complex recipe, with pale, amber, chocolate, Munich and wheat malts, with Bramling Cross and Northdown hops. It has a superb aroma of peppery hops, vinous fruit and biscuity malt, with sappy malt, hop resins and ripe fruit dominating the mouth. The long finish is indeed a joy, bitter-sweet to start but ending on a high note of tart fruit and bitter hops.

TASTING NOTES
Appearance
Aroma
Taste
Overall score

Young's Bitter

Source: Young and Co's Ram Brewery, Wandsworth, London, England
Strength: 3.7%
Website: www.youngs.co.uk

TASTING NOTES
Appearance
Aroma
Taste
Overall score

Young's is held in great affection by British beer lovers, Londoners in particular. In the dog days of the 1960s and '70s, when brewery after brewery was going over to keg beer – filtered, pasteurised and artificially carbonated – Young's declared it would remain true to cask ale. Other brewers mocked John Young, chairman of the family-owned brewery, but he has had the last laugh. The company is successful and profitable. It has substantially grown its estate of 206 pubs out of London and into the Home Counties, and has won many awards for its beers. Most of the brewers who mocked John Young are no longer in business but his company forges ahead.

Young's stands on a site with deep brewing roots. Beer has been brewed alongside the River Wandle since 1581. The present brewery was founded in 1675 and was bought by Charles Young and a partner in 1831. Eventually it became wholly owned by the Young family. It is a remarkable site to visit, a zoo cum brewery. There are stables for horses that still deliver beer by drays to local pubs. There are other animals and birds, including a ram, which is the company logo and mascot. Members of the Young family are always in evidence, often in the 'sample room' where fresh brews can be enjoyed. Head brewer Ken Don admits that John Young, still a hands-on chairman, will tell him in no uncertain terms if he considers a batch of beer to be below standard. The brewhouse and fermenting rooms are achingly traditional, with wooden and copper vessels.

No corners are cut where ingredients are concerned. In the 1990s, when Maris Otter malting barley was de-listed by farmers and maltsters in favour of more modern and higher-yielding varieties, Young's had Maris Otter specially grown for the brewery. Bitter is brewed with pale and crystal malts, torrefied barley and brewing sugar. It is extremely pale for the style, with 14 colour units. Fuggles and Goldings whole hops contribute 32 to 34 units of bitterness. Here is another bitter dubbed 'Ordinary' by drinkers but it is a beer packed with character. The aroma is dominated by earthy Fuggles and peppery Goldings hops, balanced by biscuity malt and tart citrus fruit. Bitter hops fill the mouth but there is a good underpinning of bready malt and tangy fruit. Hops defeat all-comers in the finish: bitter, flowery, resinous and piny. A tremendous beer from a company that was in the vanguard of the 'real ale revolution' that helped save Britain's brewing heritage.

Best Bitters

It is a curiosity of British brewing that brewers will dismiss their bitters as 'ordinary' or 'cooking' but will puff out their chests with pride when discussing the merits of stronger members of the family. '*Best* Bitter', they proclaim, as though the stronger beers live in a different world from their weaker brethren. It is all the more odd when you consider that in many cases Best and Ordinary use identical grains, hops and brewing sugars, as can be seen with Brakspear Bitter and Special. In some cases, a brewer will make a strong wort and then add water or 'brewing liquor' to achieve the desired strength for Bitter and Best.

'Bigger Bitter' would never catch on in a world obsessed with marketing and obesity, but that is effectively what we are talking about: beers with bigger aromas and flavours, richer in malt and hops.

I am often asked at public beer tastings and seminars how stronger beers are made. The answer is that a brewer will add more malt and perhaps special sugars to encourage the yeast to produce more alcohol. There is a limit to how much malt can be packed into a mash tun, so brewing sugars are added during the copper boil. A higher level of alcohol will create a rich malt character, with perhaps overtones of vinous fruit, toffee and butterscotch. To balance the maltiness, a generous addition of hops will give a powerful bitterness with pronounced spicy, peppery, grassy and floral notes.

It would be wrong, however, to give the impression that all Best Bitters are merely stronger clones of Bitter. A brewer, given the opportunity to make a beer between 4 and 5% alcohol, may produce something radically different. While his standard Bitter may be copper or amber coloured,

his Best may be straw coloured or pale bronze, using pale malt only. He may use a new balance of hops or just a single one to give a different aroma and flavour, perhaps importing hops from North America or mainland Europe in place of traditional English varieties.

One of the many fascinating developments in brewing in recent years has been the two-way flow of hops between Britain and the United States. While many American craft brewers use English Fuggles and Goldings in their interpretations of pale ale, their British counterparts have learned to treasure the pungent citrussy nature of American varieties.

ABOVE
Honker's Ale is a modern bitter produced by a craft brewery in Chicago.

LEFT
Bishop's Finger comes from Shepherd Neame, the oldest English brewery based in the heart of the Kent hop fields.

Adnams Broadside

Source: Adnams Sole Bay Brewery, Southwold, Suffolk, England
Strength: 4.7%
Website: www.adnams.co.uk

Southwold has two faces. There is the town centre with its market place surrounded by some fine Georgian buildings, including Adnams' Swan Hotel, and the harbour area where fishermen still set sail to search for fish and seafood in the North Sea (their produce can be bought fresh from huts alongside the banks of the river Blyth).

While Southwold attracts mainly tourists to its town centre pubs, its workaday aspect can be seen in the Harbour Inn and the Bell across the river in Walberswick, where fisherfolk sink a few pints after a day's gruelling work. After a glass of Bitter, they might move up a notch to Broadside, a beer that commemorates an important piece of history. Southwold traces its roots back to the 15th century, when it was granted a royal charter by Henry VII. In 1672, the English and French fleets combined to defeat the Dutch in the Battle of Sole Bay, off Southwold. Men o' War in those days would place all their guns along one deck of a ship and fire them by turning broadside to the enemy's vessels.

The beer that recalls this famous battle is made from 100% Maris Otter pale malt with just a tiny addition of caramel for colour adjustment. It has 38 units of colour. The hops are First Gold, Fuggles and Goldings, which create 33 units of bitterness. First Gold is one of a new type of 'hedgerow' hops pioneered in England that grow to only half the height of conventional varieties, are easier to pick as a result and are less prone to attack by disease and pests.

Broadside has a superb aroma of tangy fruit, floral and resinous hops and biscuity malt, with the Adnams' hallmark of a whiff of seaside salt. Sappy malt, tart orange fruit and spicy hops fill the mouth, while the finish is deep and long, dominated by tangy fruit, biscuity malt and great depth of hop bitterness. The poet John Masefield, who wrote several epics about the sea and ships, told one young seaman in the poem *Dauber* to 'grow some hair upon thy chest'. He should have advised a regular diet of Broadside to speed the process. A filtered version of Broadside in bottle is considerably stronger at 6.3%.

Bateman XXXB

Source: George Bateman & Son, Salem Bridge Brewery, Wainfleet All Saints, Lincolnshire, England
Strength: 4.8%
Website: www.bateman.co.uk

TASTING NOTES
Appearance
Aroma
Taste
Overall score

There is a lot of emotion attached to Bateman's XXXB. As I explained in the section on brown and mild beers (see page 36), the family-owned brewery almost closed in the 1980s as a result of a split in the family, with some members anxious to sell up and retire on the proceeds. Chairman George Bateman and his side of the family finally raised the cash to buy out their relatives and keep the flag flying above the windmill that marks the brewery as you enter the small market town of Wainfleet.

Nobody who was present will ever forget the rousing speech George Bateman made to the annual meeting of CAMRA, when he appealed for support to keep his brewery going. And then, with victory secure, guess which beer won the title of Supreme Champion Beer of Britain at CAMRA's Great British Beer Festival in 1986? As I said to George at the time: 'Who writes your script?'

Within a few years, Bateman's had gone from relative obscurity to national celebrity and XXXB became the flag bearer. The brewery also produces an XB bitter, and the names mark the time before brand images when casks were stamped with Xs to denote strength. In this case the name means a strong triple X bitter.

XXXB is brewed in classic mash tuns, coppers and wooden fermenters with Maris Otter pale malt, crystal malt and wheat malt and a small amount of wheat syrup. The colour is 38 units. Two hop varieties, Challenger and Goldings, create a robust 41 units of bitterness. This superb and complex beer has a rich aroma of biscuity malt, vinous fruit and tangy hop resins. The full-bodied palate is a fine blend of ripe fruit, ripe malt and peppery hops, followed by a big and long finish with a luscious bitter-sweet character that conjures forth creamy fruit with even a hint of banana, biscuity malt and a powerful peppery and earthy bitter hop note.

Black Sheep Emmerdale Ale

Source: Black Sheep Brewery, Masham, Yorkshire, England
Strength: 5%
Website: www.blacksheep.co.uk

TASTING NOTES
Appearance
Aroma
Taste
Overall score

It is symptomatic of the deep roots that the pub holds in the British way of life that licensed premises form the focus for three famous TV soaps: *Coronation Street* has the Rovers Return, *EastEnders* the Queen Victoria, and *Emmerdale* the Woolpack. *Emmerdale* is set in rural Yorkshire, and Black Sheep saluted the saga's success by naming a beer in its honour in 2003.

Emmerdale Ale is highly distinctive due to the use of Demerara sugar, which accounts for 16% of the recipe. In the 17th and 18th centuries, sugar from the West Indies was widely used in Yorkshire beers at a time when English landlords owned sugar plantations in the Caribbean. Sugar was cheap, as slaves were used to plant and harvest it. When slavery was abolished in the 19th century, sugar had to be bought and sold at a commercial rate and it lost its attraction to brewers. Demerara, a brown crystalline sugar used chiefly in rum production, takes its name from the Demerara River in Guyana that runs into the Atlantic at Georgetown.

Paul Ambler, the head brewer at Black Sheep, gives us a taste of what beers were like three or four centuries ago, though they would have been considerably darker before the advent of pale malt. As well as brown sugar, Emmerdale Ale is brewed with Maris Otter pale malt, crystal malt and torrefied wheat. It has 21 units of colour. Only one hop, Whitbread Goldings Variety, is used, with 36 units of bitterness. In spite of its name, the hop is an offshoot of the Fuggle and was developed by the national brewer Whitbread on its farms in Kent. They are still grown today, even though Whitbread sold its brewing interests in 2000. The beer has an aroma of biscuity malt, leafy and earthy hop resins and a touch of honey sweetness. There is a warming rum-like note in the mouth that blends with tart and bitter hops and juicy malt. The lengthy finish has tangy fruit, spicy hops, creamy malt and a continuing hint of rum. The wheel of history has turned full circle: today Demerara sugar is four times as expensive as barley malt.

Brains SA

Source: S A Brain, The Cardiff Brewery, Cardiff, Wales
Strength: 4.2%
Website: www.sabrain.com

The label for SA shows a red-and-black quartered motif, evoking the image of a rugby shirt. The Welsh are passionate about Rugby Union and beer, a fact underscored by the large number of pubs in the vicinity of both Cardiff Arms Park and the National Stadium. American readers, whose version of armour-plated football developed out of the British oval ball game, will be astonished to learn that rugby is played with a minimum of protective clothing. This could be one reason why beer lovers in Wales claim SA stands for 'Skull Attack', though overconsumption and the resulting hangover are a more likely cause.

The brewery is not keen on the nickname and prefers to suggest that SA is drawn either from the initials of the founder of the company, Samuel Arthur, or for Special Ale. These alternatives cut no ice with the beer's devotees. I wrote a magazine profile about the Welsh National Opera some years ago and interviewed members of the chorus. When they heard about my interest in beer, they waxed lyrical about Skull Attack, which they drank in such copious amounts in Cardiff it was a wonder they could sing in tune.

The beer that gives them so much delight is not, despite its name, especially strong and, in the Welsh tradition, is malt accented, recalling the time when beer was fashioned to meet the needs of coal miners and steel workers. It is brewed with Pearl and Regina pale malts, 8% crystal malt and some brewing sugar. It has 27 colour units. The three hops are all English varieties: Challenger, Fuggles and Goldings (27 units of bitterness). The deep amber beer has a ripe aroma of biscuity malt, a nutty note from the crystal malt and a light but firm spicy hop presence. A digestive biscuit maltiness, a touch of barley sugar sweetness, and a good underpinning of hop resins fill the mouth, followed by a long finish that is bitter-sweet, with sappy malt, light but persistent spicy hops and a pear-drop fruitiness.

TASTING NOTES
Appearance
Aroma
Taste
Overall score

Brakspear Special

Source: Brakspear Brewing Co, Witney, Oxfordshire, England
Strength: 4.3%
Website: www.brakspear-beers.co.uk

TASTING NOTES
Appearance
Aroma
Taste
Overall score

Here is the classic example of a Best Bitter that is the grown-up version of ordinary Bitter and yet takes on a character all its own as a result of the increase in the proportions of malt and hops used. In common with Brakspear Bitter, Special is not a particularly strong beer but the 'double drop' fermentation system leads to a cleanness of aroma and flavour that allows the key ingredients to boom and sing in perfect harmony.

The two-storey fermenters at Witney, rescued from the original home of Brakspear in Henley-on-Thames, recall a time when the likes of William Henry Brakspear could allow his beers to develop slowly and naturally, free from the pressure of marketing departments and accountants to rush beer into trade. The dropping of the beer from one storey to the second leaves behind dead yeast cells and protein that would impede a powerful, continuing fermentation. The purity of the wort, or hopped extract, gives free rein to the yeast, malt and hops.

Special is brewed with Maris Otter pale and crystal malts and invert sugar. The whole hop flowers are Fuggles and Goldings. The colour is 27, bitterness units a resounding 46: it's a best bitter that is generously hopped to balance the sweetness of the malt to avoid any cloying. The beer is dry hopped in cask, meaning a handful of hops is added to each cask as it leaves the brewery to intensify aroma. The result is a beer of awesome complexity with biscuity malt, tangy orange zest and banana fruit and peppery hops on the nose, sappy malt, earthy, bitter hop resins and fruit in the mouth. The long finish starts bitter-sweet with a powerful punch of creamy malt and citrus fruit, but finally becoming dry and bitter.

Cains Formidable Ale

Source: Robert Cain & Co, Liverpool, Merseyside, England
Strength: 5%
Website: www.cainsbeers.com

The beer is known as FA for short, which gives free rein to practitioners of demotic English. FA is also short for Football Association, the governing body of English soccer, while the term 'sweet FA' means a total lack of knowledge or understanding of a subject, which many football supporters think sums up the FA's guidance of the game. In this context, F stands for one of the most widely used vulgar words in the language and A is for All. As Merseysiders are among the most passionate of football supporters and have been known to utter the occasional expletive, Cains was on sure ground with the name of the beer.

Unlike Brakspear Bitter and Special, FA is a radically different beer from the company's 4% Bitter, which is a deep copper-coloured member of the family, using chocolate malt and dark cane sugar and with 30 units of colour. FA, on the other hand, is brewed using only Maris Otter pale malt, with a touch of wheat malt for head retention and a small amount of brewing sugar. The result is an exceptionally pale beer with just 14 colour units. Target hops are used for bitterness and the hopped wort, or extract, is late hopped in the copper with Goldings for aroma, and then dry hopped in cask with Northdown. The bitterness units are 30. The beer has a tempting aroma of rich 'wine gums' fruit, juicy malt and floral hops, with orange and lemon fruit dominating the mouth but with a solid backing of biscuity malt and bitter hop resins. The lingering finish enjoys a fine balance of sappy malt, bitter hop resins and bitter-sweet fruit, leaving a tart and tangy impression with a hint of clean sweetness. It is a splendidly refreshing beer.

Freeminer Speculation

Source: Freeminer Brewery, Cinderford, Gloucestershire, England
Strength: 4.7%
Website: www.freeminer.com

TASTING NOTES
Appearance
Aroma
Taste
Overall score

Freeminer is one of the most successful and long-established of Britain's new wave of micro-breweries. Don Burgess founded it in 1992 in the remote Royal Forest of Dean, an area made famous by such legendary television plays by Dennis Potter as *Blue Remembered Hills*, *Pennies from Heaven* and *The Singing Detective*. The medieval royal connection to the forest confers certain rights on the men born in the area. Any male born within the Hundred of St Briavels – a hundred being an ancient division of a county – can dig for coal or iron ore in the forest without charge on reaching the age of 21 and working for a year and a day in one of the drift mines dug from the hillsides.

Many of Freeminer's beers carry the names of now defunct mines: as well as Speculation, there are also Deep Shaft, Pot Lid, Shakemantle, Trafalgar and Waterloo, while Strip And At It describes the tough nature of the work.

Freeminer has won several awards for its beers, including two in the Champion Beer of Britain competition and one from the annual Beauty of Hops contest. Several of the beers, including Speculation, are available in bottle-fermented as well as cask form.

Speculation is brewed with Maris Otter pale, crystal and chocolate malts and roasted barley, and hopped with Fuggles and Goldings from Worcestershire. The colour rating is 34 and the bitterness 40. The deep copper-coloured beer has peppery and resiny hops on the nose with sultana fruit, roasted grain and a hint of chocolate. The mouth is filled with rich and pungent flavours of roasted grain, chocolate, bitter hops resins and tangy fruit, followed by a long and complex finish in which hop bitterness starts to dominate but with good contributions from roast grain, chocolate and fruit. A full-bodied, rich and rewarding beer.

Fuller's London Pride

Source: Fuller, Smith and Turner's Griffin Brewery, Chiswick, London, England
Strength: 4.1%
Website: www.fullers.co.uk

The family-run brewery close to the banks of the Thames is a marvel of the brewing world. Created more than 350 years ago and still run by members of the three founding families, Fuller's has grown from a relatively small London regional to a company owning 238 pubs and hotels, along with 600 national free trade accounts. In spite of its success, the company refuses to compromise, remaining true to traditional brewing methods and the use of the finest raw materials.

London Pride is the flagship beer. Its quality has been recognised in such competitions as the Beer and Cider Competition, where it was named Supreme Champion Beer in 2000 and won gold medals in the two following years, and in the Champion Beer of Britain Competition, where it has twice been named Champion Best Bitter and was the overall Supreme Champion in 1979. Perhaps its most remarkable achievement has been to become the best-selling premium cask bitter in Britain, with sales growing from 80,000 barrels a year in 2000 to 130,000 by 2004.

It is brewed with Optic pale malt (90%), 3% crystal malt and 7% flaked maize. The colour rating is 24. A complex hop recipe involves Challenger, Northdown and Target varieties, with Target used primarily for bitterness, and Challenger and Northdown added late in the copper boil for maximum aroma: 30 units of bitterness. London Pride has the Fuller's yeast signature of a rich orange fruitiness that dominates nose, palate and finish but is superbly balanced throughout by biscuity malt and a firm and very English floral, spicy and resiny hop attack.

It is the genius of British brewers to fashion beers that are complex and also highly quaffable, thanks to low carbonation and the brilliant balance of ingredients. Too malty, and the beer would be cloying; too bitter and it would close down the throat. The balance of London Pride means that several pints will slip down easily but with maximum enjoyment. Raise a glass to head brewer John Keeling and his team.

TASTING NOTES
Appearance
Aroma
Taste
Overall score

TASTING NOTES
Appearance
Aroma
Taste
Overall score

TASTING NOTES
Appearance
Aroma
Taste
Overall score

Goose Island Honker's Ale

Source: Goose Island Beer Company, Chicago, Illinois, USA
Strength: 5%
Website: www.gooseisland.com

As well as the renowned IPA (see page 15), Goose Island brews a wide range of beers, including Kilgubbin Red Ale to salute the Irish settlers who made their home on Goose Island in Chicago (Kilgubbin is Gaelic for goose). But the brewery's biggest brand is Honker's Ale, brewed in the style of an English bitter. The beer has driven the success of the company that produces 1.6 million cases a year for distribution throughout the US – not bad going for an enterprise that started out as a simple brew-pub.

Head brewer Greg Hall and his brewing team studied at the brewing faculty of the world-famous Siebels Institute in Chicago and have a wide-ranging knowledge of beer styles and ingredients. They source malts and hops from Britain and mainland Europe. Honker's uses malts from the American Midwest and just one hop, the Styrian Golding from Slovenia. Styrians are an offshoot of the English Fuggle. When the Slovenes developed their hop industry, they found that traditional European hop varieties from the German Hallertau region and Czechoslovakia would not grow in Slovenia's soil. Hardy English Fuggles adapted without difficulty and became the main variety grown there. But the Slovenes struggled with the odd name Fuggles and called the hops Goldings after another English variety.

Honker's Ale (14.5 colour, 35 bitterness) has a touch of crystal malt and wheat, and offers a pleasing and tempting pale copper colour. It has a rich almond nut aroma balanced by a cracker biscuit maltiness and a spicy hop note. Juicy malt, a developing tart citrus fruit note and bitter hop resins fill the mouth, while the finish is a fine balance between tangy fruit, biscuity malt and bitter hops, with the almond note reappearing.

Greene King Abbot Ale

Source: Greene King Westgate Brewery, Bury St Edmunds, Suffolk, England
Strength: 5%
Website: www.greeneking.co.uk

To mark its religious connections, Abbot Ale is given 'two Sabbaths' in the fermenters to ensure each brew is properly blessed by whichever god looks after the brewing process.

Bury St Edmunds has long been an important brewing and malting town, with ale making dating from the time of the monks who built a monastery in the area in the seventh century. King Canute, who famously failed to hold back the encroaching tide, founded a Benedictine community in 1020 to commemorate St Edmund. Edmund was the king of East Anglia who was slain in battle with the Danes in the ninth century. His shrine developed into the town of St Emundsbury, later Bury St Edmunds.

Centuries later, Benjamin Greene opened a brewery in 1799 on Westgate and eventually moved into a mansion that had been the home of the last abbot of the town following the dissolution of abbeys and monasteries under Henry VIII. A rival King brewery opened also on Westgate in 1868 and the two companies merged in 1887. The Greenes still play an active role. The chairman in the 1970s and '80s was Sir Hugh Greene, a former Director-General of the BBC. The novelist Graham Greene was fond of beer, mentioned it regularly in his books, and mashed a special ale at the brewery to mark his 80th birthday.

Abbot Ale therefore has a bit of history on its side and is brewed in a highly traditional brewhouse with copper vessels, using Halcyon and Pipkin pale malts, amber and crystal malts and brewing sugar. Colour units are 30. The all-English hop recipe is made up of Challenger, Fuggles and Northdown pellets, which create 26 units of bitterness. After the copper boil, the hopped extract percolates through a deep bed of hops in the hop back for additional aroma and bitterness. The beer has a pronounced biscuit malt, vinous fruit and spicy hops aroma, with more tangy fruit, bitter hop resins and juicy malt in the mouth. The long finish has the fullness and richness of malt and fruit beautifully balanced by a deep hop bitterness.

Hook Norton Old Hooky

Source: Hook Norton Brewery Co, Hook Norton, near Banbury, Oxfordshire, England
Strength: 4.6%
Website: www.hook-norton-brewery.co.uk

Hook Norton seems to exist in a time warp. Village and brewery are almost lost down narrow country lanes. The red-brick Victorian tower brewery is powered by a 19th-century steam engine, while mashing, boiling and fermentation take place in superb wood and copper vessels. Local deliveries are made by horse-drawn drays, with the horses kept in stables within the grounds. But the company founded in 1849 by a farmer and maltster, John Harris, and still run by his descendants, the Clarkes, is no slouch when it comes to selling beer. It owns 43 pubs and distributes to a further 500 free trade accounts. It has turned the brewery into a tourist attraction with a museum and visitor centre. The museum tells the fascinating story of how Harris brewed for his farm workers and family but was forced to expand production when gangs of navvies arrived in the area to build a railway line, which has since been axed. The brewery has been expanded and overhauled in recent years to enable production to grow to meet demand – a demand based on cask beer. One of Hook Norton's proud boasts is that it has never sold a drop of keg beer in its life, and its bottled beers account for only a tiny proportion of production.

Brewing water is drawn from a well on site, and only the finest raw materials are used. Old Hooky, despite the name, is not an old ale but a strong bitter. It is brewed from Maris Otter pale and crystal malts, with malted wheat (34 colour units). The hops are Challenger, Fuggles and Goldings, which create 32 units of bitterness. The deep copper-coloured beer has a rich aroma of fresh bread maltiness, fruitiness reminiscent of raisins and sultanas, and tangy hops resins. Fruit, malt and hop bitterness build in the mouth while the finish has a bitter-sweet start with malt and fruit dominating, but hop bitterness provides a firm base that prevents any cloying sweetness.

Iceni Fine Soft Day

Source: Iceni Brewery, Ickburgh, near Thetford, Norfolk, England
Strength: 4%
Website: www.icenibrewery.co.uk

TASTING NOTES
Appearance
Aroma
Taste
Overall score

Brendan Moore is an Ulsterman brewing in deepest Norfolk who has helped change the way in which small craft breweries get their beers to market. He supplies around 35 pubs but in general stays clear of a pub trade increasingly dominated by national groups that demand deep discounts from suppliers. Brendan has set up the East Anglian Brewers' Co-operative that delivers to beer festivals and farmers' markets in the region. Bottled beer and gift packs are a major part of Brendan's business, and all his draught beers are available in bottle-fermented form as well. His beers are on sale in the tourist shop in Thetford Forest, which attracts large numbers of visitors, and he grows barley and hops on a plot alongside the brewery as a further tourist attraction.

Brendan was encouraged to turn his home-brewing skills into a commercial venture when he had a dream in which Boudicca, or Boadicea, the legendary Queen of the Iceni tribe who fought many battles with the occupying Romans, urged him to brew good ale in an attempt to stop cheap European lager that was flooding into Britain as a result of the European Union's 'open borders' policy. He may not have stopped cheap Stella arriving in Dover from Calais but he has certainly added to the sum of beer drinkers' pleasures with his potable ales, several of which commemorate the Iceni, while Fine Soft Day is a Norfolk greeting.

In common with all the bottled beers, Fine Soft Day is kräusened with a blend of unfermented sugary extract and yeast to encourage a vigorous second fermentation in bottle. In the case of Fine Soft Day, maple syrup is also added to the brew to give the smoothness and softness demanded by the title. The other ingredients are Halcyon pale malt and caramalt, with Challenger and Fuggles hops. The beer is bronze coloured and has a tempting aroma of peppery hops, citrus/lemon fruit and biscuity malt. Juicy malt, tart fruit and hop resins fill the mouth, while the long finish has a touch of sweetness from the maple syrup but is balanced by an increasing hop bitterness and tangy fruit.

Mordue Workie Ticket

Source: Mordue Brewery, Shiremoor, Tyne & Wear, England
Strength: 4.5%
Website: www.morduebrewery.com

Two brothers, Gary and Matthew Fawson, revived a Geordie brewing tradition when they opened their tiny brewery in 1995, using the name of Joseph Mordue's 19th-century brewery on Wallsend village green. Their world changed two years later when Workie Ticket was named CAMRA's Champion Beer of Britain at the Great British Beer Festival. The brothers were media-friendly and their fame spread quickly as Workie Ticket went on sale in pubs far from its North-east home. In 1998, the Fawsons moved across the road to a new 20-barrel site and they now supply some 150 accounts.

Their beers stress their roots, with such names as Five Bridge Bitter – marking the bridges across the River Tyne in Newcastle – Geordie Pride and the outrageous pun in A'l Wheat Pet. Workie Ticket is a Geordie expression for someone who

is workshy or works his ticket. It is not an accusation that can be levelled at the Fawson brothers, who have worked mightily to build the success of their brewery.

Their prize beer and leading brand is brewed with Halcyon pale malt, pale chocolate malt and torrefied wheat. A complex hop recipe is comprised of Challenger, Fuggles and East Kent Goldings. Both colour and bitterness units are in the 30s. The beer has a rich and tempting aroma of creamy malt, vanilla, a hint of chocolate and peppery hops. Pungent hop resins dominate the palate but are balanced by biscuity malt and tart fruit. The lengthy finish is dry and hoppy, but with good contributions from juicy malt, vanilla and tangy fruit.

TASTING NOTES
Appearance
Aroma
Taste
Overall score

Rooster's Yankee

Source: Rooster's Brewing Co, Knaresborough. North Yorkshire, England
Strength: 4.3%
Website: www.roosters.co.uk

Sean Franklin, who runs Rooster's with his wife Alison, put hops on the map in the 1990s when he described them as 'the grapes of brewing'. Until then, brewers and even beer writers thought of hops as a plant that added bitterness to beer and helped prevent infections. Sean's comment made everyone think more carefully about the role of hops in the brewing process. He is a self-confessed 'hop head'. He loves the fascinating diversity of aromas and flavours that hops give to beer, and will blend English varieties – herbal, spicy and peppery – with the more citrus, floral and perfumy character of American and mainland European ones.

All his regular beers are pale in colour: he avoids the use of dark malt, as he wants the hops to dominate and shine through. He pumps nitrogen into his beers during the mashing process to stop oxidation and emphasise their

pallor. With Yankee, he says his aim is to develop a powerful Muscat grapes and lychees nose and palate, which is due to the exclusive use of American Cascade hops. They are added at the start of the copper boil and at the end, with a further addition in the hop back, a vessel where the hopped wort rests after the boil. The main grain is Maris Otter pale malt with a touch of crystal. The colour is 12, bitterness 28 units. The beer has a delightful aroma of tropical fruits and light juicy malt. There is light biscuity malt In the mouth but the emphasis is on the pungent grapefruit note from the hops. The finish is long, bitter and hoppy, with continuing citrus fruit. It is a wonderfully refreshing beer.

The Franklins opened the brewery in 1993 and moved to bigger premises in 2001, where they supply 500 outlets.

TASTING NOTES
Appearance
Aroma
Taste
Overall score

St Austell HSD

Source: St Austell Brewery Co, St Austell, Cornwall, England
Strength: 5%
Website: www.staustellbrewery.co.uk

TASTING NOTES
Appearance
Aroma
Taste
Overall score

HSD stands officially for Hicks Special Draught, named in honour of the founder of the brewery, Walter Hicks. But to legions of West Country drinkers the beer is known affectionately, if somewhat alarmingly, as High Speed Diesel. Careful consumption is strongly advised.

Hicks founded the brewery in 1851 and its current site is built from mellow Cornish stone. It is still run by Hicks's descendants, with his great-great-grandson James Staughton at the helm. St Austell is a powerful presence in Cornwall. It is one of the county's biggest employers, owns 150 pubs and has extensive free trade. In recent years both the brewery and its products have been overhauled. Distribution has expanded into Devon and Somerset, and an attractive visitor centre has been added. Production takes place in a superb brewhouse and fermenting area, with traditional copper and wooden vessels. A Celtic Beer Festival is staged every winter in the brewery's extensive cellars, with beers and ciders from other producers in the region.

HSD is brewed with Maris Otter pale and crystal malts and roasted barley (colour 40 units). The hops are the whole flowers of Fuggles and Goldings, which create 30 units of bitterness. The deep copper-coloured beer has a toasted and biscuit malt aroma with sultana fruit and floral, spicy hops. A digestive biscuit maltiness and ripe dried fruits fill the mouth with a solid underpinning of bitter hop resins. The deep finish has ripe fruit and malt but the initial sweetness is offset by a firm undercurrent of lingering hop resins.

St Peter's Organic Best Bitter

Source: St Peter's Brewery, St Peter South Elmham, near Bungay, Suffolk, England
Strength: 4.1%
Website: www.stpetersbrewery.co.uk

St Peter's brewery enjoys a magnificent setting behind a moated Tudor farmhouse. The farm dates from 1280, with the moat dug to stop an invasion by marauding Vikings. Its Tudor design is the result of the dissolution of nearby Flixton Priory by Cardinal Wolsey, an act that prompted Henry VIII to embark on a widespread wrecking of abbeys and priories to break the back of the church and fill his depleted coffers. Fixtures and fittings from Flixton were taken to St Peter's, which now enjoys a façade of Caen stone from Normandy, a great chimney, latticed windows and a porched entrance complete with a tombstone. Inside, the Great Hall has an imposing raftered ceiling, a 15th-century tapestry depicting manna from heaven, and a carved madonna and child. A dining room has a portrait of St Peter before the Basilica in Rome.

The building now belongs to John Murphy, a marketing expert who advises – clearly with great success – companies and corporations on how to improve their branding and image. He decided to add a brewery at St Peter's, as the poor showing of British beers abroad disappointed him and he decided to fashion his own brands for export. The brewery is fortunate to have its own borehole that draws fine brewing water from an aquifer 90m (300ft) below ground.

St Peter's beers, which include fruit beers and a honey porter, are now exported to the US, Europe, Japan, Scandinavia and Australia. All the beers appear in distinctive green flagon-shaped bottles, which are based on an 18th-century flagon that John Murphy found in a shop in Gibbstown near Philadelphia. Cask-conditioned versions are available in Britain and can be enjoyed in St Peter's London pub, the Jerusalem Tavern at 55 Britton Street, EC1, a faithful re-creation of an 18th-century coffee house. In 2002, the brewery doubled in size to meet demand for the beers, and a new bottling hall and brewing copper have since been added.

Organic Best Bitter has joined the growing number of British beers that use malts and hops grown without agri-chemicals. The grains are Scottish Regina pale and crystal malts, with New Zealand Hallertauer hops. The colour is 34 units, bitterness 35 units.

The pale bronze beer has a biscuity malt and peppery hops aroma, followed by an explosion of spicy, bitter hop resins on the tongue with a good balance of sappy malt and tart fruit. The long finish has good juicy malt and citrus fruit but is dominated by an iodine-like hop bitterness.

TASTING NOTES
Appearance
Aroma
Taste
Overall score

Shepherd Neame Bishop's Finger

Source: Shepherd Neame Brewery, Faversham, Kent, England
Strength: 5%
Website: www.shepherd-neame.co.uk

There was an abbey in Faversham for many centuries and the monks would have brewed ale for their own consumption. It would be historically fascinating if Shepherd Neame's strong bitter had a religious connection, but Bishop's Finger has more prosaic roots. It is named after an ancient roadside signpost shaped liked a clenched hand with the forefinger extended to point visitors in the right direction.

Since the travellers in *The Canterbury Tales* made their way through Kent to their destination, there is something Chaucerian about the bawdy local nickname for the beer: Nun's Delight. The soubriquet is not mentioned in the hallowed halls of the Faversham brewery, where wood-panelled walls and a visitors' reception area housed in a restored medieval hall demand respect and contemplation. In spite of its impressive age, Shepherd Neame is a company with its eye focussed on future success. In 2000 it invested £2.2 million in a new brewhouse that has increased annual production to 200,000 barrels a year. It owns 372 pubs in London and the South-east, and supplies 2,000 free trade accounts.

For many years, Bishop's Finger was available only in bottle but interest from beer lovers encouraged the brewery to produce a cask version as well. It is brewed with Halcyon pale malt and crystal malt, and Goldings and target hops plucked from the surrounding hop fields. It has 41 units of colour and a powerful 43 units of bitterness. It has a rich and tempting aroma of fruit reminiscent of raisins and sultanas, a warm Ovaltine* maltiness and tangy hop resins. Vinous fruit, biscuity malt and peppery hops fill the mouth, while the long finish interweaves between dried fruit, rich malt and a deep and drying hop bitterness.

*For non-British readers, Ovaltine is a bedtime drink made from malted barley and hot milk.

Timothy Taylor's Landlord

Source: Timothy Taylor's Knowle Spring Brewery, Keighley, West Yorkshire, England
Strength: 4.3%
Website: www.timothy-taylor.co.uk

The importance of pure water in the brewing process is underscored by the experience of Timothy Taylor. He was a maltster who opened a small brewery in the wool town of Keighley in 1858 and established new premises in 1863 to use the Pennine waters that flowed from the Knowle Spring. Taylor's grandson, John Taylor, was ennobled as Lord Ingrow and he thinks so highly of the spring water that he bottles it and takes it home to mix with his whisky.

Taylors, based in attractive stone buildings and with highly traditional brewing vessels, brews a wide range of beers, from light and dark milds to strong dark ales, but its flagship is Landlord, which holds the record of winning the CAMRA Champion Beer of Britain no fewer than four times. So successful is the beer that £11 million has been invested in the brewery over the past decade to expand production. Its fortunes were given an unexpected boost in the

Upper Canada Dark Ale
Source: Upper Canada Brewing Co,
Toronto, Ontario, Canada
Strength: 5%
Website: www.uppercanada.com

TASTING NOTES
Appearance
Aroma
Taste
Overall score

Upper Canada is the settlers' name for Ontario. The brewery of that name was founded in 1985 by Frank Heaps and has grown into a sizeable commercial company with splendid copper brewing vessels. Its first brewer was trained at Weihenstephan in Germany but his successors have been British with a love of ale, though the portfolio includes a lager and a wheat beer. The brewery has sunk deep roots in Toronto's artistic life. Since 2000, Upper Canada has run an annual Writers' Craft Awards for local novelists and short story writers. It also stages art, music and theatre festivals.

Dark Ale has an attractive chestnut hue and is brewed with pale, roasted and black malts, and is hopped with a single variety, English Challenger. It is an all-malt beer, as Upper Canada avoids the use of sugars and cheaper grains. It has a robust roasted grain aroma with a touch of sour fruit and a good attack of bitter, floral hop resins. Rich roasted grain, tart fruit, a hint of bitter coffee and tart hops fill the mouth, while the long finish has a solid base of bitter hops with smoky malt notes and sour fruit.

It's a good quenching beer, one that Upper Canada recommends as a base for Cheddar Cheese Soup, made with carrots, onions, celery, butter, flour, chicken or vegetable stock, Parmesan and grated Cheddar and a generous helping of the beer.

early 21st century when the singer Madonna, who has a home in England, said Landlord was her favourite beer. With phlegmatic Northern humour, Taylors changed its truck signs from 'Pedigree – loved by Yorkshiremen' to 'Pedigree – loved by Yorkshiremen… and Madonna'.

Landlord is brewed with just one grain, Scottish Golden Promise, with some brewing sugar and a touch of caramel for colour adjustment. The hops are Fuggles, Styrian Goldings and Whitbread Goldings Variety. The intense hop bitterness of the beer is achieved by circulating the hopped wort over a deep bed of Styrians in the hop back. The finished beer has a superb aroma of juicy malt, spicy and earthy hop resins and tart citrus fruit. Tangy fruit, juicy malt and bitter hops pack the mouth, while the long finish is beautifully balanced between biscuity malt, lemon fruit and bitter hops. To confuse the issue, the bottled verslon of Landlord is called a pale ale. Pale ale or bitter – you pays your money and you takes your choice. Let's just settle for a world classic beer.

Wadworth 6X

Source: Wadworth & Co, Devizes, Wiltshire, England
Strength: 4.3%
Website: www.wadworth.co.uk

TASTING NOTES
Appearance
Aroma
Taste
Overall score

Wadworth 6X is a fine example of an English bitter in which the blend of malts and hops produces a subtle beer with low carbonation and great drinkability. It comes from one of the handsomest breweries in England, a Victorian red-brick pile constructed on the tower principle, with the stages of the brewing process flowing logically from floor to floor.

Henry Wadworth founded the brewery in 1885 in an ancient market town with a name of Norman-French origin that means boundaries or divisions. Wadworth is still family owned, employs a cooper who fashions wooden casks, uses dray horses to deliver beer to local pubs, as well as traditional coppers and mash tuns. It is not stuck in a time warp, however. Considerable investment in recent years has enabled production to grow to 200,000 barrels a year, the bulk of which is made up of 6X. The beer is supplied to Wadworth's own estate of 256 pubs and free trade throughout the country.

The name 6X recalls the time when medieval monks blessed casks of ale with Xs, with the number of crosses indicating strength: a true six X would be considerably higher in alcohol than Wadworth's brand. It is brewed with Fanfare pale malt and a small amount (4%) of crystal, with 3% cane sugar (colour 28 units). The complex hop recipe is made up of four English varieties: First Gold, Fuggles, Goldings and Progress, of which the main hop is Fuggles (67%). The hopped extract filters through a bed of Goldings in the hop back after the copper boil (23 bitterness units).

The copper-coloured beer has a tempting aroma of spicy and earthy hop resins, biscuit malt and a hint of vanilla. It fills the mouth with sappy malt, a touch of barley sugar sweetness and a growing bitter and peppery hop note. The long finish is finely balanced between rich, juicy malt, hints of barley sugar and vanilla, and a firm hop bitterness.

Wellington Arkell Best Bitter

Source: Wellington Brewery, Guelph, Ontario, Canada
Strength: 4%
Website: www.wellingtonbrewery.ca

The name Arkell will be familiar to British beer drinkers, as the family of that name runs a respected regional brewery in Swindon, Wiltshire (see page 103). A member of the family emigrated to Canada and founded a community near Guelph in Wellington County. He is honoured by a beer branded Arkell, brewed in a town that is a centre of agriculture, boasts an agricultural university and has long been an important brewing centre.

Wellington Brewery specialises in English-style beers, including an Imperial Stout, County Ale, Special Pale Ale and, inevitably, an Iron Duke. The brewery was founded in 1985 by a group of British beer devotees, and they import malts and hops from Britain and mainland Europe to give their brews authentic flavours. At first they produced their beers in cask-conditioned form but quickly found that many bar owners had no idea how to look after beers that require careful monitoring in the cellar. Filtered keg beers replaced the cask ones, though a few outlets have overcome their initial resistance and now take the naturally conditioned versions.

Arkell Best, which offers more profound aromas and flavour in its cask form, is brewed with pale and crystal malts, and is hopped with Goldings and Styrian Goldings. It has a distinctive peppery Goldings hop aroma, with biscuity malt and a raisin-like fruitiness. It has a firm palate with a rich juicy malt note, ripe fruit and bitter hop resins. The lingering finish has creamy malt and rich fruit but finally becomes dry, bitter and hoppy.

TASTING NOTES
Appearance
Aroma
Taste
Overall score

Wells Bombardier

Source: Charles Wells Eagle Brewery, Bedford, England
Strength: 4.3%
Website: www.charleswells.co.uk

Charles Wells, a merchant seaman, gave up his career to found a brewery in Bedford that is still run by his descendants. It is now the only independent brewing concern in Bedfordshire's county town, the home of John Bunyan. It moved from its original site in 1976 to a modern and highly flexible new brewery that can produce both ale and lager. Part of the site once housed a building where Glenn Miller and his United States Army Orchestra recorded concerts during World War Two. Bing Crosby was among many American entertainers who appeared there with the orchestra. It is now a canning line: *sic transit gloria mundi!*

Wells is the largest independent family-owned brewery in Britain and it produces under licence such international lager brands as Cobra, Kirin and Red Stripe. It has not ignored its ale brands, though: it has a sizeable pub estate of 255 to supply, as well as extensive free trade.

Adroit marketing has turned Bombardier into one of the country's Top Ten premium cask beers. When it was launched, the beer had an image on its labels of a famous boxer called Bombardier Billy Wells, who has no connection with the brewing family: it was his rank when he was a soldier in the Royal Artillery.

The beer is brewed with Fanfare pale malt, crystal malt and invert sugar: colour 30 units. The hops are Challenger and Styrian Goldings in pellet form: 31 units of bitterness. The rich and complex copper-coloured beer has a superb aroma of wholemeal biscuits, tangy raisin and sultana fruit, floral hops and a touch of sulphur from the water. In the mouth there is a good solid base of hop bitterness, with juicy malt and vinous fruit. The finish has good length, with a final bitter hoppiness but preceded by tangy fruit and rich malt. Export bottled versions of the beer are considerably stronger. The company has pioneered draught cask beer for home consumption with vented cans.

Wolf Granny Wouldn't Like It

Source: Wolf Brewery, Attleborough, Norfolk, England
Strength: 4.8%
Website: www.wolf-brewery.ltd.uk

TASTING NOTES
Appearance
Aroma
Taste
Overall score

One of the many fine contributions craft brewers have made to British beer drinking is humour. They have got away from simple brand names such as Bitter and Best Bitter and come up with titles that bring a smile of pleasure to the lips as well as the tastebuds. The Wolf Brewery, which started life as the Reindeer brew-pub in Norwich, moved to its new site in 1996 with a 20-barrel plant based in the former Gaymer cider factory and orchards. It's a site with nostalgic appeal for me: I was evacuated from London to Norfolk during World War Two and can still recall as a small child the large cider works alongside the railway line from Norwich to London.

Wolf Witham owns the brewery, and his beers have many lupine connections, including Wolf in Sheep's Clothing, Coyote Bitter and Lupus Lupus. The last named is a pointer to the fact that the Latin name for the hop means 'wolf plant' because, untamed, it will run wild over the countryside. The pump clip and label for Granny Wouldn't Like It show a cartoon representation of Red Riding Hood and the wolf.

The beer is brewed with Halcyon pale, chocolate and wheat malts and hopped with Challenger and Goldings. The amber-red beer has a rich aroma of peppery hops, vinous fruit, biscuity malt and chocolate. The full palate is dominated by wholemeal biscuits, rich fruit, increasing hop bitterness and a hint of chocolate and roasted grain. The chocolate and roast notes persist into the long and deep finish, accompanied by ripe, sweet fruit and a solid underpinning of bitter hop resins.

Wolf Witham is wrong: I know for a fact that my late grandmother would have adored the beer. All Wolf's cask beers are also available in bottle-fermented form.

Extra Strong Beers & Bitters

Extra Strong Bitter is a style that has come in from the cold. Many brewers produced strong ales but were shy of admitting the fact. At the end of a brewery tour I have often been told, in an almost shame-faced manner, 'We do have an interesting high-gravity beer if you'd fancy a small glass.' These were beers for special occasions and only rarely allowed out into pubs and bars.

the early 20th century when a limited form of prohibition banned the sale of spirits in bars. Brewers responded by producing strong beers that soothed the loss felt by brandy, gin and whisky drinkers.

The success of strong beers has encouraged brewers to pay great attention to the style. One objection to the category in the past was that the beers tended to be sweet and cloying, with a liquid barley sugar flavour. Brewers have turned, yet again, to the hop for help. A generous addition of hops, in the copper, the hop back and even in the cask, tempers the richness and sweetness of beers made with substantial amounts of malt and other grains and sugars. The careful marriage of malt and hops, the balance of sweetness, fruit and bitterness, make this style of beer one that constantly surprises and delights.

Although it just falls outside this category, Courage has a beer called Directors Bitter (4.8%) that was first brewed solely for the directors of the company's plant in Alton in Hampshire. Then, from the late 1970s, one English beer, Fuller's Extra Special Bitter, caught beer drinkers' fancies so much so that it won several awards in CAMRA's Champion Beer of Britain competition. It crossed the Atlantic and became a cult beer in the United States, to such an extent that the Great American Beer Festival now has a category called Extra Special Bitter. In Britain, the title belongs exclusively to Fuller's and it rigorously protects the brand name.

In mainland Europe there is less reticence about strong beers. They are part of the everyday drinking experience. In Belgium, in particular, with its deep-rooted beer culture, strong beers reflect a period in

Arkell's Kingsdown Ale

Source: Arkell's Brewery, Kingsdown, Swindon, Wiltshire, England
Strength: 5.2%
Website: www.arkells.co.uk

Arkell's is one of the unassuming family-owned breweries, little known outside their trading areas, that form the backbone of traditional, high-quality brewing in England. John Arkell founded the company in 1843. He came from a farming family and emigrated to Canada, where he helped set up a community in Ontario that still exists today (see Wellington Arkell Best Bitter, page 99). John, however, returned to England and married his fiancée, who had become homesick in the New World.

John started to farm, grew barley, and took the next logical step of building a modest brewery in the Kingsdown area of Swindon. His timing was perfect. The great railway builder and architect Isambard Kingdom Brunel had chosen Swindon as the site for his works as he developed the Great Western railway line. Swindon rapidly grew from a sleepy market town into a thriving industrial one, with many thirsty throats to relieve.

To keep pace with demand, the Kingsdown brewery has been rebuilt and developed several times but it retains its Victorian charm, with an imposing tall chimney and a steam engine that can still be used in the event of a power cut.

Brewing takes place in traditional wood-jacketed mash tuns, copper boiling kettles and open square fermenters. Kingsdown Ale was introduced in 1969 when Swindon Town football club won the Football League Cup. The football team has not had much to celebrate since then but the beer has become a popular member of the brewery's portfolio.

Head brewer Don Bracher makes the beer as a 'parti-gyle' with his premium bitter 3B. This means he makes a strong wort, or extract, then adds brewing water to create the two different beers. Kingsdown is fashioned from Maris Otter pale and crystal malts with a small amount of brewing sugar (30 units of colour). The hops are Fuggles and Goldings, with a late addition of Goldings at the end of the copper boil (36 bitterness units). The generous use of Goldings gives a peppery bitterness to the amber-coloured beer that brilliantly balances biscuity malt and pear drop fruitiness. Hops and fruit offer an enticing aroma, and then fill the mouth alongside juicy malt. The deep and complex finish is bitter-sweet, with sappy malt, ripe fruit and peppery hops working in harmony.

TASTING NOTES
Appearance
Aroma
Taste
Overall score

Fuller's ESB

Source: Fuller Smith and Turner's Griffin Brewery, Chiswick, London, England
Strength: 5.5%
Website: www.fullers.co.uk

TASTING NOTES
Appearance
Aroma
Taste
Overall score

This is the beer that gave its name to an international style. While there are many American ESBs, the brand name is now unique to Fuller's in Britain and it defends the name with legal vigour in its home market.

It started life as Winter Beer in 1969 and became a regular brew under its current name two years later. Three times winner of CAMRA's Champion Beer of Britain award, ESB is renowned for its classic Fuller's house style of a deep, rich fruitiness balanced by tangy hops. Some years ago, I described ESB as 'liquid Cooper's marmalade', which to my surprise rather pleased the brewery. In 2004, I was invited – as a beer and marmalade expert – to the Chiswick brewery to taste a revamped version of the beer. The changes were the result of a slight fall in sales. Market research showed that many drinkers rejected ESB on the grounds that it was too strong. It is a curiosity of beer drinking that people will down several glasses of lager of 5% or more but will baulk at an ale of similar strength.

Head brewer John Keeling and his team tackled the problem by keeping the strength at 5.5% but extended the time the beer matures in the brewery before going out to trade. Following fermentation, the beer rests for 21 days in conditioning tanks on a deep bed of Goldings hops. The result is an increased peppery hop note that better balances the beer's intense fruitiness. The brewery has cleverly developed a new branded glass for the beer that looks like an over-sized half-pint measure but actually contains a full pint. It makes a pint of ESB look less daunting to drinkers worried about its strength.

ESB is brewed from 90% Optic pale malt, 3% crystal malt and 7% flaked maize (colour units 30). The complex hop recipe includes Challenger, Goldings, Northdown and Target. The beer is late hopped in the copper with Challenger and Northdown, matured over Goldings that are then used to dry hop in the cask (34 units of bitterness). The finished beer has an explosion of rich malt, marmalade fruit and peppery hops on the nose, with an enormous attack of juicy malt, orange peel and bitter hop resins in the mouth. The deep, complex and lingering finish is beautifully balanced between malt, hops and tangy fruit, finally becoming dry with a good bitter hop resins note. A world classic.

Jennings Sneck Lifter

Source: Jennings Brothers, Cockermouth, Cumbria, England
Strength: 5.1%
Website: www.jenningsbrewery.co.uk

TASTING NOTES
Appearance
Aroma
Taste
Overall score

Cumbria has a substantial number of breweries, 15 at the last count. But most of them are relatively new 'micros' and Jennings is the sole large commercial operator. It dates from 1828, when John Jennings, the son of a maltster, opened a small brewery in the village of Lorton. He was sufficiently successful to have to move in 1874 to bigger premises in Cockermouth, most famous as the home town of Fletcher Christian, leader of the mutiny on the *Bounty*.

The brewery enjoys a spectacular base at the foot of Cockermouth Castle (see picture) – home to the Egremont family that includes the celebrated science fiction writer John Wyndham – and alongside the confluence of the rivers Cocker and Derwent. There are no Jennings left to run the company, but the brewery still has a strong local base, and in 2005 it was bought by the national group Wolverhampton & Dudley Breweries. The modern company owns 120 pubs and has a large trade throughout the North-west and across the Pennines into Northumbria. £1 million was invested in the brewery in 1999 but it remains staunchly traditional in its brewing methods and remains committed to both cask-conditioned draught beer and the best brewing materials. It draws pure 'brewing liquor' from a well on the site.

Sneck Lifter, Jennings' strongest regular beer, takes its name from a dialect expression for someone who lifts the sneck, or catch, on the door to enter a pub. I have also been told that it means someone who doesn't buy his round of beer and hurries out of the pub by lifting the sneck. The beer is dark for a bitter and some people consider it to be close to a porter, though I doubt the London style ever found its way to such a remote area. It is brewed with Maris Otter pale malt, torrefied wheat, invert sugar and a small amount of black malt (50 colour units). The hops, used in whole flower form, are Fuggles and Goldings, which contribute 40 units of bitterness. It has a rich wholemeal and fresh bread aroma backed by spicy and peppery hops and espresso coffee notes from the black malt. The dark malt character builds in the mouth, adding some dried fruit notes, with a good balancing note of peppery hops. The finish is deep and complex, with a bitter-sweet fruitiness, a hint of coffee and chocolate, and a final lingering hop bitterness.

Moorhouse's Pendle Witches Brew

Source: Moorhouse's Brewery, Burnley, Lancashire, England
Strength: 5.1%
Website: www.moorhouses.co.uk

TASTING NOTES
Appearance
Aroma
Taste
Overall score

The journey to Burnley is one of the unsung great railway journeys of the world. I caught a train at Leeds that took a circuitous route past small towns with redundant mills and their tall, forlorn chimneys, then climbed steeply as it made for the peaks of the Pennine hills, England's rocky backbone. Brown moors and hills rose on either side, interspersed by tumbling rivers and streams. Then the train reached the summit and started the long glide down into Burnley, a mill town once so important that it had three railway stations. It was among the Pendle Hills that glower over Burnley that witches are alleged to have practised their dark arts in the 16th century. The reality is that many women, caught up in the turbulence of the times, were wrongly accused of witchcraft. James I had survived the Gunpowder Plot that failed to blow him and the Houses of Parliament to Kingdom Come. He then launched a campaign against such rebellious and staunchly Roman Catholic areas as Lancashire. In his book *Daemonology* he told the prosecuting authorities how to spot the 'devil's mark' on suspects' bodies. In most cases, birthmarks and blemishes were sufficient 'evidence' for women to be arrested. Several women from the Burnley area were tried on trumped-up charges and hanged.

The story should not distract us from the pleasures of the beer that recalls this grim period of English history. Pendle Witches Brew has won awards in CAMRA's Champion Beer of Britain competition and a silver medal in the Brewing International Awards. It is brewed with Halcyon pale malt, crystal malt, invert sugar and torrefied wheat, and hopped with just one variety, Fuggles. A pale bronze beer, it has a fine aroma of biscuity malt, spicy hops, pear-like fruit and a faint hint of vanilla. The mouth is filled with interweaving bitter-sweet flavours of fruit, malt and hop resins. The lengthy finish has some sweetness from malt and fruit but is balanced by a powerful and spicy hop character.

Pauwel Kwak

Source: Brouwerij Bosteels, Buggenhout, Belgium
Strength: 8%
Website: www.karmeliet.be

The idiosyncratic glass in its wooden serving shoe has tended to overshadow the quality of the beer itself. It comes from a family-owned brewery in the Dendermonde area, founded in 1791 by Evarist Bosteels. The company is run today by the sixth generation of the family, Ivo Bosteels and his son Antoine, and is based in the family's former mansion, which includes a small tower brewery.

The brewery's celebrated strong beer takes its name from a tavern keeper called Pauwel Kwak – literally Fat Paul – who owned De Hoorn (the Horn) on the busy road from Ghent to Mechelen. This was in the days of horse-drawn coaches. Mail coaches stopped at the tavern three times a day but the coachmen were not allowed to leave their vehicles for security reasons. So Fat Paul devised a glass with an oval base that the coach driver could place in his stirrup. As coach travel died out, the beer disappeared but Bosteels revived it, using the traditional oval-bottomed glass. As the glass cannot stand on its own, the brewery devised the wooden shoe to hold it.

The brewery has its own well in the grounds that supplies water from a depth of more than

100m (330ft). The water is soft and low in salts, and imparts a mellow note to the beer, which is made from three grains, including wheat. In the Belgian tradition, white candy sugar is added in the brew kettle to encourage a strong fermentation. The brewer does not want too much bitterness and therefore uses Styrian Goldings primarily for aroma. The finished beer is a burnished amber colour, with a dense rocky head of foam, a gentle spicy hop aroma, sappy malt and a big vanilla character from the house yeast. Malt, vanilla and a banana fruit note fill the mouth, while the big finish has a restrained spicy hop note, a rich maltiness and a lingering hint of liquorice, banana and vanilla.

TASTING NOTES
Appearance
Aroma
Taste
Overall score

Ridley's Old Bob

Source: T D Ridley & Sons, Hartford End, near Chelmsford, Essex, England
Strength: 5.1%
Website: www.ridleys.co.uk

TASTING NOTES
Appearance
Aroma
Taste
Overall score

The address may say 'near Chelmsford' but Ridley's is in a remote locality, hidden down country lanes. You come across it almost by accident: as your car breasts a slight rise in the road, there, suddenly, is the brewery, a huddle of brownstone buildings topped by an imposing chimney. It is one of the oldest beer makers in England and is a now rare example of a farm brewery. William Ridley ran a mill on the site alongside the River Chelmer. His son Thomas Dixon Ridley expanded the malting and milling business and then added a tower brewery downstream from the mill in 1842.

The brewery remains splendidly traditional. Some worn-out vessels have been replaced – the copper and hop back are made of modern stainless steel – but there are eight wooden fermenters with copper linings as well as a cast-iron mash tun. Sacks of malt are lifted by chains from the ground floor, while a malt weighing machine dates from the 19th century and is one of the oldest pieces of weighing equipment in the country. But the brewery's history pales into insignificance when compared to the Ridley family's, which can be traced back to the rugged border country of Northumbria in the 10th century. One of the most famous members of the family was Bishop Nicholas Ridley, who was burnt at the stake during the reign of Mary Tudor, when he refused to renege on his Protestant beliefs. The present chairman is also named Nicholas in the bishop's honour.

Old Bob, named after a former head brewer, was for decades a bottled beer but interest among consumers encouraged the brewery to make it available on draught as well. It is made with Maris Otter pale malt (75%), crystal malt (12.5%) and torrefied wheat (12.5%): 45 colour units. It is hopped with Fuggles and Goldings for bitterness, with Styrian Goldings used in the hop back for aroma (35 bitterness units). While it is 5.1% in strength, the original gravity – a measurement of the malt sugars prior to fermentation – is 1055 degrees. This indicates that fermentation is stopped before all the sugars have turned to alcohol, leaving some sweetness in the beer. The aroma is rich and redolent of such dried vine fruits as raisins and sultanas, with wholemeal maltiness and a light spicy hop note. Ripe fruit and sweet malt fill the mouth, but spicy and earthy hop notes in the finish stop the beer from being cloying: the hops balance the dried fruit and biscuity malt character.

* In July 2005, Greene King bought Ridley's and planned to close the brewery but said that it would maintain production of Old Bob.

Ringwood Old Thumper

Source: Ringwood Brewery, Ringwood, Hampshire, England
Strength: 5.6%
Website: www.ringwoodbrewery.co.uk

TASTING NOTES
Appearance
Aroma
Taste
Overall score

Ringwood is a remarkable success story, one that proves that small craft breweries can succeed against all the odds in a market place increasingly dominated by giant global producers. The brewery was launched in 1978 by the legendary 'father' of micro-brewing, Peter Austin, who went on to build small breweries in the United States, France and even China. On my first visit to the brewery, it was based in an old bakery near the railway station. While I interviewed Peter, I noticed a quiet young man cleaning one of the brewing vessels. He was David Welsh who went on to run the company when Peter retired.

Under David's guiding hand, Ringwood moved in 1986 to part of the old Tunk's brewery site. To keep up with demand, a new brewhouse was commissioned in 1994 and a new fermenting room was added a year later. Demand continued to increase and further fermenters were added in 2002. Ringwood now produces around 30,000 barrels of beer a year, making it a regional rather than a micro producer. Best Bitter is its biggest seller but there is no doubt that the company was put on the map and went on to greater success as a result of winning CAMRA's Champion Beer of Britain competition in 1988 with Old Thumper.

It is brewed from Maris Otter pale malt with small amounts of chocolate and crystal malts and some torrefied wheat (33 units of colour). The hops are a blend of all English varieties, Challenger, Goldings and Progress (32 units of bitterness). The deep bronze beer has a big peppery and spicy hop aroma balanced by biscuity and nutty malt with a hint of tart apple fruit. Rich juicy malt, tangy fruit and bitter hop resins fill the mouth, followed by a long finish that ends dry and bitter but with compensating notes of sappy malt, nuts and fruit. The beer is brewed under licence in the US by Shipyard Breweries (see also next entry).

Shipyard Longfellow Winter Ale

Source: Shipyard Breweries, Portland, Maine, USA
Strength: 5.5%
Website: www.shipyard.com

TASTING NOTES
Appearance
Aroma
Taste
Overall score

Shipyard, as explained in the IPA section (see page 20), was inspired by British micro-brewer Peter Austin and one of his brewers, Alan Pugsley, who is now a partner in the company, in which giant brewer Miller also has a stake.

Winter Ale is a seasonal speciality, one that beer lovers in New England await with keen anticipation. The Shipyard website was inundated in 2004 with requests to know whether the beer had been discontinued, as the brewery had launched a new Winter Ale. Alan Pugsley himself had to take to the airwaves to assure the worried drinkers that Longfellow was on the way. The beer is named after the celebrated poet Henry Wadsworth Longfellow, who lived in Portland, a major fishing harbour and port. He is most famous for the epic *Hiawatha* but he also wrote poems about the sea, including *The Wreck of the Hesperus*.

Longfellow Winter Ale employs pale, crystal and chocolate malts and roasted barley (colour 44) and is hopped with Cascade, East Kent Goldings, German Tettnanger and Warrior (40 bitterness units). The house yeast strain, imported from Ringwood in England, imparts a typical fruity character. The rich amber beer has a spicy cinnamon and roasted grain aroma, with hints of bitter chocolate and coffee in the mouth, roasted grain, fresh apple and earthy hops. The long finish is deep and complex, with vine fruits, spices, earthy hop resins and roasted grain.

Wild River Extra Special Bitter

Source: Wild River Brewing, Grants Pass, Oregon, USA
Strength: 5.3%
Website: www.wildriverbrewing.com

TASTING NOTES
Appearance
Aroma
Taste
Overall score

The first head brewer at Wild River, Hubert Smith, was a frequent visitor to Britain and I met him regularly at the Great British Beer Festival where he graced my annual beer seminars. He had a passion for strong English pale ales and he poured that passion into his interpretation of Extra Strong Bitter.

Wild River started life as a Pizza Deli in 1975, founded by Jerry and Bertha Miller at Brookings Harbor with the toe-curling slogan, 'Blame us if your life goes to Pizzas'. They flourished in their attractive river setting close to the California border and eventually opened new premises at Cave Junction and Grants Pass. Realising that pizza and strong malty/hoppy beers are a marriage made in heaven, the Millers added in-house brewing facilities first at Cave Junction and then at a bigger plant at Grants Pass, which has a 15-barrel kit. The breweries produce a wide range of beers, which are also widely distributed in bottle, and include Kölsch, Hefe Weizen and Russian Imperial Stout.

The stand-out beer is the ESB, brewed from pale, Munich, crystal and wheat malts and hopped with American Chinook and English Fuggles. The copper-coloured beer throws a dense, rocky head of foam and has an enthralling, complex aroma of tangy hop resins, tart citrus fruit and biscuity malt. Rich creamy malt fills the mouth with a good balance of earthy hop resins and tart fruit, while the long and deep finish is a fine balance between juicy malt, lemon fruit and a lingering hop-leaf bitterness.

Wychwood Hobgoblin

Source: Wychwood Brewery, Eagle Maltings, Witney, Oxfordshire, England
Strength: 5.2% (bottle); 5% (cask)
Website: www.wychwood.co.uk

Wychwood was set up in 1983 in the maltings of the old Clinch's brewery that dated from the 1800s. The founders of Wychwood were Paddy Glenny and the late head brewer Chris Moss, who was much loved in brewing and CAMRA circles. Chris fashioned the first version of Hobgoblin with a striking label based on the legends and myths of the Royal Forest of Wychwood that covered most of West Oxfordshire in medieval times. In common with the New Forest in Hampshire, Wychwood was reserved for the sovereign and his court to go hunting. Fairies, demons and hobgoblins roamed the forest: hobgoblins were bigger versions of goblins and, despite their terrifying appearance, acted as guardians of farm and country folk, though apparently they could turn nasty if thwarted. Sounds like the Stella drinkers in my local.

Over the years, Hobgoblin has ranged from 4.5% to 5.5%. I have included it in this section because of the strength of the bottled version, though it's a moveable feast. It is brewed from 90% Maris Otter pale malt, with 7% crystal malt and 3% torrefied wheat (40 colour units). The hops are Fuggles and Styrian Goldings, which create 28 units of bitterness. The amber-red beer has a tempting aroma of biscuity malt, vinous fruit and spicy hop resins. Full-bodied malt, sultana fruit and earthy hops coat the mouth, while the complex finish has a bitter-sweet start, with creamy malt and ripe fruit, but spicy hops linger at the back of the tongue.

TASTING NOTES
Appearance
Aroma
Taste
Overall score

Old Ales, Barley Wines & Vintage Ales

It is tempting – and many beer writers have fallen for the temptation – to list Old Ales and Barley Wines as though they are the same style of strong beer. They are not. The designation Old Ale does not necessarily imply strength (they can be as low as 4.5%), whereas Barley Wine clearly suggests a beer that is a rival to the fermented juice of the grape. Both are English styles and they have quite different histories, though they do have in common the need to be matured for a considerable period.

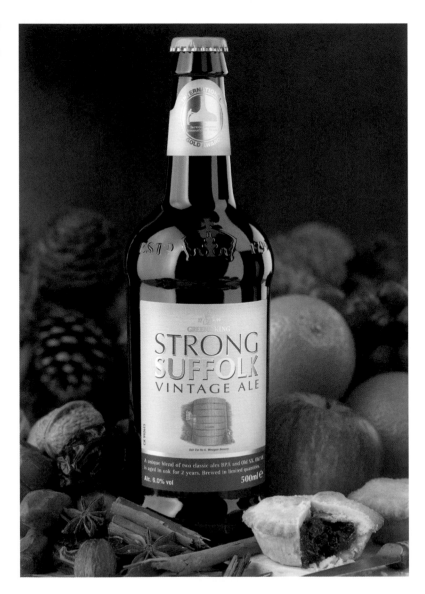

Old Ales in the 18th century were also known as 'stale' as a result of maturing for many months or years in wooden tuns, where the beer was attacked by wild yeasts and acetified by lactobacilli and tannins in the wood. The sour flavour of stale was much appreciated at the time and lives on in the form of the sour red beers of Belgium (see page 201). Stale was an important constituent of the early types of porter (see page 136) and was also blended with the young, fresh mild ales of the 18th century to give them some semblance of maturity.

Once brewers in the late 19th and early 20th centuries stopped vatting or maturing beer for long periods, old and stale disappeared. Old reappeared as part of the revival of interest in beer styles created by CAMRA and the 'real ale revolution' of the 1970s. Many of the new-wave old ales are reserved for the winter period, others are now brewed all year round. The classic of the style is the remarkable Greene King Strong Suffolk Ale, a genuine old ale or 'country ale' from the 18th century. It is a blend of two beers, one of which is still matured in ancient wooden vats. Some old ales are 'vatted' in the sense that they mature naturally on their yeast under glass. The best-known examples are Gale's Prize Old Ale in its corked bottle and the celebrated Thomas Hardy's Ale, rescued from oblivion by a micro-brewery a few years ago.

Barley wine for centuries was the preserve of the English aristocracy. While the labouring classes made do with cheap brown ales, the nobility drank beer matured for long periods that had the potency of wine. Such beers were also known as October beers – October being considered the best month to make good beer, using the new malts and hops of the harvest – Dorchester beers, malt liquors or malt wines, but by the early 18th century the term barley wine was in vogue. As a result of the interminable wars with France, it was the patriotic duty of noble Englishmen and women to drink the 'wine of the country'. Fine cut-glass goblets adorned the tables of the aristocracy and, deprived of their beloved claret, they turned to beers made as strong as wine. In *Every Man His Own Brewer*, published in London in 1768, the author commented on 'The Method of Manufacturing Pure Malt Wines': 'Laying aside vulgar opinion, that foreign wines are used by the rich, rather from vanity than taste, it must be observed that experience will always be superior to custom. Our business then is to prepare our malt drinks as nearly as possible to answer the like purpose of foreign wines.'

Commercial, or 'common', brewers supplied barley wines to the nobility but the landed gentry had their own breweries in their country mansions. In her book *Country House Brewing in England 1500–1900* (Hambledon Press), Pamela Seabrook paints a fascinating picture of beer making in small brewhouses usually attached to the kitchens of stately homes. Brewing was often one of the many tasks of the butler. An 1820s training manual for butlers said: 'The keys of the wine and ale cellars are specially kept by him, and the management of the wine, the keeping of the stock book, and also of ale in stock, or in brewing, are in his particular charge. This duty he generally performs in the morning before he is dressed to receive company... While these duties and those of brewing are in hand, he leaves the parlour and waiting duties to the under-butler and footman.'

October beers, or barley wines, of the period were exceedingly strong. One recipe called for 23 bushels of malt to make two 54-gallon hogsheads of beer, one bushel being the equivalent of eight imperial gallons. There was considerable dispute over how long the beers should be left to mature. One 18th-century writer considered that a beer brewed in October should be left until spring, when the increase in temperature would encourage a second fermentation. The beer would then be 'very fine, strong, mellow, well-tasted and wholesome' by Michaelmas (i.e. the end of September). But another writer was of the opinion that the beer would be at its best by midsummer, although it would keep for five or even 10 years.

The decline of the English aristocracy in the 20th century – only Lord Lichfield's estate at Shugborough in Staffordshire has a working brewery today – left the brewing of barley wines to commercial producers. The brand leader in Britain for decades was Whitbread's Gold Label, now reduced to a canned product, while Bass No1 Barley Wine is an occasional brew from a pilot plant in the Coors complex at Burton-on-Trent. The style has crossed the Atlantic, where it is brewed with enthusiasm by craft brewers. It has also been the inspiration for strong Belgian beers (see Bush, page 119).

Brewers enjoy challenges. The opportunity to brew vintage ale moves them from the world of mainstream beers to a level where the adroit blending of massive amounts of malts and hops can produce beers with astonishingly complex and rewarding aromas and flavours. The brewer is more fortunate than the wine maker: as Fuller's shows with its Vintage Ale, it is possible to take different malts, sugar and hop varieties once a year to produce beers that have a recognisable house style but which vary subtly and often sublimely from one vintage to the next.

ABOVE
Gale's Brewery in Hampshire has its 'brewery tap' pub next door, the Ship & Bell. Gale's brews a classic bottle-fermented old ale.

Anchor Old Foghorn

Source: Anchor Brewing Co, San Francisco, California, USA
Strength: 8.7%
Website: www.anchorbrewing.com

TASTING NOTES
Appearance
Aroma
Taste
Overall score

The beer's inspiration is the throaty growl of a ship's horn as it navigates the fog-wreathed waters of San Francisco. Owner Fritz Maytag discovered barley wine on his seminal trip to England, where he also fell in love with well-hopped pale ales (see page 53).

Old Foghorn was introduced in 1975 and has become an American classic, building on the English experience but adding new depths of richness due to an emphatic American hop character. The beer is certainly well matured: it rests on a deep bed of Cascade hops for up to 10 months before it is released to the public. It is brewed from pale and crystal malts, and – unusually – only the 'first runnings' from the mash tun are used. This means the spent grain is not sparged, or washed, with a further addition of hot water to rinse out any remaining malt sugars. Cascades produce 65 units of bitterness. Fermentation is in deep vessels, where the yeast is regularly roused to prevent it from falling asleep on the job as it creates such a high level of alcohol. The beer is pasteurised but this does not prevent it developing in bottle, and some drinkers prefer to lay down some small nip bottles for several years. It is also available on draught. The burnished mahogany ale has a pronounced ripe fruit aroma reminiscent of apricots and raisins, balanced by a ripe malt loaf note and tangy, bitter hops. Malt and fruit build in the mouth but the crescendo is reached in the finish, which lingers on the tongue and the throat with massive vinous fruit, plump grain and bitter hop resins. It's a sipping beer, to be appreciated like a fine Cognac or single malt whisky, and is a fine companion for blue cheese.

Ballard's Wassail

Source: Ballard's Brewery, Nyewood, West Sussex, England
Strength: 6%
Website: www.ballardsbrewery.org.uk

Carola Brown is a stalwart of craft brewing in Britain. She launched Ballard's in 1980 at her farm, Cumbers, and moved to an old sawmill in Nyewood in 1988. She was a founder of SIBA, which stood for Small Independent Brewers' Association but is known today as the Society of Independent Brewers. SIBA was created to give small brewers a voice in both the brewing industry and the pub trade. It has achieved remarkable success. It has persuaded the British government to introduce Progressive Beer Duty, which means smaller producers pay less tax on their products than giant national and regional brewers, and has also reached agreements with the powerful pub chains, several of which now buy beer from SIBA members.

Ballard's produces 1,500 gallons of beer a week from a smart and compact brewhouse. It brews only with malt and hops, avoiding sugars and cheaper grains. Several of its draught beers are also available in bottle-fermented form. The bottled versions are filtered, reseeded with fresh yeast and conditioned in the brewery for two weeks before release to trade.

Wassail is both a greeting – from the Middle English *waes aeil*, which means 'good health' – and also an ancient type of spiced or mulled wine drunk to celebrate Christmas Eve and Twelfth Night. Ballard's Wassail has a picturesque label that features Hengist, fifth-century leader of the Jutes, who, with his brother Horsa, brought the first Germanic settlers to England and with them the language that became English. The label also shows Vortigern, King of the Britons, and Rowena, Hengist's daughter, who seduced Vortigern.

The label is as complex as the beer, which is brewed with Pipkin pale and crystal malts and hopped with Fuggles and Goldings. The amber-red beer has a powerful aroma of dried vine fruits, a freshly-baked bread maltiness and earthy and spicy hops. Raisin and sultana fruit, ripe malt and hop resins coat the tongue, while the finish is deep and long, interweaving between rich fruit, malt and tangy, spicy hops.

TASTING NOTES
Appearance
Aroma
Taste
Overall score

Blue Anchor Spingo Special

Source: Blue Anchor, Helston, Cornwall, England
Strength: 6.6%
Website: www.spingoales.com

TASTING NOTES
Appearance
Aroma
Taste
Overall score

Beer has been brewed for 600 years or more on the site of the present inn. It started life as a monks' hospice around the year 1400. The monks brewed ale to refresh and sustain themselves, and they chose the site because it had a well with a plentiful supply of fresh water. Even a humble monks' resting place did not escape the dissolution of religious houses under the Tudors. It became a secular inn and took on the name of Blue Anchor at a time when Helston was an important port. The symbol of an anchor is weaved in the thatch on the pub roof.

The Blue Anchor remains gloriously unspoilt and has protected status as a Grade I listed building. The bars have flagstone floors, beamed ceilings and open fires. At the rear of the pub, a two-storey block houses the brewery, which has a mash tun that was installed in the 1920s and was originally a French wine cask. Opposite the tun is a venerable old lagged vessel that doubles as hot liquor tank and boiling copper.

The hopped wort is cooled in an open tray known as a cool ship and is then dropped down one storey into four small fermenting vessels.

The name Spingo was introduced following World War One and was based perhaps on a strong style of beer brewed in Yorkshire called Stingo. Spingo Special is brewed from Pipkin pale malt and Goldings hops. Although only pale malt is used, the beer has an amber-red colour, as some of the malt sugars caramelise during the long copper boil. The aroma is earthy and spicy with rich vine fruits. Peppery hops, biscuity malt and blackcurrant fruit pack the mouth, leading to a complex finish with massive tart fruit notes balanced by malt and bitter hops and hints of caramel and vanilla.

Special versions of Spingo are brewed for Easter and Christmas, and all the beers are available in bottle-fermented as well as draught form. Bottles are available from the pub and specialist shops.

BridgePort Old Knucklehead

Source: BridgePort Brewery, Portland, Oregon, USA
Strength: 9%
Website: www.bridgeportbrew.com

If you call someone a knucklehead, you will insult them; the British would use bonehead in its place for someone short on brains and thick on top. And yet the dignitaries of Portland queue up to get their face on the label of this annual vintage barley wine. To date they include the Mayor of Portland – some may think that voting for a knucklehead is not confined to one city in Oregon – and the doyen of American beer writers, Fred Eckhardt.

The beer is brewed in the autumn, using the new malts and hops of the harvest, and released in nip bottles in November. I have given 9% as the most recent rating but over the years it has varied from 8.7% to 9.1%. The malts come from the Pacific North-west region and include pale, crystal and a touch of chocolate. The hops are imported East Kent Goldings from England, with locally grown Chinook used for aroma as a late hop during the copper boil. The generous hop rate is important to balance the richness of the malt. At such a high level of alcohol, the beer has a massive fruity and vinous aroma: apple, apricot, pear and even banana can be detected with a hint of grapefruit from the Chinooks. The fruit is balanced by a rich and biscuity malt character and a blast of peppery Goldings. Ripe flavours of malt loaf, spicy hop resins and a persistent jammy fruitiness fill the mouth, while the long and lingering finish has some welcome dryness and bitterness from the hops that offset the continuing vine fruits and ripe malt. Sip carefully or you may emulate the name on the label.

TASTING NOTES
Appearance
Aroma
Taste
Overall score

Broughton Old Jock

Source: Broughton Ales, Broughton, Peebles-shire, Scotland
Strength: 6.7%
Website: www.broughtonales.co.uk

TASTING NOTES
Appearance
Aroma
Taste
Overall score

Broughton, brewery and small town, are in the Scottish Borders, a region of low hills that was fought over for centuries by the English and the Scots. There are still the remains of ancient keeps and small castles, built to halt the advancing British troops. The fortifications have a history of ale brewing, where women known as ale wives made hearty beers from local barley and oats to help sustain their fighting men folk. The tradition is maintained at Broughton, which brews an Oatmeal Stout (see page 141) as well as Old Jock.

The brewery, down a rutted lane and surrounded by fields where sheep graze, was founded in 1979 by David Younger, a member of the Younger brewing clan that once had a major plant in Alloa and was also part of the Scottish & Newcastle dynasty. He was supported by James Collins of the famous Scottish publishing house that became part of the Murdoch empire. There is a literary connection in Broughton, too: it was the birthplace of John Buchan, the adventure story writer, most famous for *The Thirty-Nine Steps*. The town has a Buchan Museum and the brewery produces a Greenmantle Ale in memory of one of his novels.

Old Jock is a member of a Scottish style known as a wee heavy, which indicates a strong bitter beer sold in nip bottles (though Old Jock is also available on draught). It is named in honour of Scottish soldiers, known as Jocks, who, once the Border disputes were settled, fought alongside the English in many battles.

The beer is brewed from Maris Otter pale malt and roasted barley (55 colour units) and hopped with Fuggles and Goldings for aroma and Target for bitterness (30 units of bitterness). It has a dark ruby colour and a rich aroma of roasted grain, vine fruits and spicy hops. Dark fruit, bitter roasted grain and hop resins fill the mouth, followed by a long finish with a good underpinning of bitterness to balance the increasing dominance of rich fruit and malt flavours. The bottled version of the beer has struggled in American markets, where the name is thought to refer to an item of male sportswear.

Bush Ambrée

Source: Brasserie Dubuisson, Pipaix, Belgium
Strength: 12%
Website: www.br-dubuisson.com

TASTING NOTES
Appearance
Aroma
Taste
Overall score

Dubuisson is a classic example of a Belgian farm brewery, in an area packed with small brewers, close to Tournai and Lille across the border in France. The brewery stands on the Mons road and, although farming no longer takes place, its origins are clear from the tiled roof and green-painted shutters at the windows.

In 1769, Joseph Leroy, an ancestor of the Dubuisson family that still runs the company, decided to brew at the farm to supply beer to his labourers and the local village. In 1931, Alfred Dubuisson took the decision to stop farming and concentrate on brewing. Two years later he changed the name of his single beer to Bush, which is the English for 'Buisson'. There are two theories for the name change. One says it was a way of paying homage to the British troops who liberated the farm and brewery at the end of World War One. The second says it was done in order to meet the increased competition from British beer imports. As there is a rather big gap between 1918 and 1933, I tend to accept the second theory.

In a country famous for strong beer, Bush is one of the strongest. It is brewed in an attractive brewhouse, with mash tun and copper set in tiled surrounds, the hallmark of many small, traditional Belgian breweries. The beer is brewed with pale malt and caramalt: the last named gives a luscious sweet and nutty character to the beer as well as its amber colour. The hops are East Kent Goldings and Styrian Goldings. The finished beer has a rich barley sugar, nutty and peppery hop aroma, with malt, fruit and hops filling the mouth, and a lingering finish in which the richness of the malt and fruit is balanced by peppery hop resins. It is a warming and alcoholic beer, the perfect aperitif, according to the brewers.

As a result of objections from Anheuser-Busch, the beer is sold in the United States under the name of Scaldis, the Latin name for the Scheldt, Belgium's main river. Anheuser-Busch is best known for American Budweiser and it is difficult to imagine that any self-respecting beer drinker could confuse the two beers.

Chiltern 300s Old Ale

Source: Chiltern Brewery, Terrick, near Aylesbury, Buckinghamshire, England
Strength: 4.9%
Website: www.chilternbrewery.co.uk

TASTING NOTES
Appearance
Aroma
Taste
Overall score

This beer and the next one listed provide an excellent example of Old Ale and Barley Wine from the same producer. Chiltern is an old-established craft brewery founded in 1980 by Richard Jenkinson. He was a City of London businessman who grew tired of the daily commute and decided to settle down in the delightful Buckinghamshire countryside and raise a rare breed of white rabbit. That enterprise failed to get out of the warren, so Richard turned instead to brewing and did so with some success.

He has been joined by the younger generation of his family, and sales of the beers encouraged a major investment in 2004 in a new brewhouse and temperature-controlled cold store. The brewery is visitor-friendly, with tours every Saturday at 12 noon and weekday visits by arrangement. There is a small brewery museum and a shop where draught and bottled beers can be taken away, along with beer-based cheeses, pickles and mustards. Richard has a passion for local history, and 300s Old Ale records the ancient practice of dividing English counties into areas known as hundreds, each one controlled by a steward. The Buckinghamshire divisions still have an important role to play in modern times: any Member of Parliament who wishes to resign his or her seat must apply for permission to do so to the Steward of the Chiltern Hundreds.

The beer that pays homage to this curious example of English political practice is brewed from Maris Otter pale malt (86%) and a substantial proportion of crystal malt (14%). The whole flower hops are Challenger for bitterness, and Fuggles and Goldings for aroma. The deep copper colour and the luscious nutty and vinous aroma and palate derive from the generous use of crystal malt. This is balanced by a tart hop and earthy hop resins character with a fine, full-bodied juicy malt note in the mouth. The finish lingers, finely balanced between tart fruit, biscuity malt and a good, solid underpinning of spicy hop resins.

Chiltern Bodgers Barley Wine

Source: Chiltern Brewery, Terrick, near Aylesbury, Buckinghamshire, England
Strength: 8.5%
Website: www.chilternbrewery.co.uk

Chiltern's sense of history pervades its beers. As well as celebrating the Chiltern Hundreds, another beer recalls Aylesbury's key role in the English Civil War, when England was briefly a republic under Oliver Cromwell. John Hampden's Ale pays tribute to a local Member of Parliament who was a leading supporter of the republican cause and opponent of Charles I. But the brewery does not ignore more humble but equally important citizens. A bodger was a craftsman who built chain fences in the Chiltern beechwoods, and it's a shame that the title has been devalued in modern times to mean someone who produces inferior work, usually as a house builder or decorator.

The bottle-fermented beer was first brewed in 1990 to mark the 10th anniversary of the brewery. It proves that strong beers do not have to be dark. It is made solely from Maris Otter pale malt and is hopped with Fuggles and Goldings. The pale bronze beer has a tempting aroma of ripe citrus fruits, juicy malt and spicy hops. Luscious malt and fruit fill the mouth, balanced by good hop bitterness. The lingering finish is beautifully balanced between sappy malt, ripe, tart fruit and a persistent bitter hop note. Each batch of beer is conditioned for a month and then bottled by hand. The numbered bottles are kept for a further month at the brewery before they are released to trade. Chiltern recommends a bottle should be consumed within a year of bottling but it is tempting to lay some down for a longer period. It is a fine aperitif beer or a good companion for strong cheeses or meats.

TASTING NOTES
Appearance
Aroma
Taste
Overall score

Cottage Norman's Conquest

Source: Cottage Brewing Co, Lovington, near Castle Carey, Somerset, England
Strength: 7%
Website: None

TASTING NOTES
Appearance
Aroma
Taste
Overall score

There are subtle jokes associated with this beer. The original gravity – the measure of the fermentable sugars before fermentation – is 1066, the year of the Norman conquest of England, which is depicted on the label of the bottle-fermented version. Norman is also the name of Chris Norman, who founded the brewery with his wife Helen in 1993.

Chris had been both an airline pilot and a keen home-brewer who took early retirement in order to pursue commercial brewing. Just two years later, the Normans hit the jackpot when Norman's Conquest won CAMRA's Supreme Champion Beer of Britain competition. When I went to see them a few weeks later, I found they ran a truly cottage, or garage, industry from the garden of their home in Somerset. My next visit was as a guest at a party to celebrate 20 years of successful brewing at a new site in a former cheese dairy with a 30-barrel plant that supplies some 1,500 customers.

Several new beers have been added to the range, including some with a steam railway theme, such as Golden Arrow. But Norman's Conquest remains the brewery's best-known product, even though it is made in small batches. The bottled version is filtered, reseeded with yeast and primed with brewing sugar to encourage a secondary fermentation. Drinkers should be patient and wait a couple of months to allow the beer to reach optimum condition, but check the 'best before' date on the label.

Norman's Conquest is brewed with Maris Otter pale, crystal and chocolate malts and hopped with just one variety, Challenger. The deep ruby beer has a digestive biscuit, dark fruits and bitter hop resins aroma. The full-bodied palate has delicious hints of chocolate, bitter orange and vine fruits, juicy malt and tangy hop resins. The long, deep finish offers chocolate, tart fruit, sappy malt, a hint of liquorice and an abiding undercurrent of bitter hop resins. A wonderfully warming yet refreshing sipping beer.

Fuller's Vintage Ale

Source: Fuller, Smith and Turner's Griffin Brewery, Chiswick, London, England
Strength: 8.5%
Website: www.fullers.co.uk

Vintage Ale has been a revelation. It was introduced in 1997 by the company's revered head brewer Reg Drury and continued by his successor John Keeling. The aim was to produce a strong bottle-fermented beer every September using different varieties of malted barley and hops. Fuller's house yeast strain adds the familiar signature of rich orange fruit, but there are subtle and even profound differences between one vintage and the next. The beer will also improve and develop over time, which means that tasting notes based on a young or mature beer will be radically different.

Vintage Ale is based on Fuller's Golden Pride barley wine, which is a pasteurised bottled beer. Vintage comes from the same mash but is conditioned in the brewery for four weeks at the end of fermentation and is then filtered and reseeded with fresh yeast. Some 50,000 bottles are produced every year, individually numbered and presented in an attractive claret box.

In 2004, I enjoyed a tasting of Vintage Ale at the brewery in the company of wine writer Oz Clarke, and we both revelled in the complexity and diversity of aromas and flavours presented to us. We found fresh tobacco, citrus fruits – orange in particular – liquorice, marzipan, vanilla, peppers and spices, to name just a few of the characteristics.

To give an indication of the different recipes used, the 2002 vintage – which marked the Queen's Golden Jubilee – was brewed with Golden Promise malt from Scotland and Goldings hops. Tobacco, cherries, marzipan, oranges and peppery hops were among the aromas and flavours detected. The 2003 vintage was dramatically different, using Optic malt and three hop varieties, Challenger, Northdown and Target. It was paler in colour, with a pronounced amber tone, and a richer malt character, but balanced by tart hop resins on the nose and a big hop bitterness in the finish, with orange and cherry fruit. The 2004 vintage had reverted to a single hop, Goldings again, with Maris Otter malt. Drunk young, the beer had a burnished ruby-red colour, with a massive biscuity malt, peppery hops and orange fruit aroma and palate, and a long, complex finish with vanilla notes adding to the complexity. And it will get better. Who says beer is a simple refresher?

TASTING NOTES
Appearance
Aroma
Taste
Overall score

Gale's Prize Old Ale

Source: George Gale & Co, The Hampshire Brewery, Horndean, Hampshire, England
Strength: 9%
Website: www.gales.co.uk

This is an old ale in the true sense of the word, with the beer matured in tanks in the brewery for between six and 12 months before it is bottled. It is one of a large portfolio of beers fermented with Gale's hearty, three-strain house yeast that imparts a rich and fruity aroma and flavour, which is most in evidence in Old Ale.

The brewery dates from 1847 when Richard Gale started brewing in the Ship & Bell. His son George expanded the business by buying local inns and farm buildings next to the Ship & Bell. Brewing moved out of the inn and into the farm but this timber building burnt down and was rebuilt. Its tower dominates the small town 10 miles from Portsmouth.

Soft water from the brewery's own well feeds the mash tuns and coppers, with separate vessels used to produce Prize Old Ale, which has been brewed since the 1920s, when a new head brewer brought the recipe with him from Yorkshire. Maris Otter pale malt and black malt are used, with around 10% brewing sugar. The hops are Worcestershire Fuggles and East Kent Goldings (colour 90 units, bitterness 53 units). Following the long maturation, the beer is bottled with corks and wire cradles (if the beer is stored, bottles should be laid down horizontally to keep the corks moist). The original yeast strain creates a powerful second fermentation in bottle and the declared strength of 9% could rise to as high as 12%.

While the brewery is required to put a 'best before' date on each bottle, the beer will come into its best form after five years and remain drinkable for at least 20. After a few years, the beer takes on a renowned Cognac note. Drunk younger, it is fruity (raisins, sultanas and dates) with a solid underpinning of earthy and spicy hops.

During one visit to the brewery, I was shown a fermenter where a former brewer committed suicide by jumping into the vessel, where he was overcome by alcohol and carbon dioxide. Is it the origin of the term 'stiff drink'?

Greene King Strong Suffolk Ale

Source: Greene King, Westgate Brewery, Bury St Edmunds, Suffolk, England

Strength: 6%

Website: www.greeneking.co.uk

Strong Suffolk Ale is a potent link with brewing practice in the 18th century. It is a now rare example of a 'country beer', a style that depended on long, slow maturation in wooden casks. The beer that emerged from slow ageing was used to blend with younger beers, and this is still the case at Greene King. The beer, matured for between one and five years in giant, 60-barrel tuns in the Westgate Brewery, is used as the base for St Edmund barley wine and the draught Winter Ale. The most notable and intriguing blend, however, is Strong Suffolk.

The tuns that hold the strong ale component are reached by a daunting clamber up narrow ladders and catwalks in tunnels at the rear of the brewery. It's thought that the tunnels once linked the monastery and the abbot's house, where the brewery now stands. Monks may have taken shelter in the tunnels at the time of the dissolution of the monasteries. The lids of the vats are covered in marl, a dialect word for the sandy gravel that covers much of Suffolk. I was told that the marl keeps wild yeast and other bacteria from infecting the beer. In spite of this protective covering, the 12% beer, known as Old 5X, that emerges from the untreated wooden vessels has a slight lactic sourness and hint of iodine. This beer is not sold commercially but small bottles are sometimes made available to visitors who show an interest in the subject. Old 5X is blended with another beer, the 5% BPA, or Best Pale Ale. This is another brew that is not found outside the brewery but I was given a taste of this rich, creamy and predominantly malty ale.

The two beers are brewed with Halycon and Pipkin pale malts, crystal malt and brewing sugar (100 colour units). The hops used are Northdown for bitterness and Target for aroma (32 units of bitterness). The blended beer has a spicy, oaky, sherry wine and iron-like intensity on aroma and palate with a hint of sourness.

The finish is big and complex, with malt, a vinous sweetness and some tannins balanced by bitter and earthy hop resins and the continuing hint of lactic sourness. The beer is filtered and pasteurised, and I have failed to convince the brewery that it would take the beer an extra mile if it were produced in bottle-fermented form.

In 2002, Strong Suffolk was made available as a cask-conditioned draught winter ale, but the experiment has not been repeated. Greene King recommends that Strong Suffolk is a good companion with pickled herring. Tangy cheese, blue Stilton in particular, would be an equally interesting match. The beer is sold in the United States as Olde Suffolk.

TASTING NOTES
Appearance
Aroma
Taste
Overall score

Highgate Old Ale

Source: Highgate Brewery, Walsall, West Midlands, England
Strength: 5.3%
Website: None

TASTING NOTES
Appearance
Aroma
Taste
Overall score

Highgate has had two changes of ownership in recent years. It was bought by its senior management in 1955, when the former owner, Bass, wanted to close the Victorian site, and then it was sold on to Aston Manor in Birmingham. There were initial worries that Aston Manor, which specialises in packaged beers and ciders, would change Highgate's portfolio of beers, but tradition has survived intact.

In order to survive, Highgate is no longer a dark ale specialist. It has added three bitters to its range but has also won a lucrative contract with Coors of Burton-on-Trent to brew the major West Midlands brand M&B Mild. But Highgate Dark and Old remain the bedrock of the small red-brick brewery, with its impressive wooden mash tuns and fermenters as well as copper boiling kettles.

Highgate Dark and Old are 'parti-gyled', which means a strong beer is made and then watered down with pure, iron-rich brewing liquor from a borehole on the site. Old Ale is made with Pearl pale malt, crystal and black malts, with Fuggles and Progress whole hops. Highly fermentable maltose syrup is added to encourage a powerful fermentation with the complex, four-strain house yeast, with each strain attacking different sugars in the wort. Colour units are 111, bitterness 30. The beer has a rich dark and roasted malt aroma with ripe dried fruits, bitter chocolate and grassy hops. Vinous fruit, luscious flavours of chocolate, liquorice and burnt malt fill the mouth, while the long finish has a good underpinning of gentle hop bitterness to balance the sweetness and richness of the malt character. The draught version of Old Ale is available only in the winter months but a filtered bottled version is sold all year round.

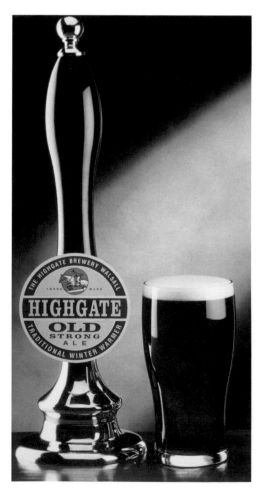

Lees Harvest Ale

Source: J W Lees, Greengate Brewery, Middleton Junction, Greater Manchester, England
Strength: 11.5%
Website: www.jwlees.co.uk

TASTING NOTES
Appearance
Aroma
Taste
Overall score

Brewers are a special breed. Not only do they have rare skills, honed over long years, but they also rise from their beds every day to begin work when most sensible folk are still slumbering. When I was invited to 'start the mash' for the annual brew of Harvest Ale at J W Lees, I booked into a convenient bed and breakfast near the brewery and was picked up the next morning by head brewer Giles Dennis at 5.30am. He was bright, cheerful and alert, while I was barely capable of speech.

In the brewery, I put on the regulation white coat and obediently followed the instructions of Giles and his fellow brewers, pushing the right buttons and pulling the correct levers to deliver malt and hot brewing liquor to the mash tun. Then I was hustled off to the inner sanctum, the brewers' 'sample room', and was taken through a tasting of several vintages of Harvest Ale. This was followed by a sumptuous brewers' breakfast before we returned to the brewhouse to check that the mash had successfully converted malt starch to sugar and we could transfer the wort to the copper for the boil with hops.

Harvests may seem remote from Lees' brewery in the outskirts of Manchester but Middleton Junction was a rural area in 1828, when John Lees, a retired cotton manufacturer, bought the site and started to brew beer as the industrial revolution spawned a thirsty army of cotton workers. His grandson, John Willie Lees, who built a new brewhouse to cope with demand, busily expanded the business. Today, his descendants still run the brewery.

Harvest Ale is brewed every autumn with fresh crops of Maris Otter malt and East Kent Goldings hops from the harvest. Each vintage is then released in 275ml bottles in time for Christmas. The beer is filtered and pasteurised but will develop in bottle.

A 2002 vintage is russet coloured, with an intense peppery aroma from the Goldings (35 bitterness units), a surprising hint of chocolate – no doubt caused by some caramelisation of the brewing sugars during the copper boil – and bitter orange fruitiness. A massive vinous richness reminiscent of Oloroso sherry fills the mouth, underscored by the continuing orange (Seville, of course) note. The finish is deep and long, with fruit, barley sugar, a hint of vanilla and a gentle spicy hop bitterness.

Moor Old Freddy Walker

Source: Moor Beer Company, Ashcott, Bridgwater, Somerset, England
Strength: 7.3%
Website: www.moorbeer.co.uk

TASTING NOTES
Appearance
Aroma
Taste
Overall score

Large companies would pay a lot of money to marketing gurus for a name such as 'Moor Beer Company'. But no money changed hands in this case. The small, 10-barrel plant was the idea of farmer Arthur Frampton and his wife Annette. They installed the kit in a workshop on their dairy farm. Sales of beer to local pubs prompted the Framptons to set up a wholesaling business to expand deliveries. They were given a major boost in 2004 when Old Freddy Walker won the top award in CAMRA's Great Winter Beer Festival. The Frampton's daughter, Holly, who works full time for the brewery, brewed the winning batch of beer.

Freddy Walker has no connection with brewing. He is a retired seaman who lives in Ashcott and is a keen consumer of Moor beers. The beer named in his honour is brewed with Maris Otter pale, crystal and black malts. The hops are Liberty from the US and Nugget.

The use of Nugget is intriguing: grown in England, Germany and the US, it is a modern 'high alpha' hop, developed to give a high level of bitterness without much aroma. It is a variety used principally by big brewers who want to extract as much bitterness as possible by using the smallest possible amount of hops, but without the delightful piny, earthy, fruity and resinous character of traditional varieties.

The Framptons use Nugget for a quite different reason: they want a powerful bitterness to balance the richness of dark malts and they provide hop aroma with the Liberty variety. The beer is russet coloured, with a barley-white head and a full and tempting aroma of vine fruits, dark, roasted grain, espresso coffee and spicy hops. Roasted grain, bitter coffee, ripe fruit and hop bitterness fill the mouth, followed by a long finish that starts bitter-sweet and then blossoms with late bitterness and a continuing fruit and coffee note.

O'Hanlon's Thomas Hardy's Ale

Source: O'Hanlon's Brewing Co, Whimple, Devon, England
Strength: 12%
Website: www.ohanlons.co.uk

Some years ago I took part in a memorable tasting of several vintages of Thomas Hardy's Ale, conducted by Christopher Pope, chairman of the large Dorchester brewery Eldridge Pope. Pope's finely tuned palate and elegant phrases discovered such aromas and flavours as 'a library of old books' and 'fresh tobacco leaves'. Christopher Pope was so enthusiastic about his strong Old Ale that I was shocked to learn that the 1999 vintage would be the last, followed by the equally distressing news that the company was leaving brewing completely. It seemed we would lose forever a classic bottle-fermented beer first brewed in 1968 to commemorate a literary festival in honour of Thomas Hardy, the novelist and poet who lived in Dorset and praised the ales of Dorchester (renamed Casterbridge in his Wessex novels).

Then an unlikely hero in the shape of a former Irish Rugby player rode to the rescue. John O'Hanlon ran a highly regarded pub and small brewery in London until 2000, when he and his wife Liz moved to a farm in Devon and installed their brewery in out buildings. John added Thomas Hardy's Ale to his portfolio when the American company Phoenix Imports said it was anxious to make the beer available in the United States, where it had a cult following. John's unenviable task was to re-create the beer to the satisfaction of its devotees on both sides of the Atlantic, and he has succeeded brilliantly.

The beer is brewed with pale and crystal malts and hopped with Challenger, Goldings, Northdown and Styrian Goldings: the hops create an astonishing 75 units of bitterness. Slow brewing and long maturation create the character of the beer. Primary fermentation lasts for two and a half weeks: most ales have no more than seven days. Maturation and secondary fermentation account for a further three months, followed by a month of cold conditioning to allow the yeast to settle. The beer is then bottled and released with the firm suggestion that it should mature for a further nine months before being consumed. The red-brown beer is smoky, intensely fruity (citrus and blackcurrant) with earthy, piny hop notes. Rich vinous fruits and sweet grain fill the mouth, with a good underpinning of hops. The finish has enormous length and is dominated by sweet fruit, dark grain and peppery hops.

TASTING NOTES
Appearance
Aroma
Taste
Overall score

Robinson's Old Tom

Source: Frederic Robinson Unicorn Brewery, Stockport, Cheshire, England
Strength: 8.5%
Website: www.frederic-robinson.com

TASTING NOTES
Appearance
Aroma
Taste
Overall score

It's a brave brewer who names his strong beer after a cat and even puts a cat's face on the label. Imagine the guffaws of laughter if a batch of beer developed a fault and tasted like... I leave the rest to your imagination. But the family-owned Robinson's brewery is a highly professional one that has been producing beer since 1838 and there are few complaints about the quality of its brews.

Frederic Robinson founded his brewery at the Unicorn Inn in the centre of Stockport. The present impressive red-brick brewery was built in the 1920s and it has stayed firmly in family ownership ever since. Five sixth-generation members of the family were appointed to the board in 2003 to ensure continuity.

The beers are notably fruity and this is most in evidence in Old Tom, whose name may stem from the fact that breweries have always kept cats on the premises to kill rodents that would otherwise run riot in malt stores. It is available on draught and in filtered bottled forms, and is brewed with Halcyon pale malt, crystal malt and a small amount of chocolate malt (100 units of colour). The beer is hopped with a single variety, Goldings, and the beer has 35 units of bitterness. Old Tom has a ripe vine fruits aroma with a delicious hint of chocolate as well as peppery hop resins. Port wine, dark malt, chocolate and bitter hops fill the mouth, while the long and complex finish offers an increasing rich vinous fruitiness and a solid underpinning of bitter hops. The draught version of the beer won CAMRA's Champion Winter Beer of Britain award in 2005.

Sierra Nevada Bigfoot Ale

Source: Sierra Nevada Brewing Company, Chico, California, USA
Strength: 9.6%
Website: www.sierranevada.com

This is a big beast of a beer named after the wild man-cum-animal that is supposed to roam the mountainous regions of California. Even he might stop his rampaging and sleep for a while if he supped a glass of the beer that bears his name.

In the American fashion, Sierra Nevada has taken the English style of barley wine and added its own interpretation, in particular a profound bitter hop character to balance the sweetness of the massive amount of malt used to create the alcohol. 9.6% is nominal: some years the beer has reached more than 12%, and since each vintage is bottle fermented it will increase in strength as a result of a secondary fermentation under glass.

The beer is also produced on draught and should, like its namesake, be approached with caution. For several years, Bigfoot was the strongest beer made in the US but several other brewers have attempted to outbid it.

The beer is brewed with two-row pale malt from the Pacific North-west, imported English crystal malt and an addition of dextrin, a type of malt sugar that cannot be fermented by conventional brewer's yeast and which adds 'body', or mouthfeel, and sweetness. The beer has a complex hop recipe, with Chinook for bitterness, and Cascade and Centennial used at the end of the copper boil. The beer is then dry hopped in the maturation tank with all three varieties grown in Oregon and Washington State. Unusually for a barley wine, it is the hops that dominate, bursting on to the nose with bitter and piny resins and tart citrus fruit. Malt struggles to make an appearance on the aroma but starts to build in the mouth with rich grain and warming alcohol. The finish leaves tyre marks on the back of the throat due to the massive hop attack, but there is a good balancing malty and nutty note from the grain. The beer will improve for around a year in bottle.

TASTING NOTES
Appearance
Aroma
Taste
Overall score

Theakston's Old Peculier

Source: T & R Theakston, Masham, North Yorkshire, England
Strength: 5.7%
Website: www.theakstons.co.uk

The beer with the peculiar spelling has a few centuries of history behind it. In the 12th century, Sir Roger de Mowbray from Masham was captured while fighting in the Crusades and held prisoner for seven years. When he was released, he expressed his gratitude for his safe return home by giving 'the living' – the priest's position and income – of the church in Masham to St Peter's in York. But the Bishop of York was not prepared to make the long and arduous journey to Masham, with the strong possibility of being attacked by footpads. He released Masham from 'all the customs and claims of his archdeacons and officials' and set up the Peculier Court of Masham to deal with church and local law. Peculier is an old Norman-French word meaning particular, not odd, and indicated a parish outside the control of a bishop. The chairman of the court had a great seal made to mark his power. The seal shows the kneeling figure of Sir Roger de Mowbray and is still in use as the brewery's logo. The court, made up of 24 'good men from the parish' and chaired by the vicar, still sits to adjudicate on parish matters.

The beer that carries this heavy weight of history on its shoulders is probably the best-known old ale in the world, as it is widely exported, to the US in particular. It is brewed with pale and crystal malts, with some cane sugar, maize and caramel (95 colour units). The hops are Challenger, Fuggles and Goldings, which create 29 units of bitterness. Brewed in traditional vessels, including high-sided wooden fermenters, the beer has a big vinous fruit bouquet balanced by peppery hops and nutty malt. Raisin and sultana fruit, roasted grain and gentle hop bitterness fill the mouth, with a finish that is bitter-sweet and dominated by roasted and nutty malt and vinous fruit with a lingering touch of hop resins.

Traquair House Ale

Source: Traquair House Brewery, Innerleithen, Peebles-shire, Scotland
Strength: 7.2%
Website: www.traquair.co.uk

TASTING NOTES
Appearance
Aroma
Taste
Overall score

Parts of the mellow stone buildings that make up the Traquair estate date from 1107, though the main house was extended in the 17th century. It is Scotland's oldest inhabited stately home and was visited by Mary Stuart, Queen of Scots, and Prince Charles Edward Stuart – Bonnie Prince Charlie – who came to the house to seek support for the Jacobite cause.

Ale has been brewed at Traquair for centuries in an old brewhouse in outbuildings alongside the stream that flows into the River Tweed, the boundary between Scotland and England. The estate is owned by a branch of the Stuart clan, the Maxwell Stuarts, and they keep the main Bear Gates locked until a Stuart returns to the British throne.

In 1965, the 20th Laird, or Lord, of Traquair, David Maxwell Stuart, discovered the disused brewhouse. It had a four-barrel capacity, since extended, and an open copper or kettle installed in 1738 – there is a receipt for it in the house archives. With advice from the Belhaven brewery, Maxwell Stuart started to brew again. House Ale quickly became a cult brew and is exported to Japan and the US. Lady Catherine Maxwell Stuart, who gave up a career in the theatre to administer the house and brewery, took over when her father died.

Brewing water comes from a spring in the valley of the Tweed, and the main grain is pale malt with just 1% black malt. The hops are exclusively East Kent Goldings, sourced from the farm of Tony Redsell near Faversham, renowned for the quality of his hops. The beer has 34 units of bitterness, a tawny colour and a ripe aroma of marmalade fruit, chocolate and peppery hops. Rich orange, lemon and lime fruits fill the mouth, with nuts, chocolate and hop resins. The finish has warming alcohol, tart fruit, nuts and a lingering peppery hop note.

Woodforde's Norfolk Nip

Source: Woodforde's Norfolk Ales, Broadland Brewery, Woodbastwick, Norfolk, England
Strength: 8.5%
Website: www.woodfordes.co.uk

TASTING NOTES
Appearance
Aroma
Taste
Overall score

Woodforde's, founded in 1981, is one of England's longest-surviving craft breweries and today has reached the status of a small regional. It has led a peripatetic existence and is now at its third home, close to the chain of reed-fringed, ancient inland waterways known as the Norfolk Broads. The site was expanded at the turn of the new century to double production and now includes a shop, visitor centre and on-site pub, the Fur & Feather. Woodforde's has twice won CAMRA's Champion Beer of Britain competition with Wherry Best Bitter and Norfolk Nog. Most of its regular draught beers are now also available in bottle-fermented form.

Norfolk Nip revives a beer brewed from the late 1920s by the large Norwich brewery Steward & Patteson. S&P had the great misfortune to fall into the clutches of the infamous London brewer Watneys, which ran rampage in Norfolk in the 1960s, buying and closing Norwich's three

breweries and axing hundreds of pubs in the county. Woodforde's restored the beer in 1992 to mark the 10th anniversary of the local CAMRA newsletter, *Norfolk Nips*. Brewing now takes place annually on St Valentine's Day, making it a true loving cup.

The beer is matured in cask in the brewery prior to bottling and will improve for at least two years. It is brewed from Maris Otter pale, crystal and chocolate malts and a touch of roasted barley. The hop is exclusively Goldings. The mahogany-coloured beer has a warm and embracing aroma of vine and citrus fruits, roasted grain and peppery hop resins. Fruits, ranging from pineapple to melon and cherry, coat the tongue, balanced by bitter chocolate and roast, with an underpinning of hop bitterness. The long and complex finish is ripe and fruity, with lingering roast and chocolate notes and a final tingle of bitter hops.

Young's Old Nick

Source: Young & Co's Ram Brewery, Wandsworth, London, England
Strength: 7.2%
Website: www.youngs.co.uk

An 'old' beer that is a barley wine. Old Nick proves that the devil not only has the best tunes but the finest beers as well, though the name has caused Young's a few problems. It was one of several small-volume beers in the brewery's portfolio that were reserved for high days and holidays until a few bottles were exported to the United States, where sales took off like an alcohol-fuelled rocket. Young's could sell more, save for the fact that it is banned in some 'Bible Belt' regions because of the depiction of Satan on the label. The firmly traditional London brewery, a flag-bearer for cask ale in the 1960s and '70s, when other brewers were phasing it out, is not prepared to change the name or image of Old Nick.

The beer has all the hallmarks of the Young's house style: a no-nonsense beer with a profound hop bitterness from the finest Fuggles and Goldings from the nearby Kentish fields. The grains are pale Maris Otter and a darker variety of crystal malt that give a rich toffee and nuts character to the beer. The colour is 75–80 units, bitterness 50–55. Toffee, nuts, tart fruit and spicy and peppery hops tempt the nose and palate, with a creamy banana-like note in the finish that finally becomes dry with a solid earthy, peppery hop note. A hell of a good beer.

TASTING NOTES
Appearance
Aroma
Taste
Overall score

Porters & Stouts

It is a significant indication of the revival of interest in beer styles that the biggest section of this book is devoted to porter, which had once all but disappeared from the world's brewing scene, and stout, which to most people means Guinness in all its manifestations. Yet in my book *Classic Stout and Porter* (Prion, 1997), the index listed close to 100 porters and stouts in Britain and more than 250 in the United States. In the US, it was a style that had been wiped out in the 1920s by Prohibition and the subsequent domination of the market by bland national lager brands. But from the 1980s, the craft-brewing revolution in both countries spawned enormous interest in traditional styles, and no more so than in the case of porter and stout.

If he can say as you can
Guinness is good for you
How grand to be a Toucan
Just think what Toucan do

The domination of the stout market by Guinness has led many people to assume that stout and its offshoot porter are Irish types of beer. The origins, however, are in London. Early in the 18th century, as the capital was changing rapidly from a loose connection of small towns into a vibrant commercial and industrial hub, the new, burgeoning working class developed a taste for a beer known as three threads, or three thirds. It was a blend of three beers, twopenny pale ale, brown ale and 'stale', or well-matured old ale.

Specialist country brewers with the space to mature beer in large oak tuns supplied both twopenny – so-called because it was twice as dear as other beers – and stale to London. Brewers there, based chiefly in cramped taverns with small brewhouses attached, were anxious to break the power of the country suppliers and their expensive malts by making a beer that replicated the flavours of three threads without the need to blend beers in their cellars. They were aided by the development of an improved type of brown malt from the malting towns of Hertfordshire that supplied London via barges and canals. London brewers grasped the new malt to fashion a beer that came from one cask, or butt, that suited the demands of their customers. The brewers called the beer 'entire butt' but it quickly acquired the nickname of porter.

Much energy has gone into debating the origins of the name porter. I have heard such risible suggestions that it was a corruption of export or even the Latin *portare*, working-class Londoners at the time being fluent Latin speakers. It is always best to go to contemporary sources. A Swiss called César de Saussure wrote to his family: 'Another kind of beer [in London] is called porter... because the greater quantity of this beer is consumed by the working class.' A retired brewer who wrote under the pen name Obadiah Poundage noted that 'the labouring people, porters etc, experienced its wholesomeness and utility, they assumed to themselves the use thereof, from whence it was called Porter.' What is beyond dispute is that the early porters, or entires, were dark brown rather than black. And, following the fashion at the time to call the strongest beer in a brewery stout, the higher gravity versions of porter were dubbed stout porter, eventually shortened to just stout. In the early 19th century, around 100 years after porter and stout first appeared, the invention of roasting machines produced the black and chocolate malts that turned porter and stout into the jet-black beers we recognise today.

The clamour for porter and stout created a new breed of commercial brewers in London and other urban areas of Britain. Brewers such as Ben Truman and Sam Whitbread built their fame and fortune on porter. From 1760, Whitbread's brewery in London's Barbican had a system of vast underground cisterns, each containing the equivalent of 4,000 barrels of beer.

Porter and stout from London and Bristol were supplied to all parts of the United Kingdom, which then included the whole of Ireland. By 1787, Arthur Guinness was brewing porter and, in 1799, he took the momentous decision to phase out all other types of ale. In Cork, Beamish & Crawford also abandoned ale in favour of porter. The Murphy brothers, who moved from whiskey distilling to brewing, followed Beamish in Cork. At one stage in the 19th century, Beamish and Guinness were the two biggest brewers in the United Kingdom, such was the demand for porter and stout in Ireland.

The terrible famine in the 1850s devastated the Irish economy. Beamish never recovered its position but Guinness rebuilt its trade by using the canal system and then the railway to take porter – known as X or plain – and stout, branded XX, to all parts of Ireland. It was exported to Britain, to other parts of the Empire and also to the US. By the close of the 19th century, Guinness was the biggest brewer in Europe. By the end of World War One, it achieved the astonishing feat, in a country of just five million people, of becoming the biggest brewer in the world.

LEFT
RCH's Porter was named after slugs found when the brewery moved to a new site. They are not used in the brewing process!

BELOW
Castlemaine is best known for lager in Australia but still makes a full-bodied stout named after a race horse

Guinness was aided by the decision of the British government during World War One to curb the use of dark malts, which used more energy. Coal, gas and electricity were needed by the munitions industry, and brewers had to switch to lighter beers for the duration. The British dared not impose such restrictions on the increasingly mutinous Irish with their demand for Home Rule. As a result, Guinness and other Irish brewers had the market in porter and stout to themselves.

Guinness had also refashioned porter and stout into a distinctive Irish style. Before changes were made in the 1880s, brewers paid tax not on the strength of their products but on the malt they used. Arthur Guinness II realised he would pay less tax to the British government if he used a small amount of unmalted – and therefore untaxed – roasted barley in his beer. The result was stout with a pronounced roasted and bitter flavour that became known as 'Dry Irish Stout'.

Pale ale and golden lagers eventually ate into sales of porter and stout. Even mighty Guinness eventually abandoned plain to concentrate on stout. But the styles never went away. Stout remains an iconic drink in Ireland, a symbol of its nationhood, while the British are the biggest consumers of stout in the world. And now today, thanks to the spirit and enterprise of craft brewers, we can revel in the many interpretations of the dark beers that changed the face of brewing 300 years ago.

Alaskan Smoked Porter

Source: Alaskan Brewing Company, Juneau, Alaska, USA
Strength: 5.5%
Website: www.alaskanbeer.com

TASTING NOTES
Appearance
Aroma
Taste
Overall score

By happy coincidence, the first beer in this section may give us a glimpse of what the early London porters tasted like, when malts cured over wood fires had a smoky tang. The inspiration for the beer came from the Bamberg region of Germany, where *rauch* beers are still made with smoked malts. But smoked porter is an ale, not a lager. It comes from a brewery, founded in 1988 by Geoff and Marcy Larson, which restored the brewing tradition to an isolated part of the US. During the 19th-century Gold Rush, Alaska at one time had 50 breweries, but many disappeared when the miners left and the breweries that remained closed during Prohibition. The Larsons built their business on the back of an Amber beer that was based on the German Alt style (see page 210). They were aware that over the road from the brewery, the

Taku fish smokery produced fine-tasting smoked salmon. The Larsons asked the owner if they could use his smokery to lay dark malts on racks heated by an alderwood fire.

The result was a sensational beer made with two-row Klages pale, black, chocolate and crystal malts, and hopped with Chinook and Willamette varieties. Smoked porter has a smoky and woody aroma, with spicy hops, dark grain, coffee and chocolate. The dark, smoky malts dominate the palate, with a growing contribution from chocolate and coffee, but spicy hops come through strongly in the finish.

The porter has won more major awards at the Great American Beer Festival than any other beer. It is brewed once a year and vintage dated. The Larsons recommend it as a good companion for smoked fish or tangy cheeses.

Bridge of Allan Glencoe Wild Oat Stout

Source: Bridge of Allan Brewery, Bridge of Allan, Stirlingshire, Scotland
Strength: 4.5%
Website: www.bridgeofallan.co.uk

TASTING NOTES
Appearance
Aroma
Taste
Overall score

Scottish stouts have their own distinctive character, which is less bitter than the Irish style, not so hoppy as English versions and with a creamy note from the use of oats. Bridge of Allan's stout goes a step further: it is an organic beer and the oats used in its production grow wild in the Forth Valley.

The area where the brewery is based is of historic importance, with Stirling Castle, the Wallace Monument and the Trossachs close by. The Forth Valley is known as the Gateway to the Highlands, and invading armies marched through the area to do battle with the Scots. It was once an important brewing area, too, with 32 producers in the valley able to make use of the pure water from the Ochil Hills and high-quality malting barley from the fields. Douglas Ross restored the

brewing tradition in 1997, when he opened Bridge of Allan in the spa town of the same name. He brews half a dozen regular cask beers and several seasonals, with many of them available in bottled form as well. His original five-barrel plant has been expanded and he has added a visitor centre.

Wild Oat Stout, suitable for vegetarians and vegans, is brewed with a rich and complex blend of Maris Otter pale, crystal, amber, dark roast and chocolate malts, with oats and wheat. The hop variety is Hallertauer Hersbrucker from Bavaria. The black beer with a ruby edge has a big aroma of burnt and roasted malt with hints of cappuccino coffee and raisins. Bitter dark fruit, creamy oats and spicy hops dominate the mouth, while the long finish has roasted grain, creamy oats, spicy hops and a late note of sour fruit.

Brooklyn Chocolate Stout

Source: Brooklyn Brewery, Brooklyn, New York City, USA
Strength: 8.7%
Website: www.brooklynbrewery.com

TASTING NOTES
Appearance
Aroma
Taste
Overall score

This is a big beer and it belongs to a style known as imperial stout, brewed in England in the 19th century for the Russian court. Such beers were brewed to high strengths and heavily hopped to withstand the long, often hazardous, sea journeys.

Garrett Oliver created the Brooklyn beer in 1994 while he brewed at the Manhattan Brewing Company in the SoHo district. Steve Hindy owned the Brooklyn Brewery but his beers were produced under licence in upstate New York. He wanted to open his own brewery and hoped to lure Garrett over the bridge to Brooklyn to become his brewmaster. Steve asked Garrett to develop a strong and memorable beer that would help put the new brewery on the map. Garrett recalls: 'Steve decided that this beer should be a strong stout. Within several days, I had written a recipe and brewed a seven-barrel batch at Manhattan Brewing Company. A few weeks later, I brought the beer to a meeting at Brooklyn Brewery. We originally thought we might actually add chocolate to the beer, but it turned out to be unnecessary – the blend of roasted malts gave the beer a flavour Steve and I had been looking for.' Garrett was hired and a few months later produced the first batch of Black Chocolate Stout.

It is brewed in the winter and has a long and complex mashing regime. The 'first runnings' – the concentrated wort extracted from the mash of grain before it is sparged or rinsed with water – is removed from the mash, which is discarded. The undiluted wort is then fermented into stout, which is aged for more than two months before it leaves the brewery. It has an intense aroma of Belgian chocolate with espresso coffee notes and bitter hops. In the mouth, rich, dark, roasted malts battle for supremacy with chocolate, spicy hops and a vinous fruitiness. The finish is long, with liquorice notes coming through to join vine fruits, bitter, spicy hops, chocolate and roasted grain. The malts used are American two-row pale, caramel, wheat, chocolate and black malts; the hops are American Fuggles and Willamette.

Broughton Scottish Oatmeal Stout

Source: Broughton Ales, Broughton, Peebles-shire, Scotland
Strength: 4.2%
Website: www.broughtonales.co.uk

Scotland has a cold climate and the people have developed grain-based food and drink to warm them. Whisky – the water of life – is a distillation of ale made without hops. Porridge is made from oats and the grain has been used for centuries in the country's distinctive strong, rich and lightly hopped ales. Oatmeal stout, a meal in itself, was a staple member of the portfolios of most Scottish breweries until 20th-century mergers created brewing giants that concentrated on light lagers and keg beers. The craft brewing revolution in Scotland – there are now more than 30 from the Borders to Orkney and Shetland – has restored pride and tradition to brewing and with it several versions of stout.

Broughton, founded in 1979, is one of the oldest independent breweries in Scotland and its Oatmeal Stout is considered to be the classic of the style, so much so that the bottled version is exported to the United States and several other countries. Hops were once brewed in the Borders, where Broughton is based – records show that home-grown hops were once used at the Traquair House brewery – but as the climate grew colder, the plant withered on the bine. As a result, Scottish brewers tend to be parsimonious with the use of the plant, imported from England. Lightly hopped stouts give free rein to the rich flavours of pale and dark malts and the creamy, nutty texture of oats or oatmeal.

The Broughton beer is brewed with Maris Otter pale malt, black malt, roasted barley and pinhead oats. It has 170 units of bitterness. The hops are

Fuggles and Goldings for aroma and Target for bitterness: 30 units of bitterness. It has a freshly ground roasted coffee beans and chocolate aroma with a gentle hint of spicy hops. Roasted and creamy grain, coffee and chocolate fill the mouth, while the finish has a silky smoothness with an underpinning of gentle hop spices, chocolate and bitter coffee.

TASTING NOTES
Appearance
Aroma
Taste
Overall score

Carlsberg Carls Stout Porter

Source: Carlsberg Breweries, Copenhagen, Denmark
Strength: 7.8%
Website: www.carlsberg.com

Carlsberg is celebrated as the company that perfected the first pure strain of yeast that enabled brewers throughout the world to brew lager beers free from infection. It may seem curious to find Carlsberg listed in this section, but many brewers in Scandinavia in the 19th century produced porters and stouts. Some of the strong imperial stouts brewed in England and destined for Russia found their way en route to Scandinavia. The popularity of the beers encouraged domestic brewers to produce the style themselves. As they had switched their production methods to cold fermentation, they brewed, in effect, dark lagers but with the roasted grain and bitter hop character that are typical of porters and stouts produced by conventional warm fermentation.

The story of Carlsberg dates from the early 19th century when Christian Jacobsen opened a small brewery in Copenhagen. His son, Jacob Christian Jacobsen, the driving force of the company, went to Munich to study the new cold-fermented brown beers that had been developed there. He brought back a supply of Munich yeast and by 1847 had opened a new brewery on the outskirts of Copenhagen that produced, to popular acclaim, a brown lager. Once the technology existed, the company concentrated on golden lager beers in the Pilsner style. Jacobsen built a second brewery for his son Carl and, as the new plant stood on a hill, it was called Carlsberg.

The original brewery is now a museum, while Carl's plant remains one of the finest in the world with superb copper vessels in spacious tiled rooms. It was in the Carlsberg laboratories that the famous brewing scientist Emil Christian Hansen isolated the first pure strain of yeast that enabled both Carlsberg and eventually all other breweries to make consistent beers free from infection.

In spite of the success of pale lagers, Carlsberg continues to produce a wide range of beers, including the rather confusingly labelled Stout Porter that is in reality an imperial stout. It is brewed from pale and roasted malts, and hopped with German Hallertauer varieties. It has the clean flavours of a lager but with molasses and liquorice on the aroma, woody and bitter coffee character in the mouth, with a spicy hop note developing in the mouth and finish, and a final rich, warming deep roasted grain note.

Carnegie Stark Porter

Source: Pripps Brewery, Stockholm, Sweden
Strength: 3.5%/5.6%
Website: www.pripps.se

The Scandinavian love-hate relationship with alcohol has had a profound impact on this remarkable 'stark', or strong, beer. For a period, it was available only on doctor's prescription as a tonic, but in recent years it has been let out of the surgery and back into bars and is now available at a strength of 3.5% (which does not do the beer justice) and an annual vintage of 5.6% that places it firmly in the ranks of genuine porters.

The beer dates from 1803 when a Scot named David Carnegie opened a small brewery in Gothenburg. There had been strong trading links between Scotland and Sweden for centuries, and Carnegie, who also created a banking group in Scandinavia, launched his porter to meet the demand for the dark beer style among the Swedes. Eventually he sold the brewery to the giant Pripps group, which continued to brew at Gothenburg for a while before closing the plant. Pripps, a state-owned enterprise until the 1990s

that produces stunningly bland and uninteresting pale lagers, was expected to phase out Carnegie Porter, especially as it is brewed with a warm-fermenting ale yeast strain. But Pripps resurrected the beer in the 1990s, won the top prize for dark beers in the 1992 International Brewers' Exhibition, and introduced the annual vintage in a club-shaped bottle in 1995.

The beer is filtered and pasteurised but the brewers feel that it nevertheless does improve in bottle and eventually takes on a port wine note. When I visited the brewery and was able to sample several vintages, I was able to detect subtle differences between one brew and the next.

The beer is made from pale and roasted malts and hopped with German varieties. It has a roasted grain, cappuccino coffee and spicy hop aroma and palate, with a Dundee Cake fruitiness in the finish – appropriate given the founder's ethnic origins – and a hint of rich dark wine.

TASTING NOTES
Appearance
Aroma
Taste
Overall score

ÅRGÅNG 2000
STARKÖL
RECEPT FRÅN PORTERBRYGGERIET
GRUNDAT 1836
D. CARNEGIE & Co.
AB PRIPPS BRYGGERIER
KORKSTÄMPEL
III
STARK·PORTER

Castlemaine Carbine Stout

Source: Castlemaine Perkins Brewery, Brisbane, Queensland, Australia
Strength: 5.1%
Website: www.lion-nathan.com

TASTING NOTES
Appearance
Aroma
Taste
Overall score

It may come as a surprise to those who think Australians drink only pale, sweet lagers that the country has a rich tradition of dark stouts. Many have disappeared in recent decades as the country's brewing industry has fallen under the sway of two giant combines, Castlemaine and Foster's. Castlemaine was owned by the Bond Corporation but when that company collapsed as the result of financial skulduggery, it suffered the ultimate indignity of being taken over by the New Zealand drinks group Lion Nathan, which also owns Toohey's and Swan.

To many people's surprise, Lion Nathan has preserved a wide portfolio of beers, including the country's best-known dark beer, Carbine Stout. It was first brewed in 1925 by the Perkins Brewery before it merged with Castlemaine. The beer is named after a remarkable racehorse Carbine, which won the Melbourne Cup in 1890 and 32 other races, and was the sire of the Derby winner Spearmint. Carbine's bloodline can be traced to 70% of Australian thoroughbreds racing today.

The original recipe for the beer named in the horse's honour included pale, amber, crystal and black malts with cane sugar as an adjunct. It was fermented with an ale yeast culture. In the 1950s, the beer was dumbed down with a simplified malt blend and cold fermentation was introduced. More recently, however, dark malts, wheat and roasted barley have been introduced, though cold fermentation remains. The beer is hopped with Tasmanian and New Zealand varieties. It has a pleasing coffee, liquorice and roasted grain aroma, with spicy hops in the mouth and finish, and a bitter-sweet palate with hints of dried fruits.

Coopers Best Extra Stout

Source: Coopers Brewery, Adelaide, South Australia, Australia
Strength: 6.8%
Website: www.coopers.co.au

TASTING NOTES
Appearance
Aroma
Taste
Overall score

The brewery founded by Thomas Cooper in the 19th century and still run today by members of his family may be best known for its Sparkling Ale (see page 56) but it also produces a magnificent stout, a world classic. Like the pale ale, it is a sedimented beer in keg and bottle, maturing on its yeast. It is an uncompromising beer: the attitude at Coopers is that the company brews spectacular beers bursting with aroma and flavour, and any drinkers deterred by such characteristics should turn instead to the 'national blands' produced by bigger producers.

Extra Stout is made with pale, crystal and roasted malts, with an addition of cane sugar in the copper in the Australian fashion to encourage a full fermentation. The hops are Pride of Ringwood in pellet form. The colour rating is 175, bitterness 40. The beer has a full and tempting bouquet of roasted malt, with a pronounced oily, tarry note from the dark grain, balanced by coffee and bitter chocolate. The hops provide a firm underpinning of spicy and earthy resins in the mouth topped by coffee, chocolate and dark dried fruits. The big and complex finish is dry and bitter but balanced by rich malt and dark fruit flavours.

Nick Sterenberg of Coopers told me: 'The popularity of unfiltered bottled and keg-conditioned ales is increasing in Australia, the land of ice-cold, crystal-clear lager. We are now 2.5% of the national market and growing.'

Darwin Flag Porter

Source: Darwin Brewery, Sunderland, England
Strength: 5%
Website: www.darwinbrewery.com

TASTING NOTES
Appearance
Aroma
Taste
Overall score

The frequently asked question, 'What did the early porters really taste like?' is answered to some extent by this fascinating beer.

In 1988, deep-sea divers from the City of London Polytechnic were investigating the wreck of a ship that had sunk in the English Channel in 1825 and they brought to the surface several bottles of porter. They were handed over to Dr Keith Thomas who at the time ran the Brewers' Laboratory (Brewlab for short) at the same polytechnic.

The beer had been contaminated by sea water and was undrinkable, but Keith was able to isolate a few living yeast cells from one bottle. He cultured them in his laboratory and, with the help of Whitbread, was able to track down an 1850s porter recipe from the group's former brewery in Chiswell Street in London. The recipe that Keith Thomas then devised, which was based on the original Whitbread one, uses pale, brown, crystal and black malts and is hopped with just one variety, Fuggles. One of the many interesting facts discovered in the Whitbread archive was that the company was still using wood-kilned brown malt as late as 1850. The beer that Keith created had another surprise:

it was not jet-black but dark ruby-red in colour; he suspects the original may have been even paler. This fits with the belief that as late as the mid-19th century there were two styles: brown porter and black porter. Flag Porter, as Keith called the beer, was first brewed by a London micro then moved to Elgood's in Wisbech, before finding its latest home at Darwin in Sunderland, where Brewlab is now also located at the university.

The beer has 34 units of bitterness: there is no direct comparison with Whitbread's Porter in 1850, as such measurements were not made. Fuggles did not exist as a variety at that time but, with a low bitterness, would not be dissimilar to mid-19th century hops. Keith Thomas, for the sake of historical accuracy, also points out that stewed crystal malt did not exist in 1850 and replaces a type called amber.

The beer is enormously complex. It has a dark tangy, slightly smoky and nutty aroma underpinned by spicy Fuggles. In the mouth there is a distinct fruitiness reminiscent of blood oranges, and the finish is rich in fruit, hops and bitter chocolate, becoming finally intensely dry with a herbal note. The beer is available in the United States: see the website legendslimited.com.

Foster's Sheaf Stout

Source: Tooth's Brewery, Sydney, New South Wales, Australia
Strength: 5.7%
Website: www.fosters.com.au

TASTING NOTES
Appearance
Aroma
Taste
Overall score

Who knows Foster's who only Foster's knows? The brewery famous for a global lager brand has a surprisingly large portfolio of beers in its own country as a result of mergers and takeovers. When it acquired Tooth's it found itself with a fine example of a genuine warm-fermented stout from a brewery founded by John Tooth. He came originally from Kent in South-east England and for many years he used the symbol of the White Horse of Kent, still embossed on hop sacks from the county. The white horse was the battle flag of Hengist and Horsa, the tribal leaders from Jutland who conquered Kent in the fifth century: their names mean Stallion and Horse.

When Tooth's was taken over by Carlton and United Breweries, since renamed Foster's, the beer's title has been shortened to Sheaf Stout, possibly on the grounds that Tooth's Sheaf was difficult to say when sober and impossible after a few pints. It has lost nothing else. Brewed from pale and crystal malts and roasted barley, with domestic hops, it has 200 units of colour and 35 units of bitterness. It is almost jet-black in colour with a woody, earthy aroma and a powerful punch of roasted grain, an oily and perfumy palate with strong hints of coffee and chocolate, and a long fruity finish with good spicy hop notes and continuing hints of chocolate, coffee and roasted grain.

Grant's Perfect Porter/Imperial Stout

Source: Grant's Yakima Brewing and Malting Company, Yakima, Washington, USA
Strength: 4.8%/7%
Website: www.grant.com

TASTING NOTES
Appearance
Aroma
Taste
Overall score

The late Bert Grant was not the shy, retiring type. He wore his heart on his sleeve and on his car. When I visited him, he picked me up from Yakima's small airport in his Oldsmobile car with the licence plates REAL ALE. His beers were, he argued, 'simply the best' and to underscore the point he brewed the Perfect Porter.

With his knowledge and experience of malting, Bert imported some peated malt from Scotland, which is used in the whisky trade, to give a smoky note to the beer. It joins pale, crystal and black malts in the mash tun and is hopped with Cascade and Willamette varieties, which are also used to dry hop the beer in cask (30 units of bitterness). The beer has a smoky aroma with powerful notes of chocolate and liquorice, and a blast of earthy hop resins. Tart fruit from the hops develops in the mouth along with peated malt and chocolate. The finish is dry and bitter – the bitterness coming from dark malts as well as hops – with further contributions from fruit and chocolate.

Grant's Imperial Stout takes no prisoners. With 100 units of bitterness created by local hop varieties, the beer is shatteringly dry and bitter. As well as pale and roasted malts, a touch of honey is used, which recalls an old American tradition dating from the days of the Founding Fathers.

This amazing beer has aromas and flavours redolent of fresh leather, dark tobacco, espresso coffee, freshly varnished wood, dried vine fruits, roasted grain, bitter chocolate, hop resins and a gentle hint of honey sweetness lurking beneath all the grain and hop characteristics.

In his brew-pub in Yakima, alongside the old railroad station, Bert took me through a tasting of all his cask beers and demanded to know my views. As people tote guns and wear big hats in this part of the world, I thought it advisable to agree that the porter was indeed perfect, while the stout was the stuff of which great empires are built.

TASTING NOTES	
Appearance	
Aroma	
Taste	
Overall score	

Great Lakes The Edmund Fitzgerald Porter

Source: Great Lakes Brewing Co, Cleveland, Ohio, USA
Strength: 5.8%
Website: www.greatlakesbrewing.com

The Edmund Fitzgerald was a freighter that sank with all hands in Lake Superior in 1975. Several members of the crew came from Cleveland, once a mighty brewing city that lost its beery tradition as a result of Prohibition and subsequent takeovers and closures. The brothers Patrick and Daniel Conway, former teacher and banker respectively, have restored the tradition. They share a passion for European beer styles. In 1988 they pooled their resources to open Great Lakes in the heart of Cleveland's old brewing district and hired Thaine Johnson, who had been head brewer at the city's last major commercial brewery, Christian Schmidt.

The success of the enterprise led to the brothers moving into two former brewers' premises where they installed a 75-barrel plant capable of producing 70,000 barrels a year.

They have also kept open their original brew-pub in Market Avenue (see page 281).

The Edmund Fitzgerald Porter is brewed with two-row pale, crystal and chocolate malts and roasted barley, and is hopped with Cascade, Northern Brewer and Willamette varieties (60 bitterness units). The dark brown beer with a hefty collar of foam has a big chocolate and orange fruit bouquet, with hop bitterness, juicy malt, tart fruit and chocolate in the mouth, and a long, complex finish with roasted grain notes and a final burst of bitter hop resins and tangy fruit.

TASTING NOTES	
Appearance	
Aroma	
Taste	
Overall score	

Guinness Foreign Extra Stout

Source: Guinness Brewing, Dublin, Ireland
Strength: 7.5%
Website: www.guinness.com

TASTING NOTES
Appearance
Aroma
Taste
Overall score

Guinness is a phenomenon. In a world dominated by golden lagers, it remains a global giant. Ten million pints of Guinness Stout are drunk every day. There are some 19 versions of the beer, and Foreign Extra Stout (FES) is sold in 55 countries and brewed under licence in a further 44. It is all a long way removed from the humble origins of Arthur Guinness, who opened a small brewery in Leixlip in 1756 with the help of a £100 gift from the local rector. Three years later, Guinness moved to Dublin, where he took a lease on a disused brewery in St James's Gate, an area packed with breweries as a result of the fine local water. By 1787 he was brewing porter as well as ale, and in 1799 he phased out ale in order to get a more lucrative share of the porter and stout market. His business expanded rapidly and he became the official supplier of porter to Dublin Castle, the seat of British power and authority. His son, also called Arthur, continued the expansion. As well as using roasted barley in the recipe (see introduction, page 137), he developed a strong beer for the export market called Foreign Extra Porter Stout, today's FES.

The beer today remains a palpable link with brewing practice in the 19th century. Tucked away in the vast Dublin brewery, which produces 2½ million pints of beer a day, are two wooden tuns that are more than 100 years old. Beer that will form part of FES is matured in the vats for up to three months. This is 'stale beer' that picks up some lactic sourness from the action of wild Brettanomyces yeast. Stale is then blended with fresh young stout, bottled and kept in the brewery for a further month before it is released.

FES is made from pale malt, 25% flaked barley and 10% roasted barley. The hops are a blend of several varieties, including Galena, Nugget and Target (60 bitterness units). The finished beer has the slightly sour and musty aroma that brewers call 'horse blanket' and which is the result of the action of wild yeasts in the wooden tuns. The bouquet is highly complex, with bitter roasted grain, a woody and vinous note and spicy hop resins. The palate is bitter from roast and hops, balanced by dark fruit, with a long, dry and bitter finish with hints of liquorice and dark mysterious fruits, including something akin to sour bananas.

FES is the base for the strong versions of Guinness produced for the Belgian market, brewed in Africa, where Guinness owns several plants, and under licence in other countries. For Africa, a dehydrated hopped wort is sent in cans to the Guinness breweries, where it is blended with a local beer made from barley malt and sorghum. Samples of all the beers brewed abroad are kept for analysis in Dublin and I once spent a happy hour there sampling beers from Nigeria and other African countries. It's dark and lonely work, but someone has to do it.

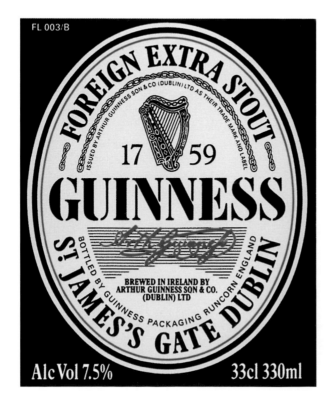

Hambleton Nightmare

Source: Nick Stafford Hambleton Ales, Holme-on-Swale, North Yorkshire, England
Strength: 5%
Website: www.hambletonales.co.uk

Hambleton was placed firmly on the map of British craft brewing when Nightmare won CAMRA's first-ever Champion Winter Beer of Britain award in 1996.

Nick Stafford's brewery on the banks of the River Swale in the picturesque Vale of York – with an ancient white horse carved in the chalk hillside – started life in outbuildings at the home of his wife Sally's parents. Capacity doubled to 100 barrels a week when new brewing equipment was installed in 2000 in a large barn in the village. Bottled beers can be bought direct from the brewery via the website.

Nightmare, with a dark ruby-red colour, is brewed with Halcyon pale malt, 8% crystal, 3% pale chocolate and 3% roasted barley. A single hop variety, Northdown, contributes 25 units of bitterness. The beer has a roasted grain and spicy hop bouquet with hints of chocolate and dried fruit. The palate is complex, with roast, bitter fruits, chocolate and earthy hop resins to the fore. The finish has great length and becomes finally dry, bitter and roasty, but there are continuing contributions from raisin fruit and smooth chocolate.

This flavoursome and refreshing beer was first called Nightmare Porter and is firmly in the 18th-century style of a well-hopped and quenching dark brown entire. Nick thinks it is a 'stout porter' but the alcoholic strength places it in the porter class.

Harveys Imperial Extra Double Stout

Source: Harvey & Son, Bridge Wharf Brewery, Lewes, East Sussex, England
Strength: 9%
Website: www.harveys.org.uk

This brilliant re-creation of a 19th-century beer restores a style lost to drinkers when Courage stopped brewing Imperial Russian Stout, a brand it had acquired from the great London brewer Barclay Perkins.

In mid-Victorian Britain, some 10 London brewers produced strong stouts for export to Russia and the Baltic states. The Thrale family owned the principal brewery on the banks of the Thames, which became Barclay Perkins. One consignment of Barclay's Imperial Russian Stout ended up on the seabed in 1869 when the Prussian ship *Oliva* was wrecked. In 1974, divers brought some bottles from the wreck to the surface bearing the mysterious name A Le Coq. Research showed that this was a Belgian called Albert Le Coq who had earned a living exporting imperial stout to Russia. He had been granted an imperial warrant from a grateful tsar for donating bottles of stout to Russian soldiers wounded in the Crimea. Early in the 20th century, Le Coq built a brewery in Tartu, now in modern Estonia, to increase the supply of stout, but the company was nationalised by the Bolshevik government in 1917. When Courage, by now part of the giant Scottish & Newcastle group, phased out its Imperial Stout in the 1990s, Harvey's negotiated with descendants of Le Coq's family to acquire the original recipe for the beer.

It is brewed with Maris Otter pale, amber, brown and black malt, and hopped with East Kent Goldings and Fuggles. It is bottle fermented, has a cork stopper and is matured for 12 months before release to trade. It has a rich bouquet of vinous fruits, fresh leather, tobacco, smoky malt and peppery hops. Vinous fruits, hop resins, liquorice, roasted grain and bitter hops dominate the palate with a long and complex finish with warming alcohol, dark fruits, fresh tobacco, roasted grain and spicy hops to the fore. B United imports the beer to the US.

TASTING NOTES
Appearance
Aroma
Taste
Overall score

TASTING NOTES
Appearance
Aroma
Taste
Overall score

Hook Norton Double Stout
Source: Hook Norton Brewery, Hook Norton, Oxfordshire, England
Strength: 4.8%
Website: www.hook-norton-brewery.co.uk

This is such a brilliant example of a full-bodied, characterful English stout that it is a pity Hook Norton produces it only for the months of January and February every year.

The beer would have both refreshed and restored the farm labourers for whom the brewery was first built and then the army of navvies engaged in the back-breaking task of constructing a railway line that linked Hook Norton with Banbury and Oxford. The railway line has gone but the stout has been brewed since 1996 and has built up a legion of admirers as a result of its robust, punchy flavours produced by achingly traditional brewing methods, including fermentation in wood-jacketed hooped round vessels.

Double Stout is brewed with Maris Otter pale, mild ale, brown and black malts and brewing sugar. It has 110 units of colour. Challenger, Fuggles and Goldings whole hops produce 34 units of bitterness. The beer has a tempting aroma of dark, roasted grain, espresso coffee, liquorice and spicy and earthy hops. Coffee, liquorice, dark fruits, bitter grain and peppery hop resins fill the mouth, while the lingering finish is dominated by burnt fruit, roasted grain, bitter hops and a continuing coffee and bitter chocolate note.

'Double' in the title recalls the period in the 18th and 19th centuries when porters and stouts were labelled X and XX.

Koff Porter
Source: Sinebrychoff Brewery, Helsinki, Finland
Strength: 7.2%
Website: www.koff.fi

Koff Porter is not a cold cure – though it could bring pleasant relief – but a beer that is more in the imperial stout class. It is the strongest beer brewed in Finland and it comes from the country's oldest brewery. A Russian, Nikolai Synebrychoff, built the brewery in 1819. As a result of the distrust of the 'Big Bear' over the border, the Finns shortened the name to Koff and it stuck as the brand image. Synebrychoff, far from being Russian controlled, is now part of the Danish Carlsberg group. The brewery began life with warm-fermented porter and other ales, but as early as 1853 had switched to cold fermentation. In 1952, timed to coincide with the Helsinki Olympics, Synebrychoff revived Koff Porter, one of its founding beers. The brewers were keen to make it in true warm fermenting style but they lacked an ale yeast. They claim they saved the deposit from a bottle of Guinness and made a culture that is still going strong.

Koff Porter is brewed with four malts, including black and roast, and hopped with Northern Brewer and Hersbrucker varieties. The colour rating is 250 to 300, making it extremely dark; the bitterness units are 50. It is conditioned at a warm temperature for six weeks, bottled without filtration but then pasteurised. It has a roasty, vinous and bitter aroma, a big, slightly oily and perfumy body, and a long finish packed with dark fruit, roasted grain and intensely bitter, iron-like hops. The brewery now produces a vintage edition of the beer in an attractive club-shaped bottle.

The original brewery site still stands in Helsinki but a new brewery has been built in the suburbs. When I visited this computer-controlled stainless-steel factory geared to undistinguished pale lagers, I feared Koff Porter had been discontinued but, eventually, in a sampling room some bottles appeared to my great relief. A few years later, when I bumped into a director of Synebrychoff in St Petersburg, I suggested he should export Koff Porter to Russia. He shrugged and said: 'That's a beer for Finns.' Old prejudices die hard.

Larkins Porter

Source: Larkins Brewery, Larkins Farm, Chiddingstone, Kent, England
Strength: 5.2%
Website: None

When you consider the beer comes from a small craft brewery and is brewed only between November and April, Larkins Porter has established a remarkable national reputation as one of the finest of the revivalist members of the style. It helps when the owners grow their own hops, the classic Kentish Fuggles and Goldings.

Ted and Marjorie Dockerty come from a family that has been growing hops in Kent since Tudor times. In 1986, they bought the Royal Tunbridge Wells Brewery that, despite its grand title, was a micro based in lock-up garages. The Dockerty's son Bob, a keen home brewer, started to brew on the plant and moved it a year later to a converted oast house at his parents' farm. The brewery has been expanded to cope with the demand for the traditional ales and porter, which is delivered to some 70 pubs in the area.

Porter is brewed from Halcyon pale, crystal and chocolate malts. Fuggles and Goldings hops create a massive 59 units of bitterness. The beer has an intense aroma of roasted grain, pungent hop resins and bitter chocolate. Dark dried and vinous fruits coat the mouth, balanced by roasted grain and peppery hops. The punchy finish is long, dry and bitter but with balancing fruit and roast.

I enjoyed a glass of the beer in the Castle Inn in Chiddingstone, a beamed pub with lattice windows close to the Dockerty's farm. The castle in question was Hever, home of Anne Boleyn, who had the great misfortune to be one of Henry VIII's wives. The village has some fine examples of Tudor buildings.

TASTING NOTES
Appearance
Aroma
Taste
Overall score

Le Coq Porter

Source: A Le Coq Tartu Oletehas Brewery, Tallinn, Estonia
Strength: 6.5%
Website: www.tartu.oletehas.est

TASTING NOTES
Appearance
Aroma
Taste
Overall score

The Tartu brewery has had a roller-coaster history. It was founded in 1823 and by the close of the century had switched to cold fermentation and lager beers. But, as explained in the entry for Harvey's (see page 149), Albert Le Coq, the importer of Barclay's Imperial Russian Stout, bought the brewery and started to brew porter by 1910 to avoid paying import duties on beer. His ownership of the brewery was short-lived. In 1917, the Bolshevik government in Moscow nationalised the plant and phased out porter. In 1971, following years of legal wrangling over compensation, the Soviet government paid £240,000 to Le Coq's family. Following the collapse of the Soviet Union, the brewery started regular production of porter in the 1990s and opened a London office to sell both lager and porter in Britain, a neat reversal of history.

At 6.5%, Le Coq Porter is clearly in the imperial Russian stout camp. It is brewed from pale, black, chocolate and roasted grain, and hopped with German varieties. It has a deep bouquet of roasted grain, bitter chocolate, molasses and liquorice, underpinned by spicy hops. Rich flavours – roast, burnt fruit, chocolate and earthy hop resins – fill the mouth. The finish is rich, rewarding and warming, dominated by dark fruits, bitter roasted grain, espresso coffee and a firm hop bitterness.

Lion Dark

Source: Lion Brewery, Nuwara Eliya, Sri Lanka
Strength: 8%
Website: None

When English tea planters in Ceylon – the colonial name for Sri Lanka – needed more than tea to refresh them, they built a brewery high in the mountains, close to the holy city of Kandy. Brewing liquor comes from the nearby Lovers Leap waterfall, while Czech, Danish and English malts, along with Styrian hops from Slovenia and English ale yeast, are transported along precarious roads 1070m (3,500ft) above sea level. The journey from Colombo, the capital and main port, takes seven hours.

In Kandy and surrounding towns, Lion Dark is served in cask-conditioned form, while the rest of the world is supplied with the beer in bottles. It is a true warm fermented beer, with production taking place in wooden vessels. The malts are pale, chocolate and roasted barley, and the single hop is the Styrian Golding. It has an immense aroma of rich melting chocolate, cappuccino coffee, roasted grain and spicy hops. Coffee and hops build in the mouth with chocolate liqueur and hop resins. The finish is long and complex, offering warming alcohol alongside the liqueur, coffee, roasted grain and hop notes.

The beer used to be bottle-fermented but is now pasteurised, while the name has been changed from Lion Stout to Lion Dark, with a label that recommends it as a companion for curry dishes. I feel the brewery may be misreading the market for the beer. In Sri Lanka, fishermen like to blend the stout with arrack, distilled from coconut.

TASTING NOTES
Appearance
Aroma
Taste
Overall score

Mackeson Stout

Source: Interbrew UK, Luton, Bedfordshire, England
Strength: 3%
Website: www.interbrew.com

TASTING NOTES
Appearance
Aroma
Taste
Overall score

Interbrew, the world's biggest brewer (known as InBev outside Britain) is sitting on a classic beer but does little with it. Mackeson is the only major survivor of a once widely produced type of dark beer known as 'milk stout'.

Mackeson was an ancient brewery that dated from 1669 and was based in the small Kentish port of Hythe. In 1907, it launched Mackeson Milk Stout with the help of a dietician and promoted it as a healthy beer. The first label had an image of a milk churn and the proclamation: 'Each pint contains the energising carbohydrates of 10 ounces of pure dairy milk.' In fact, the beer does not contain milk as such but lactose, or milk sugar. Lactose cannot be fermented by brewer's yeast and therefore gives a smooth, creamy and milky note to the beer. The beer was such a success that many other brewers rushed to produce their own versions of milk stout.

Mackeson was taken over several times and eventually became part of the national Whitbread group in the 1930s. The stout became a national brand and by the 1960s it accounted for half of the group's annual production. One of the earliest television commercials featured the voice of the actor Sir Bernard Miles, founder of London's

Mermaid Theatre, who announced in a rich country burr: 'Mackeson – it looks good, it tastes good and, by golly, it does you good.' By this time, 'milk' had disappeared from the title, as the government frowned on the misleading labelling. The milk churn, however, remained.

Mackeson once rivalled Guinness in popularity but today sales are small and the beer is brewed for Interbrew by Young's in London. It is made from pale and chocolate malts, caramel and around 9% lactose. Lactose is added as powder in the copper. The lack of fermentability of the lactose can be seen by the fact that, while the stout has an original gravity (strength before fermentation) of 1042 degrees, the finished alcohol is a modest 3%. Target hops produce 26 units of bitterness, destroying the belief that milk stouts are sweet. The dark, almost jet-black beer, has a coffeeish aroma and palate with a gentle fruitiness and distinct hint of that ancient form of confectionery known as milk drops. An export version of the beer is 4.2% alcohol and has 34 units of bitterness. That is quite a beer – but you will have to go to Japan to drink it. Interbrew should not let Mackeson wither but should promote it as an English classic.

Mendocino Black Hawk Stout

Source: Mendocino Brewing Company, Hopland, California, USA
Strength: 5%
Website: www.mendobrew.com

Mendocino, alongside California's main artery Highway 101 South and in wine country 90 miles north of San Francisco, is based in attractive single-storey rustic buildings that include a restaurant as well as the brewery.

Mendocino's predecessor, the New Albion Brewery, has an important footnote in the history of brewing in the US. Its owner had to challenge Californian state law to permit a craft brewery to sell its products in its own bar rather than through distribution. New Albion was the first micro-brewery in California since Prohibition, and its success in changing the law helped dozens of other craft breweries to get off the ground. The law also annoyed the giant national brewers who tie up bars and restaurants through their distribution deals and lock smaller producers

out of the market. All in all, it's a small triumph worth toasting with a glass of Mendocino's Black Hawk Stout, named in the company style after an indigenous bird.

Black Hawk is brewed from two-row pale, crystal and black malts, and hopped with Cascade and Cluster varieties from the Pacific North-west: the hops are added three times during the kettle boil. This full-flavoured, rich beer has an entrancing aroma of old leather, fresh tobacco, dried fruits, coffee and tangy, bitter hop resins. Dark roasted malt fills the mouth with bitter dried fruit, liquorice and tangy hops. The big finish has creamy malt, burnt fruit, a further burst of leather and tobacco and a great punch of bitter hop resins. The brewery also produces an annual Yuletide Porter.

TASTING NOTES
Appearance
Aroma
Taste
Overall score

Nethergate Old Growler/Umbel Magna

Source: Nethergate Brewery, Pentlow, Essex, England
Strength: 5%/5.5%
Website: www.nethergate.co.uk

TASTING NOTES
Appearance
Aroma
Taste
Overall score

TASTING NOTES
Appearance
Aroma
Taste
Overall score

hops aroma, with bitter chocolate, liquorice and dried fruits. The palate is intensely fruity (raisins and sultanas) with a big spicy hop bitterness. The finish is hoppy with a rich chocolate note balanced by dark fruits and roasted grain. The beer was an instant success on draught and in bottle but Ian wasn't satisfied.

Other ingredients in the original recipe, which included coriander and bog myrtle, intrigued Ian. He was unable to find bog myrtle (though it does still grow) but he added ground coriander seeds to a batch of Old Growler. The result was a beer with all the character of the original but with a big herbal and spicy note. It was meant as a one-off brew but when I wrote a newspaper article about it, drinkers pleaded with the brewery to make it on a regular basis. The result is Umbel Magna, named after the shape of the coriander leaf. The Taylor Walker recipe shows that, even as late as the mid-18th century, brewers were still using other plants and herbs alongside hops in their beers.

Old Growler is based on the oldest-known porter recipe in England. Dr Ian Hornsey is a micro-biologist and former head brewer at Nethergate who has a fascination with brewing styles. His research unearthed the recipe for a porter brewed in the 1750s by the leading London company Taylor Walker.

Adapting the recipe to modern ingredients, he used Maris Otter pale malt (85%), wheat flour, crystal malt and black malt. Taylor Walker would have relied heavily on wood-cured brown malt. The colour of the beer is 70, while Challenger hops create 27 units of bitterness. Old Growler, named in honour of Ian's dog, has a peppery

North Coast Brewing Old No 38 Stout/Old Rasputin Russian Imperial Stout

Source: North Coast Brewing Company, Fort Bragg, California, USA
Strength: 5.5%/8.9%
Website: www.ncoast-brewing.com

North Coast Brewing is a near neighbour of Mendocino Brewing and is based in Fort Bragg, once a fort in the mid-19th century and then a whaling port. Fine brewing water comes from the River Noyo that feeds the town. The brewery is sited in an old Presbyterian church and mortuary (no jokes, please, about live beer raising the dead).

Founder Mark Ruedrich acquired a taste for English ales as a result of his marriage to a British woman, and he opened his brewery, taproom and grill in 1987 to brew warm-fermented beers. He has two stouts in his range, though Old No 38 is described as 'Dublin Dry Stout' rather than an English style. It is named after a retired locomotive on a rail line known as the Skunk from the diesel fumes and which runs through the Californian redwoods, linking Fort Bragg with Willits.

Old No 38 is brewed with an English ale culture and uses pale, crystal and black malts with roasted barley. It is hopped with American Cluster and German Hallertauer varieties (50 units of bitterness). It has a wonderfully aromatic bouquet of bitter roasted grain, espresso coffee and tart hop resins. Hops, dried fruit, roasted grain and bitter chocolate build in the mouth, while the finish is deep with complex dark vine fruits, bitter grain and tangy hops, finally becoming dry.

Old Rasputin is firmly in the style of an English imperial stout and honours, if that is the word, Grigori Rasputin, the wild monk who had an unhealthy relationship with the Russian royal family and helped spark the Russian Revolution. To break his grip on the Tsarina and her children, Rasputin's enemies attempted to poison and shoot him. When he survived, they pushed him through a hole in the ice into the River Neva in St Petersburg.

The beer is brewed with a similar recipe to Old No 38, with the hops creating a whopping 75 units of bitterness. It has a tarry and oily aroma with massive earthy hop resins along with liquorice, bitter chocolate and fresh leather. Burnt grain, dark fruits, bitter roasted coffee beans and fruity hops fill the mouth, followed by an explosive finish packed with warming alcohol with a Cognac note, burnt grain and fruit, leather, tobacco and bitter hop resins.

TASTING NOTES
Appearance
Aroma
Taste
Overall score

TASTING NOTES
Appearance
Aroma
Taste
Overall score

O'Hanlon Original Port Stout

Source: O'Hanlon's Brewing Company, Great Barton Farm, Whimple, Devon, England
Strength: 4.8%
Website: www.ohanlons.co.uk

John O'Hanlon grew up in a pub in County Kerry and spent some time in Dublin playing rugby and doing the sort of social things associated with the game. So when he says his Port Stout is known in Ireland as a 'corpse reviver', we know we are listening to the voice of experience.

He uses top-quality Ferreira port at the rate of two bottles for every 36 gallons of stout. The wine raises the strength of the beer from 4.6% to 4.8%. When he owned a pub in London, John introduced this characterful version of stout to distinguish it from the Guinness he also sold. His point is that stout is more than just one brand.

The beer has done well for him. In 2001, it won the gold medal at Tucker's Maltings Bottled Beer Competition in Newton Abbot, Devon. The draught version took the top prize for stout in CAMRA's Champion Winter Beer of Britain awards in 2002, and the bottled version walked away with the national Champion Bottled Beer of Britain award in 2003. It is brewed with Optic pale malt, crystal malt and caramalt, with flaked barley and roasted barley. Phoenix hops are used for bitterness, Styrian Goldings for aroma. The beer has a superb fruity, vinous aroma with earthy hop resins and roasted grain. The delightful winy fruitiness continues through the palate and into the finish, accompanied by luscious tangy hops, roasted grain, coffee and chocolate. Hold the coffin!

Pitfield Shoreditch Stout/ 1850 London Porter/ 1792 Imperial Stout

Source: Pitfield Brewery/London Beer Co, London, England
Strength: 4%/5%/9.3%
Website: www.pitfieldbeershop.co.uk

It's fitting that a range of porters and stouts should come from a brewery in this part of north London, for Sam Whitbread first brewed in the area before moving to the Barbican, while – according to legend – Ralph Harwood brewed his 'entire butt' nearby in Shoreditch and delivered it to the Old Blue Last in Great Eastern Street, a pub that survives to this day.

Pitfield, which is run by the energetic Martin Kemp, started life as the specialist Beer Shop in 1990 and the small brewery was added two years later. Pitfield converted its beers to organic ingredients in 2000 but has since added a range of 'historic beers' based on genuine recipes from the 18th, 19th and 20th centuries. As these beers cannot be created with organic malts and hops, they are produced under the name of the London Beer Co but all the beers come from the same plant.

Shoreditch Stout, an organic beer, is brewed with Maris Otter pale malt, flaked barley and roasted barley, and hopped with Challenger, Fuggles and Target hops. The dark brown beer has a roasty and smoky bouquet balanced by spicy hop resins and a luscious malt note. Roast and dark fruits build in the mouth with a solid

ORGANIC

PITFIELD's

SHOREDITCH STOUT

ABV 4.0%   50cl

TASTING NOTES	
Appearance	
Aroma	
Taste	
Overall score	

TASTING NOTES	
Appearance	
Aroma	
Taste	
Overall score	

underpinning of floral and peppery hops. The finish has more smoked and roast malt notes, with dried fruits and tangy hops.

1850 London Porter is based on a Whitbread recipe and is brewed with Maris Otter pale and brown malt with roasted barley. Goldings are the single hop variety. The beer is deep ruby-red in colour, and the aroma is full of nutty malt, coffee and roasted grain notes, with a big waft of peppery hops. Pungent dark fruits build in the mouth with continuing roasted grain and bitter hops notes. The finish is lingering, quenching – as a good porter should be – with coffee, roast and nutty malt and peppery hops.

The 1792 Imperial Stout is another original London recipe, and is brewed with Maris Otter pale malt, wheat malt and roasted barley. Northdown is the single hop variety. This strong beer is jet-black in colour with a rich liquorice and dark fruits aroma, tangy hop resins and hints of leather and tobacco. Oily, tarry notes develop in the mouth as the dark fruits and tobacco build. The finish has enormous length with raisin fruit to the fore, backed by roasted grain, liquorice, oily and tarry notes, bitter coffee and earthy hops.

The beers are available by mail order within Britain: see website.

Pyramid Espresso Stout

Source: Pyramid Brewing Company, Seattle, USA
Strength: 5.6%
Website: www.pyramidbrew.com

TASTING NOTES
Appearance
Aroma
Taste
Overall score

The Starbucks coffee revolution began in Seattle. Waiting in the city's airport in the early 1990s, I was delighted to find a Starbucks outlet selling rich and flavoursome cappuccinos, espressos and mochas, as mainstream American coffee tends to be thin and watery. The coffee flavours in Pyramid's Stout are created by the adroit use of dark and roasted grains, and the beer has a coffee-coloured foam that endears itself to the 'coffeeholics' in the city. I just hope they don't start drinking it from Styrofoam cups and straws.

The complex recipe includes pale, caramel, Munich and black malts plus roasted barley. The hops are Liberty and Nugget from the fertile hop-growing region of the Yakima Valley on the other side of the Cascade mountains. Nugget is a modern high 'alpha hop', which means it offers intense bitterness without much aroma, whereas Liberty delivers the piny and citrus characters that are typical of traditional American varieties. The beer has a lilting aroma of cappuccino coffee and smooth chocolate, with dark fruits and piny hop resins. Fruit, spicy hops, roasted grain and rich coffee fill the mouth while the finish is smooth, creamy, lingering with dark fruits, roast and hop bitterness and a delicious hint of chocolate ice-cream.

RCH Old Slug Porter

Source: RCH Brewery, West Huish, Weston-super-Mare, Somerset, England
Strength: 4.5%
Website: www.rchbrewery.com

TASTING NOTES
Appearance
Aroma
Taste
Overall score

If a brewery paid a slick marketing company to devise a name for a beer, I don't think Old Slug would be well received. But the name hasn't inhibited success of the RCH beer, which won a gold medal in the Tucker's Maltings Bottled Beer Competition in 1998. It is available in cask and bottle-fermented versions.

The brewery was once part of the Royal Clarence Hotel in Burnham-on-Sea but since the early 1990s has had a separate site near Weston. It was the slugs that thrived in the soil around the new brewery that encouraged the staff to give the curious name to the porter. The slugs have gone but the beer flourishes. It is brewed from pale, crystal and black malts, and hopped with Fuggles and Goldings. It is a dark ruby in colour and has a woody, grainy and fruity hop aroma. Cappuccino coffee notes break through in the mouth, balanced by bitter, tangy dark fruit and earthy and spicy hop resins. The long, quenching finish offers an increasingly dry and bitter hop note, with burnt fruit and coffee notes. There is also a hint of sourness, which comes from the black malt and shows how the use of heavily roasted malts in the 19th century delivered the lactic sourness porter drinkers expected from the beer, a sourness previously supplied by long-matured stale, or old, ale.

Ridley's Witchfinder Porter

Source: T D Ridley & Sons, Hartford End, near Chelmsford, Essex, England
Strength: 4.3%
Website: www.ridleys.co.uk

The hunting of witches was a bleak and terrible period of English history. The Ridley family knows about religious persecution, as Bishop Nicholas Ridley was burnt at the stake by Mary Tudor for his Protestant beliefs. Many of the people harried, persecuted and hanged for witchcraft were religious dissenters. After the failure of the Gunpowder Plot in 1605, James I ruthlessly pursued so-called witches in Lancashire (see Moorhouse's Pendle Witches Brew, page 106) who were adherents to the 'old' Roman Catholic religion. The worst examples of witch-hunting were in eastern England, including Essex, between 1645 and 1647, when Matthew Hopkins adopted the title of Witchfinder General and caught and executed 200 or more 'witches'.

Perhaps it is fitting that a black beer commemorates this period of history. But let us be of good cheer, for this is a fine example of the style, available on draught in the autumn and winter but all year round in filtered bottle form. It is brewed from Maris Otter pale, crystal and chocolate malts, and hopped with Fuggles, Goldings and Styrian Goldings varieties. Colour units are 100, bitterness 44. It has a tempting aroma of roasted malts, dark fruit and peppery hop resins. Chocolate builds in the mouth with a solid base of spicy hops, burnt fruit and roast grain. The long finish becomes finally dry and bitter but with pleasing contributions from chocolate, dark fruits and rich roasted grain.

* See also Ridley's Old Bob, page 108.

TASTING NOTES
Appearance
Aroma
Taste
Overall score

Rogue Shakespeare Stout/Imperial Stout

Source: Rogue Brewing Company, Newport, Oregon, USA
Strength: 6.1%/11%
Website: www.rogue.com

TASTING NOTES
Appearance
Aroma
Taste
Overall score

TASTING NOTES
Appearance
Aroma
Taste
Overall score

Brewmaster John Maier is so determined to create the correct English character for his dark beers that he imports specialist malts from the old country to get the required results. The use of hops from Oregon and Washington, however, give the two stouts a definable American quality.

Shakespeare Stout, a style of beer quite unknown to the Bard, is brewed with pale, crystal, English chocolate malt, rolled oats and roasted barley. The hops create a mighty 69 units of bitterness. The beer is unfiltered and throws a dense orange-brown foam and has a smooth chocolate aroma with a creamy note from the oats. Burnt currants, roasted grain, chocolate and bitter hops fill the mouth, while the deep and complex finish has tangy, tart hops, dark fruits, roasted grain and silky oats.

The Imperial Stout has a massive hop attack, with Cascade, Chinook and Willamette creating 87 units of bitterness. It is made from pale malt, Hugh Baird's crystal malt from England, chocolate malt also from England, black and Munich malts. It pours viscously into the glass like black Cognac, and the big, booming aroma conjures up dark and mysterious spices, espresso coffee, black chocolate and bitter oranges. It is chewy, oily and perfumy in the mouth followed by a long finish that has some surprisingly sweet glacé fruit notes balanced by dark grain and bitter hops, burnt fruit, smoky and roasted grain. This memorable mouthful is unfiltered and unfined and will improve in bottle. John Maier recommends letting it develop for a year before drinking.

Samuel Smith's Taddy Porter/Oatmeal Stout/ Imperial Stout

Source: Samuel Smith Old Brewery, Tadcaster, North Yorkshire, England
Strength: 5%/5%/7%
Website: www.merchantduvin.com

Samuel Smith spearheaded the dark beer revival in the 1980s with three superb beers available only in bottle. They were originally designed for the American market, so much so that Charles Finkel, the founder of the Merchant du Vin import agency in Seattle, designed the label for Imperial Stout. In the late 1990s, however, Sam Smith's launched a special promotion for the beers in Britain complete with tasting notes and cooking recipes. The notoriously reclusive company does not release recipe information for its bottled products, though the brewery is known to favour the traditional English hop varieties Fuggles and Goldings. The beers are fermented in Yorkshire Square vessels described in the entry for the brewery's Pale Ale (see page 63).

Taddy is an affectionate diminutive for the small town of Tadcaster, where the brewery is based. Taddy Porter has the rich malty character that is typical of the brewery's beers. The aroma has a coffee and tart fruit nose, with more bitter fruit, roasted grain and hop spicy

TASTING NOTES
Appearance
Aroma
Taste
Overall score

TASTING NOTES
Appearance
Aroma
Taste
Overall score

TASTING NOTES	
Appearance	
Aroma	
Taste	
Overall score	

resins in the mouth. The finish is quenching, beautifully balanced between a luscious bitter-sweet dark malt character, dark fruits and tangy hops.

Oatmeal Stout recalls a style of beer popular early in the 20th century, when brewers were anxious to promote the healthiness of their products. Oats are a difficult grain to brew with, as they gelatinise during mashing and tend to clog up pipes and valves. They have to be used sparingly but add a delicious creamy and grainy note to beer. Sam Smith's Oatmeal Stout has a smooth and silky palate with hints of chocolate and espresso coffee on the nose, a full, rich palate dominated by rich and creamy dark grain, coffee and earthy hop resins. The finish has

nutty dark malt, roasted grain, coffee, chocolate and bitter hop notes.

Samuel Smith's describes its Imperial Stout as the ideal digestif, the perfect replacement for Cognac. It even recommends serving it in a brandy balloon. Suggestions for companions at the dining table include Stilton and walnuts, baked sultana and lemon cheesecake, caviar, apricot-glazed bread and butter pudding, and chocolate trifle with roasted almonds. It has a complex roasted barley, burnt currants, cappuccino coffee and lactic sourness bouquet. Creamy malt, bitter and spicy hop resins and burnt fruit fill the mouth, while the finish bursts with sour fruit, roasted grain, bitter coffee and tangy hops.

Stepan Razin Porter

Source: Stepan Razin Brewery, St Petersburg, Russia
Strength: 8%
Website: www.razin.ru

Stepan Razin is one of the oldest breweries in Russia, founded in the late 18th century by a Swede named Abraham Krohn. He supplied beer to the palace of Tsar Peter I, who encouraged the spread of commercial brewing. The brewery was called Kalinkin after a bridge over the Neva River, and at first it brewed English-style ales, porters and stouts, and continued to do so when it switched to cold fermentation and Pilsner-style lagers as well in the late 19th century. Following the Russian Revolution, the brewery was renamed in honour of Stepan Razin, a Cossack who led a failed attempt on the life of the Tsar and was put to death in 1671. The brewery was encouraged to expand in the 1920s by Leon Trotsky, the former Commissar for War, who helped obtain new equipment from Germany.

The brewery today enjoys a major presence in St Petersburg and many other towns and cities, and is one of few to remain in Russian hands. Global brewers have moved into Russia and bought many breweries but Stepan Razin has thwarted a bid from Heineken.

The porter is an outstanding beer, in reality a dark lager that is matured for 90 days. Brewed with pale, roasted malt and caramalt, the beer is hopped with Nugget and Goldings varieties. It has a superb aroma of roasted grain, coffee, chocolate and vinous fruit, with dark grain, coffee and spicy hops building in the mouth. The long, complex finish is balanced between rich malt and bitter hops, with powerful contributions from dark fruit, chocolate and coffee.

The brewery has an excellent museum that traces the history of both Stepan Razin and brewing in Russia, with some fascinating artefacts from the Soviet period.

TASTING NOTES
Appearance
Aroma
Taste
Overall score

Titanic Stout

Source: Titanic Brewery Co, Burslem, Stoke-on-Trent, Staffordshire, England
Strength: 4.5%
Website: www.titanicbrewery.co.uk

TASTING NOTES
Appearance
Aroma
Taste
Overall score

Titanic is one of the fastest-growing micro-breweries in England and has grown to small regional status. It was founded in 1985 and named in honour of the hapless Captain Smith of the Titanic, who was born in Stoke.

The brewery has uprooted three times to cope with demand for the beers and, in 2002, moved into former school premises with greatly expanded brewing and fermenting capacity. Owner Keith Bott is chairman of the Society of Independent Brewers, the umbrella organisation that looks after the interests of Britain's small producers. He also brews regularly at the ancient brewhouse at Shugborough Hall in Staffordshire, home of Lord Lichfield, the last country estate in England still to have a working house brewery.

Titanic Stout is available in both cask and bottle-fermented form. It is brewed with Maris Otter pale malt, wheat malt and roasted barley, and is hopped with Goldings, Northdown and Willamette varieties. This full-tasting and characterful beer has a big roasted grain, coffee, liquorice and tangy hop resins aroma, with dark dried fruits developing in the mouth alongside bitter hops and luscious dark malt. The finish is smoky, woody, hoppy, dry, fruity and quenching. Suggestions that Titanic beers go down well are not met with approval.

Wye Valley Brewery Dorothy Goodbody's Wholesome Stout

Source: Wye Valley Brewery, Stoke Lacey, Herefordshire, England
Strength: 4.6%
Website: www.wyevalleybrewery.co.uk

TASTING NOTES
Appearance
Aroma
Taste
Overall score

Dorothy Goodbody is not stout. With a complete disregard for political correctness, Wye Valley uses the image of a remarkably cantilevered blonde to adorn some of the specialist beers, the sort of image that used to appear on the fuselages of World War Two Spitfires.

The brewery had humble beginnings as a brew-pub, the Nags Head in Canon Pyon. It has moved twice and is now based in premises that enable 80 barrels a day to be produced. Wye Valley owns two pubs and supplies around 500 other outlets.

Stout is available both in cask and bottled fermented forms. The bottled version is filtered, kräusened and reseeded with fresh yeast to encourage continuing fermentation and maturation under glass. It is brewed with Maris Otter pale malt, flaked barley and roasted barley, and hopped with Northdowns. It is a deep nut-brown in colour with a big bouquet of roasted grain, tangy hops, chocolate and burnt currants. Chocolate, roast, bitter hop resins and rich fruit fill the mouth, while the long finish has smooth, silky malt, dried fruit, chocolate and earthy hop resins.

Miss Goodbody claims she found the recipe in her grandfather's brewing records, as he was once a brewer. The reality is that Wye Valley's founder Peter Amor once worked for a well-known Irish brewery whose stout was the inspiration for his beer, which was named Supreme Champion Winter Beer of Britain by CAMRA in 2002.

Young's Double Chocolate Stout

Source: Young & Co's Ram Brewery, Wandsworth, London, England
Strength: 5%
Website: www.youngs.co.uk

TASTING NOTES
Appearance
Aroma
Taste
Overall score

Young's, best known for its robust bitters, introduced Double Chocolate Stout in 1997 as a one-off brew but it found such favour that it is now a regular beer. It is principally a bottled beer in Britain, though it is occasionally on sale in Young's pubs on handpump and is also made available in cask form to CAMRA beer festivals. A draught version in the United States is filtered and pasteurised.

While most 'chocolate' stouts derive their flavour from the use of roasted malts, Young's head brewer Ken Don uses Cadbury's chocolate in both bar and essence form. Solid chocolate is added during the boil with hops, while essence is inserted as the beer is racked into casks. The grains used are Maris Otter pale, chocolate and crystal malts with roasted barley. The hops are Fuggles and Goldings. The beer is sweet by the standards of conventional stouts but not cloyingly so. The aroma has a creamy confectionery appeal, balanced by dark fruit and bitter hops. Rich chocolate fudge cake, tart hops and dark grains fill the mouth, while the long and complex finish offers intense chocolate flavours balanced by dark fruit and earthy hop resins. It is thought that this is the only stout in the world to use real chocolate as opposed to dark malt, and the bottle label pays homage to the chocolate's maker by using a similar design and typeface.

Golden Ales

Golden ales in both Belgium and Britain were created with one major aim in mind: to counter the growth of mass-advertised global lager brands. In Belgium, the first golden ale, Duvel, is the clear market leader and has spawned a legion of similar strong, warm-fermenting beers. It was the inexorable rise of Pilsner-style beers in Belgium that encouraged smaller brewers, who lacked the ability or capital investment to make lager, to add strong golden ales to their portfolios. The use of lighter varieties of malt allows hops to shine through, giving pulsating floral, piny, spicy and citrus aromas and flavours. The warming alcohol of beers such as Duvel, at 8.5%, along with deep malt, fruit and hop flavours, singles them out from Pilsner beers, whose only similarity is that of colour.

In Britain, consumers drink by the pint rather than sip reflectively from elegant, branded glassware, a habit that restricts the strength of beer. But more modest British golden ales have enabled craft brewers to set out their stall as producers of beers that are both pale in colour but packed with character. Many golden ales started life as summer refreshers. One of the best known of the breed, Hop Back's Summer Lightning, still suggests its seasonality in its name, though it is now brewed all year round.

The success of golden ales has enabled smaller British brewers to hang on to and even grow their market share at a time when giant global brewers exercise greater hegemony over the beer scene and flood both pubs and supermarkets with their bland and insipid interpretations of lager. There should be an International Court of Bibulous Rectitude that consigns to outer darkness some of the beers brewed in Britain that claim to have some tenuous connection to genuine European cold-fermented styles. Failing that, we should savour instead beers that manage to be both pale and interesting.

LEFT
Hop Back's Summer Lightning was one of the first of the new breed of Golden Ales in England and is now brewed all year round.

Achouffe La Chouffe

Source: Brasserie d'Achouffe, Achouffe, Belgium
Strength: 8%
Website: www.achouffe.be

TASTING NOTES
Appearance
Aroma
Taste
Overall score

Achouffe proves that brewing can be fun. The brewery and its products are based on the *Chouffe*, a bearded dwarf with a red hat, not dissimilar to a Smurf, who lives in the dense forest of the Ardennes in the Belgian province of Luxembourg and close to the Grand Duchy of the same name. In the late 1970s, the brothers-in-law Pierre Gobron and Chris Bauweraerts, keen home brewers, decided to launch a brewery and based their plant with borrowed farm and kitchen utensils in a small building in the then unknown village of Achouffe. Their strong, complex and bottle-fermented ales, with their striking labels depicting the dwarf, were sufficiently successful for the founders to give up their day jobs to brew full time and move into old farm buildings in 1986 with much improved equipment and a brew-length of 70 hectolitres (1,540 gallons). Sales improved dramatically when the company started to export to French Canada and they were able to open a new brewhouse and fermenting hall.

La Chouffe, the main product, is brewed with pure Ardennes water, Pilsner and crystal malts, white candy sugar and coriander. The hops are Czech Saaz and Styrian Goldings. The beer is deep gold with a rich sweet citrus fruit and coriander aroma. Vinous fruit builds in the mouth, balanced by juicy malt, herbal notes and gentle hop resins. The long finish is fruity and malty with light hop resins and a final powerful reminder of coriander. The beer is cold matured and then run into corked Champagne bottles, while a magnum version is called Big Chouffe. The beer will improve and develop greater fruit notes over time.

The brewery has added a bar and restaurant where the beers can be sampled with rustic dishes.

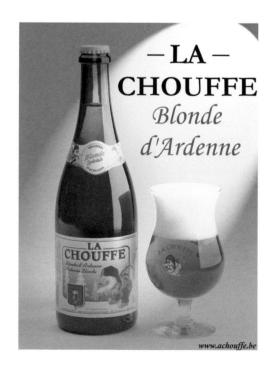

Caledonian Golden Promise

Source: Caledonian Brewing Company, Edinburgh, Scotland
Strength: 5%
Website: www.caledonian-brewery.co.uk

The attention to detail at Caledonian and the pride in a brewing process that includes the only coppers heated by direct flame left in Britain explains why the brewery opted for organic materials when it launched Golden Promise in the early 1990s. Britain now leads the world in the number of organic beers it produces, but for many years Golden Promise ploughed a lonely, if pesticide-free, furrow. It is, not surprisingly, the market leader.

There were concerns about Caledonian's future in 2004, when the country's biggest brewer, Scottish & Newcastle, announced it would close its Edinburgh brewery and had taken a 30% stake in Caledonian and owned all the company's assets. The original Caledonian management, however, has remained firmly in control, as I found when I visited the brewery shortly after the S&N announcement. Golden Promise and the other traditional Caledonian beers remain in production and will be given greater prominence throughout Britain as a result of S&N's wholesaling muscle.

Golden Promise takes its name from a Scottish variety of malting barley that was used when the beer was first brewed. Supplies are now hard to find and the brewery has had to switch to a different variety of organic malt, though it is working with farmers and whisky distillers to grow more organic Golden Promise. The beer at present is brewed with 100% Optic pale malt and is hopped with New Zealand Hallertauer. Colour units are 11 and bitterness units 26. The beer has a biscuity malt aroma balanced by floral hop resins and tangy orange fruit. Fruit and hop bitterness build in the mouth but are underscored by juicy malt. The finish is long and quenching, with a good hoppy dryness and bitterness but with continuing sappy malt and tart citrus fruit.

TASTING NOTES
Appearance
Aroma
Taste
Overall score

Castle Rock Nottingham Gold

Source: Castle Rock Brewery, Nottingham, England
Strength: 3.5%
Website: www.castlerockbrewery.co.uk

TASTING NOTES
Appearance
Aroma
Taste
Overall score

Castle Rock is the brewing division of the Tynemill pub group and both prove there is genuine demand for full-tasting beer. Tynemill was launched by Chris Holmes, a CAMRA pioneer and the campaign's energetic chairman in the formative years of the 1970s. His company owns 17 pubs in the East Midlands and all are based on a good range of cask beers from craft producers. While bigger pub groups concentrate on lager and keg beers, Tynemill sells more than 1,500 cask beers a year and is mightily successful as a result.

Castle Rock is a natural extension of the Tynemill philosophy and is equally successful. The brewery opened in 1996 and moved five years later to buildings alongside Tynemill's Vat & Fiddle pub, close to the local tax office and handily placed a few yards from Nottingham's main railway station. In 2003, in order to keep pace with demand, the brewery expanded from 30 barrels a week to 100. The brewing process can be viewed through windows in the pub wall.

Castle Rock produces a wide range of beers, but Nottingham Gold is a flagship beer, sold throughout the Tynemill estate and often under house names: Meadows Gold, for example, in the Vat & Fiddle. It is brewed from Maris Otter pale and crystal malts with a little torrefied wheat for a good head of foam. The hops are Goldings and Styrian Goldings. The beer has a rich and tempting aroma of peppery hops, tart citrus fruit and biscuit malt. Bitter hops resins, lemon jelly fruitiness and juicy malt fill the mouth while the lingering finish has tangy fruit, sappy malt and peppery hops.

Ceredigion Blodeuwedd
Source: Bragdy Ceredigion, New Quay, Ceredigion, Wales
Strength: 4.5%
Website: www.bestofruralwales.co.uk

Crouch Vale Brewers Gold
Source: Crouch Vale Brewery, South Woodham Ferrers, Essex, England
Strength: 4%
Website: www.crouch-vale.co.uk

First, some quick translation for those unused to Welsh: *Ceredigion* means Cardigan; there was once a Welsh county called Cardiganshire, and Cardigan remains an important town in West Wales. *Blodeuwedd* stands for Flower Face, while *bragdy* is the Welsh for brewery. The curious name comes from a legend that says two magicians created a beautiful girl from flowers. Tragedy struck when she plotted with her lover to kill her husband. As punishment, she was turned into an owl, 'a creature of the night'. The Welsh for owl is *blodeuwedd*, although the literal meaning is 'flower face', as mentioned above.

Brian and Julia Tilby opened the brewery in 1997 in a converted barn on Wervil Grange Farm. Julia is responsible for the hand-drawn labels on the bottled versions of the beers, all of which are suitable for vegetarians. The Tilbys refuse to use any chemical additives in the brewing process. Their beers, aimed primarily at the tourist trade in a region with a long and attractive coastline, are available in both cask and bottle-fermented versions.

Blodeuwedd is an organic beer with a certificate from the Soil Association. The beer is brewed with organic pale malt and Hallertauer hops and is primed with organic Demerara sugar to encourage a strong fermentation in bottle. Blodeuwedd has a citrus fruit, floral hop and biscuity malt bouquet, with juicy malt, tart fruit and hop resins building in the mouth. The lingering finish is hoppy and bitter, with creamy malt and a continuing tang of citrus fruit.

Golden ales challenge the domination of lager beers in Britain, and Brewers Gold does so in a fascinating fashion, as the only grain used is lager malt and the single hop variety – and hence the name of the beer – is the German Brewers Gold.

The beer is one of a portfolio developed over 20 years by one of the longest-running and most successful micros. Run by Colin Bocking and Ollie Graham, Crouch Vale has built its success on the quality of its beers and also by acting as a wholesaler for other craft brewers, whose products they supply to some 250 pubs as well as beer festivals.

Crouch Vale owns one pub, the Queen's Head in Chelmsford, which is a fine watering hole for visitors to the Essex cricket ground. Brewers Gold boosted the fortunes of the brewery in 2003, when it won the Best Bitter class in CAMRA's Champion Beer of Britain competition: the success of golden ales in the competition prompted CAMRA to add a new and separate class for such beers in 2005.

Brewers Gold has a pungent aroma of cornflour and vanilla from the use of lager malt, balanced by a massive punch of citrus fruit and hop resins from the hops. Grapefruit bursts on the tongue, balanced by juicy malt and hop bitterness. The finish is intensely bitter with a further citrus fruit tang and rich, sappy malt. It is a beautifully balanced and wonderfully refreshing beer.

TASTING NOTES
Appearance
Aroma
Taste
Overall score

TASTING NOTES
Appearance
Aroma
Taste
Overall score

De Dolle Arabier

Source: De Dolle Brouwers, Esen, Belgium
Strength: 7%
Website: www.dedollebrouwers.be

TASTING NOTES
Appearance
Aroma
Taste
Overall score

There cannot be a style called 'mad beer' but the De Dolle Brouwers, the Mad Brewers, have carved out their own distinctive and eccentric niche in the world of brewing. The Herteleer family and friends may be eccentric but their madness is more akin to passion and enthusiasm than lunacy. The brewery is in Esen, near Diksmuide, not far from Ostend, and is on the site of a brewery that dates from the 1840s and seemed destined to close in 1980, when the owner was taken ill. But a group of keen home brewers, who started out with a kit from Boots the Chemist bought on a visit to England, took over the site and started to brew at weekends.

The driving force is Kris Herteleer, an architect by trade but now also a brewer of some experience. The brewery is open to visitors on Sundays with occasional group visits on other days. On my first visit I was shown round by Kris's mother, who shared her son's passion for beer and announced: 'Water is medicine, malt is medicine, hops are medicine, therefore beer is medicine', though her warning against 'savage yeasts' chilled the blood. I think she meant wild yeasts. The brewhouse is tiny and filled with antique equipment: a pre-World War One mash tun, a copper fired by direct flame, and an open wort cooler.

Arabier started life as a summer beer but is now brewed all year round. The name is a Flemish joke about parrots that's impossible to translate. The beer is brewed with pale, amber and Munich malts, and hopped with the Nugget variety from Poperinge in Belgium. It is dry hopped using Kentish Goldings. It is a hazy gold/bronze colour with a damson jam and spicy hops aroma, rich fruit, juicy malt and peppery hops in the mouth, and a big finish that ends peppery and bitter but along the way offers further tart fruit and sappy malt notes.

The brewery ran into problems at the turn of the century when Rodenbach stopped supplying yeast to De Dolle but Kris has since managed to get a different supply and has cultured it to suit the character of his beers.

Duvel

Source: Brouwerij Moortgat, Breendonk, Belgium
Strength: 8.5%
Website: www.duvel.com

A sign in Flemish outside the Moortgat brewery says 'Ssh... Duvel is ripening'. This strong, infinitely complex and superbly aromatic beer is conditioned, refermented and matured by a long, slow and painstaking process. When I was allowed to sit in on a sampling of the beer by the brewing staff, I was amazed by the way the beer developed over weeks and months, moving from yeasty and estery when young, taking on malt, fruit and hop notes before finally blossoming into ripe and full-bodied maturity with its famous Poire William signature. In spite of its extreme pallor, Duvel (pronounced Doo-v'l, with the emphasis on the first syllable) is a warm-fermented ale.

The brewery, founded by Jan-Léonard Moortgat in 1871, has always been a specialist ale producer. Between the World Wars, when Scotch Ales were popular in Belgium, Moortgat asked the renowned brewing scientist Jean De Clerck from the brewing faculty at Leuven University to analyse a bottle of McEwan's Export. McEwan's in those days was bottle fermented, and De Clerck was able to isolate the yeast in the sediment and culture it for use at Moortgat. De Clerck discovered it had up to 15 different strains. The result was an amber-brown beer that, according to legend, was greeted by one brewery worker with the cry 'This is a devil of a beer'. Devil is duvel in Flemish. The name stuck and was used when Moortgat decided to add a golden beer to its portfolio in 1970, again with the help of De Clerck, who recultured the original yeast down to two strains.

Two-row summer French and Belgian barleys are specially malted for Moortgat. Duvel has a colour rating of seven to nine, only fractionally higher than a Pilsner's. The beer is infusion mashed and has an original gravity of 1056. Czech Saaz and Styrian Goldings hops are added to the copper boil in three stages and create between 29 to 31 units of bitterness. Dextrose is added before primary fermentation to boost the level of alcohol and encourage a full attenuation by the yeast. This lifts the gravity to 1066.

The two strains of yeast are used for primary fermentation, and the hopped wort is split into two batches in order to be attacked by the different strains. Primary fermentation lasts for six days followed by three days' secondary fermentation at cold temperature. The beer is then cold conditioned for a month, filtered, given an addition of dextrose and a dosage of one of the original yeasts. The gravity is once again boosted, this time to around 1073 degrees. The beer is bottled and held for two weeks, during which time it undergoes its third fermentation. The end result is a beer of 8.5% alcohol.

Duvel has a full, rich bouquet of hop resins, pear fruit and lightly toasted, biscuity malt. Fruit and hops dominate the mouth before the immensely long, warming finish develops an astonishing array of perfumy hops, rich pear fruit and juicy malt characteristics. The beer is poured into a special glass like an oversized brandy balloon in order to contain the vast head of foam. Some bars keep the glass in the refrigerator along with the beer. You may prefer Duvel chilled but I think its sublime character is best appreciated if served at an ale temperature.

The devil is a lucky man: not only does he have all the best tunes but one of the world's classic beers as well.

TASTING NOTES
Appearance
Aroma
Taste
Overall score

Exmoor Gold

Source: Exmoor Ales, Golden Hill Brewery, Wiveliscombe, Somerset, England
Strength: 4.5%
Website: www.www.exmoorales.co.uk

TASTING NOTES
Appearance
Aroma
Taste
Overall score

Exmoor Gold was the first of the new wave of golden ales in Britain but it wasn't meant to be a permanent beer. The brewery produced it in the early 1990s to mark its 1,000th brew. The enormous interest aroused by a beer that was as pale as lager and was a single malt ale with an intensely hoppy aroma and flavour led to it becoming a regular member of the company's portfolio. It has gone on to win some 30 awards for its quality.

Exmoor Ales was founded in 1980 in part of the old Hancock's Brewery that had closed in 1959. The omens were not good. The founders moved into a building in the depths of winter and found snow blowing in through an open wall. But the 13th brew of Exmoor Ale, to the astonishment of the brewing industry,

won CAMRA's Champion Beer of Britain competition that year. Since then the brewery has changed hands, and energetic new owners have expanded the site and now supply beer to 250 pubs in South-west England and nationally through wholesalers.

Exmoor Gold is brewed with 100% pale malt from the West Country and hopped with Challenger, Fuggles and Goldings. Colour units are 10, bitterness a resounding 40. The beer has a powerful punch of earthy hop resins, lemon fruit, juicy malt and a hint of butterscotch. Hops and fruit burst across the tongue, underscored by sappy malt and butterscotch. The finish lingers, becomes dry and intensely bitter but juicy malt continues to make its mark on a memorable and refreshing beer.

Gold Miner

Source: Freeminer Brewery, Cinderford, Gloucestershire, England
Strength: 5%
Website: www.freeminer.com

Gold Miner was launched in 2003 as a bottle-fermented beer exclusively for the Co-op supermarket group. The beer had existed in cask form previously as Gold Standard and won the 1998 Beauty of Hops competition, where the judges praised the 'orange and apricot' character contributed by the hops. Beauty of Hops is an annual competition sponsored by growers who have increased public knowledge and appreciation of hops by describing the aromas and flavours of individual varieties. The growers encourage brewers to experiment with different blends of hops or to make 'single varietal' beers with just one variety.

Gold Miner is a single varietal beer, brewed with First Gold, the most successful of the new breed of hedgerow hops that grow to only half the height of conventional varieties. They are easier to pick and less prone to attack by pests and disease. Gold Miner is brewed with Optic pale malt and a touch of pale crystal malt. It has a tart and tangy bouquet of fresh orange peel, earthy hop resins and lightly toasted grain. Tart fruit, bitter hops and juicy malt fill the mouth, followed by a finish of great length that becomes hoppy and bitter but is balanced by a continuing tangy citrus fruit element and a rich malt note.

The Co-op was founded in the 19th century to provide goods and services – including funerals – at affordable prices for working people. In recent years, it has pioneered information for its customers with detailed labelling. The back labels of beer bottles include useful dietary information and even have a Braille section.

TASTING NOTES
Appearance
Aroma
Taste
Overall score

Hesket Newmarket Helvellyn Gold

Source: Hesket Newmarket Brewery, Hesket Newmarket, Wigton, Cumbria, England
Strength: 4%
Website: www.hesketbrewery.co.uk

TASTING NOTES
Appearance
Aroma
Taste
Overall score

Hesket Newmarket Brewery was saved from closure in 1999, when both local people and drinkers from further afield formed a co-operative to run it. The brewery hadn't failed, but the couple that had run it since 1988 wanted to retire.

The tiny brewery supplies beer to the Old Crown Inn, which is also owned by a co-operative that includes locals and people from as far away as the United States and South Africa who have visited the area and fallen in love with the old inn, the beer and the surrounding fells and mountains. Both pub and brewery have featured in the national press and on television. They were visited in 2004 by the Prince of Wales who heads the Pub is the Hub campaign that seeks to maintain rural pubs as vital centres of their communities. The publicity has encouraged the brewery to expand. Mike Parker, a former brewer with Bass, is now in charge and has increased production to 120 barrels a week and added a temperature-controlled beer store. As well as supplying the Old Crown and other pubs in the area, the brewery will sell beer to visitors who bring suitable containers (016974 78066). The beers are named after local mountains and fells, including Blencathra, Skiddaw and Old Carrock.

Helvellyn Gold is a recent addition to the range and is brewed with a skilful blend of ingredients. Maris Otter pale malt is the main grain with 3% malted oats to balance hop bitterness and 2% aromatic pale malt. Mike Parker described aromatic malt as similar to crystal malt, which means it is a stewed malt that doesn't need mashing. He says aromatic pale is less cooked than crystal and has a bitter-sweet character. The hops are Cascade, Fuggles and Goldings, added twice during the copper boil, with Styrian Goldings put into the copper at the end of the boil. The beer has a rich and pungent aroma of lemon jelly fruit, biscuity malt and hop resins. Creamy malt, bitter hop resins and tart fruit fill the mouth, followed by a lingering finish with a delicate and delicious creamy maltiness balanced by tangy citrus fruit and bitter hops.

Hop Back Summer Lightning

Source: Hop Back Brewery, Downton, Salisbury, Wiltshire, England
Strength: 5%
Website: www.hopback.co.uk

Hop Back brews a wide range of beers but it is true to say that its success has been driven by Summer Lightning, a beer that has won a multitude of awards at CAMRA's Great British Beer Festival and other competitions. The brewery is yet another success story for British micros.

It started life in 1987, when John Gilbert added a tiny brewhouse to the Wyndham Arms pub in Salisbury. With support from the government's Business Expansion Scheme, the brewery moved to an industrial estate on the outskirts of Salisbury and now has a modern 20-barrel production line. It owns 11 pubs and supplies more than 200 other outlets. In the late 1980s, John decided to introduce a strong golden beer as an antidote to other beers of that strength, which, in his opinion, were both too dark and too sweet. The success of Summer Lightning, named after an obscure play of that title by P G Wodehouse, encouraged many other brewers, large and small, to add golden ales to their portfolios.

Now brewed all the year round, Summer Lightning is available in both cask and bottle fermented versions. It is brewed with 100% Maris Otter pale malt and has 14 units of colour. The cask version uses both Challenger and East Kent Goldings hops, while in bottle it is a single varietal beer with Goldings alone. Bitterness units are a powerful 38. The cask version has a massive aroma of peppery Goldings, tart citrus fruit and lightly toasted malt, with sappy malt, lemon and gooseberry fruit and earthy hop resins in the mouth. The big finish is intensely hoppy and bitter, balanced by tart fruit and juicy malt. The bottled version has a higher level of natural carbonation and a pronounced Goldings aroma and palate.

Kelham Island Pale Rider

Source: Kelham Island Brewery, Sheffield, South Yorkshire, England
Strength: 5.2%
Website: www.kelhambrewery.co.uk

Dave Wickett, an economics lecturer at Sheffield Hallam University and a long-standing member of CAMRA, launched Kelham Island in 1990. He wanted to restore Sheffield's proud brewing tradition that had disappeared when Bass and Whitbread closed their breweries in the city. He built his small brewery alongside the Fat Cat pub on an island formed by a mill race adjacent to the River Don. The success of the beers prompted a move a few yards away to new, purpose-built premises with a greatly increased capacity.

In 2004, Pale Rider was named Champion Beer of Britain by CAMRA, and Dave found his phone was red-hot with orders for the beers from as far away as Chicago. He was approached by Ridley's Brewery in Essex, and an agreement was swiftly reached whereby Ridley's would supplement Kelham Island's 25 barrels a week of Pale Rider with 60 additional barrels. Dave only gave the go-ahead to the deal when he was satisfied the Ridley's beer was a perfect match. I went to the brewery and found I could not detect the slightest difference between the two brews. However, as Dave is determined to counter any claims that he is passing off Ridley's version as his own, the beer from the Essex brewery is called Pale Island rather than Pale Rider.

Both versions are brewed with Maris Otter pale malt and a touch of wheat malt, and the only hop is the American Willamette. The beer has a pungent aroma of perfumy floral hops, tangy citrus fruit and biscuity malt. Hop resins, piny notes, tart fruit and sappy malt fill the mouth. Creamy and juicy malt builds in the long finish, balanced by a continuing citrus fruit note and bitter hop resins.

TASTING NOTES
Appearance
Aroma
Taste
Overall score

TASTING NOTES
Appearance
Aroma
Taste
Overall score

Oakham JHB

Source: Oakham Ales, Peterborough, Cambridgeshire, England
Strength: 3.8%
Website: www.oakham-ales.co.uk

JHB has won five awards in CAMRA's Champion Beer of Britain competition, including Supreme Champion in 2001. It comes from the Brewery Tap (90 Westgate), the biggest brew-pub in Europe, based in central Peterborough and close to the railway station. The brewery can be seen behind the bar on the ground floor and there is a spectacular view from the mezzanine. The pub and brewery have been threatened for years by closure to make way for a road-widening scheme. But nothing has yet happened to spoil the pleasure of drinkers who come from far and wide to enjoy the home-brewed ales, a fine selection of Belgian beers and excellent Thai food.

JHB stands for Jeffery Hudson Bitter. Hudson was a midget from Peterborough who found favour at the court of Charles I. He was placed inside a large pie – but only after it was cooked – and he burst from it at the royal table, much to the amusement of the royal couple and their guests. Hudson was a staunch monarchist and supported the king during the English Civil War, which earned him a spell in the Tower of London when the parliamentary forces under Oliver Cromwell defeated the royalists.

The beer may be named in his honour but it is not short on aroma and flavour. It is brewed with Maris Otter pale malt with 5% wheat malt for clarity and head retention. The hops are Challenger for bitterness and American Mount Hood for aroma, and they create 33 units of bitterness. JHB has a profound citrus fruit, creamy malt and earthy hop resins bouquet with a big hop bitterness building in the mouth and almost overpowering the juicy malt and fruit notes. The finish is intensely dry and bitter but is balanced by sappy and creamy malt with a continuing tart fruit note. This is a big, full-bodied beer that drinks more than its strength would suggest and is for lovers of the hop.

Silly Double Enghien Blonde

Source: Brasserie de Silly, Silly, Hainaut, Belgium
Strength: 7.5%
Website: www.silly-beer.com

Silly is a perfectly sensible name if you happen to be a Belgian from Wallonia, though it causes considerable mirth to English speakers. The village takes its name from the local river, the Sylle, in Hainaut province south of Brussels. In the 19th century, some of the bigger farms in the region not only grew barley and hops but also added small breweries to make beer for their families and workers. The Meynsbrughen family in Silly continued to farm until after World War Two but then decided to concentrate on brewing. The style of buildings and the cobbled yard still suggest a farm, and this type of brewing is known in Belgium as artisanal or rustic. In 1975, Silly bought the Tennstedt Decroes brewery in neighbouring Enghien and added its range of beers to its own. The main beers are all warm-fermented ales though the company – controlled by the fifth generation of the family – has recently added a Silly Pils: I have drunk a fair number of those over the years.

One of the Double Enghien beers is the mightily strong Blonde, brewed with pale malts from Belgium and France, and hopped with English Challenger and German Hallertauer. It has a stunning aroma of juicy malt, lemon jelly fruit and floral and spicy hops. Rich flavours of malt and fruit build in the mouth but are underpinned by a firm, spicy hop character. The finish has enormous length, with complex flavours of sappy malt, lemon fruit and a deep and intense spicy hop note. The beer for years was filtered but the brewery has bowed to demand and it is now bottle fermented and will improve and deepen its flavours over the months.

After a visit to the brewery, I enjoyed some of the brewery's beers and an excellent rustic lunch in the Café Titien in Bassilly, or Lower Silly. The bar has a version of bar billiards with the familiar mushroom-shaped guardians of the holes replaced by Champagne corks. I enjoyed a few silly games…

TASTING NOTES
Appearance
Aroma
Taste
Overall score

Unibroue Maudite

Source: Brasserie Unibroue, Chambly, Montréal, Québec, Canada
Strength: 8%
Website: www.unibroue.com

TASTING NOTES
Appearance
Aroma
Taste
Overall score

Some of the early French settlers in Canada came from Flanders and Normandy, and brought with them a beer rather than a wine culture. In the past 20 years, a number of craft breweries have sprung up to offer authentic French- and Belgian-style beers for the Francophone region, with Unibroue the clear market leader.

André Dion and Serge Racine founded the brewery and from its first tiny base moved to bigger premises in the Montréal suburb of Chambly. They worked at first in association with the Belgian brewing group Riva, which advised on the recipe of the first beer, Blanche de Chambly, a wheat, or white, beer launched in 1992. The brewery received a major injection of capital from the Canadian rock star Robert Charlebois and started to expand the range of products, which are exported to the United States and Europe.

The beers are bottle fermented and have eye-catching labels showing Canadian scenes and legends. *Maudite* means damned in French, and the name is taken from a fantastical French-Canadian story about a group of lumberjacks who sign a pact with the devil that allows them to fly their canoe home. But Satan reneges on the deal and leads them to their death.

Maudite is based on the Belgian golden ale style, and the brewers clearly had Duvel in mind when they devised their recipe, but they added coriander and spices to give their beer its distinctive bouquet and palate. American and European hops are used sparingly to allow full expression to the herbs and spices. Pale and Munich malts produce the deep red-gold colour. It has a rich and tempting nose of spices and nutty malt, with coriander and orange zest building strongly in the mouth. The complex finish is long, with nutty and juicy malt and a dry, herbal finale. The beer undergoes three fermentations and will improve in bottle for eight years.

Scottish Ales

As a result of temperament and temperature, the Scots have for centuries brewed ales that are distinctively different from those made south of the border. A cold climate requires beers that are hearty and warming; as a result Scottish ales tend to be dark, often brewed with the addition of heavily roasted malts, oats and other cereals, and rich with unfermented sugar.

The first brewers were Picts, not Celts. Their heather ale survived long after they were ethnically cleansed, and the style has recently been resurrected (see page 247). Ale brewed in a more conventional way had a poor reputation. In 1598, Fynes Morrison wrote that the local ale would 'distemper a strange body', while an 18th-century English traveller, Thomas Kirke, described it as 'sorry stuff, tunned up in a small vessel called a cogue [mash tun]; after it has stood a few hours, they drink it out of the cogue, yest and all'. Imports of ale from England reached such proportions that, in 1625, the Scottish Parliament passed an Act forbidding the 'Hamebringing of Foreyn Beir' but nobody paid any attention to the law. The probable reason for the superiority of English ale was the use of the hop, which gave it better keeping qualities. The Scottish climate was not conducive to the development of a hop industry and brewers used them sparingly or not at all.

Commercial brewing in Scotland took off almost by default. As a result of the Auld Alliance between Scotland and France, the Scots consumed substantial amounts of imported French claret and Burgundy. But supplies dwindled during the Napoleonic wars and entrepreneurial brewers, as distinct from brewers in inns and on farms, appeared to fill the gap. They also met a growing demand for beer from Scottish emigrants. The Highland Clearances had sent many landless and destitute Scots abroad to look for work, and their descendants in Australasia, the Caribbean and North America demanded ale from the old country. 'Export' – a darker and sweeter version of India Pale Ale – became a definitive brewing style. The best-known of the breed, McEwan's Export, remains a major brand for the Scottish & Newcastle group.

The brewing industry settled in the Lowlands around the cities of Alloa, Edinburgh and Glasgow, making use of the best-quality barley grown in the region. The names for beer are different from the English ones: mild in Scotland is called light, even when it is dark in colour; bitter and best bitter are known as heavy, while a wee heavy is a strong beer sold in nip bottles. Such beers are also known as 60, 70, 80 and 90 shilling ales from a 19th-century method of stating the wholesale price for beer per barrel. The names, however, should not detract from the more important fact that Scottish ales are brewed in a different way from English ones. The copper boil lasts for a shorter time. As fewer hops are used, it is important not to boil away the delicate aromas and flavours of the plant. Fermentation is at a lower temperature of 10°C (50°F), compared to 20°C (70°F) in England. As a result, the yeast works slowly, does not create a large head, does not need to be skimmed and eventually settles at the bottom of the fermenter. Fermentation lasts for around three weeks and the green beer is then stored for several more. The similarities with lager brewing are obvious. The system developed empirically before the Industrial Revolution, when brewing took place only in winter. It was the exceptionally cold weather in Scotland that created cold ferments and the system continued when refrigeration appeared. It is not difficult to understand why lager brewing took off so much earlier in Scotland than in England. Hugh Tennent's Wellpark Brewery, for example, started to brew lager beer in 1885.

As late as the 1960s, there were 16 breweries in Edinburgh alone. But Scottish brewing was devastated by mergers and takeovers even more effectively than in England. From the ashes of dozens of closures, two giants, Scottish & Newcastle and Tennent Caledonian, appeared and rapidly dominated the country with lager and keg beers. But choice and tradition have made a sturdy comeback. Today, Scotland, from the Borders to Orkney and Shetland, has around 36 craft breweries. Some concentrate on traditional 'Heavies', while newer arrivals have introduced Scottish drinkers to paler and hoppier brews.

Belhaven 80 Shilling/St Andrews Ale

Source: Belhaven Brewing Co, Dunbar, East Lothian, Scotland
Strength: 4.2%/4.9%
Website: www.belhaven.co.uk

TASTING NOTES
Appearance
Aroma
Taste
Overall score

TASTING NOTES
Appearance
Aroma
Taste
Overall score

Benedictine monks built a monastery with its own brewery in the 14th century on land close to the sea and the English border. The community that developed around the monastery became the small harbour town of Belhaven. Brewing on the same site restarted in 1719 and continues in mellow brownstone buildings that

once included a maltings. Belhaven's ales were exported widely and were prized in London and Vienna, where the Emperor praised them as 'the Burgundy of Scotland'. James Boswell, Dr Samuel Johnson's travelling companion and biographer, described the brewery's ale as 'the best small beer ever tasted'.

Today's Belhaven's 80 Shilling Ale is considered to be the classic of the style. It is brewed with Pipkin pale, black and crystal malts with liquid brewing sugar. The colour units are 33. Whitbread Goldings Variety hops are used for bitterness, Fuggles and Goldings for aroma. Bitterness units are 29. The beer is renowned for its luscious tart gooseberry fruit aroma and palate, balanced by toasted malt and spicy hops. Rich grain, tangy fruit and hop resins dominate the palate, with a finish that is dry, with good hop notes but dominated by nutty malt and a continuing presence of gooseberry fruit.

The original label of St Andrews Ale showed the Saltire, Scotland's flag. According to a legend, in 832AD, the Scottish army under King Angus mac Fergus was preparing for battle against the troops of Athelstane, King of Northumbria. On the eve of the battle, the Scots soldiers saw a cloud formation that resembled the cross of St Andrew, their patron saint. They duly went on to score a major victory the following day. The beer that commemorates this historic event is brewed with Pipkin pale, black and crystal malts, with liquid brewing sugar. The colour is 35. Fuggles, Goldings and WGV hops are used and create 36 units of bitterness. It is the only beer in the Belhaven range that is dry hopped in cask, and this gives it a big peppery note from aroma to finish. Toasted and nutty grain and tart fruit are also evident on aroma and palate, with a long, bitter-sweet finish packed with rich grain and fruit notes that finally becomes dry and bitter.

Grant's Scottish Ale

Source: Grant's Yakima Brewing and Malting Company, Yakima, Washington State, USA

Strength: 5.6%

Website: www.grants.com

TASTING NOTES
Appearance
Aroma
Taste
Overall score

The first beer Bert Grant made when he opened his brewery in Yakima was a Scottish Ale, on the grounds that he was a Scot by birth. This was factually correct, though his sojourn in Dundee was brief, as his parents moved to Canada when he was still a baby. Bert was nevertheless proud of his roots and on occasion would surprise customers in his brew-pub, who were more used to Stetsons and six guns, by turning up in the full Scottish regalia of kilt and tam-o'-shanter.

Bert described his Scottish Ale as 'the best beer in the world': Bert didn't lack chutzpah. It has the amber colour and generous nutty roastiness of dark crystal malt but is, perhaps, a shade too hoppy to be genuinely Scottish in style. But it is difficult not to end up with a hop-accented beer if you use Cascades in the kettle and Willamettes for dry hopping in cask or keg. It has a mighty 45 units of bitterness. It may or may not be, depending on your vote, the best beer in the world but it is certainly one of the bitterest. It has a rich sultana fruitiness balanced by pungent hop resins on the nose, with more dark fruit, roasted grain and tangy hops in the mouth. The finish is long and complex, with vinous fruit, nuts and roast and a big punch of bitter hops.

Harviestoun Bitter & Twisted

Source: Harviestoun Brewery, Alva, Clackmannanshire, Scotland
Strength: 3.8%
Website: None

TASTING NOTES
Appearance
Aroma
Taste
Overall score

Bitter & Twisted won CAMRA's title of Supreme Champion Beer of Britain in 2003, an award that turned the media spotlight on the advances made by small craft breweries in Scotland. Harviestoun has been brewing since 1985 and at first concentrated on beers that were firmly in the Scottish tradition. But in recent years owner Ken Brooker has redefined his product range and is reaching out to a younger audience with beers that are paler and have a strong hop presence.

Ken is an Englishman – though he now wears a kilt on formal occasion – and came to Scotland from Dagenham to work as a representative of the Ford Motor Company. He had been a keen home brewer for years, and when he got bored with selling cars, he set up a small brewery in an old cow byre on a farm in Dollar. In 2004, the success of the company allowed Ken to move into custom-built premises in Alva, where he has a production line of 50 to 60 barrels. Ken has

a dry sense of humour – he uses Hersbrucker hops, for example, in his multi-award winning cask lager, Schiehallion – but he was not in a laughing mood when he named Bitter & Twisted. He had lost an appeal against a conviction for speeding and was feeling distinctly bitter and twisted – Essex man's version of angry – when he launched his new beer.

It is brewed with Pipkin pale and crystal malts, with 16% wheat and a small amount of oats: the recipe should satisfy Scottish traditionalists. The hops are Challenger and Hallertauer Hersbrucker for bitterness and Styrian Goldings for aroma. The colour rating is 10, bitterness 30. The beer has a rich creamy malt and spicy hop bouquet with underlying tangy citrus fruit. Hop resins and citrus fruit attack the tongue with a mellow but firm malt note. The long and deep finish is packed with fruity hop character and juicy malt. It is a splendidly refreshing beer.

Innis & Gunn Oak Aged Beer

Source: Innis & Gunn Brewing Co, Edinburgh, Scotland
Strength: 6.6%
Website: www.innisandgunn.com

This remarkable beer marries the techniques of both brewing and whisky distilling. Whisky, wine and Cognac are the drinks most closely associated with ageing in wood. It is now rare in the world of beer, though the lambic beers of Belgium (see page 240) are stored in wood for up to three years in casks bought from the port wine and Cognac makers. Innis & Gunn has restored the tradition.

Dougal Sharp is the former head brewer at the Caledonian Brewery, while his father, Russell, founded Caledonian and also worked for the whisky maker Chivas Regal, where he made a study of oak ageing. The Sharps developed their beer in association with the distiller William Grant & Sons. Grants aroused the interest of the brewing industry when the distiller bought beer to assist in developing its Cask Reserve Scotch Whisky. The beer was brewed solely to age the casks but Dougal Sharp was intrigued by the flavour and decided to make a commercial oak-aged beer. His beer enjoys a 77-day maturation process, 10 times the average for ale. This includes a 30-day rest period in lightly toasted American white oak casks, the preferred wood for maturing wine and spirits. After 30 days, the beer continues to age in a 'marrying tun', where the flavours infuse and mellow, and natural carbonation takes place.

The beer is brewed with Golden Promise pale and crystal malts, and is hopped with the Phoenix variety. It has a luscious amber colour, a dense and lasting collar of foam, and a tightly beaded, Champagne-style carbonation. The aroma is smoky and oaky, underscored by ripe malt, vanilla and

tart hops. There is more smoky malt on the palate with a blast of orange fruit and earthy hop resins, while the lingering finish is bitter-sweet, with an intriguing hint of Cognac. It is sold only in bottle, though a cask-conditioned version has been made available for CAMRA beer festivals. The beer, launched in 2003, made history by winning gold medals in two categories and the overall Supreme Champion prize at the 2004 International Beer Competition. In the same year the beer collected the Safeway Consumer Beer of the Year award.

TASTING NOTES
Appearance
Aroma
Taste
Overall score

TASTING NOTES

Appearance
Aroma
Taste
Overall score

TASTING NOTES

Appearance
Aroma
Taste
Overall score

Islay Saligo Ale

Source: Islay Ales, Islay, Scotland
Strength: 4.4%
Website: www.islayales.com

Islay is world-famous for its whiskies and the island has seven distilleries, including the sublime Laphroaig. When Paul Hathaway, Paul Capper and Walter Schobert came to settle on the island, they brought with them a love of beer and whisky, and they decided to use the famously peaty waters of the island to make beer. Walter is from Germany and he has written extensively about both beer and whisky. Islay Ales was launched in 2003 and, in such a romantic spot, is based on an extremely unromantic former tractor shed on a farm. Beers are produced in both cask and bottle-fermented versions for sale to visitors to the island and further afield. A visitor centre for the brewery is planned. The beers are named after landmarks and beauty spots on the island, such as Dun Hogs Head, Loch Finlaggan and Black Rock.

Saligo takes its name from Saligo Bay on the west coast of the island. It is brewed with pale, lager and wheat malts and hopped with Bramling Cross and Goldings. It has a pale bronze colour and a ripe pear and apricot aroma, balanced by juicy malt and peppery hops. Bitter, spicy hops burst across the tongue, balanced by sappy malt and tangy fruit. The finish is bitter but not dry, with a good balance of juicy malt, hop resins and fruit. And underpinning all the flavours there is a light but distinct hint of peat from the water.

Orkney Dark Island

Source: Orkney Brewery, Quoyloo,
Sandwick, Orkney, Scotland
Strength: 4.6%
Website: www.orkneybrewery.co.uk

Roger White has won so many awards for his beers that it seems a pity he can't taste them, as he is teetotal. In all my travels, I have never come across another teetotal brewer. I look upon Roger as the Beethoven of the beer world, composing beautiful symphonies from malts and hops, but in common with the deaf maestro, unable to enjoy them to the full.

Roger is an engineer by trade and opened Orkney's first brewery for 50 years in 1988 in a former schoolhouse. At first he brewed only keg beers, as locals preferred cold, fizzy drinks. On one trip to the island I was told in no uncertain terms by sailors on the ferry: 'We don't drink that real ale!' But Roger built up good sales on the mainland and even across the border into England and, more for visitors than locals, now sells his beer properly cask conditioned in several Orkney bars and hotels. His success enabled him to expand in 1994 and can now brew 150 barrels at a time. The beers celebrate the island and its Viking past: the strong Skullsplitter, for example, is named after Thorfin Hausakliuuf, the seventh Viking earl of the island.

Dark Island is a true ruby-red Scottish 'Heavy' and is brewed with Maris Otter pale, chocolate and crystal malts, torrefied wheat and cane sugar: 100–120 units of colour. Omega hops for bitterness and Goldings for aroma contribute 20–24 units of bitterness. It has a fruity blackcurrant aroma with roasted grain and earthy hop resins. Dark roasted grain dominates the mouth along with peppery hop notes and tart fruit. The complex finish has vinous fruit, hop resins and rich dark grain, finally becoming dry but not overly bitter.

Wheat Beers

Munich & Bavaria

The Bavarians are famous not only as great consumers of beer but also as the people who have kept faith with the world's oldest beer law, the Reinheitsgebot. The 'Purity Pledge' of 1516 stipulates that only barley, water and yeast can be used in brewing. You will notice that wheat is missing. The reason is simple: it was the Bavarian royal family, the House of Wittelsbach, who drew up the terms of the Reinheitsgebot and their attitude was not altruistic.

The Bavarian royals drank wheat beer and they were determined that no one else should join them. The masses could make do with brown beers made from wood-cured malts but the princes and their families would enjoy the paler delights of wheat beer. The monarchy, in feudal fashion, held the monopoly to grow both barley and wheat, and refused to release wheat for brewing for the hoi polloi.

The Royal Court Brewery, the Hofbräuhaus, opened in Munich in 1589 to make wheat beer. At one stage there were 30 royal brewhouses in Bavaria dedicated to making the style for the aristocracy. Wheat beer only became available for general consumption in 1859, when the royal family licensed a Munich brewer named Georg Schneider to brew it: perhaps the royals were beginning to switch allegiance to the new lager beer brewed at Sedlmayr's Spaten brewery. Once wheat beer became available to the masses its sales soared. Schneider moved to new premises in the Tal (the Dale) close to Munich's Gothic town hall, the Rathaus, and demand forced him to open a second brewery at Kelheim in the heart of the Hallertau hop-growing region.

Many Bavarian brewers followed in Schneider's footsteps and added wheat beer to their range. But, by the late 20th century, the domination of the market by golden lager sent sales of wheat beer into steep and apparently terminal decline. In the 1970s, a German newspaper described it dismissively as a beer 'fit only for old ladies and those with nervous stomachs'. But a decade later, wheat beer enjoyed a remarkable revival. It was discovered by the young 'green generation', who believed that a beer sold mainly in bottle with natural yeast sediment and which was rich in protein was healthier than lager beer. Sales of wheat beer grew to such an extent that by the 1990s they accounted for 30% of the Bavarian beer market.

In spite of the name, wheat beer is made by a blend of wheat and barley malts. In Bavaria, wheat malt by law must make up at least half of the grain used in brewing wheat beer. Barley malt is essential, as it has a greater level of the enzymes that turn starch into fermentable sugar. Barley also has a husk that acts as a filter during mashing. Wheat is a huskless grain and is difficult to brew with, as it can become mushy and clog up the brewing vessels: the presence of barley malt in the mash prevents this happening. The main contribution wheat malt makes to beer is an appealing pale and hazy gold/yellow colour, and a characteristic aroma and flavour of spices and fruit: clove is the dominant spice, while apple and banana are typical fruit aromas.

Bavarian wheat beers also have a flavour characteristic that resembles bubblegum or Juicy Fruit. This is the result of the special yeast cultures used in its production. During fermentation, the yeast produces natural compounds called phenols and guaiacols that resemble the sap produced by tropical trees used in the manufacture of chewing gum. Hops are used sparingly, as bitterness and the floral and piny nature of hops do not blend well with the aromas and flavours produced by wheat and its special yeast cultures.

In Bavaria, the style is known either as Weizenbier – wheat beer – or Weisse, which means white and comes from the pale colour of the beer and its white collar of foam. In spite of the descriptor 'white', wheat beers come in dark

– dunkel – versions as well as pale ones, and in varying strengths, including strong Weizenbocks. Most brewers produce two versions of wheat beers: Hefe or Mit Hefe, which means 'with yeast'; and Kristall or Ohne Hefe, which mean clear or without yeast. The unfiltered versions are by far the most popular and flavourful. Connoisseurs like to pour the beer slowly until the glass is almost full, then twirl the bottle and deposit the sediment of yeast in the glass. This is performed with great and even dramatic skill by experienced waiters.

*Visitors to Munich will find the original Hofbräuhaus at 9 Platzl. It is now owned by the government and no longer brews on the premises. Beer is supplied by a brewery on the outskirts of the city. The Schneider Weisshaus is at 10 Tal, close to the Marienplatz. The brewery was destroyed in World War Two and beer is now supplied by the Schneider brewery in Kelheim.

Berlin

When Napoleon's troops reached Berlin, they described the local wheat beers as the 'Champagne of the North'. It was a fitting and perceptive description, for the Chardonnay and Pinot grapes of the Champagne region produce such a tart wine that it becomes drinkable only as the result of a long, slow process in which a secondary fermentation in bottle involves some lactic activity and finally becomes sparkling. Berliner Weisse beers are so tart and lactic that drinkers add a dash of woodruff or

raspberry syrup to cut the acidity. The style is traditionally low in alcohol, around 3%, is extremely pale in colour, has a light fruitiness and little hop aroma.

The origins of the style are unknown but one theory is that Huguenots fleeing persecution in the 16th and 17th centuries picked up the skill of brewing sour beer as they migrated north from France and Switzerland through Flanders, where they came across lambic and gueuze beers made by spontaneous fermentation.

Weisse was brewed by no fewer than 700 producers in the Berlin area at the height of its popularity. Today there are just two breweries left. The lactic cultures that work with a conventional warm-fermenting yeast to produce the style were isolated early in the 20th century by scientists who founded Berlin's university research and brewing school, the Versuchs und Lehranstadt für Brauerei, or VLB for short. The culture is named lactobacillus delbrücki after Professor Max Delbrück, the leading research scientist who studied the culture.

In Berlin bars, Weisse is served in a number of attractive glasses, some – most fittingly – shaped like a Champagne saucer. The beer is served with a Schuss, or shot of syrup, that, depending on the colour, will turn the beer red, green or amber: glasses of all three on the table will bring forth a joke among drinkers about traffic lights. Waiters will put a finger to the temple if you decline the syrup. My first-ever taste of Berliner Weisse was in a bar in Amsterdam, an equally cosmopolitan city to Berlin. I persuaded the waiter to serve it *au naturel*. It tasted like the health drink PLJ, or Pure Lemon Juice, and I was happy to add a shot of woodruff.

LEFT
The wheat beer from the Holy Stephen Brewery near Munich is highly regarded and comes from the oldest brewery in the world.

Berliner Kindl Weiss

Source: Berliner Kindl Brauerei, Neu Kölln, Berlin, Germany
Strength: 2.7%
Website: www.Berliner-kindl.de

The Kindl brewery dates from 1872 and is a magnificent example of the Bauhaus school of minimalist and functional architecture and design founded by Walter Gropius in 1919. Although the Nazis closed the Bauhaus school in 1933, the ideas live on in such masterpieces as Templehof airport and at Kindl. In fact, the copper vessels at the brewery were seized by the Russian Red Army and sent to the Soviet Union at the end of World War Two. But the plant was rebuilt along classic Bauhaus lines and copper was used rather than modern stainless steel.

Kindl uses well water, which is softened for brewing. The proportion of wheat malt is around 30%. Bitterness units measure a modest 10 from Northern Brewer hops, but the brewer is not looking for high bitterness. After mashing and boiling, the lactobacillus is added to start acidification, followed by a warm-fermenting yeast culture. Fermentation lasts for a week followed by several days of cold conditioning. The beer is then filtered, bottled with a fresh dosage of yeast and kräusened with partially fermented wort. The finished beer has a hazy pale gold colour with a complex and intriguing aroma of fresh lemons and rose petals. It is mouth-puckeringly acidic on the palate with a big lemon fruit bite and no discernible hop character. The finish is short, acidic and with a further blast of tart fruit.

The brewery is now part of the national Binding group but 'economies of scale' have not yet endangered weiss beer production.

TASTING NOTES
Appearance
Aroma
Taste
Overall score

Franziskaner Weissbier

Source: Gabriel Sedlmayr Spaten-Franziskaner-Bräu, Munich, Bavaria, Germany
Strength: 5%
Website: www.franziskaner.com

In Munich, the Spaten brewery has seen its world turned upside down. It is famous as the site where Gabriel Sedlmayr, a member of the ruling family, developed commercial lager brewing in the 19th century, but it now devotes half its capacity to wheat beer. They are sold under the Franziskaner label and have a separate website to avoid any confusion with Spaten's Pils and other lager brands.

The bottle labels for Franziskaner show a cheerful monk holding a mug of beer. The original wheat beer brewery was bought by Joseph Sedlmayr. The site dates from 1363 and was one of the oldest in Munich. It was next door to a Franciscan monastery, which gave its name and image to the beer. Joseph Sedlmayr eventually closed the site and merged with brother Gabriel's Spaten site. Production of wheat beer and lager are kept separate to avoid any cross fertilisation of yeast cultures.

Weissbier has a high wheat malt content of 75%. The brewers admit this can cause problems during mashing but they feel it gives a better flavour. The other Franziskaner beers, including Dunkel (dark) and Bock (strong) are made more conventionally from a 50:50 blend barley and wheat malts. A complex hop recipe is used of Orion, Perle, Spalt and Tettnang varieties. Fermentation takes place in conical vessels. The beer that emerges is centrifuged to remove the ale yeast and is re-seeded with a lager culture for bottle fermentation. Spaten is not alone in using a lager yeast in bottle, as brewers feel it gives greater stability and shelf life, though at some small cost to flavour. Still, the beer has a fruity aroma with hints of coriander. Creamy malt dominates the mouth but with powerful hints of spice and banana. The finish is long, quenching, spicy and fruity.

TASTING NOTES
Appearance
Aroma
Taste
Overall score

Hopf Export

Source: Hopf Weissbierbrauerei, Miesbach, Obberbayern, Bavaria, Germany
Strength: 5.3%
Website: www.hopsweisse.de

TASTING NOTES
Appearance
Aroma
Taste
Overall score

I have made many journeys in the quest for good beer but few have been more memorable than the trip from Munich to Miesbach in Obberbayern, or Upper Bavaria, a region of snow-capped mountains and deep, tree-fringed lakes. Hans Hopf, the owner of the family brewery, has a name marketing companies would drool over, for Hopf is almost identical to *Hopfen*, the German for hops. He even employs a brewmaster called Robert Weizbauer at a company that brews nothing but Weizenbier. And all this brilliant public relations comes free!

Hans's family started to brew in the Bavarian town of Garmish-Partenkirchen, where the arena for Hitler's Winter Olympics has been left as a grim reminder of that terrible period. The family moved to Miesbach in the 1930s. When I visited the brewery, production was running at 45,000 hectolitres (990,000 gallons) a year. Hans thinks that demand for his beers at home and abroad – they are available in the United States – will see volumes grow to 70,000 hectos (1½m gallons) but he would not want to go beyond that figure. He has a horror of getting too big and becoming prey to a bigger brewing combine. The brewhouse has already been extended to keep pace with demand, and old copper vessels nestle alongside modern stainless-steel ones.

Hans and Robert have access to the purest Alpine spring water and use French and German malts. Wheat malt accounts for 65% of the mash. Hops come from the Hallertau and are mainly the Spalt variety. The unusually shaped fermenting vessels look like a cross between Michelin men and the Daleks from the British TV science fiction series *Dr Who*. The stainless-steel vessels are closed save for openings like visors at the top, where the yeast can be seen vigorously at work. After primary fermentation, the beer in bottles and kegs is cooled to 10–15°C (50–59°F) to enable a second fermentation to start, encouraged by kräusening with wort from the brewhouse. The beer is kept at 12°C (54°F) for a week to purge diacetyl – toffee flavours – and the temperature is then raised to 15°C (59°F) for three weeks. A blend of both top and bottom yeasts is used for secondary fermentation.

Hopf Export, the main brand, has 12 units of bitterness and a vast peppery and spicy aroma, overlain by banana and bubblegum. It is tart and spicy in the mouth, with rich and creamy malt, and has a long, quenching, fruity and spicy finish. Banana is very evident in the finish and is much relished in the bars in and round Miesbach.

Matilda Bay Redback

Source: Matilda Bay Brewing Company, North Fremantle, Western Australia, Australia

Strength: 4.8%

Website: www.matildabay.com.au

Matilda Bay was the creation of Philip Sexton, a former brewer with Swan. He installed a brewery in the Sail and Anchor pub in Fremantle in 1984 and created such demand for his beers that he opened the Matilda Bay micro-brewery in neighbouring Nedlands. In 1988, with Aus$4m of investment from the Carlton/Foster's group, a brand new brewery was added in Perth in a former Ford Motor Company building. The brewing equipment made a long journey, from the De Clerck brewery in northern France.

Matilda Bay was the first new brewery in Australia since World War Two and is thought to be the first to make wheat beer. Redback is named after a dangerous and extremely poisonous spider but the name did not deter drinkers. The refreshing nature of the beer in a hot country and its sharply different flavours from mainstream lagers created a large following. Redback is made from 65% malted wheat, grown in the Avon Valley with two-row barley malt (colour units eight). The hops are European Saaz and locally grown Pride of Ringwood (18 units of bitterness).

The beer has a fruity aroma with hints of spice and some gentle hop bitterness. Tart fruit and spices build in the mouth, with a rich creamy malt note. The finish is long with spices and tart fruit dominating, but there are some lingering light hop resins. In 1993, Redback was named Supreme Champion in the Australian International Beer Awards and it won a gold medal in the AIBA in 2003. The beer brewed in Western Australia is filtered but a new brewery in Melbourne produces a bottle-fermented version.

TASTING NOTES
Appearance
Aroma
Taste
Overall score

REDBACK & PRAWNS
~ AUSTRALIA'S CULINARY COAT OF ARMS ~

Schneider Weisse/Aventinus

Source: Privatbrauerei G Schneider & Sohn, Kelheim, Bavaria, Germany
Strength: 5.4%/8%
Website: www.Schneider-weisse.com

TASTING NOTES
Appearance
Aroma
Taste
Overall score

TASTING NOTES
Appearance
Aroma
Taste
Overall score

The Kelheim brewery is a curious but pleasing blend of Spanish and Gothic architecture. It was built in 1607 and is almost certainly the oldest continuous wheat beer brewery in the world. It is the tradition that the sons of the Schneider family are called Georg in order to maintain a link with the founder of the company. I met Georg V, his elegant wife Margareta who is in charge of public relations, and their son Georg VI, who, since my visit, has taken charge.

The brewery has open fermenters, a rare sight in Germany, where the fear of wild yeasts and contamination keeps most beers covered. Production is divided 90% for Weisse beer and 10% for Aventinus. Malts are blended in the proportion 60% wheat and 40% barley. Some Vienna and darks are added to give the Weisse its appealing bronze/copper colour. Hersbrucker hops from the neighbouring Hallertau are used in pellet form. Weisse has 14–15 units of bitterness. Water comes from local wells and is softened to remove some of the natural salts.

The modern brewhouse was installed in 1988 with stainless-steel mashing vessels and kettles standing on marble floors. In the fermenting hall, the atmosphere is ripe with fruity aromas as the yeast goes to work on the sugars. Banana is the most obvious of the Weisse aromas, with a powerful waft of apple as well. Fermentation lasts for between three and five days, after which the unfiltered beer is bottled at warm temperature. Yeast – the house culture, not a lager strain – and some unfermented wort are added. The beer is matured at 20°C (68°F) for a week. This produces a lively carbonation as secondary fermentation begins. The beer then has 14 days of cold conditioning at 8°C (46°F) to stabilise it. The beer that finally leaves the brewery has a pronounced banana, cloves and nutmeg aroma with a tart, spicy and slightly acidic flavour in the mouth. The quenching finish has creamy malt, spices, fruit and gentle hop notes.

Aventinus is a Weizenbock, or strong wheat beer, with a label depicting Johannes Aventinus, the historian of Bavaria. The beer is bronze-red due to the use of caramalt (43 colour units) and has a rich spices, raisins and chocolate aroma and palate, with more spices, fruit and cloves in the finish. Schneider prefers its beers to be drunk within eight months but says they will remain in drinkable condition for eight years if they are kept cool in a dark place.

Georg Schneider VI told me Aventinus tastes like port wine after 25 years. He must have started drinking at an early age.

Schultheiss Berliner Weisse

Source: Schultheiss Brauerei, Hohenschönhausen, Berlin, Germany
Strength: 3%
Website: www.oetker.com

Since Berlin became one city again following the reunification of Germany, Schultheiss has closed two of its plants and moved production of its beers to a brewery dating from 1902 in the former eastern sector. The company became part of the national Brau und Brunnen group. In January 2004, the group's brewing interests, which includes a large brewery in Dortmund as well, was bought by the giant food and drinks combine Oetker. As Weisse accounts for a tiny proportion of Schultheiss's production, there is concern for the future of Berlin's second example of the style.

The beer is made by a blend of equal amounts of malted barley and wheat. Hallertau hop varieties create four to eight units of bitterness. Warm fermenting yeast and lactobacilli are blended together with a portion of wort that is between three and six months old. The blend encourages a lively fermentation that lasts for three or four days. The beer is warm conditioned for three to six months and is then kräusened and lactobacillus added for bottling. The result is an astonishingly complex, fruity, sour and quenching beer, with tart lemon fruit and floral notes on the aroma, stunning acidity and tangy fruit in the mouth and a dry, tart finish with more citrus fruit notes. As the beer is bottle fermented it will improve with age.

It would be tragedy if mergers in the German brewing industry were to rob drinkers of this classic beer. It would be advisable to lay in a stock and store it in a cellar.

Weihenstephaner Hefe Weissbier

Source: Weihenstephan Brauerei, Freising, Munich, Germany
Strength: 5.4%
Website: www.weihenstephaner.de

The 'Holy Stephen' brewery – the oldest brewery in the world – has already featured in this book with its superb Pilsener (see page 32). But it is primarily a wheat beer brewery and produces several versions of the style, including a Dunkel, or dark, beer and a filtered Kristall.

Its most revered beer is the unfiltered 'Hefe', or yeast beer. It is made from a blend of French and German barley and wheat malts, and is lightly hopped with varieties from the Hallertau region. The hazy orange/gold beer has a rich and tempting aroma of banana, cloves, nutmeg and gentle hop resins. Creamy malt fills the mouth, balanced by fruit and spices, with a long, refreshing, complex finish in which ripe malt competes with the growing influence of spices and fruit, with a late hint of hops.

The brewhouse is modern but the narrow windows with curved tops give an ecclesiastic touch that recalls the history of the complex of buildings that has been sacked, stripped of its religious roots, controlled by the Bavarian royal family and now by the state. One beer, Korbinian, recalls a legend about the founder of the monastery, an Irish Benedictine. He was en route to the Vatican when a bear ate his horse, which made the journey to Rome even more daunting. The monk, no doubt with some help from above, tamed the bear and made it carry his bags to the holy city. Today students make even longer journeys to the brewing faculty at Freising. It was encouraging to see young people from North America and the Far East attending classes and acquiring the skills to make good beer for future generations to enjoy.

TASTING NOTES
Appearance
Aroma
Taste
Overall score

TASTING NOTES
Appearance
Aroma
Taste
Overall score

Belgian-style Wheat Beers

While Bavarian wheat beers have enjoyed a remarkable recovery, their equivalents in Belgium have become cult drinks. The 'white beers' of the Brabant region – known as *bière blanche* or *wit bier* – were once a major beer style but it had all but disappeared until its fortunes were revived by Pierre Celis in the town of Hoegaarden.

Hoegaarden is a small town but in the 19th century it had no fewer than 30 breweries producing wheat beer. The town had its own brewers' guild and it exported its products to other parts of the Low Countries. Brabant has rich soil that produces an abundance of barley, oats and wheat, and farmers, peasants and monks took the products of the fields to fashion their beers. Monks were brewing in the region in the 15th century.

The beers took on a distinctive character when Dutch traders brought back spices from the east. The country known today as Belgium was part of the Netherlands at the height of Dutch seafaring, and spices and other exotic ingredients found their way into the cuisine of the Low Countries and its drinks. At a time when hops were used either sparingly or not at all in beer, coriander seeds and orange peel not only added spice but also countered the richness and inherent sweetness of malt. As in England, the habit of adding herbs and spices to beer continued for several centuries after the wide-scale adoption of the hop for bitterness.

The spices also balanced the sourness of the early white beers, which were made by spontaneous fermentation, allowing wild yeasts to turn malt sugars into alcohol. This style of natural fermentation survives in the lambic and gueuze beers of the Senne Valley area but it was once in wider use. White beers were also fermented in wood where they would have picked up additional sour notes from lactobacilli.

White beers today are brewed conventionally using warm-fermenting ale yeast cultures. The success of Hoegaarden has been a double-edged sword: it has brought the world's attention to the cloudy, quenching, spicy and complex beers of Belgium but, in an age of slick marketing and big brewers' insatiable quest for ever bigger volumes, it has also led to beers with less character in order to appeal to drinkers who find complexity too challenging.

As in Bavaria, the labelling of Belgian wheat beers can be confusing. As well as *bière blanche* or *wit bier*, they are also known as *bière de froment* or *tarwebier*, the French and the Flemish respectively for wheat beer.

LEFT
The symbol of a snail on the label suggests Troublette is slow brewed. It is an excellent example of the new breed of spicy Belgian wheat beers.

L'Abbaye des Rocs Blanche des Honnelles

Source: Brasserie de l'Abbaye des Rocs, Montignies-sur-Roc, Belgium
Strength: 6%
Website: www.abbaye-des-rocs.com

In spite of the impressive name, this is not a monastic brewery. It began life in the garage of the owner of a farm that, centuries ago, was a monastery: there are still a few ruins in the vicinity. The brewery is in a village in Hainaut province, close to Mons and the French border.

From tiny beginnings, the brewery has grown and for a time was run as a co-operative but has since been turned into a limited company. It is best known for its Abbaye des Rocs abbey beer, one of the better examples of beers that trade on the Trappist tradition.

All the beers are unfiltered and re-ferment in the bottle, and they also use pure local well water with no sugars or additives. Abbaye des Rocs has restored the tradition of using malted oats in its wheat beer, which adds a smooth, creamy and slightly oily note. It is strong for the style, is a hazy blond colour and has an appetising aroma of ripe or even overripe fruit, with orange and lemon to the fore. Hops give a pronounced peppery note to the aroma and palate, and the finish lingers, with delicious tangy fruit (orange-and-lemon slices) and juicy and creamy malt. The beer is named after two small local rivers called the Honnelles.

TASTING NOTES
Appearance
Aroma
Taste
Overall score

La Caracole Troublette

Source: Brasserie la Caracole, Falmignoul, Belgium
Strength: 5%
Website: www.caracole.be

The snail (*caracole*) symbol used on the label of La Caracole's beers does not suggest that trouble is brewing, but troublette is a brewing term implying haze, or turbidity, in beer. Perhaps the snail – the symbol of the Namur region – was too slow to get the proteins out of the beer.

The brewery was founded by childhood friends Jean-Pierre Debras and François Tonglet in 1990 in Namur, but four years later they moved to Falmignoul in the Meuse Valley near Dinant. They found an ancient brewery dating from around 1776 that last brewed in 1971. The friends painstakingly restored the site and still use wood-fired mash tuns and coppers, with help from the plentiful supply of wood in the Ardennes forest. Wood, says Debras, a graduate of Leuven University's brewing faculty, has to be used with enormous care: if it flares, it will caramelise the brewing sugars and darken beers that are meant to be pale. La Troublette comes in two versions: regular and 'bio', or organic. The regular beer is brewed with pale malt and Saaz and Styrian hops varieties, while organic Spalt from Germany go into the bio version. Both beers are unfiltered and re-ferment in the bottle. They have a luscious tart and tangy lemon fruit aroma and palate, with a perfumy hop note that leads to some dryness in the finish. The Spalt hops give a spicier note to the bio beer. Both beers are wonderfully quenching.

TASTING NOTES
Appearance
Aroma
Taste
Overall score

Du Bocq Blanche de Namur

Source: Brasserie du Bocq, Purnode, Belgium
Strength: 4.5%
Website: www.bocq.be

TASTING NOTES
Appearance
Aroma
Taste
Overall score

Blanche de Namur is named after a princess from the Namur province who became the Queen of Sweden. I think Greta Garbo once starred in a film about her.

The beer comes from a brewery that, in common with many in Belgium, started life as a farm. In 1858, Martin Belot decided to brew beer for his family and farm workers, using grains from the field and pure water from a spring. It is still family-owned and fiercely independent today. After World War One, sales grew when du Bocq (the name comes from the local river) launched a brown ale called La Gaulloise. Farming stopped in 1960 as the family concentrated on its brewing operations. Production currently runs at 60,000 hectolitres (1.3m gallons) a year.

Blanche de Namur is brewed with malted barley and wheat, and spiced with coriander and bitter orange peel, with Belgian and German hop varieties. It has just five units of colour and 12 units of bitterness. In common with all the beers, Blanche de Namur is cold conditioned in the brewery for three to five weeks following fermentation, then bottled and warm conditioned for a few more weeks. It has a pleasing bouquet of coriander, bitter oranges and spicy hops. Mellow malt builds in the mouth with spices and orange fruit, while the lingering finish is deeply refreshing, with creamy malt, tangy spice and tart fruit. The brewery is open to visitors: see website.

Hoegaarden

Source: Brouwerij Hoegaarden, Hoegaarden, Belgium
Strength: 5%
Website: www.InBev.com

The brand is so famous that it no longer needs to be called Wit: just Hoegaarden will do. This is the beer that rekindled the Belgian white beer phenomenon but, in so doing, a small craft brewery became part of a large Belgian group, Interbrew, that in turn became the world's biggest brewer, InBev.

In the 1960s, Pierre Celis, a milkman in Hoegaarden, who had done some part-time work as a child in the Tomsin brewery in the town, was musing over the loss of that brewery with friends in a bar and decided to start his own brewery. He opened on the site of a former farm and was scrupulous about using a true Brabant recipe: malted barley, unmalted wheat, oats, milled coriander seeds and dried Curaçao orange peel, with East Kent Goldings and Saaz hops. The beer quickly acquired cult status among students in nearby Leuven and then spread throughout Belgium and on to the Netherlands, France and Britain.

Following a fire at the site, Celis took financial help from Interbrew to rebuild it. It would be unfair on him to call the arrangement a Faustian pact, but Interbrew ended up controlling the company, while Celis left for Texas to launch a new brewery in the unlikely setting of Austin. As sales of Hoegaarden soared, Interbrew pumped money into the brewery. The artisan brewhouse on the ground floor, with attractive burnished copper vessels, has been joined by more modern and functional stainless-steel vessels on the first floor. Oats have been dropped from the grist, which is now comprised of 55% barley malt and 45% unmalted wheat. The hops create around 20

TASTING NOTES
Appearance
Aroma
Taste
Overall score

units of bitterness. Coriander seeds and orange peel are milled to coarse powders and added with the hops during the copper boil. Following fermentation, the green beer is warm conditioned for a month, primed with sugar and a dosage of fresh yeast, and then bottled or kegged. The beer has an appetising spicy nose with a clear hint of orange. It is tart and refreshing in the mouth, followed by a clean, bitter-sweet finish with hints of apple and orange zest.

Hoegaarden can be enjoyed in the smart Kouterhof bar and restaurant that is part of the brewery complex: for information on the restaurant and brewery visits, phone 016 769 811. The beer is undoubtedly less characterful than in the early days but at least InBev continues to brew it, unlike the white beer produced by Pierre Celis in Texas. He was bought out by American giant Miller, which produced a terrible pastiche of the beer for a short time and then closed the brewery. Celis has returned to Belgium where a reincarnation of his white is brewed for him by the Bios brewery.

Unibroue Blanche de Chambly
Source: Brasserie Unibroue, Chambly, Montréal, Québec, Canada
Strength: 5%
Website: www.unibroue.com

TASTING NOTES
Appearance
Aroma
Taste
Overall score

The first beer brewed by Unibroue in 1992 was this interpretation of a Belgian white beer. The founders worked closely with the Riva group from Belgium, best known for its Liefman's brown ales (see page 45) but which also produces a widely available white beer called Dentergems. The end result of the consultation was Blanche de Chambly, the success of which enabled the company to move to bigger premises and an enlarged brewhouse and fermenting capacity.

The beer is brewed with pale barley malt and unmalted wheat from Québec. The beer is lightly hopped, and spices and other aromatics are added during the copper boil. The beer is unfiltered and ferments in bottle. It is a pale, hazy yellow-gold colour, throws a big fluffy head of foam and has a superb aroma of tart lemon fruit, rich malt and heady spices. Citrus fruit and spices build in the mouth, with some light floral hop notes. Creamy malt is evident in the long, quenching finish, with spices and aromatics balancing the dominant citrus lemon character.

On the back of the success of Blanche de Chambly and the subsequent beers, Unibroue has expanded aggressively and has set up distributors in France (Unibroue France) and the United States (Unibrew USA).

Belgian Sour Red Beer

Just as lambic and gueuze beers are confined to the region of the Senne Valley, the sour red beers are a speciality of West Flanders. They are beers with sharp and stunning flavours, the result of maturation in unlined oak vessels. They are also mysterious beers: nobody is certain where the style originated. While sour red beers are fermented with brewers' yeast cultures rather than wild yeasts, there are nevertheless similarities with lambic and gueuze. On the other hand, before the Industrial Revolution transformed brewing, the practice of storing beer in oak vessels was widespread and was certainly not confined to the Low Countries. It is an intriguing thought that it may have been a visit to England and its porter brewers that encouraged the development of the style.

Rodenbach Grand Cru
Source: Brouwerij Rodenbach, Roeselare, Belgium
Strength: 6%
Website: www.rodenbach.be

TASTING NOTES
Appearance
Aroma
Taste
Overall score

My first-ever taste of Rodenbach Grand Cru was in a restaurant in Ostend. A fellow Brit warned me: 'You may not like it – it's very sour'. But it was a case of love at first sip. Ever since, in bars and restaurants in several countries, I will call for a Rodenbach if it is available, for I delight in its tart and refreshing character.

The brewery is in the canalside town of Roeselare (Roulers in French) and the beer is the result of long maturation in unlined oak tuns. Here is yet another link with brewing's past: this is a beer that is deliberately allowed to stale from the action of wild yeasts and other micro-organisms.

The Rodenbachs are German in origin, from near Koblenz. Ferdinand Rodenbach was stationed in the Low Countries as a military surgeon when the region was under Austrian rule and he decided to settle there. The Rodenbachs threw themselves with great energy into all aspects of Belgian life, including the struggle for independence.

In 1820, Alexander Rodenbach, who was blind, bought a small brewery in Roeselare. In the 1870s, another member of the family, Eugene, went to England to study brewing techniques and his experience encouraged him to develop the stale, aged beer that is the company's hallmark.

There has been considerable speculation about which breweries Rodenbach visited. It has been suggested that he might have gone to Greene King in Suffolk, where the soured Strong Suffolk Ale is brewed (see page 125).

On one visit to Rodenbach, I took some bottles of Strong Suffolk with me for a comparative tasting. As a result, the two breweries have struck up friendly links but Rodenbach says there is nothing in the archives to suggest Eugene Rodenbach visited Greene King. The company believes he may instead have gone to the Tyneside region of Northeast England. My research suggests that he probably went to the large brewery owned by John Barras, founded in Gateshead in 1770 and which moved to Newcastle in 1860 and later became part of Newcastle Breweries. Barras produced a renowned Porter that was stored for a full 12 months in wooden tuns. As the early porters were tawny or brown rather than black, I feel there is a strong possibility that the inspiration for Rodenbach's beer was the historic English style.

Rodenbach's St George's Brewery is a handsome complex on Spanjestraat. The grounds are dominated by an old malt kiln, which has been turned into a museum. Well water comes from underground springs beneath a lake on the other side of the road, where the brewer lives in some style in a chateau provided by the company.

The beer is made from a blend of pale malts from both spring and winter varieties, and slightly darker Vienna malt that gives the beer its reddish hue. Malts make up 80% of the grist, the rest comes from corn grits. German Brewers Gold and Kent Goldings hops are used: both are low in bitterness and high in aroma. Rodenbach uses them chiefly for their preservative qualities, as it does not want too high a level of bitterness, which would not marry well with the tartness of the beer. A multi-strain warm-fermenting yeast culture carries out primary fermentation over seven days, after which the beer has a second fermentation in metal tanks.

The beer for ageing that becomes Grand Cru is then stored in ceiling-high oak tuns for at least 18 months and often as long as two years. There are more than 10 halls of giant, red-hooped tuns that stand on raised brick bases. The staves of each tun are numbered and a small army of coopers is kept busy repairing the vessels. The insides of the tuns are scraped regularly to keep the correct balance of tannins and caramels present in the oak. During the long rest in wood, lactobacilli and acetobacters are busy adding a sour, lactic quality to the beer.

Two beers are produced. Rodenbach Klassiek (5%) is a blend of fresh young beer and stale. It has a sour, winey aroma, is tart and quenching in the mouth, with more sour fruit in the finish. Grand Cru (units of colour 60, bitterness 14–18) is bottled straight from the oak tuns. The beer is bigger in all respects: oaky, woody, tannic and fruity with hints of vanilla. It is flash pasteurised. I have argued without success for an unpasteurised, bottle-fermented version. The beer is not only a superb companion for food but makes a formidable contribution to cooking.

In 1999, the Rodenbach family sold the company to the big ale brewery of Palm. This created fears about the future of the brands and, for a while, quality and consistency dipped. But more recently Grand Cru is back to its best and, with sales to the rest of Europe, the United States and Japan, it seems unlikely that Palm will lose this treasured brewery and its classic, historic beer.

Bières de Garde

Most of the beer consumed in France comes in the form of the unremarkable lagers of the Strasbourg region, with its Germanic roots and disputed boundaries. But many French people have discovered that in the flat lands between Calais and Lille there is a different tradition of farmhouse ales called bières de garde.

Translated into English, 'beer to keep' is identical to the German lager, meaning 'store'. However, the stored beers of northern France, in the Nord-Pas de Calais (comprising Artois, Flanders and Picardy), have different roots that pre-date rather than chime with the Industrial Revolution of the 19th century. Like the saisons of neighbouring Wallonia (see page 208), they were beers brewed in February and March and stored in wooden casks for summer drinking by farmers, their families and workers. In both the Calais region and in French-speaking Wallonia, farm labourers were once paid in kind, with beer and potatoes.

The French take beer seriously in an area that not only shares a common border with the Belgians but also where Flemish names abound and Lille was once the capital of medieval Flanders. One of the best known of the bières de garde brewers, Duyck, stresses the Flemish roots. Every summer, the people of Douai take to the streets for a festival celebrated with beer, a choice of drink that no doubt causes disbelief in wine-growing areas. But this is a vast area, with its flat landscape, lowering skies, marshes and rivers, that provides the essential ingredients for beer, not wine: fields of barley and hop orchards that straddle the border with Belgium. Beer is the natural drink of the people. They eat with it, they cook with it, and they welcome such special seasonal brews as Bière de mars (March beer) and Bière de Noël (Christmas beer) as joyously as Beaujolais Nouveau is greeted further south.

Beer was brewed not only for farm labourers but also for coal miners. The Lille area was once the great mining region of France but all the pits have closed and the beers of the region almost disappeared along with them. Two world wars in the 20th century ravaged Flanders and Picardy. Fields and breweries were destroyed. Invading armies took away copper vessels for the 'war effort'. The fields and their produce recovered but many of the brewery owners could not afford the costs of repair and were wary of new methods of brewing. At the same time, the big lager brewers of Strasbourg broke free of the region and began to dominate the whole of France. Today, Kronenbourg (owned by Scottish & Newcastle of Britain), Heineken from the Netherlands and InBev from everywhere on the planet have a stranglehold on beer consumption in France.

The beers of the north revived as a result of the worldwide interest in Belgian beers, a rediscovery of pride in the Pas de Calais, its history and cuisine, and the cult status of the Jenlain beers from Duyck among students in Lille from the 1970s. A consumer movement, Les Amis de la Bière (the Friends of Beer), was formed in 1986 to promote the products of the region. Being French, les Amis firmly reject any suggestion that they were inspired by CAMRA in Britain, but I suspect some cross-channel inspiration took place. As a result, existing breweries found encouragement and new producers sprang up to meet a demand for genuine French beer at home and abroad.

Bières de Garde are no longer seasonal brews, though such specialities as March and Christmas beers are by definition. A true member of the style should be made by warm fermentation, though some brewers use lager cultures but ferment at ale temperatures, or they may use lager yeast for bottle conditioning: as with some Bavarian wheat beer brewers, they talk in modern marketing terms about 'stability' and 'shelf life'. It is difficult to keep track of who uses what, as brewers seem to recant from time to time and return to the true path of traditional methods and ale yeasts. The beers are rich, malt accented, often spicy but not especially bitter. They come in blonde (pale), ambrée (amber), brune (brown) and rousse (russet) forms. Most importantly, in a vast country ground between the two millstones of wine and German-style lager, bières de garde have survived and revived.

TASTING NOTES

Appearance	
Aroma	
Taste	
Overall score	

TASTING NOTES

Appearance	
Aroma	
Taste	
Overall score	

Annoeullin Pastor Ale

**Source: Brasserie d'Annoeullin,
Annouellin, France
Strength: 6.5%
Website: None**

To find this rustic brewery, you enter through a courtyard off the town's square named in honour of General de Gaulle, who was born in Lille. Typically of the area, the brewery, founded in 1905, was once a farm, and owner Bertrand Leper's wife Yolande comes from another farm brewery at Flers. When they married, they merged the two breweries, a sort of exchange of rings writ large.

In common with many farm breweries in both France and Belgium, the mash tun doubles as the boiling copper. After mashing, the wort is clarified in a separate vessel and then returns to the tun to be boiled with hops. Fermentation takes place in horizontal tanks in cellars that were once cattle byres. Primary fermentation lasts a week, followed by two weeks of cold conditioning – *la garde*. Only pale malt is used in Pastor Ale, with Flemish and Saaz hops.

The Lepers had to revive the fortunes of a brewery that had existed for years on brewing weak table beer for families and even weaker, 2% beer for schools. He said that when the school beer was discontinued, truancy increased. In the mid-1970s, he formulated a strong bière de garde that became popular and turned the brewery into a profitable concern. Pastor Ale has nothing to do with clerics but is a pun on pastorale and the country origins of the brewery. For a time the label carried the line '*C'est une symphonie*', with a bow towards Beethoven's Pastorale Symphony, but the delightful joke has been discontinued.

The beer is golden with pronounced orange fruit and earthy hops on the nose, more tangy fruit in the mouth balanced by juicy malt, and a complex finish that is dry, fruity, malty and quite hoppy and bitter for the style. The brewery also produces a superb wheat beer called L'Angelus. Cases of beer can be bought from the brewery shop. Smaller quantities, along with other beers from the region, can be obtained from Aux Caves d'Annoeullin in the town square.

Castelain Ch'ti Blonde

**Source: Brasserie Castelain,
Bénifontaine, near Lens, France
Strength: 6.4%
Website: www.www.chti.com**

The word ch'ti is Picardy dialect, a corruption of '*c'est toi*', which roughly translates as 'it suits you'. In common usage, it has come to mean anybody or anything from this part of northern France. The brewery, as is typical in the region, started life on a farm in 1926. The Castelain family bought it in 1966 and Roland handed it on to his children Yves and Annick in the mid-1970s. It was a difficult time for small breweries. Many were closing, unable to withstand the onslaught of Strasbourg lagers. The brewery produced a weak beer of around 2% for miners to down in vast amounts after a shift underground. The small museum has a poster for the beer showing a grinning miner grasping a foaming pint with a slogan announcing it is a beer made for the workers by the workers. But the mines and the workers' way of life were disappearing and Yves Castelain knew he had to find a new audience for his beer in order to survive. In 1978, he brewed a strong, pale Christmas beer called Ch'ti, matured for eight weeks. It was well received and a year later became a regular brew. All the old beers were unceremoniously dumped, though the miner in his helmet remained on the label of Ch'ti. Amber and brown versions of Ch'ti followed.

The brewery today has attractive copper vessels in tiled surrounds, visible from the road outside. Ironically, the road is called rue Pasteur: Yves makes a point of not pasteurising his beers. A wooden carving of Saint Arnold, the patron saint of brewers, guards the brewhouse. Yves marks the saint's importance by also producing a Belgian-style abbey beer named in his honour. Ch'ti Blonde accounts for 60% of the brewery's production. Water comes from a well on site that is 40 metres deep. It is brewed with four malts of the French Esterel and Scarlett varieties in pale, Munich, caramalt and torrefied forms. The hop varieties are Flemish and German Hallertauer varieties, used for aroma rather than bitterness. The beer is fermented with a lager yeast culture but at a relatively warm temperature of 14°C (57°F). Primary fermentation lasts for eight days, and *la garde* (cold conditioning) for a minimum of six weeks. It is then filtered and bottled in attractive containers with drawn corks and wire cradles. The blonde has a rich biscuity, perfumy hop and citrus fruit aroma, with fruit and malt dominating the palate, followed by a lingering finish that is bitter-sweet with notes of tart fruit, juicy malt and spicy hops.

The brewery has grown from 3,000 hectolitres (66,000 gallons) in 1978 to 35,000 today. Sadly, the miner on the label went from black to grey and has now disappeared altogether.

La Choulette Ambrée

Source: Brasserie la Choulette, Hordain, France
Strength: 7.5%
Website: None

Alain Dhaussy has a passion not only for beer but also for the traditions of this part of France between Cambrai and Valenciennes. One of the traditions is a game called *la crosse en plain*, a type of golf in which a wooden ball, *la choulette*, is belted across the countryside. It was described in great detail by Zola in *Germinal* and inspired the French-Canadian game lacrosse. There are clubs and balls on display in the brewery's tasting room.

La Choulette is based in the former Bourgeois-Lecerf brewery, which dates from 1885. The owners made the disastrous decision to convert to lager production. They quickly discovered that the big lager brewers from Strasbourg could make it not necessarily better but cheaper, and they tied bars through loans and discounts. Alain, who had trained with a brewery in Douai, bought the redundant brewery in 1977, complete with attractive copper vessels in tiled surrounds.

His first beer was La Choulette Ambrée, launched in 1981 and still his biggest seller. Pale, Munich and caramalts are used, along with hops from Flanders and the German Hallertau. The russet-coloured beer throws a big fluffy head and has a spicy (coriander?), earthy hop resins and toffee-malt bouquet. Rich, slightly burnt grain and raisin fruit fill the mouth with a gentle hop balance. The finish is long and complex, bitter-sweet to begin but with a spicy dryness at the end, balanced by vinous fruits and chewy malt.

Alain is also a keen supporter of the French Revolution. He is equally famous for a golden Bière des Sans Culottes (6.5%), which honours the foot soldiers of the revolution, the urban poor who wore trousers, as they could not afford the culottes or silk breeches of the aristocracy. There is also an 8% Brassin Robespierre, which conjures forth jokes about not drinking too much of it in case you lose your head. In the fashion of the region, the beers are sold in attractive corked and cradled bottles.

TASTING NOTES
Appearance
Aroma
Taste
Overall score

Duyck Jenlain Ambrée
Source: Brasserie Duyck, Jenlain, France
Strength: 6.5%
Website: www.duyck.com

TASTING NOTES
Appearance
Aroma
Taste
Overall score

This is the beer that put bière de garde on the map as a classic style. It was known simply as Jenlain – the name of the village near Valenciennes – for many years but 'ambrée' was added when other Jenlain beers were added.

Four generations of the Duyck family have been involved in brewing. Léon Duyck was a farmer in Zeggers-Cappel in Flanders who added brewing to his other duties. He passed on his passion for beer to his son, Félix, who built a new brewery in farm buildings at Jenlain in 1922. He produced a bière de garde that eventually acquired the name Jenlain in the 1960s, when his son Robert took over. Robert was responsible for a considerable expansion of the site, which, now controlled by yet another son, Raymond, produces 90,000 hectolitres (2m gallons) a year. In spite of the size of the operation, every effort has been made to preserve the country farmhouse feel of the brewery, with production in traditional copper vessels.

Malts from Flanders, Champagne and Burgundy are used, along with four hop varieties from Belgium, France, Germany and Slovenia (25 units of bitterness). The russet-coloured beer has a spicy and fruity aroma, with biscuity malt, hints of vanilla and raisins in the mouth, and a long, complex finish that becomes dry with good spicy hops notes, tart fruit and sappy malt. For a time, Duyck experimented with lager yeast but has returned to the true path with an ale culture. The beer is filtered but not pasteurised and is sold throughout the world in attractive 75cl Champagne bottles with wired corks.

An abbey-style beer has joined the portfolio, along with Jenlain seasonal brands. In 2000, Duyck launched a Jenlain Blonde that was marketed in Britain as 'a lager-style beer'. After protests from myself and other beer writers, this affront to the noble heritage of classic French beer was withdrawn.

St Sylvestre 3 Monts

Source: Brasserie de St Sylvestre, St Sylvestre-Cappel, France
Strength: 8.5%
Website: www.brasserie-st-sylvestre.com

There is no doubting that we are in French Flanders, with *cappel* (chapel) in the name, in a village between Steenvorde and Hazebrouck, close to the border with Belgium. This is hop-growing country, and brewery owner Serge Ricour buys half the annual crop for his beers. Once again, we encounter the dry, ironic humour of the region. There are no mountains in this flat area. The 'three mountains' in the beer's name are no more than slight bumps but they are celebrated by the locals as if they were the Flemish version of the Alps. The hills are Monts des Cats, des Rocollets and Casel. Monts des Cats once had a Trappist monastery with its own brewery, so there is a rich tradition of beer in the area.

St Sylvestre is a fine example of an artisanal farm brewery that dates from 1860. It was inherited by Rémy Ricour from his uncle in 1920 and it has been handed down to his son, Pierre, and then on to the next generation represented by Pierre's sons Christophe and Serge. They introduced 3 Monts in 1985 and it has become one of the biggest selling and best-known members of the bière de garde family.

It is made with extremely pale Pilsner malt and some brewing sugar, and hopped with local Brewers Gold and German Hallertauer varieties. It is gold coloured, with a fruity, winey aroma balanced by biscuity malt and spicy hop resins. Tart vinous fruit, juicy malt and spicy hops fill the mouth, while the big finish has great length, with an enormous fruity, vinous note balanced by earthy hop resins and creamy malt. The beer is filtered but not pasteurised and comes in the familiar corked and cradled Champagne-style bottle. The brewery also produces an abbey-style beer called Bière des Templiers, which is bottle fermented, and seasonal March and Christmas beers.

TASTING NOTES
Appearance
Aroma
Taste
Overall score

Saison

In French-speaking Wallonia they feel their beers, with the exception of Trappist ales, are overlooked and underrated. They complain that all the attention goes to the beers brewed in the Flemish-speaking areas. Neglect can lead to decline and it would be tragic if the beers of the region were to disappear, especially the style known as saison.

In recent years, there has been some recovery of interest, with small brewers starting to export to other countries and winning acclaim for products with a fascinating tradition. Saisons, by definition, are seasonal beers. They were originally brewed – and in some cases are still brewed – by farmers who made them in the winter months and stored them for summer drinking. The style, the breweries and the tradition have powerful links with the bières de garde across the nominal border with the Nord-Pas de Calais province of France, though saisons tend to have more hop character and occasionally use spices. Saisons are warm fermented, often incorporate dark malts, have generous hop rates and a big fruity character. The more commercially minded of the producers now make them on a regular basis.

I have stayed several times in the fine city of Tournai, with its awesome cathedral, as a base for visiting the local breweries, all of them tiny and artisanal. They are continung a tradition from the 19th and early 20th centuries, when saisons were brewed to meet a variety of needs: to refresh farm labourers and as drinks to accompany family meals. In common with the beers from French Flanders, there were even extremely weak beers made for schoolchildren, a habit that would cause outrage in education circles today.

A typical saison would be quenching and at the same time brewed to leave some unfermented sugars in the beer to help restore lost energy. Research indicates that some brewers would allow their worts to acetify to give the beer a lactic tang, which gives the style common cause with both the early white beers of the Flemish area, the lambics of the Senne Valley and, further afield, the early Porters in England.

RIGHT
Saison Dupont, from a farm brewery near Tournai, is regarded as arguably the best example of a Belgian saison, or seasonal, ale.

Saison Dupont

Source: Brasserie Dupont, Tourpes-Leuze, Belgium
Strength: 6.5%
Website: www.brasserie-dupont.com

Dupont is acclaimed as the classic brewer of saison. It dates from 1844 when it was a farm brewery known as Rimaux-Deridder. Louis Dupont bought the site in 1920 and gave it to his son to run to persuade him from emigrating to Canada. Today, Marc Rosier, the grandson of Louis, runs the business with his sisters and other members of the extended family. The brewery, set among buildings that surround a cobbled courtyard, still has the feel of a farm, though a statuette of Saint Arnold indicates there is beer to watch over. An on-site well provides good quality, hard water. The brewhouse is filled with steam when mashing is underway in an open vessel that also acts as the boiling copper, another Belgian farm-brewery tradition when space is limited.

With the exception of a Pils-type lager, all the Dupont beers are bottle conditioned and are stored for six to eight weeks at a warm temperature before they are released. 6,500 hectolitres (143,000 gallons) are produced a year, and the flagship brand is Saison Dupont, with the subsidiary name of Vieille Provision, or Old Provision, which recalls the time when the beer was part of the farm's nutrition and diet. It is brewed with Pilsner malt only and hopped with East Kent Goldings and Styrian Goldings. Before warm conditioning, it is re-seeded with fresh yeast and brewing sugar. The hazy orange-gold beer has a fluffy collar of foam and a big peppery Goldings bouquet balanced by toasted malt. Hops, tart fruit and juicy malt dominate the palate, followed by a long and complex finish with a big spicy hop note, sappy malt and light fruit notes.

The Duponts acquired the neighbouring Moinette farm, which produces cheese, pâté and bread, some with beer included. Moinette means little monk and the name comes from a monastery that once stood in the area. Marc has added Moinette Blonde and Brune to his portfolio. There are also organic ('bio') versions of the beers, including the Saison.

Saison de Pipaix

Source: Brasserie à Vapeur, Pipaix, Belgium
Strength: 6.5%
Website: www.vapeur.com

Pistons clank and pulleys heave in this amazing farm steam (*vapeur*) brewery in a village that is also home to Dubuisson. The site, which included a farm and a maltings, has been traced back to the late 18th century. Power for the mash mixer and rakes in the present brewery is provided by a steam engine installed in 1885. Other equipment dates from the early 20th century.

The brewery closed in the 1980s and was rescued by two schoolteachers, Jean-Louis Dits and his wife, Anne-Marie Lemaire. The couple eventually took over the Pipaix site and worked at weekends to restore the equipment, while they continued to teach. Their first commercial beer was a saison, based on a beer produced by the former owners. Tragedy struck the new concern when Anne-Marie was killed in an accident in the brewery. Jean-Louis struggled on with the help of his two daughters, one of whom is keen to take over as manager in due course. Jean-Louis has since remarried and his new wife, Vinciane Corbisier, runs an on-site shop selling ingredients to bakers, home brewers and cheese makers.

Jean-Louis has developed a passion for spices and herbs over the years. During one visit, I was taken through a range of beers in a building like a large garden shed. This included a quite remarkable beer brewed with the addition of ginger. Today his saison includes six 'botanicals', including anis, black pepper, orange peel and medicinal lichen. He uses two or three malts and East Kent Goldings. In the old Wallonian style, he allows his mash in an open tun to gain some lactic character before the copper boil. The beer is not filtered in bottle and will improve with age. I have tasted several vintages and noticed how, over the years, it gained in depth of character, with tart orange and lemon fruit, the 'horse blanket' aroma of wild yeasts, with surprising malty sweetness in the mouth, and a shatteringly dry finish with hops and spices balancing the tart, sour fruit and rich honey malt. A magnificent beer in memorable surroundings.

TASTING NOTES
Appearance
Aroma
Taste
Overall score

TASTING NOTES
Appearance
Aroma
Taste
Overall score

Alt & Amber Beers

Germany enjoys such renown and respect for its lagers that it comes as a shock to many people to discover other styles in that country. We have already seen how the wheat beers of Bavaria, members of the ale family, have enjoyed a major revival. Now, further north, beers made by warm fermentation are acquiring greater appreciation and are being reinterpreted abroad, in the United States in particular, where a substantial number of people are of German descent. The style is often called Amber in the US.

'Alt' means old in German. In the context of beer, it means a style that predates the introduction of lagering and cold fermentation on a commercial scale in the 19th century. While Alt – sometimes labelled Altbier – is brewed in small amounts in Hanover and Münster, its traditional home is the city of Düsseldorf in North Rhine-Westphalia. Close to both the Dutch and Belgian borders, Düsseldorf was once a major coal-mining area. This may explain some similarity between the Alt beers of the city and the saisons of Wallonia and the bières de garde of Northern France: they were fashioned to refresh people after a hard day's labour at the coal face or in the fields. With their copper colour, Alt beers are also similar to British bitter or pale ale, but the resemblance should not be exaggerated. This is a classic style in its own right and its growing popularity in its heartland and throughout Germany suggests that younger people do not consider Old beer to be fit only for wrinklies. (In the United States, the style is often represented by the name Amber, a reference to the colour of the beer, rather than the type of malt used.)

Just as English bitter or pale ale will vary from brewery to brewery, there is no such thing as a typical Alt beer. Pale malt, usually of the Pilsner type, may be blended with Munich or even a tiny proportion of black malt. Fermenters may be open or closed, and both infusion and decoction mashing are used. The aim is for a firm, rounded maltiness underscored by generous aromatic hoppiness. The beers will be stored for up to a month before being released to trade.

Of all my quests for good beer, few have been more pleasurable than my search for Alt beer in Düsseldorf with its charming cobbled town centre lit by gas lamps. It is known as the Altstadt, or Old Town, a fitting name for an area with several brew pubs that specialise in Alt. Im Füschen, the Little Fox, in Ratinger Street, is a vast, cavernous building with red-tiled floors, and wooden benches and tables, where pork dishes are served alongside small glasses of Alt that come straight from casks on the bar. The beer is served by its own natural gas and as soon as one cask is drained, another is delivered by a dumb waiter to the bar. Zum Schlüssel, the Key, is in Bolker Street, birthplace of the poet Heinrich Heine. The copper brewing vessels can be seen through a window at the back. A local at the bar raised his glass and confided in me: 'After the fifth one you start to taste it.' It is not just the British who underestimate their greatest achievements.

Alaskan Amber

Source: Alaskan Brewing Company, Juneau, Alaska, USA
Strength: 5%
Website: www.alaskanbeer.com

It's a long way from Düsseldorf to Alaska but German emigrants reached even the remotest parts of the United States. In the case of the most northerly state of the union, the German presence in Alaska was almost certainly due to the Gold Rush, where the prospectors' thirst for gold was matched by their thirst for beer. There were 50 breweries in the state at the time of the frantic search for gold, and Germans ran several of them.

When Geoff and Marcy Larson opened their brewery in 1988, they discovered a recipe for Alt beer left by a German brewer, who had used Saaz hops from Bohemia. The Larsons were brave people to launch their company with a warm-fermenting ale in a vast region where imported pale lagers are the norm. But they were determined to make a beer with flavour and character. Geoff, with a background in pharmaceuticals, did painstaking research into yeast before selecting a strain that would convert the main maltose sugars in the wort into alcohol but leave some other sugars behind for body and 'mouth feel'.

He uses pure, glacier-fed water and two-row pale and crystal malts (colour units 22). The hops are American Cascade and, true to tradition, Saaz from a country now known as the Czech Republic (bitterness units 18). The copper-coloured beer has a spicy hop aroma balanced by nutty and toasted malt, with hints of orange fruit. Smooth nutty malt, tangy fruit and hop resins dominate the mouth, followed by a lingering finish with spicy hops to the fore but with a good balance of rich malt and tart fruit.

Soon after its launch, Alaskan Amber won a major prize at the Great American Beer Festival and has gone on to win many more awards. The brewery has achieved fame abroad for its Smoked Porter (see page 138), but Amber is far and way the company's biggest-selling beer.

TASTING NOTES
Appearance
Aroma
Taste
Overall score

Diebels Alt

Source: Brauerei Diebels, Issum, near Düsseldorf, Germany
Strength: 4.8%
Website: www.diebels.de

TASTING NOTES
Appearance
Aroma
Taste
Overall score

Diebels, in the village of Issum, is the biggest producer of Alt beer in Germany. Josef Diebels, a proud Westphalian, founded the company in 1878 and it passed to four generations of the family. It remained independent until the turn of the 21st century, when the ever-expanding Interbrew group, now InBev, bought it. So far, there have been no attempts to downplay the importance of Alt, which accounts for 1.5m hectolitres (34.8m gallons) a year.

The modern Steinecker brewhouse has tiled walls with a mosaic showing the old brewery at the turn of the 20th century. Four mash kettles feed four wort kettles, where the hops are added in one addition. A decoction mashing system is used. The 50-year-old yeast strain is an ale culture that works at a warm temperature but it is cropped from the base of conical fermenters. It is noticeably less fruity than typical ale yeasts and fully attenuates the malt sugars. A brewer at Diebels earnestly wrote in my notebook that he used Saccharomyces cerevisiae 'unlike you British who use Brettanomyces', which is actually the wild yeast uses in lambic brewing. Primary fermentation is rapid, lasting just two days. The green beer has a short diacetyl rest to purge it of toffee and butterscotch flavours and is then cold conditioned for between 10 days and three weeks. It is still a shock to hear Germans say they lager their beer when they are referring to ale, but the term simply means 'store'.

Diebels Alt is copper coloured with a pronounced peppery hop aroma balanced by rich malt and a gentle hint of fruit. It has earthy hop resins in the mouth with toasted malt, followed by a dry and nutty finish, a hint of orange fruit and a solid base of gently bitter hops. The grist is made up of 98% pale Pils malt with – rare for the style – 2% roasted malt. Hops are predominantly Northern Brewer for bitterness, with Perle for aroma: bitterness units are 32. Brewing liquor comes from on-site wells and calcium hydroxide (lime milk) is used to soften it. Diebels is the sixth biggest brewing company in Germany: the other five are all Pils brewers.

Duckstein

Source: Brauerei Feldschlössen, Brunswick, Germany
Strength: 4.9%
Website: www.duckstein.de

Is this the favourite beer of Count Duckula? In spite of the cartoon name, this is a beer with considerable history. Its name is a corruption of Tuffstein, a type of volcanic rock that formed around a famous spring, the Lufferquelle, in the town of Königslutter in the Elm Mountains near Brunswick (Braunschweig in German).

In the Middle Ages, some 73 small breweries were recorded in the town, using the calcium-rich water to help them make beer. In the German medieval fashion, they were probably small breweries based in houses and shared communal brewing equipment. Beer was also brewed at the local prince's court. It became fashionable and was the favourite brew of the Prussian king, Friedrich Wilhelm I. In 1987, the Feldschlössen brewery in Brunswick, part of the Carlsberg/ Holsten group, revived the style with Duckstein. It soon achieved popularity and is now widely exported to other mainland European countries, Britain and the United States.

It is brewed with pale and darker Munich malts, and is hopped with Hallertau varieties. The brewery makes much of the fact that it is matured over beechwood chips. If this has a familiar ring, it is because the American brewer Anheuser-Busch makes a similar claim for its version of Budweiser. The use of beechwood is an ancient German tradition and has little to do with maturation: the wood attracts yeast and helped clarify the beer before modern filtration methods were introduced. The bronze-red beer has a fruity, raisin-like aroma with rich malt and spicy hops. The fruit notes dominate the mouth with earthy hop resins and biscuity malt. The finish is spicy, dry, slightly vinous, with bitter hops notes and is wonderfully refreshing.

While Brunswick is some distance from Düsseldorf, the Alt style clearly travelled, as the brewery also makes a Brunswick Alt.

TASTING NOTES
Appearance
Aroma
Taste
Overall score

Full Sail Amber Ale

Source: Full Sail Brewing, Hood River, Oregon, USA
Strength: 5.8%
Website: www.fullsailbrewing.com

Full Sail is based in one of the most spectacular locations of any brewery in America. It is in an old cannery sited close to a deep gorge that is popular with windsurfers as a result of the powerful breezes that sweep along the meeting point of the Hood and Columbia rivers. The lush soil of the region produces grapes, apples, cherries and pears.

Jamie Emmerson and Irene Firmat founded the brewery in 1987 with a belief in craft beers made by hands-on methods. Even today, when the company produces 60,000 barrels a year, the production process is manual. The company is owned by its employees, who bought out the founders in 1998: the joke among the 54 staff, reworking the old Remington razor advertising gag, is 'We liked the beer so we bought the brewery.'

Amber Ale is one of the most successful and respected craft-brewed beers in the US and has won a gold medal no fewer than seven times in the World Beer Championships. It is brewed with two-row pale, crystal and chocolate malts, and is hopped with Cascade and Mount Hood varieties from the Pacific North-west. The amber-red beer has a big spicy hop, tart citrus fruit and creamy malt aroma, with sweet biscuity malt in the mouth balanced by hop resins and tangy fruit. The long, complex finish is quenching, dry and hoppy, but with good spicy, malty and fruity notes.

Full Sail also owns a brew pub of the same name in nearby Portland. I left a camera there and have been meaning ever since to go back and retrieve it.

Pinkus Müller Alt

Source: Brauerei Pinkus Müller, Münster, Nordrhein-Westfalen, Germany
Strength: 5%
Website: www.merchantduvin.com/pages/5_breweries/pinkus.html

The remarkable brewery and tavern started life in 1816 as a chocolatier and bakery as well as a brewery. Today the sixth generation of the Müller family runs the enterprise. Pinkus was a nickname given to Carl Müller, who controlled the company for many years after World War Two. Members of the family told me Pinkus is a nickname for 'the singing brewer', but I have since been told it means something saucier in the local dialect.

The tavern has four intimate wood-panelled dining rooms. The main room has a traditional Westphalian oven in a surround of blue and white tiles. Members of the family look after customers' needs for food and drink, led by Hans Müller and his son-in-law Friedhlem Langfeld, who is the brewmaster.

The brewery produces 20,000 hectolitres, or 12,000 barrels a year. Most of it is consumed in the city and surrounding area but bottled versions find their way to other mainland European countries, Britain, the US and Japan.

Since the 1990s, the family has used only organic malts and hops for all its beers. Their Alt is a classic, brewed with Bioland Pilsener malt and Tettnanger hops. After primary fermentation with an ale yeast culture, the beer is lagered for a remarkable five to seven months in horizontal tanks in the cellars. A carefully controlled lactic culture is added to give a hint of sourness and touch of vinous fruit. The beer is also kräusened with yeasty wort to encourage a strong second fermentation. The beer that emerges from this long maturation is pale with a hint of bronze and a thick and lively collar of foam. The aroma offers biscuity malt, tart fruit and gently spicy hops. Juicy malt, tangy fruit and bitter hops dominate the mouth, while the finish has enormous length with a touch of sourness, ripe fruit, toasted malt and pungent hops.

The brewery also produces a wheat beer and two cold-fermented beers, Pils and Special.

TASTING NOTES
Appearance
Aroma
Taste
Overall score

TASTING NOTES
Appearance
Aroma
Taste
Overall score

St Stan's Amber Alt/Dark Alt

Source: Stanislaus Brewing Company, Modesto, California, USA
Strength: 4.8%/6%
Website: www.st-stans.com

Modesto in central California has powerful German roots. Members of a strict German Baptist sect live in Stanislaus County and it is not surprising that the local brewery concentrates on Alt beer and is not shy of using the proper German name.

It is the biggest producer of Alt-style beer in the US. Garith Helm, an American, and his German wife, Romy Graf, launched the brewery in 1984. They brewed at first in converted dairy vessels on Garith's farm but later moved to a complex they designed that includes brewery, pub, restaurant and beer garden.

Amber Alt, with 28 units of bitterness, has a complex grain recipe that comprises pale, caramalt, carapils, chocolate malt and black malt. The hops are Cascade, Willamette and imported German Tettnanger. It has a massive punch of hops, citrus fruit and biscuit malt on the noise, with tart fruit, spicy hop resins and sappy malt in the mouth. The finish is deep and long, finally dry and bitter but punctuated by toasted grain and citrus fruit.

The strong Dark Alt has 31 bitterness units and is brewed with pale malt, caramalt, black malt and roasted malt. The hops are Bullion, Cascade and English Fuggles. There is a rich and pleasing chocolate note on the aroma and palate, with roasted grain, earthy hops and light fruit. The long finish is bitter-sweet, with more chocolate character balanced by toasted grain and spicy hops.

The pub section of the complex stages regular celebrations for such events as St Patrick's Day and Halloween. In June, the brewery produces a special Graffiti Wheat Beer to commemorate the George Lucas movie *American Graffiti* that was filmed in the area. What the strict German Baptists make of these shenanigans is anyone's guess.

TASTING NOTES
Appearance
Aroma
Taste
Overall score

TASTING NOTES
Appearance
Aroma
Taste
Overall score

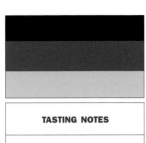

Zum Uerige Alt

Source: Obergarige Hausbrauerei Zum Uerige, Düsseldorf, Germany
Strength: 4.6%
Website: None

TASTING NOTES
Appearance
Aroma
Taste
Overall score

The Alt beer from this wonderful tavern in Berger Strasse off the Altstadt is considered by many to be the classic of the style, though others have criticised it for being too hoppy, not a charge I would make against any beer.

If the beer is a mouthful, so is the name of the tavern: *Obergarige* means 'top fermenting', while *Hausbrauerei* is 'brew-pub'. *Zum Uerige* means 'the place of the cranky fellow', which refers to the curmudgeon who opened it in the 1830s. The tavern was bombed during World War Two but rebuilt in its original style. It is a maze of rooms, some with vaulted ceilings. Others have cartoons, graffiti and photos of old Düsseldorf. The centrepiece is the spacious main bar called the Brewhouse, with copper brewing vessels forming a backdrop.

I met the energetic and enthusiastic owner Josef Schnitzler, who managed to serve beer to me and many other customers at great speed, at the same time extolling the virtues of craft brewing, the finest ingredients and that all-important element: passion.

His beer is brewed with pale malt, caramalt and a touch of black malt, and hopped with the Spalt variety. It has a big spicy hop, toasted malt and light fruit aroma, with earthy hop resins, rich malt and orange fruit in the mouth. The finish is complex and long, with toasted malt, tart fruit and bitter hops. Great beer in a brilliant setting.

Kölsch

Brewing has been a major occupation in Cologne (Köln), the capital of the Rhineland, since Roman times. The German name Köln refers to the city's colonial role during the period of the Roman Empire. Monasteries dominated production for centuries following the Roman withdrawal. When the power of the church was broken at the time of the Reformation, brewing passed into the hands of small-scale commercial producers, mainly based in taverns. A Guild of Brewers was established in 1396 and is the oldest trade association in the city.

Today, Cologne and its surrounding districts still have some 20 breweries all dedicated to the one style of pale, perfumy, warm-fermented beer. In terms of numbers, Cologne is the greatest brewing city in the world. The style is often referred to as 'wiess', which is the local rendition of white, spelt 'weiss' in other regions. This is a reference to its pale colour and heavy collar of foam, though the beer may well have been darker in previous times.

The name also suggests, as it does in Bavaria, that wheat is used, though this is not the case with all brewers. In the 20th century, Kölsch came under pressure from the spread of pale Pils-style beers. As a result, the style was tweaked: pale malts were used and beers were matured and served at lower temperatures, but warm fermentation was retained. The Cologne Association of Brewers organised the changes to the style and then, in the 1960s, took steps to protect the city's brewing tradition. They were troubled by the fact that brewers in other parts of Germany were producing beers called Kölsch. Several court cases were initiated to stop the use of the name outside its city of origin. Then, in 1985, as a result of protracted negotiations between the association and the government, the beer style was given a decree, similar to a French appellation. The brewers are rightly proud of the Kölsch Convention, printed on parchment, which guarantees the sanctity of the style and restricts it to brewers in Cologne and to a handful of other towns and cities, including Bonn. The Convention carries the signatures and seals of each of the brewers.

In common with Alt and the beers of Wallonia and northern France, Kölsch developed as beer to refresh people engaged in hard manual labour. Today it has found a new and encouragingly young audience, to such an extent that new breweries have sprung up to produce the style. A modern Kölsch is around 5% with a malty aroma, some light fruit, soft in the mouth from the local water and with delicate, perfumy hop notes. Bittering units are normally in the high 20s, but extreme bitterness is avoided. Hallertauer and Tettnanger are the preferred hop varieties. The yeast cultures attenuate the malt sugars and the beers tend to be dry in the finish.

Früh Kölsch

Source: Kölner Hofbräu P J Früh, Cologne, Germany
Strength: 4.8%
Website: www.frueh.de

TASTING NOTES
Appearance
Aroma
Taste
Overall score

P J Früh is the best-known tavern in which to relish the city's classic beer style. Service is rapid and carried out by waiters known as *Kobes*. They wear high-buttoned blue uniforms over leather jackets and carry circular trays with central tall handles that hold half a dozen or more glasses of beer. *Kobes* is a diminutive of Jakob and it assumes that all the waiters have the same name. It is a habit that reminds me of my East End upbringing in London where, if you didn't know a man's name, you called him John, as in 'Got a new motor then, John?'

The main area of the tavern is known affectionately as the *Schwemme*, which means the swimming bath. This is a standing area where tall glasses of beer are both dispensed by the *Kobes* and sunk at a rapid pace by the customers. You can escape from the *Schwemme* into the many other rooms of the tavern where beer is served at a more leisurely pace, along with snacks or full meals, based on many varieties of pork. The tavern on the Am Hof near the twin-towered cathedral used to brew on the premises but a new brewery was built just outside the city centre. The company dates from 1904 when Peter Josef Früh opened the brewhouse and it passed on to successive members of the family.

The beer is brewed only with pale malt and Hallertauer and Tettnanger hop pellets. It is a dangerously drinkable beer with a lilting aroma of biscuity malt, perfumy hops and gentle citrus fruit. Juicy malt dominates the palate but with a good balance of hop resins, while the finish is dry, full of soft malt and light fruit and hops. The beer is so popular that there is a tradition in the tavern of a male drinker telling his female companion: '*Liebling, das ist mein Lieblingsbier*', which means, roughly, 'Darling, this is my darling beer', but it may lose something in translation and could prompt divorce proceedings on the grounds that 'You love your beer more than me.'

Hellers Kölsch/Ur-Weiss

Source: Brauhaus Heller, Cologne, Germany
Strength: 4.5%
Website: www.hellers-brauhaus.de

Heller is proof of the enduring popularity of Kölsch, as the brew-pub at 33 Roon Strasse dates only from the 1990s.

Hubert Heller is a qualified engineer who developed a passion for brew-pubs as a student in Berlin in the 1960s. In the 1980s, he was at last able to turn his love into a commercial enterprise when he bought a former distillery in his home city of Cologne. In 1991, he added brewing equipment and started to produce his distinctive interpretations of the city's beer. The brewery is modern but has a fine traditional feel, with copper vessels inside wood jackets.

Two versions of the main beer are produced: a naturally-conditioned, sedimented Ur-Weiss (Original White) and a filtered version called Kölsch. Barley malt from the Rhineland and Herbrucker and Spalt hops are used in full flower form. The unfiltered version has a yeasty, fruity, creamy malt and floral hop aroma, with firm malt and earthy hop resins in the mouth. The finish is smooth and ends dry with good bitter hops notes balanced by toasted malt and tangy fruit.

The filtered Kölsch has greater malt character, is sweeter in the mouth with a more restrained hop character, but is wonderfully refreshing with some late citrus fruit notes.

The tavern has striking architecture, with a vaulted brick cellar, stained-glass windows, and gargoyles commissioned by Herr Heller and carved from basalt rock from the Eifel lakes. The coppers that can be seen behind the bar date from the 1920s and came from a former brewery in the city.

The tavern opens at 4am but closes for lunch, after which it reopens until one in the morning.

TASTING NOTES

Appearance

Aroma

Taste

Overall score

TASTING NOTES

Appearance

Aroma

Taste

Overall score

Trappist Beers

Belgium is a rich storehouse of beer but it is the ales produced by Trappist monks that have drawn the most attention in recent years. The calm and cloistered atmospheres of the abbeys are first and foremost places of worship and retreat.

Beer was brewed originally to aid the monks' work and contemplation. Small amounts were sold commercially to help renovate buildings, enable the monks to develop their missionary work far from home, and establish new communities. In a cynical world, the Trappists are frequently accused of bowing to the forces of commercialism by selling increasing amounts of beer to the outside market, of handing over production to lay workers, installing modern brewing plants, and cutting corners by using inferior raw materials.

In fact, the development of commercial sales after World War Two was on a 'survive or die' basis. The monks' breweries had been stripped of copper and other metals by the invading Nazi forces to help make bullets and tanks. Many of the abbeys had been damaged or destroyed. Income was desperately needed. Lay workers have always been involved in the brewing process: they are essential in abbeys where the monks are called to prayer, often on an hourly basis. The Orval brewery, for example, was at first run solely by workers from outside the abbey, though this is no longer the case. Where modernisation is concerned, even monastic breweries get old, start to fall apart and need to be replaced. The monks vigorously deny the charge they are using cheaper materials in their beers, and some are willing to reveal the grains, hops and sugars they permit.

The most powerful counter-argument to the cynics is the awesome dedication of the monks. They have united across the linguistic divide to defend their traditions against the flood of imitation 'abbey' beers. And they acted speedily to withdraw the Trappist credentials from the La Trappe brands produced at the Koningshoeven abbey in the Netherlands when it was bought by a commercial brewery.

St Benedict in the sixth century, at the abbey of Monte Cassino in Italy, drew up the guidelines for how monks should carry out their duties. The Benedictine philosophy was reinterpreted in the 12th century by

new ideas of stricter observance developed by St Bernard of Clairvaux at the monastery of Cîteaux near Dijon in France. The Latin name for Cîteaux is Cistercium and the monks who followed this new tradition were known as Cistercians. The monks of the Abbey of La Trappe, founded in Normandy in 1664, were Cistercians who argued for even stricter observance of monastic rules. They became the Cistercian Order of the Strict Observance, better known as Trappists.

At the time of the French Revolution, the Trappists were driven from their monasteries as their abbeys were sacked. They found refuge in the Low Countries, where they founded new abbeys,

ABOVE RIGHT
The magnificent restored Orval monastery is reflected in a lake in the grounds. The classic design includes some Art Deco touches.

lived off the produce of the fields, and set up small breweries to offer beer to guests and pilgrims, to drink with their simple meals, and sustain them during Lent. The Trappists became famous as the 'silent monks'. In fact, they not only speak but also would find it difficult to carry out their missionary work if they were mute. They prefer an atmosphere of silence in their abbeys, but they can exchange views and discuss ideas, although prayer is considered more important than speech.

The nature of the Trappists' life, working in isolated communities, and divided in Belgium between French and Flemish speakers, means there is little communication between the houses, save for occasional religious gatherings. Brewing remains unique to each abbey: the monks are at pains to stress there is no such thing as a 'Trappist style' of beer. The only similarity is that their beers are all warm-fermented, members of the ale family, but each house style has evolved in a different way.

It was remarkable, therefore, that representatives of all five Trappist breweries

in Belgium convened meetings in 1997 to discuss ways of protecting their brewing tradition. They were forced to act as a result of the confusion caused by the growing number of Abbey beers coming onto the market. These are beers brewed commercially, some under licence from non-brewing abbeys, but many with no religious connections at all. Abbey beers, in the view of the Trappists, not only confuse the public but also dilute the importance of the monks' contribution and dedication to good brewing practice.

The result was the formation, with Koningshoeven of the Netherlands, of the International Trappist Association. The association places a common seal, 'Authentic Trappist Product', on their beers. This is not an indication of a common style but something more profound. The seal is an appellation, a guarantee of origin. Koningshoeven was summarily expelled from the association in 1999 when the brewery was sold to the Dutch Bavaria group, which continues to market the beers as though they are authentically Trappist.

Achelse Blond 5/Achelse Brune 5
Source: Brouwerij St Benedictus, Abdij de Achelse, Kluis, Hamont-Achel, Belgium
Strength: 5%
Website: www.achelsekluis.org

The five Trappist breweries in Belgium became six in 1998 when the monks at Achel decided to restore brewing. The abbey is on the border with the Netherlands, and the nearest major conurbation is the Dutch city of Eindhoven. Cistercian monks settled in the area from the 12th century and cultivated the land. Trappists founded their abbey in 1845 and, somewhat confusingly, dedicated it to St Benedict. Their brewery was wrecked during World War One when the Germans dismantled the mash tuns and coppers to help build their armaments. Since then, the monks concentrated on their farm, where they grew vegetables and raised cows and pigs. In the 1990s, the brothers confronted a problem common to all monasteries today. They were getting older, farm work was demanding, and attracting new recruits to the

order was difficult. They decided it would be easier to restore brewing and raise funds for the abbey by selling beer. Some of the monks were also keen to brew, as they were unimpressed by the commercial beers available to them, mass market lagers in particular. To raise the funds for the brewery, the monks sold off a parcel of land worth £300,000. The brewing equipment was installed in a former dairy, its stainless-steel vessels in sharp contrast to the burnished copper of some of the other Trappist plants.

Unlike the other monasteries, where the beers are sold at nearby cafés and taverns, Achel has built a café in the main buildings of the abbey, restoring the traditions of centuries ago, though today's 'pilgrims' are more likely to wear shell suits and trainers than pilgrims' habits. The abbey promotes itself as the only Trappist brew-pub in

TASTING NOTES
Appearance
Aroma
Taste
Overall score

TASTING NOTES
Appearance
Aroma
Taste
Overall score

TASTING NOTES
Appearance
Aroma
Taste
Overall score

the world. The café draws large crowds, who not only enjoy the beers but are also fascinated by the view of the brewhouse. At first the beers were available only on draught at the abbey but the monks started to bottle them for commercial sale in 2004. The installation of the brewery was masterminded by one of the most revered figures in Trappist brewing. Father Thomas, the former head brewer at the Westmalle Abbey, came out of retirement to oversee the fitting of the brewing equipment. The yeast culture at Achel came from Westmalle. When Father Thomas was taken ill, another retired head brewer, this time Brother Antoine from Rochefort, took his place.

Day-to-day brewing is carried out by Tom Poncelet, who brews every 10 days and produces around 10,000 hectolitres (220,000 gallons) a year. Achelse Blond 5 is brewed with Pilsner malt, East Kent Goldings, Hallertauer-Hersbrucker and Czech Saaz hops. It is a golden beer with a pungent, spicy hop aroma balanced by clean biscuity malt, with quenching malt and floral hops in the mouth, and a long, dry finish dominated by spicy hop notes.

Achelse Brune 5 has the same ingredients, with the addition of caramalt. It is a russet-coloured beer with a toasted malt and peppery hops aroma, followed by a firm, malty palate with pronounced touches of malted loaf, and a big finish dominated by dark, roasted grain and spicy hops.

For café opening times, phone 011 800 760.

Chimay Rouge/ Blanche/Bleue
Source: Abbaye de Notre-Dame de Scourmont, Forges-les-Chimay, Hainaut, Belgium
Strength: 7%/8%/9%
Website: www.chimay.com

Chimay is the biggest of the Trappist breweries and the best known internationally. In 1850, 17 monks at the Westvleteren abbey were given permission by their abbot to leave the community and build a new one on land donated by the Prince of Chimay. The monastery was built 10 miles from the villages of Forges-les-Chimay in the Ardennes. Building work was completed in 1864, but a small brewery had been constructed two years earlier to provide sustenance for the monks and raise funds. The importance of brewing to the monks was underscored by the fact that abbey and brewery were built on the site of a well that provided copious amounts of pure water. The beer was made available in bottled form in 1885, and in 1925 the prior allowed wider commercial distribution. Labels bore the image of the abbey and the enigmatic letters ADS, which stand for Abbaye de Scourmont. It was the first time that Trappist brewers sold beer to the outside world.

German troops occupied the abbey and its brewery during World War Two, and vital brewing equipment was removed for the Nazi war effort. After the war, the monks sold their beers more vigorously to help pay for rebuilding work. The renowned brewing scientist Jean De Clerck, from Leuven University's faculty of brewing, was invited by Chimay's head brewer, Father Théodore, to advise on the design of new brewing vessels. Crucially, De Clerck took the house yeast and isolated a pure culture that developed the fruity character of their beers, with their powerful blackcurrant note.

The monks, rightly, treat their beers as seriously as wine. On my first visit, the head brewer, Father Thomas, led me to a sampling room where we tasted several vintages. He expounded on the need to allow the Grand Cru versions – sold in Bordeaux-shaped bottles with corks and wire cradles – to breathe when opened, in order to vent off some of the natural carbon dioxide produced during bottle fermentation. All three beers can be laid down to improve, but Father Thomas (who died in 2000) said that after five years the two darker ones would develop a 'port wine' character.

In 1989, the brewhouse designed by Jean De Clerck, with glowing copper vessels, was replaced by a new one based on stainless steel, with many vessels hidden from view behind tiled walls. Production is in the region of 110,000 hectolitres (2.4m gallons) a year. The local water, still drawn from the abbey well, is soft and remarkably free from agricultural and urban impurities. The beers are known by the colours of their caps: red, white and blue, and all three are also available in Grand Cru bottles. In true Trappist fashion, the monks are reluctant to say too much about the raw materials they use, but I was able to discover, over lunch in an inn in Forges-les-Chimay with lay employees from the brewery, that barley comes from the Champagne region of France, and is malted to the monks' specification in Belgium. Aroma hops come from the German Hallertau and the American North-west, with the American Galena preferred for its robust bitterness. The beers are given a dosage of yeast and sugar to encourage a strong fermentation in bottle. The monks also make soft cheese for sale, including one made with their own beer.

Red (Première in Grand Cru bottles) is brewed with pale Pilsner malt, caramalt and German Hallertauer and American Galena hops. The beer is copper coloured with blackcurrant fruit on the aroma and palate and nutmeg spice and tart hops. The finish is vinous, spicy but with a good underlying hop bitterness. White (Cinq Cents in Grand Cru bottles) is brewed with pale Pilsner malt, caramalt, and Hallertauer and Galena hops. The colour is orange/peach with a big citrus fruit aroma and palate, a hint of spice in the mouth, and a big, dry finish balanced between tart fruit and bitter hops. Blue (Grande Réserve in Grand Cru bottles) is made with pale Pilsner malt, Hallertauer and Galena hops. It has a deep copper colour, with an enormous vinous fruitiness on the aroma and palate: the brewers describe the vinous note as being similar to Zinfandel. There is also a spiciness from hops and the house yeast, and the big rich and fruity finish finally becomes dry with a good underpinning of spicy hops. The beers should be served at room temperature, not chilled.

TASTING NOTES	
Appearance	
Aroma	
Taste	
Overall score	

TASTING NOTES	
Appearance	
Aroma	
Taste	
Overall score	

Orval

Source: Brasserie de l'Abbaye Notre-Dame d'Orval, Villers-devant-Orval, Belgium
Strength: 6%
Website: www.orval.be

TASTING NOTES
Appearance
Aroma
Taste
Overall score

The Abbey of Our Lady of Orval stands in densely wooded countryside in the Ardennes, on a sharp bend in the old Roman road that runs from Trier in Germany to Rheims in France, one of the important salt routes of earlier times. The abbey and grounds are places of great beauty and serenity that belie a turbulent past that has seen the site destroyed by fire, rebuilt, and then destroyed again during the French Revolution. The present complex surrounds the ruins of the former abbey.

The abbey uses the symbol of a trout with a ring in its mouth to emphasise a legend connected to the origins of the site. Orval is a reworking of 'Val d'Or', or Golden Valley. The overlord of the region, Countess Matilda, the Duchess of Tuscany, came to the valley in 1076 to visit a small group of Benedictine monks who had made the arduous journey from Calabria in Italy to build an abbey. Matilda was in mourning for her late husband. As she sat by the side of a small lake, her wedding ring slipped from her finger into the water. Overcome with grief, she prayed that the ring would be restored to her. At that moment a trout broke the surface of the water with the ring in its mouth. 'This is truly a golden valley!' the duchess exclaimed, and she gave a generous endowment to the monks, who used it to extend the size of the abbey.

The monastery was rebuilt in the 12th century by Cistercian monks from the Champagne region of France. It burnt down soon afterwards and was rebuilt. For centuries it played an important role in the political and spiritual life of the region. Then it was sacked following an artillery barrage in 1793 by French revolutionaries who came over the border in the mistaken belief that the deposed Louis XV was hiding there.

The present buildings were constructed over a long period between 1926 and 1948. Trappist monks came from as far away as Brazil to answer the call to settle at Orval, and help re-create a place dedicated to prayer and charitable work in the community. The modern abbey was designed

by the architect Henri Vaes, a great admirer of Cistercian buildings. His impressive creation, with the main buildings reflected in an ornamental lake, is a stunning blend of Romanesque and Burgundian styles, with some startling 1920s Art Deco touches. Vaes even designed the brewery's pre-Raphaelite beer goblet and skittle-shaped bottle.

A brewery was added in 1931 to provide sustenance for the monks, and to generate finance for the construction and maintenance of the abbey. The brewhouse is in a chapel-like room with a crucifix on the wall, an obligatory icon in all the Trappist breweries. The walls are half decorated with mustard-coloured tiles, and the brewing vessels stand on bases made from the same material. The formula for the beer was devised by a German brewer named Pappenheimer, who worked to the monks' specification that includes the English method of 'dry hopping'. This entails adding a handful of hops to the finished beer for aroma and bitterness.

The brewery is unique among the Trappist establishments in producing just one beer, called, simply, Orval. Enormous care and dedication go into every stage of production, starting with the selection of four or five spring barleys from

England, France, Germany and the Netherlands. A small amount of English crystal malt is added to the pale varieties to give the beer its distinctive orange-peach colour. Pure white candy sugar is added during the copper boil to encourage a powerful fermentation. The hops used for the copper boil are German Hallertauer varieties and Styrian Goldings from Slovenia. East Kent Goldings are used for dry hopping, and are chosen for their piny, resiny aromas. Brewing liquor is still drawn from the well that gave rise to the legend of Orval. The beer has three fermentations. Primary fermentation is with a conventional ale yeast. The beer is pumped to conditioning tanks, where four or five more yeast strains are added. One of these is a wild yeast, a member of the Brettanomyces family used in making the 'spontaneous fermentation' lambic beers in the Brussels area. The yeast's signature is an aroma known as 'horse blanket'. The yeast strain, now carefully cultured in the brewery's laboratory, can attack dextrins as well as maltose sugars in the wort. The result is a beer with a high level of attenuation, strong in alcohol, and with virtually no sugars left. The beer is bottled with a dosage of the first yeast and some candy sugar, which encourages a third fermentation. It is then stored for six weeks before being released for sale. Although it is declared at 6.2% alcohol, it will reach close to 7% as a result of bottle fermentation. The acidity of the beer, especially when it is aged for months or a few years, makes it the perfect aperitif. It should be stored upright at a cellar temperature of 12°C (54°F). The monks produce some 38,000 hectolitres (836,000 gallons) of beer a year, of which around 10% is exported.

The abbey shop sells the beer as well as bread and cheese made by the monks. A rustic restaurant known as L'Ange Guardien (Guardian Angel) is just a few minutes' walk from the abbey on the main road. It sells dishes cooked in Orval, while the entrance bears the symbol of the trout with a ring in its mouth. The beer has an orange/peach colour, an aroma of peppery hops and tart fruit, followed by a palate dominated by gooseberry fruit, with a long and intensely bitter finish with hints of herbs and a touch of lactic sourness from the action of the wild yeast.

Rochefort 6/8/10
Source: Brasserie de Rochefort, Abbaye de Notre-Dame de St-Rémy, Rochefort, Belgium
Strength: 7.5%/9.2%/11.3%
Website: None

Rochefort is one of the most secluded of the Trappist monasteries. It is another settlement in the Ardennes but, unlike Orval, the abbey doesn't stand prominently on a major road but is reached along a narrow, wooded road. Perhaps in an attempt to deter visitors, the beer is labelled simply Rochefort rather than using the full name of the abbey. Rochefort is a small town near the abbey and has many shops offering bread, locally raised and made meats and chocolate, with cafés serving the local beer.

The abbey has a history almost as turbulent as Orval's. It was founded as a convent in 1230 by Gilles de Walcourt, the Count of Rochefort. The hard climate and grinding poverty proved too much for the nuns, and monks replaced them in 1464. Documents show that a small brewery existed from around 1595 to provide beer for the community, using barley and hops grown in the grounds. The monks were forced to abandon the abbey during the French Revolution, when scant attention was paid to the border between France and the Low Countries. The abbey was rebuilt in 1887 by Trappists from Achel, and a brewery was opened two years later.

The present brewhouse dates mainly from the 1960s, with some additions in the 1970s. It produces around 15,000 hectolitres (330,000 gallons) a year. Blessed by the customary crucifix on the wall and the image of St Arnold, the patron saint of brewers, the brewhouse has burnished copper vessels set amid tiled walls, with the sunlight pouring through stained-glass windows and glinting on the mashing vessels and coppers. One tun carries the warning: '*Ne pas toucher les cuivres avec les mains!*' – 'Don't touch the vessels with the hands!'

Under the long regime of head brewer Brother Antoine, the perfect blend of barleys was assembled, using Pilsner and darker Munich malts grown from grain in Belgium, France and

TASTING NOTES
Appearance
Aroma
Taste
Overall score

TASTING NOTES
Appearance
Aroma
Taste
Overall score

the Netherlands. Dark candy sugar is used in the copper, along with hops from the German Hallertau and Styrian Goldings. To make the point that there is no uniform Trappist style, the beers from Rochefort are dark and malty, unlike the pale and intensely bitter beer from Orval. Brother Antoine maintained that the character of his ales was determined by their original use as 'liquid bread' during periods of fasting.

Two strains of yeast are used for primary and bottle fermentation. The beer is given a dosage of white sugar to encourage the bottle ferment. The three beers have red, green and black crown caps and are labelled 6, 8 and 10 from an old and now defunct Belgian method of indicating strength.

Six is brewed from Pilsner and Munich malt, and hopped with German Hallertauer varieties and Styrian Goldings. It has a reddish-brown colour, with a fruity and slightly herbal aroma and palate, and a finish dominated by rich malt with gentle hop notes.

Eight has identical ingredients, is copper-brown, with a rich fruity aroma and palate reminiscent of raisins and sultanas, and a long, complex finish dominated by the dark grain and a yeasty/bread-like note.

Ten, again, has the same ingredients, is red-brown in colour, with a vast aroma and palate of toasted grain, soft, vinous fruits, nuts and chocolate. The finish is dominated by warming alcohol, with more chocolate, ripe fruit and gentle hop notes.

Westmalle Dubbel/Tripel
Source: Brouwerij Westmalle, Abdij der Trappisten van Westmalle, Malle, Belgium
Strength: 7%/9.5%
Website: www.trappistwestmalle.be

The Abbey of Our Lady of the Sacred Heart, better known as the Trappist Abbey of Westmalle, finds it more difficult to find seclusion than the monasteries further south in the Ardennes. It stands in flat, wind-swept countryside close to Antwerp. Over the centuries, tall elms and walls have grown and been built to offer some protection from both the elements and possible attack. The monks have every reason to be protective, given the stormy origins of their settlement. During the French Revolution, three Trappist monks escaped from France to Switzerland, and planned to go to Amsterdam and from there sail to Canada. But revolutionaries were active in the Low Countries, and their close links with fellow revolutionaries in America meant that a sea journey to Canada would be hazardous. Abandoning their plans, the monks accepted an invitation from the Bishop of Antwerp to establish a religious community in his bishopric. In 1794, a farmer at Westmalle donated some of his land to the brothers. They were joined by other refugee Trappists, and a dozen monks set to work to build an abbey in the hard, unyielding countryside. The mellow stone complex was completed in 1804.

A brewery was added in 1836 and for some time supplied only the monks' daily needs. In 1865, a brewing monk of Prussian origin, Ignatius Van Ham, extended the brewery in order to sell beer commercially and help finance a Trappist community in the Belgian Congo. Sales were restricted to the immediate area around Westmalle and were not sold more widely until the 1920s. In 1932, the Abbot of Westmalle, Edmond Ooms, gave his beers the appellation 'Trappistenbeer', and thus announced to the outside world, rather more emphatically than Chimay, the presence of monks and brewing in the Low Countries. Two years later Abbot Ooms commissioned a secular architect to design a new, bigger brewhouse. Classic copper vessels are set on tiled floors in a powerful 1930s design with Art Deco influences. The brew kettle is fired by direct flame, a method that gives a defining toasted malt and toffeeish character to the beers, as some of the malt sugars are caramelised during the boil with hops. The brewing liquor is hard, which suits brewers in a region where such classic pale ales as De Koninck in Antwerp are produced. The monks use Bavarian and French summer barleys that are kilned at low temperatures to produce extremely pale Pilsner malts. Whole hop flowers are used: the monks are rather reticent about naming all the varieties but will admit to putting Bavarian Tettnanger, Czech Saaz and Styrian Goldings in the kettle in three stages. Candy sugar is also added during the boil. The two beers enjoy slow secondary fermentations in tanks before being bottled with priming sugar and re-seeded with yeast.

Westmalle is the second biggest of the Trappist breweries, producing more than 100,000 hectolitres (2.2m gallons) a year. Its contribution to Belgian brewing has been profound. The monks introduced the designations Dubbel and Tripel for their two beers and the terms are now widely used. They are not so much indications of strength, though a Triple is stronger than a Double, but are taken to mean that a Double is darkish and malty, while the Triple, introduced after World War Two, is pale, hoppy and fruity. Westmalle Trippel, with just 13 units of colour, has become a world classic, the benchmark beer for strong, pale and hoppy ales.

Dubbel is brewed with Pilsner malt, highly-kilned dark malt, dark candy sugar, with Tettnanger, Saaz and Styrian Goldings hops. It is russet coloured, with a chocolaty, fruity spicy aroma and palate. The fruitiness is complex with hints of guava and other tropical products. The finish is dry and malty, with chocolate notes from the dark malt and rich fruit.

Tripel is brewed with Pilsner malt only. The hops are Tettnanger, Saaz and Styrian Goldings. It is orange coloured, with a floral Saaz-inspired aroma and orange citrus fruit, followed by a tangy, fruity palate with big spicy hop notes, and a long, lingering finish with warming alcohol, resiny hops and a tantalising herbal character.

Westvleteren Blond/Extra/Abt
Source: Abdij Sint Sixtus, Westvleteren, Belgium
Strength: 5.8%/8%/11%
Website: www.sintsixtus.be

The Abbey of Sint Sixtus is the smallest of the Trappist breweries and the most reclusive. It sells only limited amounts of its beer commercially, though they are available for collection at the abbey. Visitors, save for pilgrims, are not welcome. Nevertheless, the abbey has been a force for good and for change. It was monks from Westvleteren who founded Chimay. And, in 1997, the abbot set in train events that led to all the monastic breweries in Belgium identifying their beers as coming from the Trappist tradition. The abbot held talks with the management of the St Bernardus Brewery in neighbouring Watou and made a simple request: 'Please remove the image of a monk from your labels.' In 1946, the monastery had entered into an arrangement with St Bernardus whereby the monks restricted their production to personal consumption and for sale in a café across the road from the abbey, while the commercial brewery could sell the beers, brewed to the same specification, more widely. Confusion reigned, especially as the commercial beers carried the word 'Sixtus' on the label. When the licence to brew the Westvleteren beer expired in 1992, St Bernardus dropped the word Sixtus, but five years later the monks requested an end to any suggestion that the commercial beers came from the Trappist tradition.

The abbey was founded in 1831 in the village of Westvleteren in flat Flanders countryside near Ypres and overlooking the hop fields centred on Poperinge. A small brewery was added in 1838 solely to provide beer for the monks. In the 1920s, the abbot, Dom Bonaventure De Groote, renovated the brewery in local Flemish artisanal style, with brewing vessels set in tiled surrounds. In the early 1990s, this brewhouse was replaced with a modern one using stainless-steel vessels. Production is restricted to around 3,500 hectolitres (77,000 gallons) a year. Brewing does

TASTING NOTES
Appearance
Aroma
Taste
Overall score

TASTING NOTES
Appearance
Aroma
Taste
Overall score

TASTING NOTES
Appearance
Aroma
Taste
Overall score

TASTING NOTES
Appearance
Aroma
Taste
Overall score

not take place on a daily basis. When a new batch is ready, a message on the brewery's answerphone draws queues of drivers in cars, vans and even on bikes who wait patiently to buy their maximum allowance of 10 cases each. Only one beer is available at a time. The beer bottles carry no labels and are identified by the colours of the caps: green, blue and yellow, though the green is also known as Blond, the blue as Extra, and the yellow as Abt, which means Abbot.

While the brewhouse has changed, brewing practice has not. Only pale malt is used, and the beers achieve their colours as a result of white or dark candy sugar. The hops are Northern Brewer and the yeast strain comes from Westmalle. The beers are not filtered. Protein and yeast are allowed to drop out naturally during maturation, and the beer is then reseeded with yeast when bottled. The green cap beer is a recent addition to the range. It is extremely pale and is a sign that even the monks of Wetvleteren are aware of the demand for pale-coloured ales in Belgium, though they emphasise that the beer was introduced primarily as a lower-strength beer for their own consumption.

On my first visit to the abbey, on a rainy and blustery autumn day, cowled monks hurried out and emphatically pulled the main gates closed. I was able to speak at a side gate to an amiable

monk called Brother Mathias, and then tasted the beer range in the Café Vrede on the other side of the road from the abbey gates. A sign in the cafe says: 'The Good Lord has changed water into wine, so how can drinking beer be a sin?'

Blond (with a green cap) is brewed with pale malt, pale candy sugar and Northern Brewer hops. It has a pale gold colour. A big herbal, hoppy aroma leads to a firm malty body balanced by tart hops, followed by a hoppy, lightly fruity and finally dry finish.

Extra (with a blue cap) is brewed with pale malt, dark candy sugar and Northern Brewer hops. It has a deep russet colour with a vast aroma of tart, plummy fruit, mouth-filling malt, fruit and hops, and a complex finish of rich malt, tart hops and bitter fruit.

Abt (with a yellow cap) is made with pale malt, dark candy sugar and Northern Brewer hops. It is a dark brown beer, with a massive attack of vinous fruit, toffee and roasted grain on the nose, chewy malt, dark fruit and hops in the mouth, and a warming alcohol, toasted grain and hops finish.

*Sales from the abbey, when available, are between 10am and 12 noon and 2pm and 5pm. No sales on Friday, Sunday or public holidays, 1–14 January or the week after the third Sunday in September. Phone 057 400 376.

Abbey Beers

Abbey beers fall into two categories. In the first, an abbey that no longer brews licenses a commercial brewery to make beer for it. The monks may exercise some control over ingredients and recipes, and derive income in the form of royalties they use to further their religious work. The second category involves modern commercial breweries that produce beers with monastic-sounding names and often religious artefacts on their labels but which have little or no connection with any religious houses.

As a result, confusion reigns and many drinkers, even those with more than a passing knowledge of the world of beer, often mistake abbey beers for Trappist ales. The problem was sufficiently serious for the brewers of true Trappist ale to give their products a seal of origin (see page 220).

The abbey beers that fall into the first category have some history on their side. Many abbeys and their breweries were destroyed during the Napoleonic wars that raged over the Low Countries. Some were attacked as late as World War One. In order to raise funds to rebuild their abbeys, the monks decided to abandon brewing and to seek commercial brewers who would make beers to the monks' specifications and pay them royalties. Many of the commercial breweries were small and close to the abbeys. Unfortunately, the late 20th-century's rampant commercialism and the quest among big brewers for mergers and centralisation of production put an end to the old tradition of a close link between abbey and local brewer.

The Leffe beers are the best known and most widely marketed of abbey brands. I visited the Mont St Guibert brewery near Brussels in the early 1990s, where all but one of the Leffe beers were brewed. It was a charming, rustic brewery and, although part of the Interbrew group, seemed to enjoy a considerable degree of independence. But a few years later, Interbrew closed the site and moved production to its vast beer factory at Leuven. The beers that carry the name of the Abbey of Grimbergen have had an even more tortuous history. At one stage they were brewed by the Alken-Maes group when it was controlled by Grand Metropolitan of Britain, best known for the infamous Watney beers of the 1970s. The group passed into the hands of the French biscuit and yoghurt maker Danone, which at the turn of the 21st century sold its brewing interests to Scottish & Newcastle. When S & N unveiled the Grimbergen range at a lavish event in Edinburgh, Norbertine monks in flowing white robes from the abbey were in attendance, giving the beers a holy blessing they did not altogether deserve.

The 'second wave' of abbey beers has a more direct link to Mammon. There are no royalties to monks, only the income from commercial sales. No criticism can be levied at breweries in the United States, which is too young a country to have a monastic tradition but where several producers with a passion for Belgian beers make beers in the abbey style.

I am aware that this is the only section of the book hedged around with concerns about confusing labelling. Some labels may mislead consumers into thinking they are getting beers brewed in abbeys when they come instead from commercial companies. My concerns should in no way be taken to mean that the beers that follow are anything less than of the highest quality. If they did not meet the criteria set by the book, they would not be included. The Trappists, given their traditions and belief in quietude, have taken a bold step in setting the seal of authenticity on their products. It is high time for the rest of the Belgian brewing industry to make it clear to consumers that abbey beers are commercial products with little or no connection with religious houses. A clearer and less ambiguous labelling for these beers would be in the best interests of their owners, enabling them to be judged in their own right and not as imitations of Trappist ales.

Abbaye des Rocs

Source: Brasserie de l'Abbaye des Rocs, Montignies-sur-Roc, Belgium
Strength: 9%
Website: www.abbaye-des-rocs.com

Jean-Pierre Eloir launched his brewery at his home in 1979 as a part-time venture in a garden shed, producing 50 litres (11 gallons) of beer every other week. The first beer, and still the main product, is called simply Abbaye des Rocs. As explained in the section on Belgian-style wheat beer (see page 196), the religious connection amounts to a few stones from a monastery that became a farm.

Jean-Pierre, a former tax inspector, has a great passion for Belgian Trappist and abbey beers, and has painstakingly created his ale with due reverence. It is brewed with pale malt, several varieties of darker grains and malted oats. Jean-Pierre was one of the first craft brewers in Belgium to experiment with malted oats, a difficult grain to brew with but which gives a smooth and creamy note to the beer. The beer is hopped with Belgian, Czech and German varieties and spiced with coriander. No sugars or adjuncts are used. Abbaye des Rocs is unpasteurised and improves in bottle. It has a rich claret colour that leads to a big vinous fruit aroma with spices and dark malt notes. Ripe fruit, coriander, chewy grain and hop resins fill the mouth, followed by a big, complex finish that is sweet at first, then becomes fruity and spicy but with a solid underpinning of hops. The brewery has moved and developed over the years and now produces 2,000 hectolitres (44,000 gallons) a year. The abbey beer is exported to Italy and the United States.

Affligem Blond

Source: Affligem Brouwerij BDS, Opwijk, Belgium
Strength: 6.7%
Website: www.heinekeninternational/affligem_blond.jsp

Affligem is a Benedictine abbey in the hop-growing region of Aalst, where the monks once cultivated their own hop garden. The original abbey, now in ruins, dates from 1074, and a new site was built in the 1920s. The monks reached an agreement with the nearby brewery of De Smedt to produce beers for commercial sale. De Smedt is not as old as the original abbey but it has a history that dates from 1790 and enjoyed a good reputation for the quality of its ales, the pale Op-Ale in particular.

The success of the Affligem beers encouraged De Smedt to rename itself after the brand name. This, in turn, caught the attention of global giant Heineken, which took a 50% stake in 1999 and increased it to 95% two years later. The abbey has retained control of the Affligem brand name and has an assurance that the beers must be brewed in Belgium for the next 30 years. Will this be honoured more in the breach than the observance? Already a large proportion of draught Affligem Blond is taken in tankers to France, where it is kegged by Heineken in Lille.

There are brown and triple versions of Affligem but the Blond is far and away the biggest of the brands and, in true Heineken style, is now widely exported. It is brewed with pale malt and has a colour of 12. The hop varieties are not revealed but are thought to be local ones. Bitterness units are 24. The beer has a honey-gold colour, a juicy malt, lemon fruit and hop resins aroma, with tart fruit, sappy malt and a solid bitter hop note in the mouth. The finish is quenching, bitter-sweet, with tangy lemon, creamy malt and spicy hops. An up-rated seasonal version of the beer at 7% is called Paters Vat (the fathers' brew). Affligem/Heineken has filled its boots with abbey beers, also producing ales for the Saint Feuillien and Postel abbeys.

TASTING NOTES
Appearance
Aroma
Taste
Overall score

Bosteels Tripel Karmeliet

Source: Brouwerij Bosteels, Buggenhout, Belgium
Strength: 8%
Website: www.karmeliet.be

TASTING NOTES
Appearance
Aroma
Taste
Overall score

The name and label commemorate the Carmelites of Dendermonde who had a reputation for brewing fine ales, including one made from three grains. The Bosteels brewery was keen to brew a similar beer and happily came across detailed information about the monks' version from a recipe dated 1679. The grains in question are barley, wheat and oats, while Styrian Goldings are the chosen single variety of hop. Bosteels has enjoyed such success with the beer that it is now best known as the Karmeliet brewery, even though it had much earlier gained a reputation for its strong Pauwel Kwak ale served in its distinctive wooden 'shoe' (see page 107).

Karmeliet is one of the finest new beers I have tasted in recent years. It is accompanied by an elegant serving glass with a fleur-de-lys motif. The glass was designed by Antoine Bosteels who, with his father Ivo, represents the sixth generation to run the family brewery. The three grains are used in both malted and unmalted form and the result, not surprisingly, is a highly complex bronze-gold beer with a profound aroma of biscuity grain, vanilla and banana, and spicy hop resins. Ripe fruit, creamy malt, vanilla and hop resins fill the mouth, while the finish is long, complex, rich, fruity, malty and with a final tart, quinine-like bitterness from the hops. The vanilla and banana character comes from the house yeast culture. The beer is used as both an ingredient and a companion for meals in a restaurant also called Karmeliet in Bruges.

Koningshoeven La Trappe Blond/Dubbel/Tripel

Source: Bierbrouwerij De Koningshoeven BV, Berkel-Enschot, Tilburg, Netherlands
Strength: 6.5%/6.5%/8%
Website: www.latrappe.nl

The brewery claims the products are 'Trappisten biers' and the brewery is indeed in the grounds of the awesome, brooding abbey of Koningshoeven. But, as I explained in the previous section (see page 220), the brewery was expelled from the Trappist brewers' association when it was bought in 1999 by the Bavaria group, a large Dutch company that specialises in own-label beers for supermarkets. It is a tragic situation, as the abbey and brewery have a fascinating history and produce extremely good beers. But I have no doubt that the Belgian Trappists were right to take their action in order to protect the integrity of their tradition.

Koningshoeven means King's Gardens, and the land was given to the monks by the monarch when they moved north from La Trappe in Normandy to escape the French Revolution. The rustic-sounding Schaapskoi (Sheepfold) brewery was built in the 1880s to raise funds for the restoration of the abbey. Following World War Two, the brewery was bought by Stella Artois of Belgium, which wanted to establish a bridgehead in the Netherlands. It produced an unlikely Trappist Pils and installed a small lager plant. The beer was not a success and the monks raised funds to buy back the brewery. Perhaps it was this brush with Mammon that led the brothers down the path of unrighteousness, allowing commercial brewers to make some of their beers and signing a deal with the British supermarket group Sainsbury's to sell an own-label Trappist beer.

A new, modern brewhouse, with stainless-steel vessels, was installed in 1986; the original traditional brewhouse is depicted on the tiles of the walls. The flexibility of the site, as well as the renown of the La Trappe brands, attracted the Bavaria group, and now production of other beers, including a Pils, has been moved to Koningshoeven. Critics of the sell-out (myself included) expected the quality of the ales to decline but they are consistently good.

La Trappe Blond is a recent addition to the range and is brewed with pale malt and German Northern Brewer hops. It has a tart lemon fruit, juicy malt and spicy hop aroma, with tangy fruit, sappy malt and perfumy hops in the mouth. The finish is quenching, finally dry and hoppy but with balancing notes of malt and lemon fruit.

Dubbel is made with pale, Munich and other coloured malts and, again, the hop variety is Northern Brewer. It has a tawny colour, a powerful orange Muscat aroma and palate, overlain by peppery hops.

The copper-coloured Tripel has ripe sultana and raisin fruit on nose and palate, the fruitiness balanced by rich malt and a powerful blast of peppery Goldings hops that leads to a dry and bitter finish.

TASTING NOTES	
Appearance	
Aroma	
Taste	
Overall score	

TASTING NOTES	
Appearance	
Aroma	
Taste	
Overall score	

TASTING NOTES
Appearance
Aroma
Taste
Overall score

TASTING NOTES
Appearance
Aroma
Taste
Overall score

Leffe Triple

Source: Brouwerij Hoegaarden (Interbrew), Hoegaarden, Belgium
Strength: 8.1%
Website: www.leffe.be

Triple is the only beer in the Leffe range that is bottle fermented. It is brewed at the Hoegaarden brewery, controlled by Interbrew, which is famous for its spiced white beer and where there is expertise in the delicate area of reseeding beer with yeast in bottle.

While Interbrew busily turns Leffe Blonde and Brune into international brands, the Triple is the only beer in the range that is true to the monastic tradition and may bear some resemblance to the type of beer once brewed by the Norbertine brothers in the Abbey de Notre-Dame de Leffe.

The abbey's origins lie in the 12th century and it stands at the confluence of the Leffe and Meuse rivers near Dinant. The present buildings date from the 18th century. The abbey has enjoyed a tumultuous history: it has been ravaged by fire and then partially destroyed

during the Napoleonic wars. In the 1950s, the monks reached an agreement with a local brewer to make beers for them under licence. It is thought to be the first such agreement between representatives of the church and the outside commercial world. The original commercial brewery was eventually taken over and the Leffe beers were transferred to the Mont St-Guibert plant, best known for Vieux Temps ales. The house yeast culture was used to ferment the Leffe brands and is still used for primary fermentation of Triple. The Hoegaarden strain is used for bottle fermentation.

It is a deceptively pale, golden beer with a fruity, vinous aroma and palate, balanced by spicy hops and juicy malt. The finish is warming, rich and packed with sappy malt, spices, bitter hops and ripe fruit.

Maredsous 8/10

Source: Brouwerij Moortgat, Breendonk, Belgium
Strength: 8%/10%
Website: www.duvel.be

Maredsous is an ancient religious community based at Denée, south of Namur. It graduated from a humble community of Bavarian monks to a full-blown abbey in 1878, with striking buildings in the neo-Gothic style of the 19th century. At some time, the monks stopped brewing and, in 1963, they approached Moortgat with a view to the brewery making beer for them. Were the monks aware that Moortgat was best known for a beer called Duvel, which means devil? The beer had not then achieved world fame, as it was still a dark beer and only became golden in colour six years later. But this was still a remarkable coming together of the representatives of paradise and perdition.

The Maredsous beers produced by Moortgat are generally considered to be among the finest of the abbey beers brewed in Belgium, which is perhaps not surprising given the quality of the brewery's other products. The monks control the recipes and monitor the quality of the beers. Their intervention may account for the fact that little information is available about the grains and hops used, which is frustrating for those who revel in the aromas and flavours of the beers.

Maredsous 8 is russet coloured with a rich aroma and palate of chocolate and cappuccino coffee: colour and flavour suggest the use of well-roasted malts. The finish is sweet with more chocolate notes, with rich fruit and a gentle but firm hop bitterness.

Maredsous 10 is a burnished golden ale with massive ripe fruit notes – oranges and pears – on the aroma and palate, with good earthy and spicy hops and a long, complex finish that interweaves between rich fruit, juicy malt and earthy hops.

These bottle-fermented beers are left to ripen for two months in the brewery and will improve in bottle for three years, developing an even more profound fruit character.

TASTING NOTES
Appearance
Aroma
Taste
Overall score

TASTING NOTES
Appearance
Aroma
Taste
Overall score

Ommegang Abbey Ale

Source: Brewery Ommegang, Cooperstown, New York, USA
Strength: 8.5%
Website: www.ommegang.com

TASTING NOTES
Appearance
Aroma
Taste
Overall score

Don Feinberg and Wendy Littlefield have had a long love affair with Belgium and its beers. They were inspired by a visit to the country in 1980 and began to import Belgian beers into the US. In 1997, with the active support and advice of the Belgian brewers Affligem, Dubuisson and Moortgat, they opened their Ommegang Brewery in Cooperstown, upper New York State, world famous as the home of the Baseball Hall of Fame.

The custom-built brewery is on the site of a former hop farm: this region of New York was once a major hop-growing area but the industry was ruined by Prohibition. The brewery is designed along the lines of a Belgian abbey-cum-farmhouse and is named after the Ommegang, or walkabout, held every year in July in the Grand' Place in Brussels, where the Belgian Brewers' headquarters are based.

The Cooperstown brewery has been a great success from opening day. Don and Wendy refuse to compromise on quality, despite pressure to increase production. Their beers are matured slowly and lovingly on site before being bottled on their yeast. The Abbey Ale is in the style of a Belgian Dubbel. It is brewed with pale, Munich and caramalt grains, and hopped with American and Belgian varieties. It is a Burgundy-coloured ale with a deep collar of foam, a complex aroma of fruit, hops and spices, a palate rich in caramel, liquorice, toffee, chocolate and earthy hops, and a dry finish in which vine fruits, peppery hops and ripe grain dominate.

Stoudt's Triple

Source: Stoudt's Brewing, Adamstown, Pennsylvania, USA
Strength: 9%
Website: www.stoudtsbrewing.com

TASTING NOTES
Appearance
Aroma
Taste
Overall score

Carol Stoudt got tired of the joke that 'Stoudt's don't brew a stout', so she added a warm-fermented black ale to her portfolio. But since the brewery opened in 1987, it has built its reputation on the quality of its Belgian and German-style beers. Carol is married to Ed Stoudt. His German family came to the US as early as 1733. Ed went into the restaurant business while Carol toured Bavarian breweries and then took a university course in brewing before setting up shop in Adamstown. The area is known as 'Pennsylvania Dutch', but there is no Dutch influence: the word is a corruption of Deutsch, for a German community developed there.

Stoudt's has won many prizes and plaudits, including gold awards at the Great American Beer Festival. Carol not only brews a stout but has also added an IPA, but one of her outstanding beers is her Belgian-style abbey Triple. It is made with two-row Pilsner pale malt and Munich malt, and is hopped with four varieties from the German Hallertau. It is orange coloured with a big spicy hop and rich biscuity malt aroma, a warming malt palate rich in alcohol, fruit and spicy hops, and a long, lingering finish with earthy hop resins, ripe sappy malt and tart fruit. It is fermented with a Belgian yeast culture and is not filtered.

The Stoudt complex includes a shopping mall with a bakery and restaurant.

Tongerlo Double Brown/Triple Blond

Source: Browerij Haacht NV, Bortmeerbeek, Belgium
Strength: 6%/8%
Website: www.primus.be

The Abbey of Tongerlo is one of the most striking in Belgium, its imposing buildings rising out of the flat lands known as the Kempen close to the Dutch border. It is a Norbertine abbey, named after the followers of the migrant preacher Norbert of Gennep who became St Norbert. He founded a community at Prémontré in France in 1121. His followers built a monastery at Tongerlo in 1133 where the River Grote Nette waters the fields and meadows. From this lush countryside the monks were able to grow barley and hops to make their own beer. The abbey that grew out of the community became a major centre of religion and culture and has a replica of Leonardo da Vinci's *Last Supper*.

World War Onc put an end to brewing at Tongerlo, when the invading German troops dismantled the brewhouse and confiscated the copper vessels for the war effort. In 1989, the monks approached the Haacht brewery and asked them to produce beers for them. Haacht is best known for its Jan Primus beers named after the famously bibulous 13th-century Duke of Brabant whose name, corrupted to Gambrinus, became an inspiration for brewers in the Low Countries and further afield. The Tongerlo beers are carefully controlled by the monks and are refermented in the bottle and will improve with age.

The Double Brown has a deep copper colour, a spicy aroma with raisin and sultana fruit and spicy hops. The firm, full palate has powerful hints of coffee and liquorice with rich malt and earthy hops, followed by a long finish that is bitter-sweet, vinously fruity and ends with peppery hops.

The Triple Blond has a glowing amber colour, tart lemon fruit, juicy malt and spicy hops on the nose, and warming alcohol, citrus fruit, biscuity malt and spicy hop resins in the mouth. The finish is big, complex, with citrus fruit, rich malt and spicy hop resins.

The beers are accompanied by attractive glasses that show the image of the abbey. Several rustic restaurants in the neighbourhood of the abbey serve rustic meals with the beers.

TASTING NOTES
Appearance
Aroma
Taste
Overall score

TASTING NOTES
Appearance
Aroma
Taste
Overall score

Steam Beer

Many people assume that steam beer is a reference to the steam-driven engines that transformed brewing during the Industrial Revolution. There are a few breweries that use the word steam in this context. But in San Francisco it has a more precise meaning. It refers to a style, now confined to a single brewery, where both ale and lager techniques combine to produce a beer with the richness and fruitiness of an ale with the quenching character of a lager. It was a style created during the California Gold Rush and which survives and flourishes today due to the passion of a man who saved his local brewery and, in so doing, helped launch the American beer revolution.

Anchor Steam Beer

Source: Anchor Brewing Co, San Francisco, California, USA
Strength: 5%
Website: www.anchorbrewing.com

TASTING NOTES
Appearance
Aroma
Taste
Overall score

Fritz Maytag was a student at Stanford University in the 1960s and enjoyed a San Francisco speciality known as 'steam beer'. In 1965, he ordered a glass in his local bar and was told it would be the last because the producer, the Anchor Steam Brewery, was about to close. As a result, Fritz wrote his chapter of the American Dream. He cashed in some of his shares in the family's washing machine business, bought the brewery and created a legend.

Steam beer is unique to San Francisco. It is a style that dates from the California Gold Rush of the 1890s. When prospectors poured into the small town, they found a mainly Mexican population drinking wine or tequila. The gold diggers wanted beer and, in particular, they wanted the lager beers they enjoyed back east. Brewers in the area were desperate to meet the demand but refrigeration had not yet arrived, and the Californian coast, unlike Bavaria, does not have icy caves in which beer can be stored. The brewers tackled the problem with remarkable ingenuity by fermenting their beers with lager yeasts but at ale temperatures. They developed shallow vessels that exposed more of the beer to the atmosphere and encouraged it to cool rapidly. The beer continued a lively fermentation in casks in the bars, producing a high level of natural carbonation. As a result, when a cask was tapped, it let off such a hiss of escaping gas that drinkers said it sounded like steam.

The brewery Fritz inherited in the 1960s was on its last legs, and so strapped for cash that it used baker's yeast for fermentation and had just one employee. Fritz nursed it back to success, though it took 10 years for the Anchor Brewery to show a profit. Eventually he was able to move from a run-down site under a freeway to an impressive 1930s Art Deco building that had previously been the offices of a coffee-roasting company. Over the years, Fritz has immersed himself in the history, the culture and craft of brewing. He has re-created a beer from the Old World, using a recipe translated from cuneiform writing on stone tablets, and toured the great brewing nations. He has also built a brewery that is a shrine to the art of brewing. The reception area is like a comfortable club, with deep leather chairs, prints of old San Francisco and its brewing history, and a bar where all the Anchor beers are tapped. Plate glass windows allow visitors to view the brewhouse, with copper vessels standing on a tiled floor, handcrafted for Fritz by a German company. Anchor Steam has played a pivotal role in the American craft brewing revolution. Its success encouraged many others to fire mash tuns and kettles, revive old beer styles and develop new ones.

Fermentation for Anchor Steam takes place in open vessels just 60cm (2ft) deep, using a lager yeast culture but a warm temperature of between 16 to 21°C (60 to 70°F). The grist is a blend of pale and crystal malts with no added sugars. Hops are Northern Brewer, which are added three times during the copper boil (units of bitterness 30–35). Following fermentation, the green beer is warm conditioned for three weeks and then kräusened by adding some partially fermented wort to encourage a strong secondary fermentation.

The beer that emerges from this exhaustive process is bronze coloured, with a rich malty-nutty aroma, tart fruit and a spicy, earthy hop resins note. The firm, full palate has juicy malt, citrus fruit and tangy hops, followed by a long finish at first dominated by sappy malt and tart fruit but with a late burst of bitter hops. It is a complex and quenching beer, a world classic.

Lambic & Gueuze

Lambic and gueuze are potent symbols of brewing's past. Their vinous and cidery palate stresses the absurdity of building barriers between beer and fruit-based alcohols. Their long ageing process helps destroy the myth that beer is a rough and ready drink. And even though the act of turning sweet wort into alcohol is left to nature, the production of lambic demands the highest skill.

Lambic beers have been made for 400 years – possibly much longer. The method stretches back to 3000BC, when the first beers were made in the Old World by yeasts in the atmosphere. Today, there is only a handful of producers left, grouped in the valley of the River Senne that runs through Brussels in a region known as Payottenland. This is Breughel country, and the stolid peasant folk carousing in the paintings of Pieter the Elder are drinking lambic, not wine, from their earthenware pots.

The term 'lambic' is lost in history and has many interpretations. One theory is that the name was taken from the town of Lembeek, which has had a guild of brewers since the 15th century and an annual pilgrimage to the shrine of the patron saint of lambic brewers, Saint Veronus. One of the principal lambic producers, Frank Boon, is based in the town. Another theory is that the conquering Spanish in the 16th and 17th centuries called the farm-house breweries in the Senne Valley *alembics*, or distilleries.

What is beyond dispute is that lambic is the oldest beer style in existence. It is an agricultural beer that was once the only type drunk in Brussels and its environs. It declined in step with rural life and the spread of industry. Lambic's cause was not helped when a type of prohibition in Belgium at the turn of the 20th century prevented gin and other spirits being sold in cafés and bars. Drinkers turned to strong ales rather than the weaker lambics. The rapid spread of Pilsner-type beers did little to help lambic, either. Lambic and gueuze have been protected by Belgian law since 1965 and by a European Union ordinance of 1992. But such backing will keep the beers in production only if they are supported by consumers.

The method of production remains slow, ruminative and bucolic. Brewing does not take place in summer. In centuries past, farmers would not have brewed in the summer months, as they needed to devote all their energies to the harvest. And even spontaneous fermentation is too unpredictable and uncontrollable in hot weather.

Lambic is a type of wheat beer. Its protective laws and ordinances lay down that at least 30% wheat must be used in the mash. The wheat is not malted. The reasons are probably empirical: farmer-brewers had limited time at their disposal and knew that sufficient extract and enzymes could be provided by barley malt. Wheat also gave a tart, quenching and spicy character to the beer. The malt used in lambic breweries is exceptionally pale. As a result of the presence of wheat, the wort produced is turbid and milky white. A lambic will usually have an original gravity of around 1050 degrees and a finished alcohol of 4.5 to 5%. This can rise to 6% when fruit is added during maturation. The copper boil is a long one, often lasting for three hours. The wort is heavily hopped, using Belgian, English or German varieties. But the hops are four years old, have lost much of their aromatics and have a cheesy smell. They are used solely for their preservative qualities, as hop aroma and bitterness do not marry well with the characteristics imparted by wheat, wild yeasts and storage in oak vessels.

Following the boil, the hopped wort is pumped to the brewery attic. This is common to all lambic producers, for it is under the roof that alcohol starts to be made. The wort is run into a shallow open fermenter known as the cool ship, made either of copper or stainless steel. The room fills with steam as the wort runs into the fermenter and begins to cool. The louvred windows are left open and during the night wild yeasts enter and attack the sugars in the wort once the temperature has fallen to below 18˚C (66˚F). To encourage the yeasts, brewers even remove a few tiles to leave gaps in the roofs.

Research at the brewing faculty of Leuven University has identified two main types of *Brettanomyces* yeast, *bruxellensis* and *lambicus*. But when all the yeast strains in the atmosphere, the cellars and inside the casks are added together, they number as many as 35. When the beer reaches the maturation halls and is stored in oak casks, it is attacked by both microflora in the wood and the atmosphere. The wild organisms create a flor on top of the maturing beer similar to the flor in sherry casks that prevents oxidation.

The oak casks are bought from Portuguese port makers, Spanish sherry producers or Cognac distillers in France. The beer will stay in cask for several years: some are more than six years old. In the now closed Belle-Vue brewery I once walked down the dimly lit, cool avenues between the casks, each one chalked to indicate the year and month it was filled, and every so often tasting a small glass that had been tapped for me. A month-old lambic had a yeasty aroma and a bready taste. A year-old beer was sour on the nose, sweet and sour in the mouth and had a cheesy finish from the hops. At 18 months, the beer had taken on a delightful sherry colour, a musty Brettanomyces nose, a vinous palate and a dry finish with still a hint of cheesy hops. At 6½ years, the beer was much paler, had a sour, winey aroma, a sharp tangy palate with a pronounced sherry character and a sour, lactic finish. The cheese note had disappeared. It takes some time for Brettanomyces yeasts to dominate the other wild strains.

A straight lambic, tart, cidery and served flat, is usually on draught. The most popular form of the beer is gueuze (also spelt gueze), a blend of young and old lambics in bottle. The young lambic causes a fresh fermentation in the bottle. The result is a spritzy, foaming beer served from a bottle that has been corked with a wire cage like Champagne. The blending requires enormous skill. The blender must decide how much young lambic to marry with old: usually 60% young, but the beer will have more character if as much old lambic as possible is used. The bottles will be stored on their sides in cellars for between six and 18 months. Gueuze beers tend to be around 5.5% alcohol and are dry, tart and wonderfully refreshing. Again, no one is certain about the origin of the name but it is possible that it is a nickname derived from geyser, as the beer tends to rush and foam when released from the bottle. The Bruxellois certainly pronounce it with great force: gur-zer. On the Channel Islands, I discovered that, in Norman-French, gueuze is an old name for wheat, which may possibly provide a link to the beer style at a time when spontaneous fermentation extended beyond Payottenland.

The most exotic versions of lambic are those in which a further fermentation is caused by the addition of fruit. The two basic fruits used are cherry and raspberry. The use of these fruits is similar to the addition of juniper at a time when hops were not part of brewing. The fruit increases fermentability and adds tartness to the finished beer that blends well with the malt. And fruit seems to fuse especially well with beers in which wheat, with its fruity, apple-like flavour, is used. Small, hard cherries grow in abundance in the Brussels area. The preferred variety is the Schaarbeek, though the Gorsem is also used. The cherries are picked late so the fermentable sugars are concentrated. It is similar to the 'noble rot' grapes used in wine. As soon as the cherries are harvested they are added to casks, usually at the rate of 1kg (2¼lbs) of fruit to 5 litres (9 pints) of beer, with the addition of some young lambic. The sugars in the fruit and the young beer create a new fermentation. The tannins on the skins add to the dryness of the finished beer, while the pips impart further dryness and an almond-like note. A cherry lambic is called kriek from the Flemish word for the fruit: the French term is never used. A raspberry beer, on the other hand, is known by both Flemish and French words: frambozen or frambois.

The way in which lambic is made and blended means that aromas and flavours and even alcoholic strength will vary from one batch to another. The tasting notes are my most recent ones but expect variation. Go, drink and marvel.

Boon Geuze/Mariage Parfait Kriek
Source: Brouwerij Frank Boon, Lembeek, Belgium
Strength: 6%/6%
Website: None

Frank Boon (pronounced 'bone') has the perfect address: Fonteinstraat (Fountain Street) in Lembeek, the historic centre of lambic brewing. Frank came into the industry from running a student bar at college, then wholesaling beer, blending other producers' lambics and finally making the beer itself. He took over the De Vits brewery in Lembeek in 1975 when the owner retired. It is a site with considerable history: the present buildings date from 1810 but there had been a farm brewery and distillery since the late 17th century.

During the past 30 years, Frank's reputation has covered all the bases: eccentric, maverick, traditionalist, revivalist, innovator and, inevitably, compromiser as a result of making some filtered, sweetened and commercial lambics. Without doubt, he also makes some of the finest and most characterful traditional lambics. Blended lambics are sold under the Mariage Parfait label: perfect marriage.

Visitors are welcomed by wooden casks at the entrance, and the brewery inside is achingly traditional, down to the open cool ship in the attic, where fermentation begins when the wort is impregnated with wild yeasts. The beers have a softness and delicacy that makes them highly drinkable with less of the assertive acidity in other lambics. The Geuze (Frank's interpretation of the spelling) is a bottled blend of old and young lambics. It is spritzy and tart, with a lemon and ginger aroma, tart fruit in the mouth and a dry finish with hints of oak and fruit.

Mariage Parfait Kriek is superb, an annual vintage that is a blend of the year's young lambic and matured versions that have been in wood for between 18 months and two years. The blend enjoys a further maturation with the addition of cherries and is then held in bottle for up to two years. The beer that emerges is tart and has the toasted note that is also the signature of dry Champagne. The aroma is heady with tangy, sour cherries, and the fruit note continues through the palate into the long, quenching finish.

Cantillon Rosé de Gambrinus/Gueuze-Lambic/ Kriek/Foufoune

Source: Brasserie Cantillon, Anderlecht, Brussels, Belgium
Strength: All 5%
Website: www.cantillon.be

Cantillon dates from 1900. The present owner, Jean-Pierre Van Roy, married into the Cantillon family, took charge in 1978 and built the brewery's reputation. He is passionate about lambic to a degree that often upsets other producers of the style. 'Industrial gueuze' is not a phrase that endears Jean-Pierre to his competitors but, as he nears retirement and hands over to his son Jean, he is concerned that breweries that shorten maturation periods and use syrups rather than whole fruit will lower the standing of the lambic family. In recent years,

Jean-Pierre has switched to organic production as his contribution to saving the planet. He brews from the end of October to the end of March. 'We used to brew in May, but we've lost a whole month as a result of global warming,' he says.

Cantillon calls itself the Museum of Gueuze and maintains strict traditional brewing methods. On the ground floor, a mash of barley malt and wheat is made in a small mash tun, and the turbid wort is pumped to the copper, where it is boiled for an extraordinary four or even five hours. The hopped wort then goes to the cool

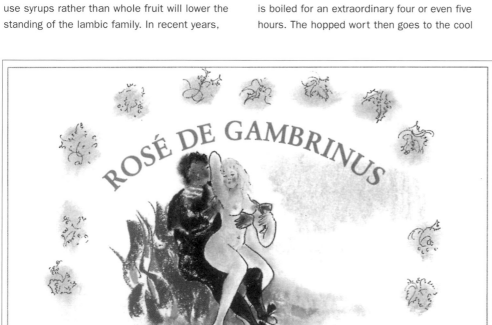

TASTING NOTES
Appearance
Aroma
Taste
Overall score

TASTING NOTES
Appearance
Aroma
Taste
Overall score

ship in the attic to invite inoculation by wild yeasts. Once fermentation is under way, the liquid is transferred to oak or chestnut casks bought from wine and Cognac makers.

Rosé de Gambrinus is a remarkable beer, a blend of raspberry lambic with a small amount of kriek. It has a superb aroma and palate of tart fruit and a bone dry and spritzy finish packed with more tart fruit, with raspberry to the fore.

The Gueuze-Lambic is sour with an almond-like nuttiness, lemon and bitter apple fruit and a deliciously mellow finish.

The Kriek has a glowing red colour, a sour fruit aroma, fresh tart fruit in the mouth and a dry and lingeringly fruity finish.

Foufoune is a recent addition to the range, a lambic made with the addition of apricots. It is extremely pale, dry, acidic, tart and bone dry in the finish. Jean-Pierre, with a wolfish grin, explained that *foufone* in the Brussels dialect means pussy. When you consider the shape of an apricot, you know he is not referring to the brewery cat.

Cantillon is five minutes from Brussels Midi, the Eurostar terminus. It is open to visitors at any time during working hours. For a fee of € 3.50, you can visit the brewery and enjoy a beer. Groups must book: tel: 0032 2521 4928; email: info@cantillon.be. Closed Sunday and public holidays.

Drie Fonteinen Oude Gueuze/Framboos/Oude Kriek

Source: Brouwerij Drie Fonteinen, Beersel, Belgium
Strength: 6%/5%
Website: None

Someone in Rome must have thrown three coins in the Trevi fountain for, lo and behold, a new lambic brewer of that name appeared and has helped breathe life back into the sector.

The Debelder family has run an acclaimed restaurant in Beersel for many years and also acted as lambic blenders, taking beer from the likes of Boon, Girardin and Lindeman, and bringing them to fruition in oak casks. Then, in 1999, the brothers Armand and Guido took the giant step of opening the first new lambic brewery for 80 years. They continue to buy in lambic from Girardin and Lindeman until their own beers have reached an acceptable maturity and are ready for blending.

As well as the beers featured here, they have made the almost-lost style of Faro, a sweetened lambic, and have also made lambics with the addition of Chardonnay and Pinot Noir grapes. The bottled beers will improve with age.

Oude Gueuze has a shockingly dry, musty, tart lemon bouquet and palate, with a long, fruity, sour, acidic finish. Framboos is a true raspberry beer, made with whole fruit, not syrup. It has a luscious pink colour, a delightfully fruity but dry aroma and palate, with tart, slightly sour fruit in the lingering finish. Anybody who thinks fruit lambics are too challenging should sample this beer and let it cast aside any preconceptions. A bottled version is 6% and has more depth of fruit flavours.

Oude Kriek has a superb aroma of bitter cherry fruit and 'horse blanket' yeast mustiness. The fruit, with an almond-like underpinning from the pips, dominates the palate, while the finish is dry, sour, fruity and nutty. Again, the bottled version is 6% and is a revelation, with enormous sour fruit, yeast bite and almonds dominating from nose to finish.

The Drie Fonteinen restaurant is round the corner from the brewery at 3 Herman Teirlinckplein (closed Tuesday and Wednesday; tel: 02 331 0652). It serves top-class food and draught gueuze and lambic.

TASTING NOTES
Appearance
Aroma
Taste
Overall score

TASTING NOTES
Appearance
Aroma
Taste
Overall score

TASTING NOTES
Appearance
Aroma
Taste
Overall score

Girardin Gueuze Black Label 1882

Source: Brouwerij Girardin, Sint Ulriks Kapelle, Belgium
Strength: 5%
Website: None

TASTING NOTES
Appearance
Aroma
Taste
Overall score

This is one of the few remaining genuine farm brewers in the Senne Valley still making lambic. The brewery was launched in 1882 by Francis Girardin and today Paul is the fourth generation of the family to run the company. The farm still grows the wheat that is blended with barley malt to make beer. The small complex is fronted by oak casks and, inside, mashing and boiling take place in attractive, burnished copper vessels, watched over by an effigy of St Arnold, the patron saint of brewers.

Fermentation begins in a cool ship and continues in oak casks. Girardin produces framboise and kriek, but the Black Label is considered to be not only the best product but also one of the finest examples of a blended gueuze. It is full-bodied, with rich and creamy malt on the nose and palate, spritzy from natural carbonation and with a tongue-tingling sour lemon fruit note that dominates from start to finish, all overlain by a musty, 'horse blanket' character from the attack by Brettanomyces yeasts.

Do not confuse Black Label with Girardin's White Label 1882, which is a filtered version, perfectly acceptable and pleasant but a shadow of the unfiltered beer with its great depth of flavours that will improve in bottle for years, if not decades.

Beers made with Fruit, Spices, Herbs & Seeds

In 1588, Jacob Theodor von Bergzabern, describing contemporary brewing practice in Europe, noted that hops were increasingly being used but added: 'The English sometimes add to the brewed beer, to make it more pleasant, sugar, cinnamon, cloves and other good spices in a small bag. The Flemings mix it with honey or sugar and precious spices and so make a drink like claret or hippocras [spiced wine]. Others mix in honey, sugar and syrup, which not only makes the beer pleasant to drink, but also gives it a fine brown colour.' He added that brewers had learned from 'the Flemings and the Netherlanders' that adding laurel, ivy or Dutch myrtle to beer strengthens it, preserves it and stops it going sour.

As late as 1750, London brewers were still using bog myrtle and coriander to flavour their beers. As we have seen, Belgian brewers continue to add spices and orange peel to white, or wheat, beers, as well as hops. The addition of sugars, herbs and spices to beer is far older than the 16th century. We know from research and the translation of hieroglyphics on clay tablets that the Ancient Egyptians used dates, honey and even mandrake – a plant that, alarmingly, is a member of the nightshade family – in beer making.

From 3000BC to modern times, brewers have grappled with the problem of how to balance the biscuity nature of malt with ingredients that add a welcome bitterness and spiciness. When European brewers discovered the hop plant, they started to use it in brewing more for commercial reasons than for those of taste.

In his *Perfite Platforme for a Hoppe Garden*, first published in 1574 in England, Reynold Scot's arguments in favour of the plant were principally commercial: 'Whereas you cannot make above 8–9 gallons of indifferent ale from 1 bushel of malt, you may draw 18–20 gallons of good beer. If your ale may endure a fortnight, your beer through the benefit of the hop shall continue a month.' In other words, hops gave beer better 'shelf life', to use an ugly modern expression, and less malt had to be used.

The cost of raw materials was an important consideration as brewing moved from being a church-based pastime to a business activity. At a royal banquet in Windsor Park in 1528, 15 gallons of ale and 15 gallons of beer were ordered. The beer cost 20 pence, the ale two shillings and sixpence. The difference in price is significant and is caused almost completely by the greater quantity of malt used in ale.

The ability of the oils, acids and tannins in the hop plant protected beer against bacterial infection, which was a major problem in a period when it was almost impossible to control fermentation temperatures. Scot, whose book ran to several editions and was highly influential, did add that one of the advantages of hopped beer was 'the grace it yieldeth to the taste all men may judge that have sense in their mouths'.

But hopped beer, as opposed to unhopped and flavoured ale, did not please all drinkers. A debate raged for several centuries in England over the benefits of ale and beer. Hops were banned in Norwich, even though many Flemish weavers, who had introduced the plant to England, had settled there. In 1519, the use of the 'wicked and pernicious weed' was prohibited in Shrewsbury. Henry VIII instructed his royal court brewer to use neither brimstone nor hops in his ale. Drinkers, from the humble to the mighty, preferred the old flavours of spices, honey, flowers, plants and herbs. Their use lingered on for several centuries. They persist in a handful of styles. And, to add to both the pleasure and a greater understanding and appreciation of beer, their use has been revived in a number of countries by craftspeople who have given us another fascinating glimpse of brewing's past.

Daleside Morocco Ale

Source: Daleside Brewery, Harrogate, North Yorkshire, England
Strength: 5.5%
Website: www.dalesidebrewery.co.uk/levenshall.co.uk

Morocco Ale is brewed to a secret recipe held at Levens Hall, a moated Elizabethan complex, famous for its topiary, near Kendal in Cumbria. The beer is thought to date from the time of Elizabeth I and was given its name by Colonel James Grahme, a courtier of Charles II. Charles's queen, Catherine of Braganza, brought Tangiers as part of her dowry, and Grahme may have associated the Moors of the region with the dark beer consumed at Levens.

The recipe for the beer had been buried in the garden of the hall under evergreens during the English Civil War. Following the restoration of the monarchy, the beer was brewed every May until 1877. Each batch was matured for 21 years and was served at feasts held in the gardens of the hall. At one stage, meat was part of the recipe in order to give the yeast nutrition to sustain it over such an extraordinary period of maturation. New guests were required to stand on one leg and empty, in a single draught, a tall 'constable' glass of the beer.

The beer was resurrected in the 1990s by the Daleside Brewery for Levens Hall and has since been made available commercially. Brewery and hall are tight-lipped about the ingredients, though they confirm meat is no longer used. It will rapidly become clear when the beer is sniffed and sipped that ginger is a major ingredient. The other spicy notes suggest nutmeg, while the rich marmalade fruit and roasted and toasted notes will come from the malts and hops used: Daleside uses Challenger and Goldings in its regular beers.

The beer is available from Levens Hall (015395 60321) and from Booths supermarkets in the north of England.

Fraoch Heather Ale/Kelpie Ale

Source: Williams Brothers Brewing Company, Alloa, Scotland
Strength: 4.1%/4.1%
Website: www.fraoch.com

The earliest brewers in Scotland were not Celts but Picts, the cave-dwelling race that raided Roman Britain but which was exterminated in a series of pogroms in the fourth century by marauders from Ireland. According to legend, the last Pict threw himself from the cliffs into the sea rather than pass on the secret of heather ale to the invading forces of the king of Ireland.

But heather ale lingered on in remote parts of the Highlands and Islands. A visitor to Islay in 1744 noted that beer there was made from malt, hops and 'heath'. Ancient Pictish kilns have been discovered in the Galloway region where heather ale was once made. In his 19th-century book *Curiosities of Ale and Beer*, John Bickerdyke described the way in which heather was used to brew: 'The blossoms of the heather are carefully gathered and cleansed, then placed in the bottom of the vessels. Wort of the ordinary kind is allowed to drain through the blossoms and gains in its passage a peculiar and agreeable flavour known to all familiar with heather honey.'

In 1993, Bruce Williams in Glasgow obtained a translation from the Gaelic of a recipe for heather ale that was in the possession of a woman in the Western Isles. Bruce's Fraoch Ale aroused enormous interest. The beer was produced under licence for him at several Scottish breweries until he and his brother were able to acquire the Forth Brewery site in Alloa.

Fraoch (pronounced 'frook', the Gaelic for heather) is available on draught and bottle. It is brewed with pale malt, carapils, flowering heather and bog myrtle, and hopped with First Gold, which produce 19 units of bitterness. The hopped wort is infused with fresh heather flowers for an hour before fermentation. The beer has a delicate flowery, fruity bouquet with flowery and minty

flavours in the mouth, balanced by gentle hop resins and juicy malt. The finish is dry, earthy, minty, floral and quenching.

Kelpie is Gaelic for seaweed. The beer recalls the time 400 years ago when coastal and island farmers used seaweed beds to grow cereal crops. Bladderwrack seaweed is used with organic pale malt and First Gold hops to produce a pale beer with an iron-like aroma and palate, balanced by juicy malt and spicy hops. The finish is lingering, tart, tangy, with a herbal and fruity intensity. The bottled beers are available in Canada and the US.

TASTING NOTES	
Appearance	
Aroma	
Taste	
Overall score	

TASTING NOTES	
Appearance	
Aroma	
Taste	
Overall score	

Jopen Koyt

Source: Jopen BV, Haarlem, Netherlands
Strength: 8.5%
Website: www.jopen.nl

TASTING NOTES
Appearance
Aroma
Taste
Overall score

For centuries, European and Scandinvian brewers added gruit, a type of bouquet garni of herbs and spices, to beer. Gruit was big business and it was controlled by the church, which fought a powerful rearguard action against the use of hops in brewing. In Cologne, the archbishop cornered the gruit market through a decree called the Grutrecht and he attempted to outlaw the use of hops. In the Low Countries, from the 14th century, the religious controllers of the gruit market placed punitive taxes on hopped beer imported from Bremen and Hamburg. But the march of history and drinkers' preference prevailed and eventually the gruit market was abandoned, though the church did well out of the deal, accepting rents or royalties in return for giving up their rights to supply gruit to brewers.

The great Dutch trading city of Haarlem was once a major brewing centre. Water from the canals was used until pollution made the supply unsafe. Pure brewing liquid was then brought to Haarlem by a new canal: it still exists today as Brewers Canal. In the 17th century, Haarlem was home to around 100 brewers. The number had

fallen to seven by the 19th century and the last brewery closed in 1916. In 1995, a group of beer enthusiasts led by Michel Ordeman launched a range of beers based on medieval recipes that used gruit. The flagship regular beer is Koyt, an old Dutch word for gruit, while jopen is another old term for a beer cask.

Koyt is brewed for Jopen by the Van Steenberge brewery in Belgium (Jopen does not brew Koyt itself). Michel and his friends wanted to brew Koyt without hops but the Dutch authorities will not permit any beer to be made without hops – a fussy, bureaucratic attitude that rather misses the point of the endeavour. So Koyt has hops but also uses sweet gale, coriander and other herbs and spices. In the medieval fashion, the grains are malted barley, wheat and oats, with a darker barley malt that gives the beer a luscious russet colour. It has a rich spicy aroma of coriander with a woody, grassy note, along with nutty and creamy malt and light hops. Spices and rich malt fill the mouth while the finish is long and complex, with spices and creamy malt dominating.

Meantime Coffee Beer/Red Beer

Source: Meantime Brewing Co, Greenwich, London, England
Strength: 4%/4.5%
Website: www.meantimebrewing.com

Meantime was created in 2000 by master brewer Alastair Hook to produce handcrafted European beers. Alastair is a graduate of both Heriot Watt brewing and distilling school in Edinburgh and of the brewing faculty at Weihenstephan in Freising near Munich, widely regarded as the finest brewing school in the world. His mission has been to brew small-batch beers to exacting standards, producing lagers with character and flavour rather than gas and gaiters, and ales that snap and crackle with hop aroma. He brews beers for the Sainsbury's supermarket group under the Taste the Difference label. Meantime owns the Greenwich Union pub (56 Royal Hill, London SE10) where draught and bottled beers can be tasted.

The Coffee Beer is brewed with the addition of Fairtrade Rwanda Maraba Bourbon coffee to East Anglian pale and dark barley malts and Fuggles hops. The coffee, like the beer, is hand-crafted, roasted by Union Coffee Roasters. It has a superb aroma of freshly roasted beans, vanilla and dark malt, with a good spicy undertow of hops. Coffee, vanilla, grain and hops pack the mouth, followed by a long, complex finish that is dry, roasty and hoppy.

Alastair's interpretation of a Belgian-style fruit beer uses fresh raspberry juice added to a beer base. It has a luscious red colour and a rich raspberry aroma balanced by sappy malt and gentle hops. The palate is spritzy, with lush and tart fruit, juicy malt and spicy hops, followed by a lingering finish packed with tangy raspberries, biscuity malt and earthy hop resins.

TASTING NOTES
Appearance
Aroma
Taste
Overall score

TASTING NOTES
Appearance
Aroma
Taste
Overall score

Nethergate Augustinian Ale

Source: Nethergate Brewery Co, Pentlow, Essex, England
Strength: 5.2%
Website: www.nethergate.co.uk

Nethergate moved to Essex in 2004. Its first base was in the attractive market town of Clare in Suffolk, where there is an Augustinian priory and a small group of monks. The brewery reached an agreement with the prior to produce what in Belgium would be called an abbey beer, using images of the church and St Augustine, one of the most influential saints. There are religious houses throughout the world where Augustinians faithfully follow his doctrines. A royalty on sales of the beer is paid to the prior in Clare.

Augustinian Ale is brewed with Maris Otter pale and crystal malts, is hopped with Fuggles and spiced with coriander. It is a rich, deep bronze in colour with a spicy aroma from the coriander, and a piny and earthy note from the Fuggles, with a solid base of biscuity malt. Citrus fruit enters on the palate with continuing notes of spice, juicy malt and hop resins. The lingering finish is spicy, with nutty and biscuity malt, bitter hops and tangy fruit. The beer is filtered and then reseeded with fresh yeast prior to bottling. It is produced principally for sale in the United States but it can be bought by mail order direct from the brewery: 01787 277244. The beer should not be confused with Nethergate's beer of the same name, which is a draught 4.5% cask-conditioned beer and is not spiced.

RCH Ale Mary

Source: RCH Brewery, West Hewish, Weston-super-Mare, Somerset, England
Strength: 6%
Website: www.rchbrewery.com

TASTING NOTES
Appearance
Aroma
Taste
Overall score

Ale Mary is a bottle-fermented version of the brewery's regular draught cask beer Firebox with the addition of spices. And what spices! Ginger, cloves, cinnamon, coriander, nutmeg and pimento join pale and chocolate malts and Progress and Target hops to produce a beer that stunned the judges – myself included – in CAMRA's 2001 Champion Bottled Beer of Britain competition, which it duly won.

Firebox has a tart and tangy orange fruit character and this comes through powerfully in the bottled version. But the fruit is fighting for attention with the spicy, peppery and almost sneeze-inducing aromatics. What a wonderful companion for Indian cuisine the beer would make instead of the insipid mock lagers most restaurants serve. Ginger and coriander in particular blast the tongue but are balanced by raisin and sultana fruit and earthy hops. The finish is warming, ripe with alcohol and lingering spices, with a dry and finally bitter end but with a solid underpinning of juicy malt and vine fruit.

The brewery firmly denies any suggestion the beer is named in honour of Lady Mary Archer, wife of the disgraced peer and novelist Lord Jeffrey Archer of Weston-super-Mare. In a famous court case, the judge described Lady Archer as 'fragrant' but probably didn't have nutmeg or pimento in mind.

St Austell Clouded Yellow

Source: St Austell Brewery Co, St Austell, Cornwall, England
Strength: 4.8%
Website: www.staustellbrewery.co.uk

When Roger Ryman, the head brewer at St Austell, decided to brew a German-style wheat beer for the brewery's annual Celtic Beer Festival in 1999, he called it Hagar the Horrible. In spite of this less than mellifluous name, the beer was well received and in 2003 Roger entered it for the Beer Challenge staged by the giant supermarket group Tesco. It won, gained shelf space with Tesco nationally and achieved wide praise and appreciation under the gentler name of Clouded Yellow, a rare butterfly that visits Britain during the summer in common with several German wheat beers.

Roger's aim was to create his interpretation of a German Weissbier but he was anxious not to introduce an imported yeast strain in case it cross-fertilised with his prized house culture.

In order to create the true flavour of a German weiss, with its banana and bubblegum character, he used vanilla pods, cloves, coriander and maple syrup alongside Maris Otter pale malt, wheat malt and spicy American Willamette hops. The spices are added in a vessel known as the hop back that receives the hopped wort after the copper boil. Maple syrup is blended with sugar and used as a priming to encourage fermentation in bottle. The burnished gold beer has a full and tempting aroma of spices, banana and vanilla with creamy malt and light hop resins. Spices and vanilla fill the mouth but there is a continuing rich malt note. The finish is quenching, lingering, rich with banana, vanilla, spices, rich malt and light earthy hops. A complex, intriguing and refreshing beer.

Wells Banana Bread Beer

Source: Charles Wells Eagle Brewery, Bedford, England
Strength: 4.5% cask/5.2% bottle
Website: www.charleswells.co.uk

TASTING NOTES	
Appearance	
Aroma	
Taste	
Overall score	

Charles Wells is England's biggest family-owned, independent regional brewery. Not satisfied with the success and growth of its premium cask beer Bombardier (see page 100), it has added to the range a beer that not only offers the ripe aroma and flavour of banana – the most popular fruit in the country – but actually uses real fruit during the production process.

The Campaign for Real Ale, ever anxious to win new supporters to the cause of cask ale, organised a tasting for women-only visitors to the Great British Beer Festival in London and found that Banana Bread Beer met with great acclaim and appreciation. Hop bitterness is one frequent reason given by women for not drinking real ale, and the lush smoothness and creaminess of banana clearly helped make the beer more acceptable.

The cask version is a seasonal beer, the stronger bottled one is available all year round. It is brewed with pale and crystal malts and hopped with Challenger and Goldings varieties. Banana pulp is added during the copper boil stage. The pale bronze beer has a rich banana aroma, while the palate has both banana and pear drop flavours, allied to juicy malt and a light tingle of hops. The finish is fruity, creamy but finishes dry with a late crackle of spicy hops and smooth, creamy malt.

Pale Lagers

Brewing in continental Europe was transformed by the development of golden lager beer in Pilsen, Bohemia, in the mid-19th century. But it was in neighbouring Bavaria that brewers grasped the potential of cold fermentation to produce a wider portfolio of beers made with the use of ice-making machines, better-quality malt and hops, and purer strains of yeast.

Such was the impact of the new beers from Munich and the surrounding region that brewers elsewhere in Europe and Scandinavia referred to 'Bavarian beer' as both a style and one they wished to emulate. It was the fame of Bavarian beers that sent J C Jacobsen, the founder of the Carlsberg brewery in Copenhagen, on a long and arduous coach journey to Munich in order to get a supply of yeast from Spaten in order to make beer by cold fermentation.

The first commercial Bavarian beers were dark in colour, a luscious, transluscent red/brown as a result of using malts kilned over wood fires. The Bavarians, more stolid and conservative than the famously unconventional Bohemians, remained loyal to dark beers they called 'dunkel'. But the success of Pilsner beer and the introduction of modern methods of kilning malt to make lighter varieties encouraged the Munich brewers to introduce paler versions of lager beer. They made their own interpretations of Pilsner beer – usually shortened to Pils to avoid legal action from Pilsen. But, just as British brewers introduced a weaker, everyday version of India Pale Ale called simply pale ale, the Bavarians developed a pale lager that was fractionally lower in alcohol than a Pils but noticeably less hoppy, perhaps 22 units of bitterness compared to the 38 of a Pils. The style is known as Helles or Hell and means pale.

This is the style of quaffing beer that is downed in beer gardens, bars and restaurants in Bavaria. Pils is seen as a beer for a special occasion or perhaps as the fitting end to a drinking session. Helles is a style that has been widely copied. Brewers throughout the world may call their golden lagers Pils or Pilsner but few have the aggressive hop bitterness of the original. Helles has even made its impact felt across the border in the modern Czech Republic, for the classic Budweiser Budvar has more in common with a Munich Helles than with a beer from Pilsen.

With the exception of the Japanese and Russian beers, the lagers listed below are brewed in accordance with the German Purity Law, the Reinheitsgebot, that stipulates that only malt, hops, water and yeast can be used in the brewing process. Sugars and cheaper grains are outlawed. Czech brewers, such as Budvar, produce 12 degree or premium beers in accordance with the Reinheitsgebot in order to sell them in Germany.

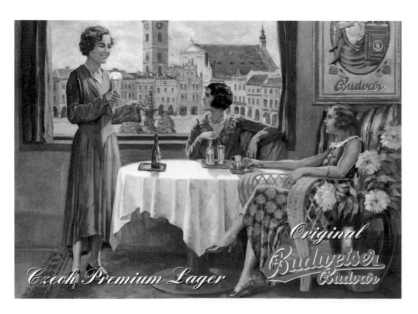

ABOVE LEFT
Baltika is a fine-tasting lager from Russia's major brewing group owned by Carlsberg and Scottish & Newcastle

LEFT
An early 20th-century promotion by Budvar for its classic golden lager was aimed at women.

Augustiner Hell

Source: Brauerei Augustiner, Munich, Bavaria, Germany
Strength: 5.2%
Website: www.augustiner-braeu.de

Munich is München in German, a corruption of Mönchen, meaning the Monks' Place. The city was founded in 1158 when a Bavarian duke built a bridge across the River Isar, enabling it to become an important trading post on the salt route from Austria to the north German ports. Benedictines and Franciscans were among the orders that built monasteries in the town but it was the Augustinians who developed a community there in 1294 and added a brewery in 1328. Augustiner can therefore lay claim to being the oldest brewery in Munich, though it has long since moved from its original site to a modern brewery in the city centre.

In common with most of the old breweries in Munich, Augustiner has had a turbulent history: secularised in 1803, taken over first by the Bavarian royal family and then by the state when the monarchy lost power after World War One, and bought by the Wagner family. Today it is a public company. While it is less known outside Bavaria than some of the other big Munich breweries, Augustiner is the most popular beer in the city and is consumed with relish in such beer gardens and bars as the Augustiner Keller on Arnulf Strasse, the brewery tap on Neuhauser Strasse and the large Hirschgarten near the Nymphenburg Palace. I have even enjoyed a glass in the pavilion of the MCC, the Munich Cricket Club, run by ex-pats in the Englischer Garten.

The beer is a burnished gold colour, is brewed with pale malt (around eight units of colour) and Hallertau hop varieties that produce 22 units of bitterness and has a rich toasted malt, light citrus fruit and floral hop aroma. Ripe, juicy malt and hop resins fill the mouth, followed by a long finish with some dryness at the end but dominated by sweet, soft malt, light but punchy hops and a delicious hint of lemon fruit.

Baltika Classic No 3

Source: Baltika Brewery, St Petersburg, Russia
Strength: 4.8%
Website: www.baltika.ru

There is a certain irony in the fact that the number of breweries in Russia has fallen by almost half since the collapse of the Soviet Union. Whisper it quietly, but there was more choice under communism than capitalism. The Russian tradition of brewing dark beers, including porters and imperial stouts, is under threat as global brewers dominate the market, centralise production and concentrate on pale lagers. As this book was being completed, the Baltika group announced it was brewing Foster's under licence. Oh, you lucky Russians! When I visited the Vena brewery in St Petersburg, a subsidiary of Baltika, and asked to taste its porter I was told it was no longer produced.

The main Baltika plant was built in 1978 on a greenfield site outside Leningrad, now St Petersburg. The state enterprise was privatised in 1992 and is now owned by Baltic Beverages Holding, a group jointly owned by Carlsberg and Scottish & Newcastle, which includes Sinebrychoff in Finland. Baltika is now the biggest brewing group in Russia with close to a quarter of the market. As well as St Petersburg, it has plants in Rostov on Don and other major urban centres. In the Russian tradition, the beers are labelled simply 1 to 7, the last one being a porter.

The pale lagers tend to be rather bland, mass market beers devoid of much aroma or taste. The exception is Classic, also branded as No 3. Vena has a similar beer called Original at 5%. Baltika uses pale malt and a touch of dark malt for colour and flavour. Hops, in the form of pellets, are imported from Germany, as the Russian hop industry is currently too small to supply sufficient quantities. The beer is exceptionally pale with a rich cornflour, vanilla and juicy malt aroma and a touch of lemon fruit. The fruit note builds in the mouth with a toasted malt note and light floral hops. The finish is dry with developing bitter hop notes balancing the tangy fruit and sappy malt.

TASTING NOTES
Appearance
Aroma
Taste
Overall score

TASTING NOTES
Appearance
Aroma
Taste
Overall score

Budweiser Budvar 12°

Source: Budějovicky Budvar, České Budějovice, Czech Republic
Strength: 5%
Website: www.budvar.cz

TASTING NOTES
Appearance
Aroma
Taste
Overall score

Controversy surrounds one of the world's classic lager beers. Budweiser Budvar is seldom out of the headlines. It is constantly involved in court battles and trade mark disputes with the giant American brewer, Anheuser-Busch, owner of the world's biggest beer brand, also called Budweiser.

The Americans claim their beer is the original, but history is not on their side. The South Bohemian town of České Budějovice has been a major brewing centre for centuries. It had 44 breweries in the 15th century and, under the town's old German name of Budweis, the beers were known generically as Budweiser, just as beers from Pilsen are called Pilsner. The royal court brewery was based in Budweis, enabling the products to be called 'the beer of kings'. In the 19th century, a major, German-owned brewery, Budweiser Burgerbrau, made and widely exported beer under the Budweiser name. It still exists but is now known as Samson.

In 1875, two German-born emigrants called Anheuser and Busch opened a brewery in St Louis, Missouri, and among its beers it had one called Budweiser, based on the Czech style, which it subsequently tagged 'the king of beers'.

Sound familiar? Twenty years later, Czech speakers in Budweis opened a new brewery, the Budějovicky Pivovar, which means the Budweis Brewery. For convenience, the name is shortened to Budvar. When the Czechs attempted to export their beer to the United States, sparks flew and litigation involving the two brewers of Budweiser has rumbled on ever since.

Today, the two beers could not be more different. The American beer lists rice before barley malt on the label, and the minute amount of hops used in production create no more than 12 units of bitterness. Budvar, on the other hand, is a pure malt beer that adheres to the German purity law. It is made in a magnificent brewhouse, with large copper mashing and brew kettles set on tiled floors. A double decoction mash is used. Primary fermentation is in small conicals, ripening or lagering in classic horizontal tanks. Lagering lasts for 90 days, one of the longest periods of cold conditioning in the world. Only pale Moravian malt and Žatec hops are used (20 units of bitterness). Soft brewing water comes from a deep underground natural reservoir that dates back several thousand years. Budvar has a rich malt and vanilla aroma, it is quenching in the mouth with a floral hop character, and the finish has a fine balance of juicy malt, tangy hop resins and a delicate hint of apple fruit. It is unquestionably one of the world's finest lager beers, sold in the United States under the name of Czechvar.

Kirin Ichiban

Source: Kirin Brewery Co, Tokyo, Japan
Strength: 5%
Website: www.kirin.com

Ichiban means 'Number One' or, literally, the best. Kirin Lager enjoys a reputation as the best Pils-style beer in Japan, but it added to the pleasure of beer drinking in 1990 with the introduction of Ichiban, fractionally stronger than the lager. It is made from the 'first running', or first pressing, of the wort in the mash tun. Instead of leaving the mash of malt and water to stand and then sparging, or sprinkling, it with more fresh water to squeeze out as much malt sugar as possible, the Kirin brewers run off the first, biscuity wort from the mashing vessels and discard the grain. The wort is clarified in a lauter tun, boiled with hops, fermented and then ripened or lagered, in this case for two months. Pale barley malt and Czech Saaz and German Hallertauer hops are used.

The delicious and refreshing beer that emerges, on draught and in bottle, has a lilting lemon grass, toasted malt and light floral hop aroma, with juicy malt, hop resins and delicate fruit in the mouth, and a lingering finish with biscuity malt, tangy fruit and spicy hops.

The beer has been so successful that it is now brewed under licence in both Britain and the US.

TASTING NOTES
Appearance
Aroma
Taste
Overall score

Spaten Münchner Hell

Source: Spaten-Franziskaner-Bräu, Munich, Bavaria, Germany
Strength: 4.8%
Website: www.spatenbraeu.com

Spaten traces its brewing roots back to 1397, with commercial rather than monastic production dating from 1522. In 1807, Gabriel Sedlmayr the Elder, master brewer at the Royal Court Brewery, bought the company, whose Spaten name means 'spade': the logo shows a maltster's shovel, used for turning grain in a maltings. In 1839, his son Gabriel the Younger took over and began energetically to transform production of beer to make use of the new technologies of the Industrial Revolution. Together with the Viennese brewer Anton Dreher, he visited Britain to see how the new pale ales were made. He built a new brewery in 1851 on the site of deep cellars and, with the aid of ice-making machines, turned his earlier experiments into full-blown commercial production of beers by the method of cold fermentation.

As I explained in the introduction to this section, the first lager beers in Munich were brown in colour but, in 1893, Sedlmayr launched the first pale or Helles beer in the city. It would be hyperbolic to suggest it marked a transformation of brewing. Most of the other Munich brewers did not begin to brew pale lagers until the 1920s, such was the consumer devotion to dark, or Dunkel, beers. But Spaten had produced the benchmark beer and that style today is the major one alongside wheat beers.

Spaten's Hell, lagered for two months, brewed from pale malt and Hallertauer hop varieties (22 units of bitterness) has a lightly toasted malt, gentle hop resins and delicate lemon fruit aroma and palate, with a quenching finish that is bitter-sweet to start and ends dry with delicate hop notes, juicy malt and tangy fruit.

TASTING NOTES
Appearance
Aroma
Taste
Overall score

Žatec 12°
Source: Žatec Brewery, Žatec, Czech Republic
Strength: 5%
Website: None

TASTING NOTES
Appearance
Aroma
Taste
Overall score

On my first visit to the brewery, it was semi-derelict, with a reception area recently vacated by the Young Communist League. Two years later, the brewery had been transformed, sparkling with fresh paint. Previously leaking lagering cellars with rusting pipework were now spick and span. The transformation is due to the energetic ownership of Anglo-Swedish businessman Rolf Munding. The town of Žatec, in the former German-speaking Sudetenland, gives its name to the surrounding hop-growing region, famous for producing some of the finest and most aromatic varieties in the world, known outside the Czech Republic by their German name of Saaz. The dark red soil, rich in ferrous oxide, is ideal for hop growing. The brewery is based in a former castle with a commanding position over the town and river. The castle cellars, 24m (80ft) below ground, proved ideal for storing beer when the site became a brewery in the 19th century, modelled on the Pilsner Urquell plant in Pilsen, where the first golden lager had been made. Žatec has a capacity of 160,000 hectolitres a year and produces 10, 11 and 12 degree beers: the 11 degree is available in selected bars and restaurants in Britain where Rolf Munding has interests, but I have chosen the 12 degree as the best of the three.

It is stored or lagered for 45 days and brewed with pale Moravian malt and local hops: the hops are added to the kettle three times, after 30 minutes, one hour and 1½ hours. Primary fermentation is in open vessels, lagering in horizontal tanks. For a Czech lager, the beer has a surprising hint of banana fruit on the nose from the house yeast culture, with massive hop resins, juicy malt and citrus lemon. Floral hops dominate the palate, and the long, dry hoppy finish has more juicy malt and lemon fruit.

A sign in the brewer's office announces: 'Where beer is brewed there is a good life' and the good life has certainly returned to a brewery that, in the early 1990s, seemed destined to close.

Black & Dark Lagers

Dark lager, in common with dark mild in England, is enjoying a renaissance. Both are beer styles that developed at the time of the Industrial Revolution and refreshed the new urban working class. They also reflect an earlier period of brewing, when all beers were brown in colour as a result of the way in which malt was prepared: cured or kilned over wood fires.

Wood fires are difficult to control. They often flare and scorch the grain, giving a smoky character to the finished beer. When coke and, later, gas replaced wood as the fuels for curing malt, brewers were able to make beers from pale malt with its far higher level of the natural enzymes that transform starch into fermentable sugar. Even dark beers started to be made from pale malt with the addition of darker grains for colouring and flavour. Dark lager – known in Bavaria as dunkel or dunkles – was different in one important respect from dark mild. It was the first beer to be made by the new system of cold fermentation. Cold conditioning took place in deep cellars cooled by ice. The wooden casks in which the beer was stored were lined with pitch and the result was a beer with a brown or russet colour and a luscious flavour reminiscent of vine fruits, nuts, liquorice and coffee. It was 'Bavarian beer' that started to transform European brewing practice and paved the way for the Pilsner revolution of the mid-19th century.

In Bavaria, home of the first dark lagers, most brewers kept a dunkel beer as part of their portfolios. But dunkel was a minority taste for older drinkers: what the English call a 'cloth cap'

beer. The style was rejuvenated by one man: Crown Prince Luitpold in his castle at Kaltenberg near Munich (see page 262). As a result of his endeavours, dunkel now enjoys a much higher profile and is brewed with some enthusiasm.

Across the border in Czechoslovakia, dark lager remained an important part of the brewing scene, partly because heavy industry lingered on for much longer than on the other side of the Iron Curtain and also as a result of the extreme conservatism of the communist regime. It was the lack of funds to invest in new brewing methods that enabled both genuine Pilsners and dark lagers to survive. We have seen that the arrival of the 'free market' in the new Czech Republic has done little to improve the quality of pale lagers but so far dark versions have survived intact and even been given a small amount of support and promotion.

Dark lager has been boosted further in the United States. A new generation of brewers, many of them of German descent, are brewing beers with enormous devotion to the original styles, including dunkel, which has brought dark lager to a new and appreciative audience.

TASTING NOTES

Appearance

Aroma

Taste

Overall score

TASTING NOTES

Appearance

Aroma

Taste

Overall score

Gordon Biersch Dunkles
**Source: Gordon Biersch Brewery,
Palo Alto, California, USA
Strength: 5%
Website: www.gordonbiersch.com**

The American Dream is alive and well in California. Dan Gordon graduated from a five-year course at the Weihenstephan faculty of brewing near Munich, the first American to do so for 40 years. When he returned to California, he met Dean Biersch, a restaurateur and beer lover, and they planned a brew-restaurant in Palo Alto that would offer first-class food, backed by Dan's faithful re-creations of German beers.

Palo Alto opened in 1988 and such has been the success of the venture that, backed by investment from a Las Vegas-based entertainment group, Dan and Dean have built a brewery with a capacity of 85,000 barrels a year in San José and opened new restaurants in Hawaii, Nevada and Washington State. Hops from the Bavarian Hallertau and a yeast strain from Weihenstephan are imported to brew and ferment the beers.

Dunkles has a rich and tempting russet-brown colour, a ripe bouquet of liquorice, coffee, dark grain and vine fruits, and a full palate dominated by raisin fruit, coffee, burnt malt and light hop resins. The lingering, complex finish is packed with rich, dark fruit, caramel, bitter-sweet grain and earthy hops.

Kaltenberg König Ludwig Dunkel
**Source: Schlossbrauerei Kaltenberg, Geltendorf, Bavaria, Germany
Strength: 5.6%
Website: www.kaltenberg.de**

His Royal Highness Crown Prince Luitpold of Kaltenberg is an unlikely brewer. But, despite the title, he has no power and with a large castle to run he decided to turn the small family brewery into a commercial enterprise that would help pay for the upkeep of the estate. He took charge of the castle and brewery in 1976 when he was in his mid-20s and is still in control today.

A castle was built on the site in the 13th century by Duke Rudolph of Bavaria and was attacked, ransacked, destroyed and rebuilt in medieval times. The current castle dates from 1670 but was redesigned in neo-Gothic style in the 1840s. Thirty years later the castle brewery spread its wings and began to supply local taverns as well as the royal household with beer. When Prince Luitpold took charge he decided to turn the local speciality, a dark lager, into the main brand to restore dunkel beer to its rightful position as a proud Bavarian style. It is named in honour of King Ludwig, one of his ancestors. The brewery at first could make just 25,000 hectolitres (550,000 gallons) a year but capacity has grown to more than 100,000 hectos (2.2m gallons).

Prince Luitpold uses Bavarian pale, dark and roasted Bavarian malts, and he hops the beer three times with Hersbrucker and Tettnanger varieties from the Hallertau (colour 40, units of bitterness 26). The mash is a long triple decoction one. After the copper boil, the beer has a primary fermentation in small conical vessels, followed by a long ripening in steel tanks in the cellars of the castle. The original wooden lagering tanks are for display only. The beer is kräusened with partially fermented wort to encourage a strong second fermentation during lagering. To avoid the sweetness associated with some dunkel beers, Prince Luitpold attenuates the beer more than most brewers, turning 80% of the malt sugars into alcohol: the Bavarian norm is around

70%. He also adds a lactic delbrücki culture (see page 190) to help counteract sweetness. Most unusually – as the practice is frowned on by German brewers – he dry hops the beer in the British manner for additional aroma and flavour before it leaves the brewery. The beer that emerges is chestnut coloured, with a pronounced roasted malt, coffee, figs and floral hops aroma. Dark grain and fruit flavours crowd the palate, followed by a long, spritzy, quenching finish dominated by vine fruits, coffee and gently bitter hops.

The Munich brewers refuse to allow Prince Luitpold to have a beer tent at the annual Oktoberfest and he has hit back by organising a remarkable jousting tournament every July, held over three weekends. It is like taking a step back in time. At night, torch flares light the sky. Ancient crafts are practised in the many tents. Troubadours, falconers and tumblers entertain the large crowds, while the jousting is full-blooded, with no quarter given by professional stuntmen. There is a pervading aroma of earth, straw and horse sweat, overlain by the richer smells of cooking. And the event is toasted by endless exquisite draughts of King Ludwig Dark Lager.

Klasterni St Norbert Dark

Source: Klasterni Pivovar St Norbert, Strahov, Prague, Czech Republic
Strength: 5.5%
Website: www.klasterni-pivovar.cz

Klasterni Pivovar means 'cloister brewery' and it stands in the grounds of the white-walled monastery of St Norbert in Strahov, an outlying district of Prague. My first visit was in the winter, and as I arrived snow was falling and the monks were singing their plain song inside the church. The centuries, unlike the snow, melted away, and for a moment I thought I was back in a time before war, religious oppression, occupation and dictatorship ravaged central Europe.

The brewery and restaurant match the monastery, its whitewashed and red-roofed buildings set round a small courtyard used as an outside drinking area in good weather. The monastery dates from 1140 when King Vladislav II donated land to followers of St Norbert. A brewery was built at some time between the 13th and 14th centuries. In 1629, Abbot Kaspar Questenberg built a new brewery on the spot where the present restaurant is located.

Following the Velvet Revolution, monks revived their community at Strahov and leased the buildings for the restaurant complex to a commercial company. The main bar includes the burnished copper vessels used for mashing, filtering and boiling. Fermentation and maturation take place in separate rooms at the rear of the complex. Brewer Martin Matuska previously worked at the famous Prague brew-pub U Fleků and therefore has considerable experience at producing a tmavé, or dark beer. He uses four malts, Pilsner, Munich, crystal and black, and hops the beer with Žatec varieties that create 37 units of bitterness. The beer is ruby/black with an aroma bursting with bitter chocolate, figs, burnt grain and floral hops. The mouth fills with rich flavours of dark fruit and grain with a solid underpinning of earthy hops. The long and complex finish is fruity, with chocolate and earthy hop notes. The beer can be taken away in attractive black bottles with gold embossed lettering and swing-top closures. The restaurant, brewery and monastery are at 302 Strahovské nádvoří.

Köstritzer Schwarzbier

Source: Köstritzer Schwarzbierbrauerei, Bad Köstritz, Thuringia, Germany
Strength: 4.6%
Website: www.koestritzer.de

On my first visit to the Bitburger brewery in Germany, I was intrigued to find, in a plant dedicated to pale Pilsner lager, some bottles of black beer in the brewer's office. I was told it was a speciality known as Schwarzbier, or black beer, from the Erfurt region of Saxony that had just emerged from the former German Democratic Republic beyond the wall. The beer style had been made in local castles in the area in the 16th and 17th centuries, and later became a commercial beer that had refreshed, among others, the German writer and poet Goethe when he visited the spa town of Bad Köstritz to recover from illness.

In its earliest form, the beer would have been warm fermented but it had become a black lager. It survived during the communist period with a low strength and was recommended for nursing mothers with the addition of egg or milk. The current chairman of Bitburger, Dr Axel Simon, remembered the beer from his childhood and he bought the brewery when it came up for sale following the collapse of the communist regime. I visited the brewery, a red-brick complex built in 1907 but in urgent need of investment. Bitburger spent a small fortune bringing the brewery up to date and making the beer available in other parts of Germany and then in export markets. The strength was increased dramatically from 3.5% to 4.6% and production was brought within the strict terms of the Reinheitsgebot purity law, which had been ignored during the communist period.

The beer is made with pale malt, Munich malt and roasted malt, and is hopped with Hüller and Hallertau Mittelfrüh varieties. The colour rating is 900 – an indication of how dark it is – and the bitterness units are 35. It has an aroma of dark fruit, malt loaf and bitter chocolate, followed by a creamy palate with roasted grain, coffee, chocolate and a hint of figs and a gentle hop note. The finish is smooth, creamy, with strong notes of burnt grain, bitter chocolate, dark fruit and spicy hops.

Meantime Chocolate Beer

Source: Meantime Brewing Co, Greenwich, London, England
Strength: 4.5%
Website: www.meantimebrewing.com

Meantime Brewery reverses Robert Louis Stevenson's claim that 'it is better to travel hopefully than to arrive'. The nearest Underground station is at the derelict and failed Millennium Dome. The brewery, when you find it, is part of an unprepossessing industrial estate. But, once inside, you are confronted by an impressive, state-of-the-art brewery where brewmaster Alastair Hook practises the skills he learned at the Weihenstephan brewing faculty near Munich.

I have toured Bavaria in his company, visiting breweries run by colleagues and former students, and quickly discovered his passion for good beer and his distaste for corner-cutting that produces inferior, mass market brews. Alastair is a perfectionist and, after a few false starts, he now has the equipment and the financial backing to produce beers of the highest quality.

His Chocolate Beer is a lager and is rooted in the dark lager style of Germany. No confectionery is used: it is heavily roasted chocolate malt that gives the colour and flavour to the beer. The roasting process produces grain that looks like coffee beans. It has no 'enzymic power', which means the high temperature in the maltings kills the enzymes in the malt that turn starch to sugar. The pale malt base does that job. The chocolate malt is there to deliver colour and flavour, which it does highly effectively. The ebony-coloured beer, with its rich barley white head, has a powerful aroma and palate of bitter chocolate, vanilla and dark grain with a good underpinning of floral, spicy hops. The finish lingers, dominated by rich chocolate and vanilla but with a pleasing dryness and spiciness from German hop varieties.

TASTING NOTES
Appearance
Aroma
Taste
Overall score

TASTING NOTES
Appearance
Aroma
Taste
Overall score

TASTING NOTES
Appearance
Aroma
Taste
Overall score

Třeboň Dark Regent

Source: Pivovar Regent, Třeboň, Czech Republic
Strength: 4.4%
Website: www.pivovar-regent.cz

My most recent visit to the Regent brewery began with an oompah band and a singer greeting me with a vivacious rendition of 'Roll Out the Barrel'. I discovered the song is of Bohemian origin and was brought to Britain by Czech fighter pilots in World War Two. It was a jolly way to start a brewery tour and was in stark contrast to my first visit in the late 1980s. I was accompanied then by a suspicious guide from the government tourist agency Čedok and I was confronted by a brewery that managed to produce excellent beer from a site in urgent need of investment.

But Regent has had a long and dramatic history. Augustinian monks brewed in Třeboň from 1367. The local aristocrats, the Rosenbergs, built a castle on the site of the monastery and, in 1482, dug new cellars for the brewery. In 1706, the brewery was moved to the castle armoury, where it stands today, though the site was rebuilt in 1888 to take account of the developments in Budweis and Pilsen that enabled cold-fermented beers to be produced. Between the two World Wars of the 20th century, the brewery was owned by another aristocratic family, the Schwarzenbergs, but they lost control when Regent became a state enterprise during the communist period. The brewery was privatised in 1992 and got the investment it needed to install new equipment. It brews golden lagers but its speciality is Dark Regent, also known as Bohemia Regent in some markets.

It is brewed from pale, caramalt and dark malts, and hopped with Saaz varieties. It has a rich garnet colour with an appealing aroma of floral, spicy hops, bitter chocolate and dark grain. Chocolate, earthy hops and burnt grain fill the mouth, while the finish is hoppy and malty with a powerful hint of cappuccino coffee.

The town of Třeboň in southern Bohemia is famous for its lakes packed with carp, and Dark Regent is traditionally drunk during the winter, at Christmas in particular, with fish.

U Fleků Flekovský Dark

Source: U Fleků Brewery and Restaurant, Prague, Czech Republic
Strength: 4.5%
Website: www.ufleku.cz

The most celebrated beer in Prague comes from the world's oldest brew-pub, U Fleků, at 11 Kremencova in the New Town, where the entrance is marked by a large hanging clock. Beer has been brewed on the premises since at least 1499, and isotopic measurements of the remains of paintings on the wooden ceiling of the brewhouse date them back to 1360.

The present name of the establishment stems from 1762 when Jakub Flekovský and his wife bought it. In the Czech fashion, the tavern was known as U Flekovskych, which was shortened over time to U Fleků: in Czech *U* serves the same purpose as *chez* in French.

The tiny brewhouse, with a capacity of 6,000 hectolitres (132,000 gallons), is the smallest in the country. With its open cool ship fermenter, it is reminiscent of a Belgian lambic brewery but no wild yeasts are encouraged here. New brewing vessels are made of copper and date from 1980. The single beer made on the premises uses Pilsner pale malt, Munich malt, caramalt and roasted malt. A double decoction mash is used and Žatec hops are added in three stages. The beer has a chocolate, coffee and liquorice aroma with floral hops. Creamy malt, roasted grain, earthy hops and coffee notes fill the mouth, while the finish is bitter-sweet at first but becomes dry with good hop notes, balanced by coffee, chocolate and liquorice.

One wall in the brewhouse has a portrait of the present brewer and the inscription 'God bless the mother who gave birth to a brewer', a statement of such profound good sense that it survived the communist period. The six rooms in the tavern have dark wood-panelled walls, benches and alcoves. Simple, filling Czech fare of the pork and dumplings variety is served. There are regular burlesque shows and occasional oompah bands dressed in military uniforms that recall the heady days of the first independent Czechoslovak republic in the early 20th century.

Bocks

Bavarians will assure you that Bock is a style of beer indissolubly linked to their country. But its origins lie in Lower Saxony, some distance from Bavaria. The historical fact is stressed by the legend above the Einbecker Brewery in Einbeck: '*Ohne Einbeck gäb's kein Bockbier*' – 'Without Einbeck there would be no Bock beer.' To emphasise the point, all the brewery's products are labelled Ur-Bock, meaning Original Bock, while the entrance to Einbeck has a sign saying 'Beer City'.

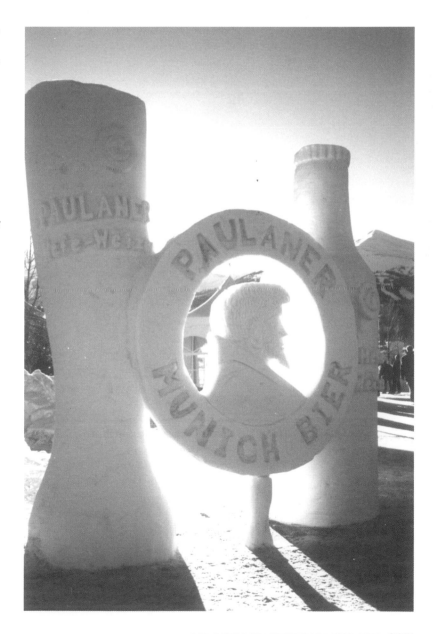

BELOW
Paulaner Bock is the benchmark for the style, brewed in the great beer city of Munich.

Einbeck was an important member of the Hanseatic League, the community of trading towns and cities of the 14th and 15th centuries in Germany, the Low Countries and Scandinavia. Each member of the league offered a special contribution, and Einbeck was famed as a brewing centre. Its citizens had been granted brewing rights from the 14th century. They spread malt and hops in the lofts of their houses to dry, while a communal brewing vessel toured the city for them to use in turn. The high arches of the houses, designed to allow the vessel to pass through, are still visible today.

The beers of Einbeck achieved fame and notoriety in the 16th century when supplies were sent to Martin Luther, an Augustinian friar, to sustain him between sessions of the Diet of Worms in 1521, where he was excommunicated for attacking the excesses of the Papal court in Rome and the sale of indulgences. Luther, the leader of the Protestant Reformation in Europe, had cause to thank the brewers of Einbeck for their nourishing beer at a trial that amounted to a witch-hunt and during which he made his defiant statement: 'Here I stand – I can do no other'.

The beer of Einbeck was called in the German fashion 'Einbecker', meaning 'of Einbeck'. The people of Munich and Bavaria first came across Einbecker beer in the 17th century when the Duke of Brunswick in Lower Saxony married the daughter of a Bavarian aristocrat. The wedding was held in Munich and the duke brought a master brewer with him to make beer for the celebration. The Bavarians took to the strong, rich style and, over the course of time, their powerful southern dialect turned Einbecker into 'Oanbocker'. By the 18th century, the Munich Hofbräuhaus, the Royal Court Brewery, was producing an Oanbock beer. This, in turn, was shortened to the simple and explosive 'Bock'. The new name was a pun. *Bock* in the Bavarian dialect means billy goat and, as a symbol of virility and strength, was the ideal name for the beer style. Many producers of Bock use the image of the goat on their labels.

The benchmark version of strong Bock beer was developed by monks at the Paulaner Brewery (see page 273). Bock beer became so engrained in the Bavarian way of life that a special version, Maibock, is brewed to herald the arrival of spring, with an even stronger version, called Doppelbock, or Double Bock, for Lent. Under Bavarian law, a Bock beer must be at least 6.4% alcohol, a Double Bock 6.9%. Monks called Bock beer 'liquid bread', as it helped sustain them during the Lenten fast. The Bock style was picked up in other European countries and eventually made its way to the United States, where it is brewed with enthusiasm and dedication by German-style brewers.

Ayinger Celebrator

Source: Brauerei Aying Franz Inselkammer, Aying, Bavaria, Germany
Strength: 6.7%
Website: www.aying-bier.de

TASTING NOTES
Appearance
Aroma
Taste
Overall score

Celebrator is a Double Bock and the point is emphasised on a label that shows two goats holding a glass of the dark chestnut-coloured beer.

Aying has built a fine reputation for its wheat beers as well as lagers, and is typical of the many small country breweries in Bavaria that first and foremost serve their local communities. In the case of Aying, founded in 1878 by the Inselkammer farming family, the community is no more than a tiny huddle of houses and a church, with a maypole on the village green, all standing at the foot of the Alps. The village of Aying is too small to sustain a brewery in the modern world and so owner Franz Inselkammer exports widely to North America, Italy, France and Scandinavia.

His powerful Celebrator is the most successful beer in export markets and is an outstanding example of the Double Bock style. It is brewed with four malts, including pale, Munich, caramalt and roast, and hopped with Hallertauer varieties. Pure water comes from the Alps. The beer enjoys a double decoction mash and then between four and six months' cold maturation in the lager cellars. The beer throws a lively and dense collar of foam that leads to an entrancing aroma of creamy and roasted grain, coffee, figs and gentle hop resins. Ripe malt, dark fruit and spicy hops fill the mouth, while the long finish has a delicious bitter-sweet character with notes of figs, coffee and dry, gently bitter hops.

The brewery complex includes a restaurant serving hearty Bavarian food, and a hotel. Herr Inselkammer organises many beer events and festivals during the course of the year.

Eggenberg Samichlaus

Source: Schlossbrauerei Eggenberg, Vorchdorf, Austria
Strength: 14%
Website: www.schlosseggenberg.at

In the Swiss-German dialect, *Samichlaus* means Santa Claus. The name is given to a powerful Swiss interpretation of Bock. The beer is called Santa Claus because it is brewed every year on 6 December, St Nicholas's Day, and lagered for nine or 10 months before being bottled and released for the following year's celebration.

Samichlaus was first made by the Hürlimann brewery in Zürich and, at 14% alcohol, is listed as the world's strongest regularly brewed beer. It was not a title sought by the brewery, which made the beer as part of scientific research into yeast. The brewery was founded in 1865 at a time when beer making was being transformed as a result of the lager revolution in Munich, Pilsen and Vienna. The dedicated research by Hürlimann's scientists into the temperatures at which yeast will turn malt sugars into alcohol complemented the work of other lager pioneers.

Unlike a wine or Champagne yeast, which can produce high levels of alcohol, brewer's yeast 'goes to sleep' at around 12%, overwhelmed by the alcohol it has produced. The researchers at Hürlimann worked for several decades to culture a strain of yeast that would continue to work above 12%. In 1979, they used a new culture to make an experimental Christmas beer and the interest created encouraged the brewery to make it on an annual basis. During the long ripening process, the beer is roused from time to time by pumping it from one tank to another to prevent the yeast from slumbering. A double decoction mash is involved and hops are added three times during the copper boil.

In the late 1990s, Hürlimann was bought by the Swiss brewing giant Feldschlössen, which said it would discontinue Samichlaus. A year later, the Austrian brewer Schloss Eggenberg announced it had won agreement to brew the beer again and the first vintage appeared, fittingly, in time for Christmas 2000. The castle (*Schloss*) brewery at Eggenberg dates from the 12th century and stands in an area of great natural beauty, with deep lakes, high mountains and dense forests. The russet-coloured Samichlaus is made from pale malt and three darker ones. It is hopped with Hallertauer, Hersbrucker and Styrian Goldings (30 units of bitterness). It has a complex aroma of port wine, dried fruit, toasted malt and peppery hops. The palate offers coffee, bitter chocolate, nuts and malts, while the finish is long, lingering, bursting with rich malt, vinous fruit and spicy hops, with a hint of Cognac. The beer is pasteurised but it will develop in bottle.

TASTING NOTES
Appearance
Aroma
Taste
Overall score

Einbecker Ur-Bock

Source: Einbecker Brauhaus, Einbeck, Lower Saxony, Germany
Strength: 6.9%
Website: www.einbecker.com

TASTING NOTES
Appearance
Aroma
Taste
Overall score

Beer has been brewed in the small town of Einbeck, near Brunswick and Hanover, since at least 1351. Einbecker beers were sold as far afield as Amsterdam and Stockholm, and they were made strong to help them withstand long journeys by road and water. The early brews would have been dark and warm fermented, probably made from a blend of barley and wheat malts. At a time when most brewing was carried out in monasteries and castles, the citizens of Einbeck brewed themselves. Every May Day, lots were drawn in the town square to decide the order in which the official brewmaster would visit more than 700 houses with the public brewing pan to help them make beer for domestic use and for public sale.

A commercial brewery was built in Einbeck in 1794 and has been rebuilt on several occasions. Three versions of Bock are produced, all with alcoholic strengths of 6.9% and all labelled, quite reasonably, Ur-Bock: Original Bock. Soft water comes from deep springs, malt from the Brunswick area, and hops – Northern Brewer, Perle and Hersbruck – from the Bavarian Hallertau. The beers are hoppier and drier than a Bavarian Bock but the main characteristic is a rich and rounded maltiness that avoids a cloying sweetness. The pale Hell (colour 15, bitterness units 38) has an appealing biscuity malt aroma and palate with a late burst of spicy hops in the finish. The dark, or Dunkel, version has 40 units of colour and the same bitterness rating. Dark grains give hints of roasted malt, figs and coffee on aroma and palate, with malt and fruit balanced in the finish by the hops. A Maibock produced for the spring has a tempting bronze colour (25 colour units, 36 bitterness), a dry and crisp aroma and palate with juicy malt, light fruit and floral hops, followed by a quenching malty and gently hoppy finish. The Hell and Dunkel are lagered for eight to 10 weeks, the Maibock for six.

The brewery houses a small museum and good beer and food are served in its tavern on the market square.

EKU Kulminator/28

Source: Erste Kulmbacher Unionbraurei, Kulmbach, Germany
Strength: 7.5%/13.5%
Website: www.eku.de

To most drinkers outside Germany, the beers from EKU are the best-known interpretations of Bock. For many years, the branded glass that accompanies 28 declared it was the 'strongest beer in the world' but as it is very slightly weaker than Samichlaus, the bottle label more modestly claims it to be one of the strongest. The name of the brewery indicates it was the first (*erste*) united brewery in the famous brewing town of Kulmbach, formed by a merger of two companies in 1872.

EKU brews a fine Pils but is best known for its two Double Bock beers. They are made with water from the surrounding mountains and local barley malt. Hops, which are added four times during the copper boil, are Hersbruck, Perle and Tettnang. Darker malts are blended with pale to produce Kulminator, which has a deep cherry red colour (65 units) and a ripe fruit, rich malt and spicy hop resins aroma. Warming alcohol fills the mouth, underscored by earthy hops and rich fruit, while the finish is fruity, malty with a gentle spicy hop note (24 bitterness units).

The even stronger 28 is known as Kulminator 28 in domestic markets but EKU 28 abroad. It is brewed from pale malt only but the sheer volume of malt and some caramelisation of the sugars in the copper give the finished beer an orange/amber glow. The alcohol produces quite a glow, too, backed by rich malt on the aroma,

some citrus fruitiness on the palate, and a long, deep, intense, rich and warming finish. The colour rating is 35, bitterness units 30.

The number 28 comes from an old method of expressing the strength of beer. The beer is lagered for nine months and towards the end of the storage period ice crystals form in the tank. The brewery does not claim the beer is an 'Ice Bock', a speciality of the region, as the beer already has sufficient alcohol without adding more from the concentration of beer and ice.

Some drinkers claim EKU is a cure for the common cold. It would certainly take your mind off the sniffles.

TASTING NOTES
Appearance
Aroma
Taste
Overall score

TASTING NOTES
Appearance
Aroma
Taste
Overall score

Hübsch Doppelbock

Source: Sudwerk Privatbrauerei Hübsch, Davis, California, USA
Strength: 7.1%
Website: www.sudwerk.com

The inspiration is clear from the name: this is a strictly German brewery based in California. *Sudwerk* is the German name for a brewhouse, and the impact of German brewing names and techniques can be measured by the fact that a widespread slang word for beer in the US is 'suds'.

Founder Ron Broward named his brewery after his German mother's maiden name: she had regaled him with stories of the wonderful beer halls in her native country. His first venture was a brew-pub in Davis in 1990. He has since opened a 20,000-barrel brewery in Sacramento, the state capital.

Ron is a stickler for detail. He brews to the German *Reinheitsgebot*, imports malts and hops from Bavaria, and uses a yeast culture from the Weinhenstephan brewing faculty near Munich. His Doppelbock is made with pale and chocolate malts, and Hallertauer and Tettnanger hop varieties. It has a deep copper colour with a massive aroma of roasted malt and chocolate that carries through to the palate, followed by a chewy malt, chocolate and light hop finish that finally becomes dry.

Ron also produces a 6.5% Maibock for the spring. It has a deep bronze colour with nutty malt and spicy hops.

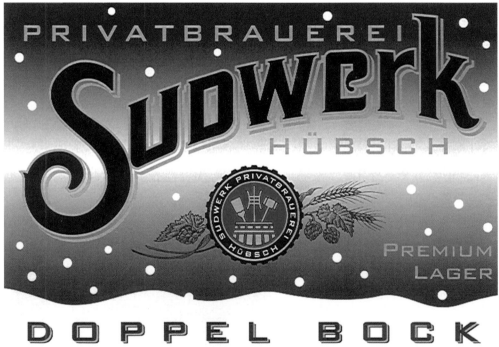

Paulaner Salvator Doppelbock

Source: Paulaner-Salvator-Thomasbräu, Munich, Bavaria, Germany
Strength: 7.5%
Website: www.paulaner.de

Paulaner produces the classic Munich Bock, the benchmark for the style. The beer is so famous that its name, Salvator, is incorporated in the company name, along with the title of a long-extinct brewery, Thomas, taken over in 1923.

The Paulaner brewery was founded in 1634 by monks who were followers of St Francis of Paula in Calabria in Italy. They were Pauline monks, not Franciscans, who are followers of another St Francis, the better-known patron saint of animals from Assisi. The monks built their Paulaner monastery on a hill on the outskirts of Munich, and added a small brewery. The hillside helped the monks defend themselves from attack: it later proved invaluable in allowing maturation cellars to be dug where beers were stored at low temperatures.

The monks made, among others, a strong beer for the Lent period called *Salvator*, which means Saviour or Holy Father. The beer was sold commercially from the late 18th century to help raise funds for the monastery. When, a century later, the monastery was secularised, the new owner, Franz-Xaver Zacherl, vigorously promoted sales of Salvator, with such success that other Munich brewers launched their own brands under the same name. Zacherl took them to court in 1894. The result was that his competitors dropped the name but gave their brands new titles ending in –or, such as Triumphator or Kulminator. Every year, three weeks before Easter, a cask of the year's first batch of Salvator is tapped by a local dignitary, such as the Mayor of Munich, in the brewery's beer garden. This heralds the '*Starkbierzeit*', or strong beer period, when people, weather permitting, invade the city's many beer gardens to sup Salvator and other rich brews that help shrug off the memories of a long Alpine winter and usher in the spring. Drinking Doppelbock is known as the *Frühlingskur* – the 'spring cure'.

Salvator is brewed with pale lager malt, caramalt and Munich malt and Hallertauer hop varieties. It has a russet-brown colour with a rich malt loaf aroma, a yeasty, bready palate, and a complex finish rich in sultana-like fruit, malt and hops. The beer is lagered for at least three months.

TASTING NOTES
Appearance
Aroma
Taste
Overall score

Vienna Red, Märzen & Oktoberfest Beers

It is a curiosity of brewing that a beer called Märzen should be identified with the world's most celebrated drinking festival, the Munich Oktoberfest. Märzenbier means March beer. The beers at the modern Oktoberfest are cold-fermented lagers but before cold storage developed in the 19th century, March was the last month in which beer could be safely brewed in Bavaria, with its long, hot summers.

The Munich tradition was to brew a strong beer in March and store it in Alpine caves, protected by the cold from the heat and wild yeast infections. Brewers noticed that the low ambient temperatures in the caves produced a long, slow second fermentation in cask. The yeast settled at the bottom of the vessels, while maturation created a lively, natural carbonation. The lagering, or cold storage, of beer was under way.

Casks of March beers were broached in late September or early October. The ceremony took on added significance in 1810 when a festival was held in a large open space in Munich to celebrate the marriage of the Crown Prince of Bavaria. The meadow was dubbed the *Theresienweise*, or Theresa's Meadow, after the royal bride. Every year since 1810 there has been an annual jamboree on the site, lasting for 16 days from late September but dubbed the Oktoberfest as the festival concludes in that month. The festival is launched by a horse-drawn parade by Munich's brewers, who sell vast amounts of Oktoberfest beer in their great tents decorated like baronial halls, with central stands for oompah bands.

The Märzen beers took on a more central role in Bavarian life as commercial lagering of beer gathered pace. March beer became a special treat, launched every year at the Oktoberfest. At first the beers were dark brown but the innovative Munich brewers Gabriel and Josef Sedlmayr worked closely with the Viennese brewer Anton Dreher, who was developing his own style of cold-fermented beer. While lagers were dark in Munich and golden in Pilsen, Dreher at his brewery in the Schwechat district of Vienna used malt kilned to a slightly higher temperature than pale lager malt to produce a beer that was dubbed 'Vienna Red'. The colour was probably amber or orange, rather than red, and not dissimilar to English pale ale. But pale ale was unknown to Austrian drinkers and Dreher's 'red beer' had such an impact that he was invited to open breweries in Bohemia, Hungary and Trieste to reproduce the style. When Mexico was briefly part of the Austrian empire, breweries there also produced Vienna Red lagers that survive today in the shape of Dos Equis and Negra Modelo.

Sedlmayr's brother Josef, who ran his own Franziskaner Brewery in Munich, studied Dreher's technique and produced a March beer for the Oktoberfest with a polished amber colour that became the benchmark for the style. The beer was brewed in March then lagered in the brewery's ice-packed cellars until the autumn. The Sedlmayr breweries merged in the 1920s and today it is Spaten that makes the benchmark version of a Märzen.

True March beers are now hard to find. Austrian brewers shrug their shoulders at the mention of Vienna Red and churn out beers in the Pilsner style. The beers sold at the Oktoberfest are also golden rather than amber. But the flag is being flown across the Atlantic by American brewers who have a passionate devotion to brewing beers strictly to style.

RIGHT
The Oktoberfest is the world's oldest and biggest beer festival. The beers brewed for the event are rich and strong.

Boston Samuel Adams Lager

Source: Boston Beer Company, Boston, Massachusetts, USA
Strength: 5%
Website: www.samueladams.com

BREWED BY THE BOSTON BEER CO., BOSTON, MA AND UNDER SPECIAL AGREEMENT PIT., OR. TO VISIT US AT OUR SMALL TRADITIONAL BREWERY, CONTACT THE BOSTON BEER CO., THE BREWERY, 30 GERMANIA ST., BOSTON, MA 02130 OR CALL 617-368-5080.

FOR BREWERY-FRESH TASTE, PURCHASE BEFORE MONTH NOTCHED. 1996
CRAFTED SLOWLY WITH CARE AND ONLY HONEST INGREDIENTS.

JAN | FEB | MAR | APR | MAY | JUN | JUL | AUG | SEP | OCT | NOV | DEC

TASTING NOTES
Appearance
Aroma
Taste
Overall score

Samuel Adams Lager was the beer that put the Boston Beer Company on the map. As the first national brand that was not produced by a brewing giant, it gave a kick-start to the craft brewing revival in the United States. The founder and owner Jim Koch is a charming, quietly spoken man, but behind the urbane exterior lurks a tough, no-nonsense entrepreneur. He has raised hackles by his aggressive selling techniques and his style – now widely copied – of having his beer brewed under licence in different centres. Waiting for planes, I have enjoyed his beers at both Dallas and St Louis airports, brewed a long distance from Boston. To have the franchise for beer at St Louis airport, the hometown of mighty Anheuser-Busch, brewer of Budweiser, takes a fair degree of chutzpah.

Koch, whose name is pronounced 'Cook' to avoid bringing a blush to the cheek of Americans who prefer rooster to cock, comes from a family of German origin who arrived in America in the 19th century. Five generations of the family ran breweries. There was a Koch brewery in St Louis that was taken over and closed down by Anheuser-Busch, which explains why Jim wanted

a franchise there. Jim won a degree in management at Harvard University, and his father, who left the brewing industry as the like of A-B tightened its noose on sales and distribution, was not best pleased when his son said he wanted to make beer. Jim didn't have a brewery and he had Boston Lager, bearing the image of patriot Sam Adams, made for him by the Pittsburgh Brewing Company. Jim launched the beer in 1985 and he sold it door to door. It was a sensation: drinkers starved of choice and used to the bland 'suds' of the nationals, suddenly discovered that lager beer could have rich aroma and flavour. Jim eventually opened his own brewery in Boston but that is used mainly to produce Boston Ale (see page 54).

His lager, based on the Bavarian March style, is still contract brewed around the country. It uses two-row American pale malt and caramalt, and is hopped with German Hallertauer 'noble' varieties, including Mittelfrüh. The amber beer has a floral hop bouquet balanced by biscuity malt. Spicy hops build in the mouth with delicious juicy malt. The lengthy finish has a superb balance of spicy, bitter hops and sappy malt but finally becomes dry with firm hop bitterness.

Brooklyn Lager

Source: Brooklyn Brewery, Brooklyn, New York City, USA
Strength: 5%
Website: www.brooklynbrewery.com

TASTING NOTES
Appearance
Aroma
Taste
Overall score

My first-ever taste of Brooklyn Lager was in a bar in Manhattan. The amber colour and the rich malt and peppery hops character of the beer entranced me. I thought it was one of the finest beers I had ever tasted and nothing since made me change my mind. At the time, the beer was brewed under licence by the F X Matt Brewery in Uttica, New York State. The beer was the brainchild of journalist Steve Hindy and banker Tom Potter who wanted to restore Brooklyn's great brewing tradition that had been wiped out by Prohibition and the Great Depression. At one time, Brooklyn had 48 breweries and they were responsible for one of every 10 barrels of beer brewed in the United States. Steve and Tom commissioned a retired German-American brewer, Bill Moeller, to develop a recipe for Brooklyn Lager. Bill's grandfather had brewed in Brooklyn and bequeathed his recipe books to his grandson. Using the old brewing books, Bill fashioned a beer that is a true Vienna Red. Its classy label was designed by Milton Glaser, best known for his I♥NY logo.

The Brooklyn Brewery now has its own plant, where brewmaster Garrett Oliver fashions the lager from two-row Pilsner malt, caramel malt and Munich malt. He hops the beer with Cascade, Hallertauer Mittelfrüh and Vanguard varieties. The beer has 14 units of colour and 30 bitterness units. It has a floral and piny hop aroma balanced by biscuity malt. The mouth is filled with juicy malt and caramel flavours and a big punch of spicy hops. The finish is a superb balance of sweet malt, a hint of tangy citrus fruit, and crisp, bitter hops. Unusually for a lager, the beer is dry hopped in the English style for additional aroma.

Hofbräu Märzen

Source: Staatliches Hofbräuhaus,
Munich, Bavaria, Germany
Strength: 5.7%
Website: www.hofbraehaus.de

It's not often that drinking beer sends a chill down my spine but it happened during one of many visits to the Hofbräuhaus. I was sitting in a side room on a comfortable wooden settle when a companion asked: 'Do you know who used to sit there?' I shook my head but I had a horrible feeling I could guess the answer: Adolf Hitler. The Nazi leader's first attempt to grab political power, the *Kapp Putsch*, was planned in that very room in the tavern. Don't be put off. This remarkable, sprawling beer hall on a small square called the Platzl, with vaulted roofs, brass bands, men in lederhosen and Alpine hats supplied by Central Casting, and a delightful beer garden shaded by chestnut trees provide one of the great drinking experiences.

The Hofbräuhaus, or Royal Court Brewery, was built in the 16th century by Duke Wilhelm V of Bavaria to supply the royal family with beer. It maintained the monopoly for more than 300 years. When the royal family lost power after World War One, the tavern and its brewery were taken over by the state. Brewing no longer takes place on the premises: a new, modern plant has been built on a greenfield site out of town. It supplies beer in large wooden casks that are tapped in the beer hall. The Hofbräu started life as a wheat beer brewery, added Bock beer along the way, and bolted on a March beer when cold fermentation held sway in Munich.

The amber beer is made from pale and Munich malts, and is hopped with Hallertauer varieties. It has a rich bready, biscuity, nutty and spicy hop aroma and palate, followed by a complex finish dominated by ripe, vinous fruit, creamy malt and piny hops.

Don't miss the beer hall, decorated in the blue and white flags of Bavaria, or the succulent beer.

Kronenbourg Premier Cru

Source: Brasseries Kronenbourg,
Obernai, Alsace, France
Strength: 6%
Website: www.brasseries-kronenbourg.com

Kronenbourg is the biggest brewer in France, accounting for 42% of the domestic market. It is based in Alsace that has twice been under German rule, most recently in World War Two. Towns and villages are packed with black-and-white medieval buildings and, running like a broad ribbon through the lush countryside, the Rhine marks the border between France and Germany. The slopes of the Vosges mountains provide grapes for the local wines but hops grow there, too.

The brewery at Obernai is enormous, the single biggest beer-making plant in Europe. It has three brewhouses, each one producing 30,000 hectolitres (660,000 gallons) of beer a day, with a new brew every two hours. The origins of the group are on a much smaller scale. In 1664, a cooper named Jerome Hatt opened a small brewery in Strasbourg. His beers were popular but the brewery was frequently flooded when the Rhine overflowed its banks. In 1850, a new site was built on higher ground in the suburb of Cronenbourg, which means the crown of a hill. It was the ideal place for digging deep lagering cellars. The spelling was eventually changed to the more Germanic Kronenbourg. The Obernai plant was opened in 1969 and the Strasbourg plant is now a museum.

Kronenbourg was bought in the 1970s by the French food group Danone, which also had brewing interests in Belgium. In 2000, Danone sold all its breweries and brands to Scottish & Newcastle. To its credit, S & N has quickly moved to improve beer quality at Obernai and introduced Premier Cru, which, unlike the mainstream Kronenbourg lagers that blend corn with barley, is an all-malt beer.

Spring barley is used with a small percentage of chocolate malt. The beer is hopped with the local Strisselspalt variety, an offshoot of the Czech Saaz. The colour rating is 16, units of bitterness 25. The beer has a luscious aroma of chocolate, vanilla pods and liquorice, with creamy malt, floral hops and citrus fruit in the mouth and a dry, toasted grain, light fruit and spicy hops finish.

TASTING NOTES
Appearance
Aroma
Taste
Overall score

TASTING NOTES
Appearance
Aroma
Taste
Overall score

Spaten Ur-Märzen

Source: Gabriel Sedlmayr Spaten-Franziskaner-Bräu, Munich, Bavaria, Germany
Strength: 5.6%
Website: www.spaten.de

TASTING NOTES
Appearance
Aroma
Taste
Overall score

Ur- in the title is short for *Urtyp*, which means 'original'. Spaten should perhaps blow its trumpet rather louder, for this is the classic Munich March beer: a rich and transluscent amber/bronze/red-tinged beer, the first to be fashioned in the city by Josef Sedlmayr in collaboration with Anton Dreher.

It became a Spaten brand when the two Sedlmayr breweries merged in the 1920s. Spaten can trace its origins back to the 14th century. Its current name is a play on word: it means spade, but stems from George Spaeth, who became the owner of the brewery in 1622. Ownership passed to Gabriel Sedlmayr the Elder, the Royal Court brewer, in 1807. It was his son, also called Gabriel, who pioneered cold fermentation in Munich. The company is now a public one but members of the Sedlmayr family retain an interest. It has merged with another famous Munich brewer, Löwenbräu [Lion Brew] but they have separate brewhouses to ensure the integrity of the beers.

The Spaten March beer is brewed with pale and Munich malts, and hopped with Hallertauer varieties. It has 32 units of colour and 21 bitterness units. It has a toasted malt, nutty, slightly vinous aroma with a gentle floral and grassy hop note. Rich biscuity malt, vinous fruit and hop resins fill the mouth, while the long and lingering finish is bitter-sweet in the start but becomes dry with good balancing juicy malt and earthy hop notes.

In a belt-and-braces style, Spaten also brews a paler Oktoberfest beer. Let us hope the March beer does not disappear. Many other Munich March beers have been replaced by golden Oktoberfest beers. Spaten's version, the benchmark, the classic, deserves to survive.

Dortmunder Export

Export is a rather over-blown description for a style of beer that is largely restricted to Dortmund and a few other towns and cities in the Ruhr and Westphalia. It crept over the border into the Netherlands and, in that narrow respect, it was exported. Dortmund has had a brewing tradition since the 13th century, specialising in dark wheat beers, often flavoured with herbs and spices.

In the 19th century, Dortmund, sited at the confluence of the small river Dort and the mighty Ruhr, grew rapidly as a major industrial city based on mining and steel industries. It had a large army of thirsty workers to satisfy, and brewing rushed to satisfy them. At one time, Dortmund had more breweries than any other German city. The Kronen Brewery switched to cold fermentation as early as the mid-1840s. Other breweries followed, and by the 1870s, the city had its signature style, Export.

The aim of Export beer was a simple one: to quench the prodigious thirsts of industrial workers and to restore energy lost after long stints digging coal or making steel. The beer style played a similar role to mild ale in England but the similarities should not be exaggerated. Export is not only a lager beer but it is also high in alcohol, slightly stronger than a Pilsner. It has a deep burnished gold colour as a result of slightly darker Munich malt being blended with pale. Brewing water is rich in calcium carbonate and sulphate, and the salts draw more flavour from the malt. The beer is not 'fully attenuated', which means some malt sugars are left to give richness and fullness to the flavour. Hop bitterness is restrained, in the mid-20s.

The Dortmund breweries in recent decades have given little support to their Export brands. They prefer to promote their Pils and seem reluctant, in some cases, to even mention they still make Export. It is true that heavy industry in the region has declined massively but that is surely no reason for downplaying a flavoursome beer with the type of tradition that other German cities, such as Cologne and Düsseldorf, cherish. The process has not been helped by considerable rationalisation of brewing in Dortmund. For most of the 20th century, the city was dominated by two fiercely independent and competitive companies, Dortmunder Actien Brauerei and Dortmunder Union Brauerei, known for short as DAB and DUB. Actien indicates a company listed on the stock market, while Union stands for a merger of several breweries.

DUB was famous for its plant in the centre of Dortmund, where the single neon-lit letter U blazed out at night from a central tower. In 1988, DUB and another local brewery, Ritter, became part of Brau und Brunnen that owns other breweries and mineral water manufacturers. The DUB site closed in 1994 and production was concentrated at the Ritter brewery, which has enjoyed considerable investment. In the meantime, the Oetker food and drinks group bought DAB. The final indignity came in 2004, when Oetker took over Brau und Brunnen and now owns both DAB and DUB. Further rationalisation can be expected.

As a result of its penetration of the Dutch market, some brewers in the Netherlands make a similar style of beer they have shortened to Dort, to avoid any suggestion the beer originates in Dortmund. And, once again, the style has crossed the Atlantic where it is brewed with an enthusiasm sadly lacking in its city of origin.

Brinkhoff Dortmunder Union Export
Source: Brauerei Brinkhoff, Dortmund, Germany
Strength: 5.3%
Website: www.brinkhoffs.de

TASTING NOTES
Appearance
Aroma
Taste
Overall score

Brinkhoff is the new name for the merged DUB and Ritter breweries. Fritz Brinkhoff was the brewmaster at DUB in the 19th century where, according to a local legend, he developed the exceptionally pale style of Export beer 'by mistake' when he was sent the wrong type of malt. Similar stories are told about both the first Pilsner and Porter, and I am sceptical about them, as I think an experienced brewer would spot if the malt had been kilned at the wrong temperature.

Brinkhoff is commemorated today by the brewery's main product, Brinkhoff's No 1, which is marketed as a Pilsner. After I toured the brewery, where seven brews a day totalling 9,000 hectolitres (198,000 gallons) of beer can be produced, I was offered glasses of No 1, for which I was truly grateful, but I had to pester the bar staff in the reception area for a sample of Export. Eventually, a keg was found and connected. The beer was pale gold, with a colour of around 10 units. It had a big rocky head of foam, an aroma reminiscent of digestive biscuits and tart hop resins, and a juicy malt and gently bitter palate with a touch of lemon fruit. The finish was bitter-sweet, beautifully balanced between malt, fruit and hops. Bitterness units are in the mid-20s. The beer is made by a decoction mashing regime, and is hopped with varieties from the Hallertau. The beer is lagered for a month.

A group of British beer importers were visiting the brewery at the same time. Encouraged by me, they suggested to the Brinkhoff management that they should export Export to Britain. The joke got lost in translation, and the Brinkhoff executives concentrated on promoting the joys of their Pils.

DAB Export
Source: Dortmunder Actien Brauerei, Dortmund, Germany
Strength: 5%
Website: www.dab.de

TASTING NOTES
Appearance
Aroma
Taste
Overall score

DAB was founded in 1868 by the Fischer family but it became a public company just four years later. It was a proud brewer of the Export style and won a gold medal for the beer at the World Fair in Paris in 1900. After World War Two, DAB began to concentrate on Pilsner and downplayed the importance of Export. In the late 1970s, DAB merged with another local brewer, Hansa, and a decade later they closed both their town-centre breweries and moved to a new combined plant in the suburbs. More recently, DAB has taken over Dortmunder Kronen, which developed cold fermentation and the Export style in the 19th century.

The spate of mergers, takeovers and closures in Dortmund, once dubbed 'the Burton of Germany', is doing little to maintain confidence in the local style of beer as more and more effort goes into marketing Pilsners. The Pils-type beers brewed in Dortmund are perfectly acceptable, but they rather miss the point. If the Kronen version of Export is still brewed, the company keeps remarkably quiet about it.

DAB Export is pale for the style, with nine units of colour. It is made from a blend of pale and Munich malt and hopped with Hallertau varieties (25 bitterness units). It has a rich toasted malt aroma with light hop resins and a touch of citrus fruit. It is smooth, creamy and malty in the mouth with a gentle touch of spicy hops. The finish is sweet to start but develops a late flourish of hop and a hint of lemon fruit.

Great Lakes Dortmunder Gold

Source: Great Lakes Brewing Co, Cleveland, Ohio, USA
Strength: 5.8%
Website: www.greatlakesbrewing.com

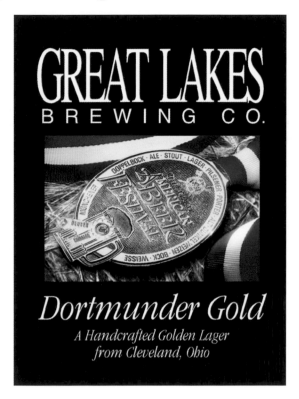

TASTING NOTES
Appearance
Aroma
Taste
Overall score

When Patrick and Daniel Conway opened their brew-pub at 2516 Market Avenue, Cleveland, in 1988, their first beer was named after a local football star but was eventually relabelled Dortmunder Gold. It was the beer that made their reputation and is still the flagship brand, brewed in the brothers' new, adjacent plant based in one of the city's last commercial breweries that were wiped out during Prohibition and subsequent bouts of merger mania. The Conways employed Thaine Johnson, who had worked at the last brewery in Cleveland, Christian Schmidt, to close its doors. Between them, they fashioned a big, full-bodied interpretation of Dortmunder Export that is recognised as the benchmark version of the style brewed in the US. It has won five gold medals in the annual World Beer Championships.

It is brewed from pale and Munich malt, and hopped with Hallertauer and Tettnanger varieties that create a robust 30 bitterness units. It is a shade darker than a German original, orange to light bronze, with a new-mown grass aroma, rich biscuity malt, tangy and spicy hops and some citrus fruit in the mouth, and a big finish with a great whack of bitter, herbal, spicy hop notes balancing the biscuity malt and gentle fruit.

It can be enjoyed in the brew-pub in several rooms on different levels, including the Rockefeller Room where John D of that ilk had his humble legal offices before branching out into the oil business.

Gulpener Dort

Source: Gulpener Bierbrouwerij BV, Gulpen, Netherlands
Strength: 6.5%
Website: www.gulpener.nl

TASTING NOTES
Appearance
Aroma
Taste
Overall score

Gulpen is a village near Maastricht in the Limburg region of the Netherlands, the narrow neck of the country that has Belgium and Germany in close proximity. The brewery was founded by the Rutten family in 1825 and over the years has built a solid reputation for both the quality and eclectic nature of its beer range. It brews ales and lagers, and they include a Dutch interpretation of a Belgian 'sour red', a spiced wheat beer, an abbey beer, a barley wine and two Pilsners. It has recently experimented with fruit beers. It must be good fun being a brewer at Gulpen: 'I'm off to work, dear. I think I may try a Pils today or, hang about, perhaps I'll have a go at a raspberry beer.' In 1995 Grolsch arrived and took a major holding in the company. The relationship has proved benign: Gulpen is free to develop its beer range, while the national company sells them far and wide.

The brewery's interpretation of a Dortmunder is fascinating. It is considerably stronger than the German template and is made with pale malt, maize and caramel, which indicates that Dortmunder Export may have crossed the border but left the Reinheitsgebot purity law behind. It is hopped with Hallertau varieties that create 20 units of bitterness. The beer is lagered for 10 weeks. The beer that emerges from the lager cellar has a bright bronze/orange colour, a heavy collar of foam, a spritzy, sappy, biscuity and creamy aroma with a delightful fresh, floral hop note. Rich juicy malt, a faint hint of liquorice and spicy hop resins fill the mouth, followed by a lingering and complex finish dominated by malt and fruit but with a good hop resin balance.

Pinkus Special

Source: Brauerei Pinkus Müller, Münster, Nordrhein-Westfalen, Germany
Strength: 5.4%
Website: www.merchantduvin.com/pages/5_breweries/pinkus.html

The Dortmunder Export style made the short journey to Münster, where it is brewed with verve and gusto at the renowned tavern and brewery of Pinkus Müller. Brewmaster Friedhelm Langfeld is a great believer in the proper lagering of beer. His beers are stored in horizontal steel tanks in his lager *Keller*. Unlike modern vertical tanks that encourage a fast second fermentation, the beer ripens more slowly in horizontal tanks, some unfermented malt sugars are left to give the beer body, and a good natural carbonation is achieved. Special is brewed with organic Bioland Pilsner malt and organic Tettnanger hops from Bavaria. As a result of the cramped conditions in the brewhouse, the mash tun also acts as the boiling copper. From the tun, the sugary extract is filtered in a lauter tun, then returns to the first vessel for the boil with hops. Following primary fermentation, Special enjoys three months in the lager *Keller*.

The pale bronze beer that emerges from this long process has a slight haze, as it is not filtered. It has a massive fruity aroma reminiscent of ripe pears, with toasted malt and floral hops. Bitter hop resins dominate the palate, balanced by juicy malt and fruit, while the long finish has tart fruit, sweet malt and bitter hops. It is a wonderfully refreshing beer, best enjoyed in the convivial atmosphere of the tavern, with its swift service and generous portions of Westphalian food. Neither the tavern nor the beer should be missed.

TASTING NOTES
Appearance
Aroma
Taste
Overall score

Sapporo Yebisu

Source: Sapporo Breweries, Hokkaido, Japan
Strength: 5%
Website: www.sapporo.jp

TASTING NOTES
Appearance
Aroma
Taste
Overall score

麦芽100%
YEBISU
ALL MALT BEER

YEBISU TRADITIONAL BREW

BORN 1887

Premium
YEBISU
ALL MALT BEER

YEBISU BEER is a rich and mellow premium beer
brewed from 100% fine malt and select hops
with Sapporo's traditional art.

500ml

Japan, with its four brewing giants Asahi, Kirin, Sapporo and Suntory, is a major force in world brewing, and it has achieved this status in a remarkably short time. Beer was unknown in the country until 1853, when an American trade mission went to Japan accompanied by ships of the US Navy under the control of Commodore Matthew Perry. When Japanese dignitaries went on board one of Perry's ships, they were offered beer. One of the visitors was sufficiently intrigued by the taste to search out a handbook on brewing, translate it from Dutch into Japanese and start brewing at home.

Following the reforms of Emperor Mutsuhito in 1868, which encouraged westernisation and industrialisation, a commercial brewing industry started to develop. The first brewery was established with American help and finance, but the Japanese looked to Europe for inspiration. As a result 'Bavarian beers' started to appear, followed by other German styles.

Sapporo, formed in 1876, is one of the oldest breweries in Japan and is named after the northern town of the same name where it started in business. It now owns five breweries in the country and many consider that Yebisu, named after a Shinto god and also a district in Tokyo, is its best beer.

Yebisu is promoted as an all-malt product and is firmly in the Dortmunder style. It is hopped with Hallertauer Mittelfrüh and Hersbrucker varieties. It is a pale gold colour, with a malty aroma balanced by floral hops and a hint of lemon fruit. Creamy and biscuity malt dominate the palate but there is a growing hop resin presence and light fruit. The finish is bitter-sweet, firmly malty but with a good hoppy and fruity finish.

Sapporo's beer can be enjoyed in the Beer Station grouping of bars and restaurants at the Yebisu site.

Švyturys Ekstra

Source: Švyturys Utenos Alus, Klaipeda, Lithuania
Strength: 5.2%
Website: None

Lithuania, one of the first republics to break away from the former Soviet Union, has a long brewing history that dates back to the Middle Ages. Commercial brewing started to develop in the 17th and 18th centuries. Švyturys was founded in 1784 and is now the oldest brewery in the country and the last remaining beer producer in Klaipeda, once a major brewing town. Following privatisation, the company has come under the wing of Carlsberg, which has a 20% share. In 1999, the European Bank for Reconstruction and Development took a similar stake and invested heavily in the brewery, which produces 350,000 hectolitres (7.7m gallons) a year. The Ekstra brand is its flagship beer and is widely distributed in the United States, where it won a gold medal in the Dortmunder Export class in the 2001 World Beer Championship.

The beer is brewed with local malt and imported German hop varieties. It is a burnished gold in colour with a grainy, malty, biscuity aroma, backed by spicy hops. The full-bodied palate is dominated by ripe, juicy grain, earthy hop resins and a touch of citrus fruit, while the lingering finish is quenching, bitter-sweet, with delicious juicy malt notes and a final attack by bitter and spicy hops.

TASTING NOTES
Appearance
Aroma
Taste
Overall score

Smoked Beer

The smoked, or Rauch, beers of the Bamberg region of German Franconia are a powerful link with brewing's past, when malt was kilned over wood-fuelled fires and beer had a smoky character as a result. Bamberg is famous for its stunning medieval architecture, a Benedictine abbey and Romanesque-Gothic cathedral. The abbey's former brewery, which dates from the 11th century, is now a brewing museum that underscores the important role the small city and its surrounding area have played in the history and development of beer. Malt is also made in Bamberg. Beechwood is collected from the surrounding forests to supply fuel for the malt kilns. As well as the main producer of Rauch beer listed here, also sample the smoked beers of the Christian Merz brew pub at 10 Obere König Strasse, and the beers of the Kaiserdom brewery.

BELOW LEFT
Rauchbier, or smoked beer, is a style confined to the Bamberg region of Germany.

BELOW RIGHT
The Schlenkerla beers are available in the handsome tavern in Bamberg.

Aecht Schlenkerla Rauchbier

Source: Brauerei Heller-Trum, Bamberg, Franconia, Germany
Strength: 5.1%
Website: www.schlenkerla.de

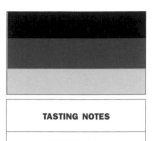

Brewing began in the Schlenkerla tavern in the city (junction of Dominikaner Strasse and Sand Strasse, beneath the cathedral) in 1678, when the beer was stored in caves in the nearby hill of Stephansberg. The need for more space in the tavern and a growing demand for the beer forced the Trum family to move to new premises nearby. The sixth generation of the family still runs the business. The brewery yard is packed with beechwood logs. Inside, there is a smokehouse where the barley malt lies on a mesh above a beechwood oven that throws up wonderful aromas reminiscent of garden fires in autumn. The copper brewhouse uses a double-decoction mashing regime. The extract is filtered in a lauter tun, then pumped to a copper brew kettle in a tiled surround where it is boiled with hops from the Hallertauer (29–32 units of bitterness). Following seven days' primary fermentation, the beer is stored for six to eight weeks.

The finished beer is dark chestnut in colour with an intense smoked malt aroma and palate, with dry malt in the mouth and a long and lingering finish, with herbal and smoky notes and a gentle underpinning of spicy hops. The word Aecht in the name of the beer means 'original'.

The brewery also produces an autumn smoky Bock and a Helles, or pale, lager. The beers can be enjoyed with hearty local dishes in the Schlenkerla tavern (9.30am–11.30pm, closed Tuesdays). The name comes from the nickname given to a former brewer who walked in a slightly odd fashion that suggested he might have over-indulged in his product.

TASTING NOTES
Appearance
Aroma
Taste
Overall score

Glossary

ABV (Alcohol by Volume): international method for measuring and declaring for tax purposes the strength of beer. In the US, a system known as Alcohol by Weight is used: 5% ABV is 4% ABW. Many American brewers now also declare the strength of beer in ABV.

Abbey beer: commercial beers – produced principally in Belgium – that may be brewed under licence from monasteries, though some have no monastic links whatsoever. Not to be confused with Trappist beers (qv). Abbey beers are labelled Abbaye (French) or Abdij (Flemish).

Adjuncts: cereals and sugars added to beer, often as a cheap substitute, but sometimes used by craft brewers for special flavours. Producers of mass-market lagers may often dilute the barley mash with corn [maize] or rice. On the other hands, Belgian brewers use candy sugar for palate, while British brewers often use caramel and invert sugar. Adjuncts are not permitted in Germany where the Reinheitsgebot (qv) allows only malted grain.

Ale: the world's oldest beer style, produced by warm or top fermentation. The term covers such styles as (in Britain, Ireland and the US) mild, bitter, porter, stout, old ale and barley wine, and in the Low Countries, Abbey and Trappist ales, and some types of Bock, or Bok.

Alpha acid: the natural acid in the cone of the hop plant that gives bitterness to beer. Some international brewers use only 'high alpha' or 'super alpha' hops that give a high level of bitterness but little aroma.

Alt & Amber: an 'old' style of warm-fermented beer from the Dusseldorf region of Germany, often known as Amber in the US.

Aroma: the 'nose' of a beer that gives an indication of the malty, hoppy and possibly fruity characteristics to be found in the mouth.

Attenuation: If a beer is 'fully attenuated', most or all of the malt sugars will have turned to alcohol. In some styles, such as English mild or Dortmunder Export, some malt sugars are left in the beer for fullness of palate and some sweetness. Such beers are not 'brewed out' or fully attenuated.

Barley: the preferred grain used by all brewers as the main ingredient in beer and source of fermentable sugar.

Beer: generic term for an alcoholic drink made from grain. It includes ale, lager and Belgian lambic/gueuze.

Bière de Garde: French 'keeping beer', a style associated with French Flanders, first brewed by farmer/brewers in spring and stored to refresh their labourers during the summer months, but now produced all year round.

Bitter: A draught English pale ale that may range in colour from gold through amber to copper. The name indicates a generous amount of hop bitterness.

Blond/blonde: term used in mainland Europe to indicate a light-coloured beer. The term is often used when a brewery produces brown and pale versions of the same or similar beers, as in the case of Leffe Blonde and Brune.

Bock: German term for a strong beer, which can be pale or dark, usually stored or lagered for several months. The term is associated with the 'liquid bread' beers brewed by monks to sustain them during Lent. In the Netherlands, the term is sometimes spelt Bok, and beers there may be warm fermented.

Bottle conditioned/bottle fermented: a beer bottled with live yeast that allows the beer to mature, gain condition ('sparkle') and extra alcohol in its glass container.

Bragget: an ancient beer style associated with the Celtic regions of the British Isles, usually brewed without hops but often with the addition of herbs and spices. A Bragget beer is occasionally brewed at the Blue Anchor brew-pub in Cornwall.

Brew-pub: a pub that brews beer on the premises.

Brune: a brown beer. See blond.

Burtonise/Burtonisation: addition of such salts as gypsum and magnesium to replicate the hard brewing waters found in Burton-on-Trent.

Campaign for Real Ale (CAMRA): Beer drinkers' organisation founded in 1971 to protect cask-conditioned beer – dubbed 'real ale'. CAMRA now has 76,000 members.

Carbon dioxide (CO_2): a gas naturally produced by fermentation. When beers are said to be 'naturally conditioned', as in cask-conditioned ale or bottle-conditioned beer, the gas is natural. When beers are filtered in the brewery, CO_2 may added either in the brewery or as part of the dispense system in a bar or pub. This can make beer too gassy.

Cask ale: also known as cask beer or real ale. A draught beer that undergoes a secondary fermentation in the cask in the pub cellar, reaching maturity as a result of natural processes. The style is mainly confined to Britain.

Condition: the level of carbon dioxide (CO_2) present in beer, which gives beer its sparkle.

Copper: vessel used to boil the sugary wort (qv) with hops. Traditionally made of copper but more often today of stainless steel. Known as a brew kettle in the US.

Decoction mashing: a system used mainly in lager brewing or German wheat beer production, in which portions of the mash are removed from the mashing vessel, heated to a higher temperature and then returned to the first vessel. Improves enzymic activity and the conversion of starch to sugar.

Doppelbock (double bock): extra strong type of Bock, usually around 7.5% ABV or more, but not – despite the name – twice the strength of an ordinary Bock.

Draught: beer served from a bulk container and drawn to the bar. Spelt 'draft' in the US.

Dry hopping: the addition of a small amount of hops to a cask of beer to improve bitterness and aroma. Usually associated with cask-conditioned beer in Britain.

Dubbel: Flemish word for double, first coined by the Westmalle Trappist brewery, to indicate a strong dark ale of around 6.5% ABV.

Dunkel: German for 'dark', indicating a lager beer in which colour is derived from well-roasted malts.

Enkel: Dutch word for single, used to indicate a beer of modest strength, as in La Trappe Enkel.

Esters: Flavour compounds produced by the action of yeast turning sugars into alcohol and carbon dioxide (CO_2). Esters are often similar to fruits, and fruitiness is associated with members of the ale family.

Fermentation: turning malt sugars into alcohol and carbon dioxide (CO_2) by the action of yeast. Ale is made by warm fermentation, lager by cold fermentation. These are often called top and bottom fermentation but the terms are misleading, as yeast works at all levels of the liquid.

Fining: Clarifying beer with the addition of finings, usually isinglass made from fish bladders. Caragheen [Irish Moss] can also be used and is preferred by vegetarians and vegans.

Finish: the aftertaste of a beer; the impression left at the back of the tongue and the throat.

Grand Cru: a term given to the finest beer of a brewery, one thought to typify the house style. Often used by Belgian brewers.

Grist: brewers' term for the milled grains to be used in a brew. The term comes from the word 'grind' and is still used in the expression 'all grist to the mill'.

Gruit: medieval method of adding a blend of herbs and spices to beer.

Gueuze: see Lambic.

Hefe: German for yeast. Beers '*mit hefe*' are naturally conditioned and not filtered. Usually applies to wheat beers.

Helles: German for light, indicating a pale beer, either lager or wheat beer.

Hops: climbing plant with cones containing acids, resins and tannins that gives aroma and bitterness to beer, and helps prevent bacterial infection.

IBU: International Units of Bitterness, a scale for measuring the bitterness of beer.

Infusion: method of mashing beer, mainly associated with British ale brewing. The grain is left to soak with pure hot water in a mash tun at a constant temperature; enzymes in the malt convert starch to sugar.

IPA: short for India Pale Ale, the first pale beer in the world, associated with Burton-on-Trent in the English Midlands in the 19th century. First brewed for soldiers and civil servants based in India, it spawned pale ale and bitter in England, and even inspired the first lager brewers of Austria and Germany.

Kräusen: The addition of some partially fermented wort (qv) to beer in the lager cellar to encourage a strong secondary fermentation.

Lager: from the German meaning store or storage place, similar to the English word larder. Following primary fermentation, beer is 'cold conditioned' in tanks where the temperature is held just above freezing. As the yeast settles at the bottom of the tanks, a slow secondary fermentation takes place, carbonation increases, and a clean, quenching, spritzy beer results, usually lacking the fruity esters associated with ale.

Lambic: Belgian beer made by 'spontaneous fermentation', using wild yeasts in the atmosphere. True lambics are confined to the area of the Senne Valley centred on Brussels. A blended lambic, using young and aged beers, is known as gueuze. When cherries or raspberries are added, the beers are known as kriek and framboise, or frambozen.

Lauter: vessel used to run off and filter the wort from the grain after mashing. The word comes from the German for clarify, and the vessels were once associated with lager or wheat beer brewing. But many ale brewers with modern equipment now employ lauter tuns, as the mash tun (qv) can be used to start a new brew once the mash has been pumped to the lauter.

Liquor: Brewers' term for the pure water used in the mashing and boiling process.

Maibock: in Germany, a strong, usually pale, lager brewed to herald the arrival of spring.

Malt: grain – usually barley – that has been partially germinated, dried and cured or toasted in a kiln. The grain contains starches that will be converted by natural enzymes into fermentable sugar during the mashing period in the brewery. The colour of malt is determined by the degree of heat in the kiln. All beers are made primarily from pale malt, which has the highest level of natural enzymes. Colour and flavour are derived from darker malts, such as amber, brown or chocolate.

Märzen: Traditional Bavarian lager brewed in March and stored until the autumn, when it is tapped at the Oktoberfest.

Mash: the mixture of malted grain and pure hot water, the first stage of the brewing process, when sugars are extracted from the malt. Mashing can be either by decoction or infusion (qv).

Mash tun: vessel in which malted grain is mixed with 'liquor' to start the brewing process.

Micro-brewery: a small brewery with a small staff, often just a couple of people, brewing batches of beer for local distribution. 'Micros' in Britain and the US have been at the forefront of the craft beer revival in the past 20–30 years. Many micros have re-created old beer styles and designed new ones. In the US, micros may be big by European standards, but are considered small when compared to giant American producers.

Mouth-feel: the sensation that beer and its constituent parts – malt, hops and fruity esters – make in the mouth. The tongue is a highly sensitive organ and can detect sweetness, sourness, saltiness and bitterness as the beer passes over it.

Oktoberfest beers: medium-strength lager beer brewed in Munich for consumption at the famous autumn beer festival.

Original Gravity (OG): system once used in Britain for measuring the level of 'fermentable material' – malt, other grains and sugars – in a beer. Tax was levied on the OG until the system was replaced by Alcohol By Volume (ABV – qv). However, many brewers still list the OG and the ABV of their beers.

Parti-gyle: making more than one beer from a brew with the addition of brewing liquor to water the wort (qv) down to the required strengths.

Pasteurisation: heating process developed by Louis Pasteur that kills bacteria and stabilises the beer. It can be done quickly by flash pasteurisation as the beer passes through a pipe or more slowly by tunnel pasteurisation when the beer comes into contact with heat. If pasteurisation is clumsy, the beer can take on unpleasant cardboard or cabbage-like aromas and flavours. Many brewers now prefer to sterile filter beer. One leading opponent of pasteurisation was Pasteur himself, who developed the method to protect wine, and said beer was too delicate to withstand it.

Pilsner/Pilsener/Pils: originally a golden, hoppy lager brewed in the city of Pilsen in Bohemia, now part of the Czech Republic. A true Pilsner is usually around 4.5–5% ABV. In Germany, many brewers either spell the word Pilsener or shorten it to Pils, to avoid any suggestion their beers come from Pilsen. In the Czech Republic, Pilsner is an 'appellation': only beers from Pilsen can use the term.

Porter: a brown (later black) beer first brewed in London early in the 18th century. Called 'entire butt' by brewers, it acquired the name of porter due to its popularity with street-market porters. The success of porter created the modern commercial brewing industry in England and later in Ireland. The strongest porters were known as stout (qv).

Priming: the addition of priming sugar to encourage a strong secondary fermentation.

Quadrupel: a Belgian beer of exceptional strength but rarely four times as strong as other beers.

Racking: running beer from a conditioning tank into a cask or keg.

Real Ale: term coined by CAMRA (qv) in Britain to denote a beer that is neither filtered nor pasteurised, which undergoes a secondary fermentation in its container and is not served by applied gas pressure.

Reinheitsgebot: The Bavarian 'Pure Beer Law' dating from 1516 that lays down that only malted barley and/or wheat, hops, yeast and water can be used in brewing. Cheaper cereals, such as corn or rice, and sugar are not permitted. The law now covers the whole of Germany, but export beers may not necessarily adhere to it.

Sparge: to rinse the grain after mashing to flush out any remaining malt sugars (from the French *esperger*, meaning to sprinkle).

Stout: Once a generic English term for the strongest or 'stoutest' beer produced in a brewery. With the rise of porter (qv) in the 18th century, strong porters were known as stout porters. Over time, the term was shortened to just stout, indicating a strong, jet-black beer, made with highly roasted malts and roasted barley, and generously hopped. The style is most closely associated today with Ireland.

Trappist: beers of the ale family made in breweries controlled by Trappist monks in Belgium.

Tripel: strong, usually pale beer, associated with the Westmalle Trappist brewery in Belgium, but now widely used throughout the Low Countries.

Tun: a large vessel once used to store beer. The term today is confined to the mash tun, the vessel in which malt and water are blended at the start of the brewing process (qv).

Vienna Red: term for the first successful commercial lager beer brewed in Austria in the 19th century. It was a halfway house between the dark lagers of Munich and the golden lagers of Bohemia. Vienna Red inspired the Munich Märzen beers (qv).

Wheat beer: known as weizen (wheat) or weiss (white) in Germany, blanche in French or wit in Dutch and Flemish. Beer made from a blend of wheat and barley malt. Wheat beers are members of the ale family and may be unfiltered and cloudy, or filtered bright.

Wort: the sweet, sugary extract produced by mashing malt and water. Wort is boiled with hops, then cooled prior to fermentation.

Yeast: a natural fungus that attacks sweet liquids such as wort, turning malt sugars into alcohol and carbon dioxide (CO_2). Brewers' yeasts are either warm or top fermenting cultures for ale brewing, or cold or bottom fermenting cultures for lager brewing. Belgian lambic brewers (qv) use wild yeasts from the atmosphere.

Index

By beer name

Darwin Flag Porter (England) 145

Darwin Rolling Hitch (England) 14

De Dolle Arabier (Belgium) 174

De Koninck (Belgium) 57

Diebels Alt (Germany) 212

Doc Hadfield's Pale Ale (Canada) 58

Double Maxim (England) 41

Drie Fonteinen Framboos (Belgium) 245

Drie Fonteinen Oude Gueuze (Belgium) 245

Drie Fonteinen Oude Kriek (Belgium) 245

Du Bocq Blanche de Namur (Belgium) 198

Duckstein (Germany) 213

Duvel (Belgium) 175 ✓

Duyck Jenlain Ambrée (France) 206

Eggenberg Samichlaus (Austria) 269

Einbecker Ur-Bock (Germany) 270

EKU 28 (Germany) 271

EKU Kulminator (Germany) 271

Elgood's Black Dog Mild (England) 42

Exmoor Gold (England) 176

Foster's Sheaf Stout (Australia) 146

Franziskaner Weissbeir (Germany) 191

Fraoch Heather Ale (Scotland) 249

Fraoch Kelpie Ale (Scotland) 249

Freeminer Speculation (England) 88

Freeminer's Gold Miner (England) 177

Früh Kölsch (Germany) 218

Full Sail Amber Ale (US) 214

Fuller's ESB (England) 104 ✓

Fuller's London Pride (England) 89 ✓

Fuller's Vintage Ale (England) 123

Gale's Prize Old Ale (England) 124 ✓

Geary's Pale Ale (US) 58

Girardin Gueuze Black Label 1882 (Belgium) 246

Goose Island Honker's Ale (US) 90

Goose Island IPA (US) 15

Gordon Biersch Dunkles (US) 262

Grant's Imperial Stout (US) 146

Grant's India Pale Ale (US) 16

Grant's Perfect Porter (US) 146

Grant's Scottish Ale (US) 185

Great Lakes Dortmunder Gold (US) 281

Great Lakes The Edmund Fitzgerald Porter (US) 147

Greene King Abbot Ale (England) 90 ✓

Greene King Strong Suffolk Ale (England) 125 ✓

Grolsch Pilsener (Netherlands) 26 ✓

Guinness Foreign Extra Stout (Ireland) 148 ✓

Gulpener Dort (Netherlands) 282

Hambleton Nightmare (England) 149

Harveys Imperial Extra Double Stout (England) 149

Harveys Sussex Best Bitter (England) 73 ✓

Harviestoun Bitter & Twisted (Scotland) 186 ✓

Hellers Kölsch (Germany) 219

Hellers Ur-Weiss (Germany) 219

Hesket Newmarket Helvellyn Gold (England) 178

Highgate Dark Mild (England) 43

Highgate Old Ale (England) 126

Hoegaarden (Belgium) 199 ✓

Hofbräu Märzen (Germany) 277 ✓

Hogs Back BSA (England) 17 ✓

Holden's Black Country Bitter (England) 74

Holt's Bitter (England) 75 ✓

Holt's Mild Ale (England) 44

Hook Norton Double Stout (England) 150 ✓

Hook Norton Old Hooky (England) 91 ✓

Hop Back Summer Lightning (England) 179

Hopf Export (Germany) 192

Hübsch Doppelbock (US) 272

Hydes Dark Mild (England) 45

Iceni Fine Soft Day (England) 92

Innis & Gunn Oak Aged Beer (Scotland) 187 ✓

Islay Saligo Ales (Scotland) 188

Jennings Sneck Lifter (England) 105 ✓

Jever Pilsener (Germany) 27

Jopen Koyt (Netherlands) 250

Kaltenberg König Ludwig Dunkel (Germany) 263

Kelham Island Pale Rider (England) 179

Kirin Ichiban (Japan) 259

Klasterni St Norbert Dark (Czech Republic) 264

Koff Porter (Finland) 150

Koningshoeven Dubbel (Netherlands) 233

- [✓] Shepherd Neame Bishop's Finger (England) 96
- [✓] Shepherd Neame Master Brew Bitter (England) 76
- [ ] Shipyard Fuggles IPA (US) 20
- [ ] Shipyard Longfellow Winter Ale (US) 110
- [ ] Sierra Nevada Bigfoot (US) 131
- [ ] Sierra Nevada Pale Ale (US) 64
- [ ] Silly Double Enghien Blonde (Belgium) 181
- [ ] Spaten Münchner Hell (Germany) 259
- [ ] Spaten Ur-Märzen (Germany) 278
- [ ] Spendrup's Old Gold (Sweden) 31
- [ ] St Austell Clouded Yellow (England) 254
- [ ] St Austell HSD (England) 94
- [ ] St Peter's Organic Best Bitter (England) 95
- [ ] St Stan's Amber Alt (US) 215
- [ ] St Stan's Dark Alt (US) 215
- [ ] St Sylvestre 3 Monts (France) 207
- [ ] Stepan Razin Porter (Russia) 165
- [ ] Stoudt's Triple (US) 236
- [ ] Švyturys Ekstra (Lithuania) 285

- [✓] Theakston Best Bitter (England) 77
- [✓] Theakston's Old Peculier (England) 122
- [✓] Timothy Taylor's Landlord (England) 96
- [✓] Titanic Stout (England) 166
- [ ] Tongerlo Double Brown (Belgium) 237
- [ ] Tongerlo Triple Blond (Belgium) 237
- [ ] Traquair House Ale (Scotland) 133
- [ ] Třeboň Dark Regent (Czech Republic) 266
- [ ] Trumer Pils (Austria) 32

- [ ] U Fleků Flekovský Dark (Czech Republic) 266
- [ ] Uley Bitter (England) 78
- [ ] Unibroue Blanche de Chambly (Canada) 200
- [ ] Unibroue Maudite (Canada) 182
- [ ] Upper Canada Dark Ale (Canada) 97

- [✓] Wadworth 6X (England) 98
- [ ] Weihenstephaner Hefe Weissbier (Germany) 105
- [ ] Weihenstephaner Pilsner (Germany) 32
- [ ] Wellington Arkell Best Bitter (Canada) 99
- [ ] Wells Banana Bread Beer (England) 255
- [✓] Wells Bombardier (England) 100
- [ ] Welton's Pridenjoy (England) 79

- [ ] Westmalle Dubbel (Belgium) 226
- [ ] Westmalle Tripel (Belgium) 226
- [ ] Westvleteren Abt (Belgium) 227
- [ ] Westvleteren Blond (Belgium) 227
- [ ] Westvleteren Extra (Belgium) 227
- [ ] Wild River Extra Special Bitter (US) 110
- [ ] Wolf Granny Wouldn't Like It (England) 101
- [ ] Woodforde's Norfolk Nip (England) 134
- [ ] Worthington's White Shield (England) 21
- [✓] Wychwood Hobgoblin (England) 111
- [ ] Wye Valley Brewery Dorothy Goodbody's Wholesome Stout (England) 167

- [✓] Young's Bitter (England) 80
- [✓] Young's Double Chocolate Stout (England) 168
- [✓] Young's Old Nick (England) 135
- [✓] Younger's Special Bitter (US) 65

- [ ] Žatec 12° (Czech Republic) 260
- [ ] Zum Uerige Alt (Germany) 216

Index

By beer style

- [ ] Greene King Abbot Ale (England) 90
- [ ] Hook Norton Old Hooky (England) 91
- [ ] Iceni Fine Soft Day (England) 92
- [ ] Mordue Workie Ticket (England) 93
- [ ] Rooster's Yankee (England) 93
- [ ] St Austell HSD (England) 94
- [ ] Shepherd Neame Bishop's Finger (England) 96
- [ ] St Peter's Organic Best Bitter (England) 95
- [ ] Timothy Taylor's Landlord (England) 96
- [ ] Upper Canada Dark Ale (Canada) 97
- [ ] Wadworth 6X (England) 98
- [ ] Wellington Arkell Best Bitter (Canada) 99
- [ ] Wells Bombardier (England) 100
- [ ] Wolf Granny Wouldn't Like It (England) 101

Extra Strong Beers & Bitters

- [ ] Arkell's Kingsdown Ale (England) 102
- [ ] Fuller's ESB (England) 104
- [ ] Jennings Sneck Lifter (England) 105
- [ ] Moorhouse's Pendle Witches Brew (England) 106
- [ ] Pauwel Kwak (Belgium) 107
- [ ] Ridleys Old Bob (England) 108
- [ ] Ringwood Old Thumper (England) 109
- [ ] Shipyard Longfellow Winter Ale (US) 110
- [ ] Wild River Extra Special Bitter (US) 110
- [ ] Wychwood Hobgoblin (England) 111

Old Ales, Barley Wines & Vintage Ales

- [ ] Anchor Old Foghorn (US) 114
- [ ] Ballard's Wassail (England) 115
- [ ] Blue Anchor Spingo Special (England) 116
- [ ] BridgePort Old Knucklehead (US) 117
- [ ] Broughton Old Jock (Scotland) 118
- [ ] Bush Ambrée (Belgium) 119
- [ ] Chiltern 300s Old Ale (England) 120
- [ ] Chiltern Bodgers Barley Wine (England) 121
- [ ] Cottage Norman's Conquest (England) 122
- [ ] Fuller's Vintage Ale (England) 123
- [ ] Gale's Prize Old Ale (England) 124
- [ ] Greene King Strong Suffolk Ale (England) 125
- [ ] Highgate Old Ale (England) 126
- [ ] Lees Harvest Ale (England) 127
- [ ] Moor Old Freddy Walker (England) 128
- [ ] O'Hanlon's Thomas Hardy's Ale (England) 129
- [ ] Robinson's Old Tom (England) 130

- [ ] Sierra Nevada Bigfoot (US) 131
- [ ] Theakston's Old Peculier (England) 132
- [ ] Traquair House Ale (Scotland) 133
- [ ] Woodforde's Norfolk Nip (England) 134
- [ ] Young's Old Nick (England) 135

Porters & Stouts

- [ ] Alaskan Smoked Porter (US) 138
- [ ] Bridge of Allan Glencoe Wild Oat Stout (Scotland) 139
- [ ] Brooklyn Chocolate Stout (US) 140
- [ ] Broughton Scottish Oatmeal Stout (Scotland) 141
- [ ] Carlsberg Carls Stout Porter (Denmark) 142
- [ ] Carnegie Stark Porter (Sweden) 143
- [ ] Castlemaine Carbine Stout (Australia) 144
- [ ] Coopers Best Extra Stout (Australia) 144
- [ ] Darwin Flag Porter (England) 145
- [ ] Foster's Sheaf Stout (Australia) 146
- [ ] Grant's Imperial Stout (US) 146
- [ ] Grant's Perfect Porter (US) 146
- [ ] Great Lakes The Edmund Fitzgerald Porter (US) 147
- [ ] Guinness Foreign Extra Stout (Ireland) 148
- [ ] Hambleton Nightmare (England) 149
- [ ] Harveys Imperial Extra Double Stout (England) 149
- [ ] Hook Norton Double Stout (England) 150
- [ ] Koff Porter (Finland) 150
- [ ] Larkins Porter (England) 151
- [ ] Le Coq Porter (Estonia) 152
- [ ] Lion Dark (Sri Lanka) 153
- [ ] Mackeson Stout (England) 154
- [ ] Mendocino Black Hawk Stout (US) 155
- [ ] Nethergate Old Growler (England) 156
- [ ] Nethergate Umbel Magna (England) 156
- [ ] North Coast Brewing Old No 38 Stout (US) 157
- [ ] North Coast Brewing Old Rasputin Russian Imperial Stout (US) 157
- [ ] O'Hanlon Original Port Stout (England) 158
- [ ] Pitfield Shoreditch Stout (England) 158
- [ ] Pitfield 1792 Imperial Stout (England) 158
- [ ] Pitfield London Beer Co 1850 London Porter (England) 158
- [ ] Pyramid Espresso Stout (US) 160
- [ ] RCH Old Slug Porter (England) 160
- [ ] Ridley's Witchfinder Porter (England) 161
- [ ] Rogue Imperial Stout (US) 162
- [ ] Rogue Shakespeare Stout (US) 162
- [ ] Samuel Smith's Imperial Stout (England) 163
- [ ] Samuel Smith's Oatmeal Stout (England) 163

Books for Beer Lovers

CAMRA Books, the publishing arm of the Campaign for Real Ale, is the leading publisher of books on beer and pubs. Key titles include:

Good Beer Guide 2006
Editor: ROGER PROTZ

The Good Beer Guide is the only guide you will need to find the right pint, in the right place, every time. It's the original and the best independent guide to around 4,500 pubs throughout the UK; the Sun newspaper rated the 2004 edition in the top 20 books of all time! Now in its 34th year, this annual publication is a comprehensive and informative guide to the best real ale pubs in the UK, researched and written exclusively by CAMRA members and fully updated every year.

£13.99   ISBN 1 85249 211 2

Good Beer Guide Belgium
Editor: TIM WEBB

Now in its 5th edition and in full colour, this book has developed a cult following among committed beer lovers and beer tourists.It is the definitive, totally independent guide to understanding and finding the best of Belgian beer and an essential companion for any beer drinker visiting Belgium or seeking out Belgian beer in Britain. Includes details of the 120 breweries and over 800 beers in regular production, as well as 500 of the best hand-picked cafes in Belgium.

£12.99   ISBN 1 85249 210 4

Good Beer Guide Germany
Editor: STEVE THOMAS

The first ever comprehensive region-by-region guide to Germany's brewers, beer and outlets. Includes more than 1,200 breweries, 1,000 brewery taps and 7,200 beers. Complete with useful travel information on how to get there, informative essays on German beer and brewing plus beer festival listings. Publication June 2006.

£14.99   ISBN 1 85249 219 8

Big Book of Beer

ADRIAN TIERNEY-JONES

Everything you could ever want to know about the world's favourite drink; this beautifully illustrated book is an eye-opener to the world of beer articulated by celebrities, chefs, beer experts and those who brew it. A perfect gift for the 'real beer' connoisseur.

£14.99   ISBN 1 85249 212 0

Good Bottled Beer Guide

Editor: JEFF EVANS

This award-winning book is the bible for all aficionados of bottle-conditioned beer. It is a comprehensive guide to the huge number of beers now available in supermarkets, off-licences and via the internet in the UK, from bitters and milds to wheat beers, stouts, porters, fruit beers and barley wines.

£9.99   ISBN 1 85249 197 3

The Book of Beer Knowledge

JEFF EVANS

A unique collection of entertaining trivia and essential wisdom, this is the perfect gift for beer lovers everywhere. More than 200 entries cover everything from the fictional 'celebrity landlords' of soap pubs to the harsh facts detailing the world's biggest brewers; from bizarre beer names to the serious subject of fermentation.

£9.99   ISBN 1 85249 198 1

CAMRA'S Good Cider Guide

The 5th edition of this title features more than 600 traditional cider producers and outlets in the UK and is an essential volume for anyone wishing to become a cider connoisseur. The popularity of real cider is permanently rising, as more and more people discover how deliciously mellow, aromatic and intoxicating the flavours of naturally-produced cider can be. CAMRA'S Good Cider Guide, revised and updated, offers a county-by-county directory of UK cider producers and outlets and provides unique, in-depth knowledge for the discerning cider consumer.

£10.99   ISBN 1 85249 195 7

Order these and other CAMRA books online at **www.camra.org.uk/books**, ask at your local bookstore, or contact: CAMRA, 230 Hatfield Road, St Albans, AL1 4LW. Telephone 01727 867201

Do you feel passionately about your pint? Then why not join CAMRA

Just fill in the application form (or a photocopy of it) and the Direct Debit form on the next page to receive three months' membership FREE!

If you wish to join but do not want to pay by Direct Debit, please fill in the application form below and send a cheque, payable to CAMRA, to CAMRA, 230 Hatfield Road, St Albans, Hertfordshire, AL1 4LW.

Please tick appropriate box

☐ Single Membership (UK & EU) £18

☐ For under-26 Membership £10

☐ For 60 and over Membership £10

For partners' joint membership add £3 (for concessionary rates both members must be eligible for the membership rate).
Life membership information is available on request.

If you join by Direct Debit you will receive three months' membership extra, free!

Title _____ Surname _____

Forename(s) _____

Address _____

_____ Postcode _____

Date of Birth _____ Email address _____

Signature _____

Partner's details if required

Title _____ Surname _____

Forename(s) _____

Date of Birth _____ Email address _____

Please tick here ☐ if you would like to receive occasional emails from CAMRA
(at no point will your details be released to a third party).
Find out more about CAMRA at **www.camra.org.uk** Telephone 01727 867201

The Direct Debit Guarantee

DIRECT Debit

This Guarantee should be detached and retained by the payer.

- This Guarantee is offered by all Banks and Building Societies that take part in the Direct Debit Scheme. The efficiency and security of the Scheme is monitored and protected by your own Bank or Building Society.

- If the amounts to be paid or the payment dates change CAMRA will notify you 7 working days in advance of your account being debited or as otherwise agreed.

- If an error is made by CAMRA or your Bank or Building Society, you are guaranteed a full and immediate refund from your branch of the amount paid.

- You can cancel a Direct Debit at any time by writing to your Bank or Building Society. Please also send a copy of your letter to us.

detached and retained this section

Instruction to your Bank or Building Society to pay by Direct Debit

DIRECT Debit

CAMPAIGN FOR REAL ALE

Please fill in the form and send to: Campaign for Real Ale Ltd. 230 Hatfield Road, St. Albans, Herts. AL1 4LW

Name and full postal address of your Bank or Building Society

To The Manager   Bank or Building Society

Address

Postcode

Name (s) of Account Holder (s)

Bank or Building Society account number

Branch Sort Code

Reference Number

Banks and Building Societies may not accept Direct Debit Instructions for some types of account

Originator's Identification Number

| 9 | 2 | 6 | 1 | 2 | 9 |

FOR CAMRA OFFICIAL USE ONLY
This is not part of the instruction to your **Bank or Building Society**

Membership Number

Name

Postcode

Instruction to your Bank or Building Society

Please pay CAMRA Direct Debits from the account detailed on this Instruction subject to the safeguards assured by the Direct Debit Guarantee. I understand that this instruction may remain with CAMRA and, if so, will be passed electronically to my Bank/Building Society

Signature(s)

Date

It takes all sorts to Campaign for Real Ale

CAMRA, the Campaign for Real Ale, is an independent not-for-profit, volunteer-led consumer group. We actively campaign for full pints and more flexible licensing hours, as well as protecting the 'local' pub and lobbying government to champion pub-goers' rights.

CAMRA has 75,000 members from all ages and backgrounds, brought together by a common belief in the issues that CAMRA deals with and their love of good quality British beer. For just £18 a year, that's less than a pint a month, you can join CAMRA and enjoy the following benefits:

A monthly colour newspaper informing you about beer and pub news and detailing events and beer festivals around the country.

Free or reduced entry to over 140 national, regional and local beer festivals.

Money off many of our publications including the *Good Beer Guide* and the *Good Bottled Beer Guide.*

Access to a members-only section of our national website, **www.camra.org.uk,** which gives up-to-the-minute news stories and includes a special offer section with regular features saving money on beer and trips away.

The opportunity to campaign to save pubs under threat of closure, for pubs to be open when people want to drink and a reduction in beer duty that will help Britain's brewing industry survive.

Log onto **www.camra.org.uk** for CAMRA membership information.